Emerging Legal Orders in the Arctic

More than ever before the changing environmental and political landscape in the Arctic requires stability and foreseeability based on resilient common norms. The emerging legal orders in the Arctic cannot be legitimately created or effectively implemented unless all relevant actors are involved. Simultaneously, it must always be based on respect for the sovereign rights of the eight Arctic states in the region, as well as the tradition and cultural livelihood of the local communities. It is this delicate balance between Arctic and non-Arctic interests that is the core problématique for the emerging legal orders in the Arctic.

Emerging Legal Orders in the Arctic critically examines the role of non-Arctic actors in this advancement of the shape and scope of the Arctic legal order. Discussing the admittance and participation of Observer states and organisations in the Arctic Council, including task force meetings where new treaties are negotiated, it details the issues and successes this can result in. Setting up the context of the current legal orders in the Arctic, the book discusses Asian, indigenous and European perspectives, amongst others. There is a strong focus on the groundbreaking fisheries agreement of November 2017 in the Central Arctic Ocean (CAO), and the impact on both Arctic and non-Arctic actors. Interests in marine living resources, scientific cooperation and the Arctic shipping regimes and governance are also thoroughly discussed from multiple perspectives.

The book combines the expertise of academics and practitioners in the fields of international law and Arctic governance, uniquely focusing on Asian actors in the Arctic legal order-making. The resulting study is a fascinating insight into the interplay between non-Arctic actors and the Arctic legal order, and will be invaluable to academics in the field of Arctic and international law.

Akiho Shibata is a Professor of International Law and Director, Polar Cooperation Research Centre (PCRC) at Kobe University, Japan.

Leilei Zou is a Professor at Shanghai Ocean University, Shanghai, China.

Nikolas P. Sellheim is a postdoctoral researcher at the Helsinki Institute of Sustainability Science (HELSUS), University of Helsinki, Finland.

Marzia Scopelliti is a PhD candidate in Law at Complutense University, Madrid, Spain.

Routledge Research in Polar Law

Emerging Legal Orders in the Arctic
The Role of Non-Arctic Actors
Edited by Akiho Shibata, Leilei Zou, Nikolas Sellheim & Marzia Scopelliti

For a full list of titles in this series, visit https://www.routledge.com/law/series/RRPL

Emerging Legal Orders in the Arctic

The Role of Non-Arctic Actors

Edited by Akiho Shibata, Leilei Zou, Nikolas Sellheim and Marzia Scopelliti

Routledge
Taylor & Francis Group
LONDON AND NEW YORK

First published 2019
by Routledge
2 Park Square, Milton Park, Abingdon, Oxon OX14 4RN

and by Routledge
605 Third Avenue, New York, NY 10017

First issued in paperback 2021

Routledge is an imprint of the Taylor & Francis Group, an informa business

Publisher's Note
The publisher has gone to great lengths to ensure the quality of this reprint but points out that some imperfections in the original copies may be apparent.

British Library Cataloguing-in-Publication Data
A catalogue record for this book is available from the British Library

Library of Congress Cataloging-in-Publication Data
Names: Shibata, Akiho, 1965–, editor.
Title: Emerging legal orders in the Arctic : the role of non-Arctic actors / Edited by Akiho Shibata, Leilei Zou, Nikolas Sellheim & Marzia Scopelliti.
Description: New York : Routledge, 2019. | Series: Routledge research in polar law | Includes index.
Identifiers: LCCN 2018052714 (print) | LCCN 2018055129 (ebook) | ISBN 9780429461170 (ebk) | ISBN 9781138618510 (hbk)
Subjects: LCSH: Arctic Regions—International status. | International law—Arctic regions. | Law of the sea—Arctic regions.
Classification: LCC KZ4110.P65 (ebook) | LCC KZ4110.P65 E44 2019 (print) | DDC 341.40911/3—dc23
LC record available at https://lccn.loc.gov/2018052714

Typeset in Galliard
by Apex CoVantage, LLC

ISBN 13: 978-1-03-224127-2 (pbk)
ISBN 13: 978-1-138-61851-0 (hbk)

DOI: 10.4324/9780429461170

Contents

Illustrations

Figures

Tables

Notes on contributors

Rasmus Gjedssø Bertelsen is Professor of Northern Studies and Barents Chair in Politics at the Department of Social Sciences, UiT The Arctic University of Norway. He was Japan Society for the Promotion of Science (JSPS) invited fellow and invited professor at Kobe University in 2017. His research in International Relations focuses on the role of knowledge in international politics.

Dalee Sambo Dorough, an Inuk from Alaska, was elected in 2018 as international Chair of the Inuit Circumpolar Council (ICC). She serves as a Senior Scholar and Special Advisor on Arctic Indigenous Peoples at University of Alaska, Anchorage (UAA), and was previously an Associate Professor of Political Science at UAA and served as the Chairperson and an Expert Member of the United Nations Permanent Forum on Indigenous Issues (UNPFII), nominated by the Arctic region.

Keiji Ide is the former Ambassador of Japan for Arctic Affairs (2017–2018). He has been posted in Croatia (as Ambassador of Japan), in Russia and in the People's Republic of China (as Minister of Embassy of Japan) and in France (as Counsellor of the Japanese Delegation to the OECD). He published a book in Japanese entitled *History of China–Russia Border Negotiations* in 2017.

Sebastian Knecht is a PhD student at the Berlin Graduate School for Transnational Studies at Freie Universität Berlin, Germany. His research areas include Arctic cooperation, authority and legitimacy of the Arctic Council, and the politics of observer inclusion in Arctic Council governance. He is the co-editor of *Governing Arctic Change: Global Perspectives* and recently co-authored a German-language textbook on international relations in the Arctic region.

Timo Koivurova is Research Professor and Director at the Arctic Centre, University of Lapland, Finland. His research work addresses the interplay between different levels of environmental law, legal status of indigenous peoples, law of the sea in the Arctic waters, integrated maritime policy in the EU, the role of law in mitigating/adapting to climate change, the function and the role of the Arctic Council in view of its future challenges.

Bjarni Már Magnússon is an Associate Professor and the chairman of the Institute of International and European Law at Reykjavík University School of

Law, Iceland. His research interest lies in public international law, especially the law of the sea, the Arctic Ocean and most recently gender equality.

Erik J. Molenaar is Deputy Director of the Netherlands Institute for the Law of the Sea (NILOS) at Utrecht University. He is also a Professor at the K.G. Jebsen Centre for the Law of the Sea (JCLOS), UiT The Arctic University of Norway. His research fields include the law of the sea, international fisheries law and the international law relating to the Antarctic and the Arctic.

Joji Morishita is Professor at the Department of Marine Policy and Culture, Tokyo University of Marine Science and Technology. Until recently he was Director-General at the National Research Institute of Far Seas Fisheries. He serves as the head of the Japanese delegation to the A5+5 Meeting on High Seas Fisheries in the Central Arctic Ocean.

Egill Thor Nielsson is Executive Secretary of the China–Nordic Arctic Research Centre (CNARC). He is a visiting scholar at the Polar Research Institute of China and Shanghai Institutes for International Studies, and a PhD candidate at the University of Iceland and University of Lapland. His research work focuses on China–Nordic relations within the context of the Arctic region from bilateral, regional and multilateral perspectives.

Yuanyuan Ren is a SJD candidate at the University of Wisconsin Law School, USA. She received her PhD in international law from Fudan University Law School (2012) and LLM from the University of Wisconsin Law School (2014). She served as an Assistant Professor at the Polar Strategic Studies Division of Polar Research Institute of China from 2012 to 2013. Her research interests are in the areas of polar law, WTO law and international dispute resolution.

Marzia Scopelliti is a PhD student in Public International Law at the Complutense University of Madrid, Spain. Her research interests include the governance of the Arctic region and international climate change law. In fall 2017, she was a Research Fellow at the Polar Cooperation Research Centre of Kobe University, Japan. In spring 2018, she held a scholarship from the University of Fribourg, Switzerland, to carry out her doctoral research at the Faculty of Law of the same university.

Nikolas Sellheim is a postdoctoral researcher at the Helsinki Institute of Sustainability Science (HELSUS), University of Helsinki, Finland. He was a Japan Society for Promotion of Science (JSPS) post-doctoral fellow at Kobe University in 2017–2018. He is the author of *The Seal Hunt: Cultures, Economies and Legal Regimes* (2018) and is a Co-Editor of *Polar Record*.

Akiho Shibata is Professor of International Law and Director, Polar Cooperation Research Centre (PCRC), Graduate School of International Cooperation Studies (GSICS), Kobe University, Japan. He specializes in international law-making process, international environmental law, Arctic international law and the Antarctic Treaty System.

Jennifer Spence is a Postdoctoral Fellow and Research Associate at Carleton University's School of Public Policy and Administration and a Fellow with the Centre for International Governance Innovation (CIGI) in Canada. She holds a PhD in public policy. An expert in international governance, institutional effectiveness and public policy, she has a particular interest in the opportunities and challenges facing the Arctic region.

Aki Tonami is Associate Professor in International Relations and Economics at the University of Tsukuba, Japan. She works on the theory and practice of economic diplomacy with a particular emphasis on foreign investment, science and technology, development aid and environment. She is the author of *Asian Foreign Policy in a Changing Arctic: The Diplomacy of Economy and Science at New Frontiers* (2016).

Leilei Zou is Professor at Shanghai Ocean University, China, and Japan Society for Promotion of Science (JSPS) post-doctoral fellow at Kobe University, 2017–2019. Her research interests include marine policies and laws, while polar living resources conservation is her research focus. She was invited as a visiting scholar at School of Law, University of Virginia in 2014–2015. She also worked as a fisheries policy analyst at OECD in France in 2012–2013.

Acknowledgements

This book is the outcome of the international symposium "The Role of Non-Arctic States/Actors in the Arctic Legal Order-Making" which we convened at the Polar Cooperation Research Centre (PCRC), Kobe University, Japan, and we would like to take this opportunity to thank all staff who made the smooth conduct of the conference possible. We would particularly like to thank Osamu Inagaki, then Assistant Professor at PCRC, and Maiko Raita and Narimitsu Kato, PhD candidates at Graduate School of International Cooperation Studies (GSICS), Kobe University, for their invaluable assistance.

The Kobe PCRC is funded by Japan's flagship Arctic research project: ArCS (Arctic Challenge for Sustainability, 2015–2020) and is headed by Akiho Shibata, the lead editor of this book. Marzia Scopelliti was a PCRC research fellow from October 2017 to February 2018, funded exclusively by the ArCS project. ArCS is unique in that it incorporates social science studies relating to the Arctic as its essential and integral component. We would therefore like to congratulate the foresight of the ArCS project in enabling us to convene a conference such as the above. In addition, Japan Society for the Promotion of Science (JSPS) was instrumental in providing funding to recruit scholars from all over the world with expertise and experience in the area of Arctic social sciences. The Kobe PCRC was very fortunate to receive two such experts, Leilei Zou from China and Nikolas Sellheim from Germany (residing in Finland), as JSPS postdoctoral fellows during the conference and much of the preparatory period of this book. One of the conference speakers was Rasmus Gjedssø Bertelsen, a JSPS invited fellow from Denmark, based at UiT-The Arctic University of Norway. We would therefore like to thank JSPS and particularly its international fellowship program. We would furthermore like to thank Yuko Osakada, Professor at Chukyo University, for her assistance.

The symposium and this book project were partially supported by JSPS KAKENHI Grant number 16H03551 entitled "Emerging Legal Orders in the Arctic" (PI: Akiho Shibata) and grant number 15K12970 entitled "International Polar Law in the Making" (PI: Akiho Shibata). Finally, we were able to invite several distinguished guest speakers and early-career scholars, as well as those from indigenous communities in the Arctic, with the generous financial support from Kobe

University Rokkodai Foundation. We would like to thank these funding agencies for making the symposium and, as its outcome, this book project possible.

We, the editors, all stem from non-Arctic countries – Japan, China, Germany and Italy. All of these countries are Observers to the Arctic Council. It appears therefore only natural for us to come together and publish a book on the role of non-Arctic actors in the Arctic legal order. But while this might be the case, we wish to express our sincerest thanks to the Arctic people and peoples that have hosted us – and still host us – on countless occasions throughout our careers. Without the hospitality of the Arctic, despite its somewhat inhospitable environment, we would not be where we are now: in regions that are below the Arctic Circle, yet looking towards it with admiration and fascination for the cold – and worryingly warming – North. We certainly hope that the present volume contributes to the world moving closer together to help us stand as one global people facing the challenges ahead.

Abbreviations

AAC	Arctic Athabaskan Council
ABNJ	Areas Beyond National Jurisdiction
AC	Arctic Council
ACIA	Arctic Climate Impact Assessment
ACOPS	Advisory Committee on Protection of the Sea
AEC	Arctic Economic Council
AEPS	Arctic Environmental Protection Strategy
AIA	Aleut International Association
AMAP	Arctic Monitoring and Assessment Programme (of the Arctic Council)
AMSA	Arctic Marine Shipping Assessment
ASM	Arctic Science Ministerial
AWRH	Association of World Reindeer Herders
BBNJ	Biodiversity Beyond National Jurisdiction
CAFF	Conservation of Arctic Flora and Fauna (of the Arctic Council)
CAO	Central Arctic Ocean
CAOF	Central Arctic Ocean Fisheries
CCAMLR	Commission for the Conservation of Antarctic Marine Living Resources
CCSBT	Commission for the Conservation of Southern Bluefin Tuna
CCU	Circumpolar Conservation Union
CLCS	Commission on the Limits of the Continental Shelf
EEZs	exclusive economic zones
EGBCM	Expert Group on Black Carbon and Methane (of the Arctic Council)
FAO	Food and Agriculture Organization
GCI	Gwich'in Council International
IASC	International Arctic Science Committee
IASSA	International Arctic Social Sciences Association
ICC	Inuit Circumpolar Council
ICES	International Council for the Exploration of the Sea
ICRW	International Convention for the Regulation of Whaling
IFAW	International Fund for Animal Welfare
IFRC	International Federation of Red Cross and Red Crescent Societies
IGOs	inter-governmental organisations
ILA	International Law Association

ILO	International Labour Organisation
IMO	International Maritime Organization
INSROP	International Northern Sea Route Programme
IPs	Indigenous Peoples
IPY	International Polar Year
IUCH	International Union for Circumpolar Health
IUCN	International Union for Conservation of Nature
IWC	International Whaling Commission
IWGIA	International Work Group for Indigenous Affairs
JNRFC	Joint Norwegian Russian Fisheries Commission
LNG	Liquefied Natural Gas
MOSPA	Marine Oil Pollution Preparedness and Response in the Arctic (Agreement on)
MPA	Marine Protected Area
NAMMCO	North Atlantic Marine Mammal Commission
NCM	Nordic Council of Ministers
NEAFC	North-East Atlantic Fisheries Commission
NEFCO	Nordic Environment Finance Corporation
NF	Northern Forum
NGOs	non-governmental organisations
NSR	Northern Sea Route
OPPRA	Oil Pollution Preparedness and Response in the Arctic (Agreement on)
PAME	Protection of the Arctic Marine Environment (of the Arctic Council)
PCRC	Polar Cooperation Research Centre (of Kobe University, Japan)
POPs	Persistent Organic Pollutants
PPs	Permanent Participants (of the Arctic Council)
PRIC	Polar Research Institute of China
RAIPON	Russian Arctic Indigenous Peoples of the North
RFMA	Regional Fisheries Management Agreement
RFMOs	Regional Fisheries Management Organisations
RoP	rules of procedure
SAOs	Senior Arctic Officials (of the Arctic Council)
SAON	Sustaining Arctic Observing Networks
SAR	search and rescue
SCPAR	Standing Committee of the Parliamentarians of the Arctic Region
SCTF	Scientific Cooperation Task Force (of the Arctic Council)
SDWG	Sustainable Development Working Group (of the Arctic Council)
SOLAS	Safety of Life at Sea (International Convention for the)
SWIPA	Snow, Water, Ice and Permafrost in the Arctic
TFAMC	Task Force on Arctic Marine Cooperation (of the Arctic Council)
TFBCM	Task Force on Black Carbon and Methane (of the Arctic Council)
TFCBF	Task Force to Facilitate the Circumpolar Business Forum (of the Arctic Council)
TFICA	Task Force on Improved Connectivity in the Arctic (of the Arctic Council)

TFOPP	Task Force on Arctic Marine Oil Pollution Prevention (of the Arctic Council)
TFSR	Task Force on Search and Rescue (of the Arctic Council)
UArctic	University of the Arctic
UNCLOS	United Nations Convention on the Law of the Sea
UNDP	United Nations Development Programme
UNECE	United Nations Economic Commission for Europe
UNEP	United Nations Environment Programme
WMO	World Meteorological Organization
WNC	West Nordic Council
WTO	World Trade Organization
WWF	World Wildlife Fund for Nature

1 An ocean in the making

Non-Arctic actors and emerging Arctic legal orders

Akiho Shibata, Leilei Zou, Nikolas Sellheim and Marzia Scopelliti

1.1 Changing tides in Arctic legal order-making

We live in times marked by remarkable change all over the world, but particularly in the Arctic. Ever since the recognition of the role of the North as a bellwether for global change[1] and the emergence of the Arctic as a distinct political and legal region,[2] global attention has shifted from the Arctic being a peripheral, frozen region to the Arctic being a centrepiece in and for global affairs. Indeed, Finger and Heininen note: "[T]he Arctic has now become global, ecologically, economically, politically and culturally."[3] As the Arctic Climate Impact Assessment (ACIA) Report has shown, environmentally the most pressing effects in the Arctic are caused by non-Arctic sources. Arctic change, it seems, is essentially of non-Arctic origin.

The changing landscape in the Arctic – both environmentally and politically – requires more than ever the stability and foreseeability based on resilient common norms and multilateral institutions applicable in the Arctic. When looking at the international legal history of the Arctic, legal orders that are relevant *for* and *in* the Arctic have not merely been drafted and shaped by the Arctic's numerous socio-political actors, but have been equally influenced by actors that are neither geographically nor politically "Arctic". Instead, these actors emerge from regions outside of the Arctic or are globally operating.[4] Thus, we argue that the emerging legal orders in the Arctic cannot be legitimately created or effectively implemented unless all the relevant actors, including states, peoples, governmental and non-governmental organisations, are involved in the processes of such order-making and implementation. Here we see a potential, and even a necessity, for non-Arctic actors to play a constructive role.

1 Arctic Climate Impact Assessment (ACIA) (2005) *Arctic Climate Impact Assessment: Impacts of a Warming Arctic*. Cambridge University Press, Cambridge.

2 E. C. H. Keskitalo (2011) *Negotiating the Arctic: The Construction of an International Region*. Routledge, London.

3 Matthias Finger and Lassi Heininen (eds) (2018) "Chapter 1: Introduction" in *The Global Arctic Handbook*. Springer, Berlin: 1–7.

4 Timo Koivurova, Qin Tianbao, Tapio Nykänen and Sébastien Duyck (eds) (2017) *Arctic Law and Governance: The Role of China, Finland and the EU*. Hart Publishing, Oxford; Kristina Schönfeldt (2017) *The Arctic in International Law and Policy*. Hart Publishing, Oxford.

The recent increase in the admittance and participation of Observer states and organisations in the Arctic Council[5] is but one such signal of expectation. In 2013, China, India, Italy, Japan, Republic of Korea and Singapore gained Observer status in the Arctic Council. At the same time, the Arctic Council has increasingly become a law-making forum where legally binding treaties are negotiated, including the most recent Agreement on Enhancing International Arctic Science Cooperation, signed in 2017 and entered into force on 23 May 2018.[6] Outside of the Arctic Council, we see the collaboration between Arctic and non-Arctic states within the International Maritime Organization (IMO) in establishing the shipping rules for ice-covered seas, the Polar Code, which came into force on 1 January 2017.[7] The five central Arctic Ocean (CAO) coastal states and five other distance fishing actors, namely China, European Union, Iceland, Japan and Republic of Korea, successfully concluded the negotiation on an Agreement to Prevent Unregulated Commercial Fishing on the High Seas of the Central Arctic Ocean in 2017, and nine of the ten negotiating parties formally signed the agreement on 3 October 2018 in Ilulissat, Greenland.[8]

These examples of recent law-making activities are relevant to the Arctic with the participation of non-Arctic actors and which we consider as forerunners of future legal orders in the Arctic. At the same time, a legitimate legal order-making in the Arctic should always be based on the respect for the sovereignty and sovereign rights of the eight Arctic states, as well as the traditions and cultural livelihoods of the indigenous peoples and the local communities. It is this delicate balance between Arctic and non-Arctic interests and perspectives that is the core problématique for the emerging legal orders in the Arctic.

5 The Arctic Council was formally established in 1996, consisting of Canada, Denmark, Finland, Iceland, Norway, the Russian Federation, Sweden and the United States. From the outset it has been designed in a progressive manner by including six indigenous organisations – Aleut International Association (AIA); Arctic Athabaskan Council (AAC); Gwich'in Council International (GCI); Inuit Circumpolar Council (ICC); Russian Association of Indigenous Peoples of the North (RAIPON); and Saami Council (SC) – as Permanent Participants.

6 As of September 2018, three legally binding agreements have been negotiated under the auspices of the Arctic Council: the Agreement on Cooperation on Aeronautical and Maritime Search and Rescue in the Arctic (2011); the Agreement on Cooperation on Marine Oil Pollution Preparedness and Response in the Arctic (2013); and the Agreement on Enhancing International Arctic Scientific Cooperation (2017).

7 Koji Sekimizu (2017) "The Polar Code and the Contribution of Non-Arctic States in its Formation and Implementation", oral presentation at the Third PCRC International Symposium on The Role of Non-Arctic States/Actors in the Arctic Legal Order-making, Kobe, Japan, 7–9 December. See also Robert C. Beckman, Tore Henriksen, Kristine Dalaker Kraabel, Erik J. Molenaar and J. Ashley Roach (eds) (2017) *Governance of Arctic Shipping: Balancing Rights and Interests of Arctic States and User States*. Brill, Leiden.

8 EU signed on 26 October 2018. See Chapter 9 by Erik Molenaar for details. For the text of the Agreement, see Appendix of this Book.

1.2 Rising waves: the Arctic and non-Arctic, particularly Asia

When examining the future design of Arctic legal orders from the perspective of actors being Arctic or non-Arctic, it becomes necessary, first and foremost, to clearly identify who the Arctic states are. Even in today's globalised world, states still hold the privileged legal status of inherent and primary subject of international law with law-making capacities. Timo Koivurova (Chapter 2: "The Current and Future Role of Non-Arctic States in Arctic Governance") demonstrates that the recognition of being an Arctic state had not been a straightforward political process. It was a hard-fought achievement over the life of the Arctic Council, spanning now more than 20 years. Today, the Arctic states are those eight states that are members of the Arctic Council, and they are the ones establishing the Arctic as a distinct political region. As a consequence, all other states are non-Arctic states, with the possibility of obtaining the Observer status in the Arctic Council. We consider this legal status as a non-Arctic state will not be influenced by, for example, such a state self-identifying as a "near-Arctic state" or something similar.

An identification of Arctic states within the governing structure of the Arctic Council leads to a clear image of who are Arctic actors other than states. According to Koivurova, the Arctic indigenous peoples and their representative non-governmental organisations (NGOs) that first started as observers in the Arctic Environmental Protection Strategy (AEPS) but came to be recognised as Permanent Participants in the Arctic Council demonstrate their strength in Arctic governance as core Arctic actors. Another category of Arctic non-state actors are the provinces and other sub-national units that actually conduct Arctic governance. The Northern Forum is the primary example.

This Arctic/non-Arctic dichotomy, however, can only highlight the actual and potential role of non-Arctic states and actors in the future of Arctic legal-order making. This is particularly the case of all major Asian states. In the face of the rise of Asian states in the Arctic region, Aki Tonami (Chapter 3: "The Rise of Asia and Arctic Legal Order-making: Political-Economic Settings") argues that Asian states are realists, placing more priority on the balance of power, diplomacy and the formation of alliances, and they are only willing to play a role if norm-making efforts serve their political/economic goals in pursuing their economic security. This depiction of potential involvement of Asian states in Arctic legal order-making is contrasted by Keiji Ide, a former Japanese Ambassador in charge of Arctic Affairs, in analysing Japan's Arctic Policy announced in October 2015 and its implementation (Chapter 4: "Japan's Role in Formation and Strengthening of Arctic Legal Orders"). Ambassador Ide explores the Japanese efforts to promote international cooperation and the rule of law in the Arctic, particularly in the elaboration and implementation of Arctic-relevant binding instruments.

On the other hand, the analysis by Egill Thor Nielsson and Bjarni Már Magnússon on the Chinese Arctic policy with its "Polar Silk Road" element announced in January 2018 (Chapter 5: "China's Arctic Policy White Paper and its Influence on the Future of Arctic Legal Developments") seems to confirm that the economic sway of China as the world's largest trader and second largest economy, alongside its tangible commitment in the Yamal LNG project, Arctic shipping and scientific achievements, already makes it a significant stakeholder in terms of Arctic affairs. According to Nielsson and Magnússon, the reaffirmation of its international legal commitments towards the Arctic in the Chinese Arctic policy white paper is a sign of potentially employing international law to strengthen its perceived position in the Arctic as a key player and downplaying its secondary status as an Observer in the main intergovernmental forum in the Arctic, the Arctic Council. Within such a complex political setting, the role of non-Arctic states and actors in the emerging legal orders in the Arctic must be analysed.

1.3 The homeland, the ocean and non-Arctic actors

While we naturally acknowledge that there are many different legal regimes impacting on the Arctic, for the people and peoples living in the Arctic it does not matter which of the different legal regimes impacts their lives – it is, after all, their homeland, their *one* Arctic, which is subject to non-Arctic influences and even forces.[9] But, as so powerfully presented by Aytalina Ivanova, Arctic peoples, in this case the Sakha people in Russia, are not passive objects for outside law-making, but they themselves are active agents and actors in the influencing of their legal environment.[10]

The centrality of Arctic indigenous peoples in the making of Arctic legal orders is reflected in the contribution of Dalee Sambo Dorough, where she assesses the history and current role of the Inuit political organisation within the frameworks of the United Nations and the Arctic Council, as well as the emergence of Inuit rights in the traditional Inuit homeland in Greenland, Canada and the United States (Chapter 6: "Our Homeland: Arctic Indigenous Peoples' Perspective of Non-Arctic States"). The chapter ends with recommendations for non-Arctic states and actors when engaging in the Arctic and with Arctic indigenous peoples, primarily to recognise and to respect the Inuit's right, role and status under international human rights law.

Environmental NGOs interested in the conservation of the Arctic wildlife are, according to Koivurova's categorisation, non-Arctic actors. While many such organisations play a constructive role particularly within the Arctic Council as

9 Marcus Carson and Garry Peterson (eds) (2016) *Arctic Resilience Report*. Arctic Council, Stockholm Environment Institute and Stockholm Resilience Centre, Stockholm.

10 Aytalina Ivanova and Florian Stammler (trans.) (2017) "100 years of Non-Arctic Development in the Arctic: Customs and Institutions of Conflict Management in Extractive Industries in Russia", paper presented at the Third PCRC International Symposium on the Role of Non-Arctic States/Actors in the Arctic Legal Order-making, Kobe, Japan, 7–9 December. See also Florian Stammler and Aytalina Ivanova (2016) "Pluralities of Governance in the Russian Arctic", *Cultural Anthropology*, 29 July 2016. https://culanth.org/fieldsights/937-pluralities-of-governance-in-the-russian-arctic (accessed 6 August 2018).

Observers in providing scientific and environmental expertise in its norm-making activities, the tensions sometimes arise not only with the Arctic state governments but also with Arctic indigenous peoples. The conflicting relationship maintained by a few of those NGOs that sustain an extreme conservationist agenda in and for the Arctic well illustrates these tensions. Marzia Scopelliti and Nikolas Sellheim have considered extreme cases of law-shaping in the context of international sealing, whaling and hydrocarbons legislation in which non-Arctic, non-governmental influence has not only challenged prevailing legal orders but also negatively impacted on Arctic indigenous peoples' traditional livelihoods (Chapter 7: "Sustaining a Conservationist Agenda? NGO Influence on Arctic Sealing, Whaling and Hydrocarbon Regimes").

The ocean in the Arctic has been the main arena of interests for non-Arctic states and actors, particularly in the business sectors pursing real and potential economic gains through shipping, investments, and direct engagement in the resource developments. For non-Arctic states, the ocean provides the legal opportunities under international law of the sea to access the Arctic for navigation and shipping, to sustainably utilise its resources and to contribute through marine scientific research to the development of knowledge on the Arctic as well as the globe. These accesses, utilisation and contribution are provided as rights under international law of ocean user states with the corresponding obligations on the coastal states. Thus, in this particular context of use of the Arctic Ocean, one could expect the Arctic and non-Arctic dichotomy being subsumed into that of user states and coastal states. However, as can be seen in the negotiations and the texts of the Arctic Science Cooperation Agreement and the central Arctic Ocean fisheries agreement, the Arctic/non-Arctic dichotomy is very much alive, as the Arctic (Ocean coastal) states declare "the special role and responsibility for marine stewardship in the Arctic region"[11] or "the special responsibilities and special interests in relation to conservation and sustainable management of fish stocks in the central Arctic Ocean".[12]

It is thus particularly pertinent in this context to examine the two legally binding international instruments specifically applicable to the Arctic Ocean, one on fisheries and another on shipping, and to analyse the role of non-Arctic states and actors in them. Non-Arctic contribution to the Agreement to Prevent Unregulated High Seas Fisheries in the Central Arctic Ocean has been analysed by Joji Morishita and Erik J. Molenaar, drawing from first-hand observations as part of the Japanese and EU delegations to the negotiations (Chapter 8: "The Five-plus-five Process on Central Arctic Ocean Fisheries Negotiations: Reflecting Interests of Arctic and Non-Arctic Actors";

11 Arctic Council, Task Force on Arctic Marine Cooperation, *Report to the Ministers of the Task Force on Arctic Marine Cooperation*, 11 May 2017, at 7. See also Tore Henriksen (2016) "The Arctic Ocean, Environmental Stewardship, and the Law of the Sea", *UC Irvine Law Review* 6: 61–82.

12 4th preambular paragraph, Agreement to Prevent Unregulated High Seas Fisheries in the Central Arctic Ocean, see Appendix of this Book.

Chapter 9: "Participation in the Central Arctic Ocean Fisheries Agreement"). The Polar Code comprises an essential component of the Arctic shipping governance. Rasmus Gjedssø Bertelsen analyses the contribution that transnational knowledge networks and epistemic communities make to Arctic shipping governance by mitigating its complexity and overall facilitating international policy cooperation in this area (Chapter 10: "The Role of Transnational Knowledge Networks and Epistemic Communities in Arctic Shipping Governance"), while Leilei Zou examines "Russia's Legislative Development Pertaining to the Northern Sea Route and Its Interaction with Sino-Russian Arctic Cooperation" (Chapter 11).

1.4 Shifting currents? Science, Arctic Council and Observers

As discussed above, the Arctic/non-Arctic dichotomy as a fundamental approach to Arctic legal order-making originates from the institutional structure of the Arctic Council. Koivurova notes that the global legal orders pertinent to the Arctic, such as the United Nations climate change and the Law of the Sea regimes, have little or no relevance to the Arctic/non-Arctic dichotomy. Also as the chapter by Nielsson and Magnússon (and to a lesser extent, that by Zou) attests, the bilateral governance-building based on concrete reciprocal merits between non-Arctic state (China in their essays) and Arctic states tends to reflect more accurately their economic, political, scientific, and/or military interests and powers, rather than their formal status as Arctic or non-Arctic. So, do we see an underlying shift in the ocean currents where important Arctic-related law-making is more likely to occur outside of the Arctic Council, where the Arctic/non-Arctic dichotomy has less relevance and thus where the latter has more leverage in the outcome?

Koivurova is very clear in situating the Arctic Council as the only standing intergovernmental forum focusing on Arctic policy issues. He states that "it is natural that any actor wanting to contribute to improving Arctic governance, needs to also be active in the Arctic Council".[13] Thus, the emerging legal orders in the Arctic will continue to occur at the crossroads of the Arctic Council on the one hand and the global, regional (e.g. UN Economic Commission on Europe (UNECE)), functional (e.g. Arctic Science Ministerial (ASM)[14]) and bilateral institutions on the other. The question is how the Arctic Council and its non-Arctic Observers have responded to such a dynamic legal order-making for the Arctic. Arctic science cooperation is a testing case for the Arctic Council and its non-Arctic Observers in demonstrating their relevance in Arctic legal order-making since the universality of

13 Chapter 2 by Timo Koivurova in this book.

14 The first ASM was held in September 2016, hosted by United States. www.arctic.gov/publications/other/supporting_arctic_science.html (accessed 5 October 2018). The second ASM was held in October 2018, co-hosted by European Commission, Finland and Germany. https://europa.eu/newsroom/events/2d-artic-science-ministerial-meeting_en (accessed 5 October 2018). The third ASM in 2020 will be co-hosted by Iceland and Japan. Conclusions of the Second Arctic Science Ministerial. www.arcticscienceministerial.org/en/conclusions-1740.html (accessed 1 December 2018).

science draws interests from many non-Arctic states and actors. And after all, the Observer scheme in the work of its Working Groups and other subsidiary bodies has been meant to incorporate such interests from the wider scientific community.

According to the analysis by Akiho Shibata on the Arctic Science Cooperation Agreement negotiated under the auspices of the Arctic Council in its Science Cooperation Task Force (SCTF), the Agreement has succeed in reflecting as much as possible the interests of non-Arctic states and their scientists actively engaged in Arctic science. Even though only the eight Arctic states had the decision-making powers in the SCTF, Arctic Council Observer states and organisations have provided substantive inputs during the negotiation. He cites the procedural and diplomatic ingenuities demonstrated by the co-chairs of the SCTF as instrumental in achieving such result (Chapter 12: "The Arctic Science Cooperation Agreement: A Perspective from Non-Arctic Actors"). At a more general level of the working methods of the Arctic Council, Sebastian Knecht and Jennifer Spence discuss the institutional and procedural reform undergone by the Arctic Council in order to accommodate a rising number of Observer states. According to their analysis, the shift from a flexible to a more formal and rule-based admission policy might result in impaired contributions from different Observers and ultimately impair the science cooperation objectives pursued by the Council (Chapter 13: "State Observers and Science Cooperation in the Arctic Council: Same Same But Different?"). Yuanyuan Ren showcases how the participation of Observer states may also face limitations. Examining China's influence in the Arctic Council, Ren claims that China has yet to find its proper way to make its voice heard due to the restriction faced by Observer states in the Council in addition to China having failed to properly leverage Arctic governance due to inadequate delegations and unclear domestic institutional competences (Chapter 14: "China in the Arctic Council: Existing Problems and Prospective Solutions").

1.5 The fountainhead

Who are the non-Arctic actors and how, where and to what degree do they influence the emerging Arctic legal order? These are questions that have not been addressed from a legal perspective. And these are the questions that have prompted us to delve more deeply. However, it became clear rather quickly that contemporary literature on the legal Arctic does not address the role of non-Arctic actors from a normative angle. To this end, we convened the conference entitled "The Role of Non-Arctic States/Actors in the Arctic Legal Order-Making" on 7–9 December 2017 at the Polar Cooperation Research Centre, Kobe University, Japan. Twenty-eight experts and scholars constituted the presenters and panellists of the symposium.[15] The present volume, which aims to fill a gap to address the normative impact of non-Arctic actors on the Arctic

15 Tony Cabus and Maiko Raita (2017) "Conference Report: The Role of Non-Arctic States/Actors in the Arctic Legal Order-Making" in *Current Developments in Arctic Law*, University of Lapland, Rovaniemi: 4–7. http://lauda.ulapland.fi/bitstream/handle/10024/63186/Cabus.Tony%3b%20Raita.Maiko.pdf?sequence=1&isAllowed=y (accessed 6 August 2018).

legal order, is a result of some of the papers presented. We have tried to present a balanced perspective on who these different actors are and in which fora and to what degree they are able to influence law- and policy-making in and for the Arctic. Since legal research on these issues is in its infancy, this book constitutes the first attempt to make the legal role of non-Arctic actors in the Arctic legal order comprehensible.

Part I

Setting the contexts

2 The current and future role of non-Arctic states in Arctic governance

*Timo Koivurova**

2.1 Introduction

This chapter ponders the role of non-Arctic actors, non-Arctic states in particular, in shaping the Arctic law and policy order. For many years, the focus has been on creating legal and policy arrangements by which the northern states influence how the Arctic is to be governed via international forums and hard- and soft-law measures. The game-changer in this respect has clearly been the melting of the Arctic Ocean sea ice, given that with open ocean, other states in the world can in principle exercise their rights and freedoms guaranteed in the Law of the Sea and the UN Convention on the Law of the Sea (UNCLOS).[1] Current estimates suggest that we will witness the first summer without any sea ice by 2030 to 2040,[2] which means that extensive navigational freedoms are going to become increasingly available in the coming two to three decades, especially in the 2.8 million square kilometre high seas portion of the Arctic Ocean.[3]

Not only economic opportunities have awakened outside interest in Arctic affairs, and many are concerned as to what will happen to the vulnerable ecosystems of the Arctic, one of the last frontier regions of our planet. Also, some have also been concerned by the possible geopolitical tensions that have risen in

* I am indebted to Krittika Singh for her research assistance.

1 UNCLOS codifies customary law of the sea (which applies to the United States as it is not a party to the UNCLOS). See Timo Koivurova (2016) "How to Improve Arctic International Governance" *UC Irvine Law Review* 6–1: 83; Tavis Potts and Clive H. Schofield (2008) "Current Legal Developments: The Arctic" *International Journal of Marine and Coastal Law* 23–1: 158. See also the The Ilulissat Declaration, Arctic Ocean Conference of 28 May 2008, *International Legal Materials* 48: 362. The declaration says: "this framework provides a solid foundation for responsible management by the five coastal States and other users of this Ocean through national implementation and application of relevant provisions".

2 See Arctic Council AMAP (2017) "Snow, Water, Ice and Permafrost in the Arctic (SWIPA)". www.amap.no/documents/doc/Snow-Water-Ice-and-Permafrost-in-the-Arctic-SWIPA-2017/1610 (accessed 6 June 2018).

3 See Lawson W. Brigham (2017) "The Changing Maritime Arctic and New Marine Operations" in *Governance of Arctic Shipping: Balancing Rights and Interests of Arctic States and User States* edited by Robert C. Beckman, Tore Henriksen, Kristine Dalaker Kraabel, Erik J. Molenaar and J. Ashley Roach. Brill, Leiden: 11–12.

the region, symbolised by the Russian flag-planting underneath the North Pole in 2007.[4]

The chapter proceeds in the following manner: since the special emphasis of this chapter is on the contribution of non-Arctic states to Arctic governance, it makes sense to establish who are the Arctic and non-Arctic states, and thereafter which non-Arctic actors have a clear policy role in the region.

Particular attention is paid to the two possible ways of framing how states can be deemed Arctic states: either as the Arctic Eight or as the Arctic Five. By defining the Arctic states, I also show which states are normally identified as non-Arctic states. It seems clear that, at present, it is the members of the Arctic Council that can be considered Arctic states, even if Arctic Ocean coastal states have occasionally challenged this conception. It is also useful to carry out a brief study of the basic rights and obligations of the observer states, and to other Observers that have an influence on the work of the Arctic Council. Finally, this chapter offers a general overview of the contribution of non-Arctic actors, in particular states, on Arctic governance.

2.2 Who are the Arctic and non-Arctic states?

In the last 50 years or so, two competing ideas have existed as to who forms Arctic states: Arctic Ocean coastal states (Arctic Five; A5) or the members of the Arctic Council that have sovereign areas above the Arctic Circle (Arctic Eight). It is fair to say that our concept of the Arctic has expanded over time, reflected for instance in the general public's view of what the Arctic actually is. The Arctic used to be defined by frozen seas, glaciers, northern reaches of tundra or barren desserts, and this meant that northern areas covered by boreal forests were not included in this public perception of the Arctic. Indeed, one of the most popular geographical definitions of the Arctic refers to the tree line or the 10°C July isotherm as forming the southern boundaries of the Arctic.[5] Over the years, this public perception of what constitutes the Arctic has expanded to include many northern regions – a process which has been partly driven by the conscious and interest-driven efforts of many actors (e.g. sub-national authorities viewing the Arctic label as being beneficial for their regions).

It is interesting to note that prior to the mid-1980s, there had been no discussion of who formed the Arctic states, and the Arctic was still to emerge as a political region. If we had had that discussion, we would have likely perceived Arctic states as being those states with coastal fronts to the Arctic Ocean. It was the Arctic range states that concluded the Polar Bear Agreement in 1973, simply

4 See Scott G. Borgerson (2008) "Arctic Meltdown" *Foreign Affairs* March/April Issue; Tavis Potts and Clive H. Schofield (2008) "Current Legal Developments: The Arctic" *International Journal of Marine and Coastal Law* 23–1: 151–176.

5 See Rosemary Rayfuse (2007) "Melting Moments: The Future of Polar Oceans Governance in a Warming World" *Review of European Community & International Environmental Law* 16–2: 196–216.

because polar bears only live in the area of these states.[6] In the whole body of the United Nations Convention on the Law of the Sea (UNCLOS), there was only one article that pertained to the Arctic region.[7] Article 234 accorded additional enforcement powers for the purpose of environmental protection over vessel traffic in exclusive economic zones (EEZs), if the ocean area was ice-covered. It was therefore the Arctic Ocean coastal states that potentially had these additional enforcement powers over their ice-covered seas. An argument has also been advanced that the Arctic Ocean could qualify as a semi-enclosed ocean under Article 122, and thereby this would entail co-operation obligations (Article 123) in various policy areas between the Arctic Ocean coastal states.[8] Even if there is disagreement as to whether the Arctic Ocean qualifies as such an ocean, it is obvious that the Arctic Ocean coastal states could have invoked this article to commence cooperation,[9] but they have not yet chosen to do so.

It is important to note that during this era an idea of the Arctic as a separate political region did not exist, and that in terms of Cold War high politics it was seen primarily as a strategic military theatre. However, this perception started to change during the mid-1980s because of several processes. First, negotiations surrounding the International Arctic Scientific Committee (IASC) commenced in 1986, and during those negotiations the Arctic Circle was seen as the decisive southern line of the Arctic. On this basis, it was decided that those states that had sovereignty above the Arctic Circle were deemed as Arctic states.[10] Another important influence was Secretary-General Gorbachev's speech in 1987 in Murmansk, which paid particular attention to environmental cooperation in northern Europe.[11] Finland utilised this opportunity and obviously wanted the Arctic Circle to serve as a criterion of membership since it was not a coastal state to the

6 See the Agreement on the Conservation of Polar Bears, signed 15 November 1973 and entered into force 26 May 1976, *International Legal Materials* 13–1: 13–18.

7 See the UN Convention on the Law of the Sea, adopted 10 December 1982 and entered into force 16 November 1994, *United Nations Treaty Series* 1833: 3.

8 Ibid. Article 122 of UNCLOS: For purposes of this Convention, "enclosed or semi-enclosed sea" means a gulf, basin or sea surrounded by two or more states and connected to another sea or the ocean by a narrow outlet or consisting entirely primarily of the territorial seas and exclusive economic zones of two or more coastal states.

9 See Rayfuse, *supra* note 5. It is a vexed question whether the Arctic Ocean is a semi-enclosed sea over which Arctic coastal states are vested with special rights and duties of cooperation as provided for in Articles 122 and 123. See also Koivurova, *supra* note 1; Donald Rothwell (1996) *The Polar Regions and the Development of International Law*. Cambridge University Press, Cambridge: 289–290.

10 See Odd Rogne et al. (2015) *IASC after 25 Years – A Quarter of a Century of International Arctic Research Cooperation*. Special Issue of the IASC Bulletin. https://iasc.info/iasc/history (accessed 6 June 2018).

11 See Michail Gorbatjov (1987) *The Speech in Murmansk: At the Ceremonial Meeting on the Occasion of the Presentation of the Order of Lenin and the Gold Star Medal to the City of Murmansk, 1 October 1987*. Novosti Press Agency, Moskva. See also Kristian Åtland (2008) "Mikhail Gorbachev, the Murmansk Initiative, and the Desecuritization of Interstate Relations in the Arctic" *Cooperation and Conflict* 43–3: 289–311.

Arctic Ocean. The power of academics to influence what we see as politically distinct regions should also not be underestimated. A widely read article by Oran Young titled "The Age of the Arctic" projected that the Arctic would establish itself as a distinct political region.[12]

Overall, it was a Finnish initiative to commence inter-governmental cooperation focused on environmental protection between the eight Arctic states that settled this matter for a while, and states that had sovereignty areas above the Arctic Circle were deemed Arctic states (Russia, the United States, Canada and the five Nordic states). They launched the Arctic Environmental Protection Strategy cooperation, which later was merged to form the Arctic Council during 1996 to 1998.[13]

This perception of who comprised the Arctic states stood for a number of years until it was challenged. In 2008, the five Arctic Ocean coastal states organised a meeting in Ilulissat Greenland, without inviting the three other member states of the Arctic Council (Finland, Sweden and Iceland), or the Permanent Participants of indigenous peoples organisations that have a unique status in the Arctic Council. In the Ilulissat Declaration, the Arctic Five defined themselves as stewards of the Arctic Ocean and envisaged cooperation in various areas.[14] This caused considerable consternation among the non-invited member states of the Arctic Council and among the Permanent Participants, especially because it seemed that the Arctic Five were in the process of establishing a permanent general forum for inter-governmental cooperation, perhaps even challenging the Arctic Council.[15] In 2010, as a result of the second meeting of the Arctic Five, the then Secretary of State of the United States, Hillary Clinton, stated that these meetings between the Arctic Five should not continue, and that focus should be put on the work of the Arctic Council. Although the Arctic Five have acted as initiators of the central Arctic Ocean fisheries agreement, they have not issued any further challenge to the role of the Arctic Council as the predominant inter-governmental forum focusing on the Arctic. However, the A5 format is still seen as useful for the purposes of fisheries and continental shelf delimitation issues.[16]

What are the practical consequences of deciding who are deemed as being Arctic states? It is obvious that if the cooperation had proceeded with only the Arctic Ocean coastal states, then the three states of Finland, Sweden and Iceland would no longer be "Arctic states". Furthermore, the focus would be on marine issues, rather than on both land and marine issues as they are currently

12 See Oran R. Young (1985) "The Age of the Arctic" *Foreign Policy* 61: 160–179.

13 See Arctic Environmental Protection Strategy (AEPS), 14 June 1991, *International Legal Materials* 30: 1624–1669.

14 The Ilulissat Declaration (2008), *supra* note 1.

15 On a personal level, I was invited to two Arctic conferences as a non-Arctic state representative.

16 See Center for Military Studies, University of Copenhagen (2018) "Learning from the Ilulissat Initiative: State Power, Institutional Legitimacy, and Governance in the Arctic Ocean 2007–18", 19 February 2018. https://cms.polsci.ku.dk/english/publications/learning-from-the-ilulissat-iniative/ (accessed 6 June 2018).

considered in the Arctic Council. As shown below, the legally binding agreements catalysed by the Arctic Council have taken the form of region-building regimes in that they always try to include all of the Arctic Eight as parties to the agreements.

The Arctic states are commonly seen to be those states that are members of the Arctic Council, and as a consequence this means that all other states are non-Arctic states. Most of the states that wish to contribute to Arctic governance are Observers to the Arctic Council, although it needs to be kept in mind that not all states that have applied for Observer status have been accepted as such. Currently, it can be evaluated that those states that take a keen interest in the Arctic have Observer status, but there are also some states that are party to the Svalbard Treaty but not yet Observers to the Arctic Council.[17] Some of these states may file to become Observers but they also need to demonstrate their Arctic interests, and show that they can fulfil the criteria for Observers by the Arctic Council. Given the Arctic Council's criterion of the Arctic Circle as forming the southernmost boundary of the Arctic, we know that when we talk of non-Arctic states, we are normally referring to Observers to the Arctic Council.

2.2.1 Who are the non-state actors that can be seen as Arctic actors?

When we talk of non-Arctic actors, it is useful to discuss who generally belongs to the non-state actor category. This means policy actors other than nation-states, and can be seen to consist of two main sub-groups – inter-governmental organisations (IGOs) and forums and non-governmental organisations (NGOs), and the many types of actors they involve.[18]

From the viewpoint of Arctic policy and law, the most relevant distinction between these actors is in those that have a clear Arctic identity, and those that do not. A good example is the International Arctic Science Committee (IASC) that was commenced in 1990, even before the whole pan-Arctic inter-governmental cooperation commenced in 1991. As such, IASC has been an observer to the pan-Arctic cooperation from the very beginning.

Perhaps most distinctively, it is the region's indigenous peoples non-governmental organisations that first started as observers in the Arctic Environmental Protection Strategy (AEPS) but came to be recognised as Permanent Participants in the Arctic Council that serve to demonstrate the strong position these non-governmental organisations have in the current Arctic Council. This is

17 See Treaty between Norway, the USA, Denmark, France, Italy, Japan, the Netherlands, Great Britain and Ireland and the British Overseas Dominions and Sweden with regard to the Archipelago of Spitsbergen, signed 9 February 1920 and entered into force 14 August 1925, *League of Nations Treaties Series* 2: 7. A total of 43 countries are registered as parties to the Svalbard Treaty (originally the Spitsbergen Treaty).

18 See Arctic Council website: "Observers – Arctic Council". www.arctic-council.org/index.php/en/observer-menu (accessed 6 June 2018).

not only shown by the fact that six indigenous peoples NGOs are now Permanent Participants in the Arctic Council and need to be consulted before decision-making by nation-states, but also that they clearly demonstrate their strength in Arctic governance as core actors.[19] The Arctic Five organised their meeting in Ilulissat, Greenland, in 2008, without the participation of Iceland, Finland and Sweden, and importantly without the participation of Permanent Participants. This caused a lot of consternation, and one of the factors that caused the US to pull out of the second meeting of the Arctic Five (in Chelsea, Canada) was that indigenous peoples organisations had protested against these meetings. Another sign of the strength of these Permanent Participants is that the Inuit Circumpolar Council (ICC, one of the Permanent Participants) has already issued international declarations of its own to influence Arctic policy and law.[20] The ICC represents the Inuit in Russia, the United States, Canada and Greenland, and as an international NGO perceives that it should have a strong say as to which direction Arctic policy and law turns, especially given that they and other Permanent Participants are the original occupants of the region.[21]

One group of non-state actors that are clearly Arctic are those provinces and sub-national units that actually conduct Arctic governance. The Northern Forum is the international non-governmental organisation that brings together many of these sub-national units (including some non-Arctic regions), and it is also an Observer to the Arctic Council. Since these sub-national bodies represent the majority of people that live in the Arctic, an argument has been made that their status in the Arctic Council should be strengthened. Tony Penikett has suggested that the Northern Forum could be elevated to the status of Permanent Participant, but this seems difficult from the viewpoint of criteria set out for Permanent Participants.[22] Another suggestion has been that the Arctic Council could catalyse a regional council, similar to the way it created the Arctic Economic Council (AEC). With this idea, regional actors – represented by an independent organisation – would be consulted by the Arctic Council when it comes to issues falling under the purview of their governance mandate.

There are many examples of Observers to the Arctic Council that have clear Arctic identity, either because of the region they represent or the issues they deal with. Among the intergovernmental and inter-parliamentary organisations, the clearest examples are the North Atlantic Marine Mammal Commission (NAMMCO); OSPAR Commission (as their scope of application of the treaty extends

19 See Dalee Sambo Dorough (2017) “The Rights, Interests and Role of the Arctic Council Permanent Participants” in *Governance of Arctic Shipping*, *supra* note 3, at 68–103.

20 Ibid., at 72. See also the Circumpolar Inuit Declaration on Sovereignty (2009). www.inuitcircumpolar.com/sovereignty-in-the-arctic.html (accessed 6 June 2018); and the Circumpolar Inuit Declaration on Resource Development Principles in the North (2011). www.inuitcircumpolar.com/uploads/3/0/5/4/30542564/declaration_on_resource_development_a3_final.pdf (accessed 6 June 2018).

21 Dorough, *supra* note 19, at 71–74. For more information on the creation of the Inuit Circumpolar Council see ICC homepage: www.inuitcircumpolar.com (accessed 6 June 2018).

22 Tony Penikett (2017) *Hunting the Northern Character*. Purich Books, Vancouver.

to the North Pole); Standing Committee of the Parliamentarians of the Arctic Region (SCPAR); Nordic Council of Ministers (NCM); Nordic Environment Finance Corporation (NEFCO); and the West Nordic Council (WNC). Among the non-governmental organisations, there are also many that have their roots and identity in the Arctic, such as the Arctic Institute of North America (AINA); Association of World Reindeer Herders (AWRH); Circumpolar Conservation Union (CCU); International Arctic Science Committee (IASC); International Arctic Social Sciences Association (IASSA); International Union for Circumpolar Health (IUCH); the Northern Forum (NF); and the University of the Arctic (UArctic).

There are also many global organisations that have a particular Arctic focus in their work. Of the Observers to the Arctic Council, many of the inter-governmental organisations have a fully global operating sphere but also conduct Arctic policy. These include bodies such as the International Council for the Exploration of the Sea (ICES); International Federation of Red Cross & Red Crescent Societies (IFRC); International Union for the Conservation of Nature (IUCN); United Nations Development Programme (UNDP); United Nations Environment Programme (UNEP); and the World Meteorological Organization (WMO).

There are also regional inter-governmental organisations that contribute to the work of the Arctic Council. At the Kiruna Ministerial Meeting in 2013, the Arctic Council "receive[d] the application of the European Union (EU) for Observer status affirmatively", but deferred a final decision. Until such time as Ministers of the Arctic states may reach a final decision, the EU may observe Council proceedings. This has meant in practice that the EU has been treated in a similar way to other Observers, even though it is not yet an Observer to the Council. Moreover, the United Nations Economic Commission for Europe (UN-ECE) is an Observer to the Arctic Council, likely because all eight Arctic states are its members. Many global non-governmental organisations are also Observers to the Council, such as the Advisory Committee on Protection of the Sea (ACOPS); International Work Group for Indigenous Affairs (IWGIA); National Geographic Society (NGS); and the Oceana conservation and advocacy group. The strongest of these global actors has been the World Wide Fund for Nature-Global Arctic Program (WWF), which has been a very effective Observer during the existence of the Arctic Council.

Other non-state actors also have an Arctic focus in their activities, and a good example is Greenpeace International, which applied for Observer status in the Arctic Council but was not approved. No reasons have been published for this rejection, but it is likely that because of its "Save the Arctic" campaign and the controversy it had with Russia over the Prirazlomnoya oil rig, Greenpeace was probably not seen as fulfilling the criteria for an Arctic Council Observer, not only by Russia, but also by some of the other states and Permanent Participants.[23]

23 See Piotr Graczyk and Timo Koivurova (2015) "The Arctic Council" in *Handbook of the Politics of the Arctic* edited by Leif Christian Jensen and Geir Hønneland, Edward Elgar, Cheltenham: 298–327; Erik J. Molenaar, (2017) "The Arctic, the Arctic Council, and the Law of the Sea" in *Governance of Arctic Shipping*, *supra* note 3, at 51–52.

2.2.2 *Why does the Arctic Council create Arctic agency for non-Arctic actors?*

It seems clear that it is the Arctic Council that defines the states and organisations that want to engage in Arctic policy,[24] and this is already laid out in the criteria for Observers:[25]

> In the determination by the Council of the general suitability of an applicant for Observer status the Council will, *inter alia*, take into account the extent to which observers:

(1) Accept and support the objectives of the Arctic Council defined in the Ottawa declaration;
(2) Recognize Arctic States' sovereignty, sovereign rights and jurisdiction in the Arctic;
(3) Recognize that an extensive legal framework applies to the Arctic Ocean including, notably, the Law of the Sea, and that this framework provides a solid foundation for responsible management of this ocean;
(4) Respect the values, interests, culture and traditions of Arctic indigenous peoples and other Arctic inhabitants;
(5) Have demonstrated a political willingness as well as financial ability to contribute to the work of the Permanent Participants and other Arctic indigenous peoples;
(6) Have demonstrated their Arctic interests and expertise relevant to the work of the Arctic Council; and
(7) Have demonstrated a concrete interest and ability to support the work of the Arctic Council, including through partnerships with member states and permanent participants bringing Arctic concerns to global decision making bodies.

What is of interest here is that non-Arctic actors have to not only accept the basic rules of Arctic governance and the special role of Permanent Participants, but also demonstrate their "Arctic interests and expertise relevant to the work of the Arctic Council". And, since the Arctic Council is the only standing intergovernmental forum focusing on Arctic policy issues, it is natural that any actor

24 See *Ottawa Declaration on the Establishment of the Arctic Council*, 19 September 1996 (especially Article 3). https://oaarchive.arctic-council.org/bitstream/handle/11374/85/EDOCS-1752-v2-ACMMCA00_Ottawa_1996_Founding_Declaration.PDF?sequence=5&isAllowed=y (accessed 6 June 2018). See also Rules 36–38, *Arctic Council Rules of Procedure*, most recent version adopted by the Kiruna Ministerial Meeting, 2013. www.arctic-council.org (accessed 6 June 2018). It is also of interest that the related institutions to the Arctic Council, those to which it has given birth, The University of the Arctic, the Arctic Economic Council and the Arctic Coastguard Forum use the same definition of which states are Arctic, reinforcing the idea that these eight states are the Arctic states.

25 Criteria for admitting Observers, "Observers – Arctic Council", *supra* note 18.

wanting to contribute to improving Arctic governance needs also to be active in the Arctic Council.[26] Notably, although Greenpeace has applied for Observer status in the Arctic Council, it has not yet been granted.[27]

2.3 What is the role of non-Arctic states in the Arctic Council?

From 2007 to 2009, a lot of anxiety existed among member states, Permanent Participants and among those countries that were Observers or candidates for such status. As examples, France was critical of the limited possibilities that Observer status offered for its contribution to the work of the Arctic Council, and the Permanent Participants were concerned with vast nation states like China sending big delegations as ad hoc Observers to the Arctic Council.[28] This happened largely because at the time there were no clear rules on who could become an Observer, and under what criteria. It was also unclear as to what rights and obligations the Observer status entailed. This challenge was resolved by revising internal rules, and the criteria for entities seeking Observer status and their rights and obligations were decided by the Arctic Council in their 2011 and 2013 ministerial meetings, respectively.[29] Now, the system is much clearer for all of the actors within the Arctic Council, and 13 states have now been accepted as Observers,[30] with an overall total of 39 Observers.

As defined by the internal rules of the Arctic Council, Observers (including major non-Arctic states) can mainly work in the Working Groups and other subsidiary bodies, where most of the work of the Arctic Council is conducted.[31]

26 See Piotr Graczyk et al. (2017) "Preparing for the Global Rush: The Arctic Council, Institutional Norms, and Socialisation of Observer Behaviour" in *Governing Arctic Change: Global Perspective* edited by Kathrin Stephen and Sebastian Knecht. Palgrave Macmillan, London: 121–139. See also Piotr Graczyk and Timo Koivurova (2014) "A New Era in the Arctic Council's External Relations? Broader Consequences of the Nuuk Observer Rules for Arctic Governance" *Polar Record* 50–3: 225–236.

27 Molenaar, *supra* note 23.

28 Graczyk and Koivurova, *supra* note 26.

29 Ibid. See also Molenaar, *supra* note 23, at 50. The 2011 Nuuk Ministerial Meeting adopted the so-called "Nuuk Observer Rules". The Task Force for Institutional Issues (TFII) established in 2011 was charged with amending the original (1998) Arctic Council Rules of Procedure to ensure the integration of the Nuuk Observer Rules and – at a later stage – with drafting an "Observer Manual". The amended Rules of Procedure and the "Observer Manual for Subsidiary Bodies" were eventually adopted in 2013 and applied to most of the then pending applications.

30 Applications made by three states: Turkey (in 2013), Mongolia (in 2013) and Greece (in 2014) for Observer status were rejected prior to the 2017 Fairbanks Ministerial Meeting. See Molenaar, *supra* note 23, at 49.

31 *Arctic Council Observer Manual for Subsidiary Bodies*, as adopted by the Arctic Council at the Eight Arctic Council Ministerial Meeting, Kiruna, Sweden, 15 May 2013. https://oaarchive.arctic-council.org/bitstream/handle/11374/939/EDOCS-3020-v1B-Observer-manual-with-addendum-finalized_Oct2016.PDF (accessed 6 June 2018).

Hence, they can participate meaningfully in the areas of action that the Arctic Council undertakes, mainly in broad fields of soft-law environmental protection and sustainable development work. Currently, Observer status is regularly reviewed, and can also be postponed or terminated.[32]

Non-Arctic state Observers can also influence the work of the Arctic Council in other ways. They have a right to make written submissions in Senior Arctic Official Meetings.[33] Outside the internal rules of the Council, non-Arctic state Observers can also influence the Arctic Council, depending on how matters are organised by the chair-state.[34] Various chair-states have used their discretion to enable different formats to engage Observers. As an example, the current chair (Finland) will make use of some of the practices used by previous chairs, but in its own manner. At the recent Oulu SAO plenary meeting in October 2017, Finland had a separate session where Observers had the opportunity to present what types of pollution prevention work they have undertaken in the Arctic Council.[35] In the next SAO meeting in Levi in March 2018, Observers will be given the possibility to directly interact with working groups of the Arctic Council.[36] As was pointed out above, the role of Observers can be very important in the subsidiary bodies of the Arctic Council, in particular in the Working Groups. Thus, a couple of examples may help to illustrate this more clearly.

The Arctic Migratory Birds Initiative (AMBI), under the Conservation of Arctic Flora and Fauna (CAFF) working group of the Arctic Council, aims to enhance the conservation status of migratory birds that breed in the Arctic.[37] Since these birds live parts of their lives much further to the south, there is also a need to work with non-Arctic state Observers to the Council, many of whom have been very active in this project.[38] Another good example of non-Arctic state participation is the framework programme on black carbon and methane, which is conducted under an expert group now headed by Finland. Since much of the

32 The previous chair (the United States) and current chair (Finland) agreed that the US reviews Observers that had been accepted as Observers before 2000, and Finland will review the rest during its chairmanship 2017 to 2019. Also see Rule 37 of the Arctic Council Rules of Procedure and Rule 4.3 of the Observer Manual.

33 Rule 38 of the Arctic Council Rules of Procedure and Rule 7.4 of the Observer Manual.

34 See Douglas C. Nord (2016) *The Arctic Council: Governance within the Far North*. Routledge, London. See also Graczyk et al., *supra* note 26.

35 Arctic Council (2017) "Summary Report, SAO Plenary meeting, Oulu, Finland, October 2017", at 10–11. https://oaarchive.arctic-council.org/handle/11374/2030 (accessed 6 June 2018).

36 This was also organised in the US chair period.

37 Arctic Council Conservation of Arctic Flora and Fauna: "Arctic Migratory Birds Initiative (AMBI)". www.caff.is/arctic-migratory-birds-initiative-ambi (accessed 6 June 2018). See also Arctic Council (2014) "Final Report on Senior Arctic Official (SAO) meeting of the Arctic Council, Yellowknife, Canada, 26–27 March 2014", at 10 (section 5.4.2, Arctic Migratory Birds Initiative (AMBI)).

38 The AMBI webpage notes: "Arctic breeding birds use as many as eight different flyways to move from Arctic breeding grounds to overwintering or stopover sites at lower latitudes". See also Timo Koivurova, Qin Tianbao, Tapio Nykänen and Sébastien Duyck (eds) (2017) *Arctic Law and Governance: The Role of China, Finland, and the EU*. Hart Publishing, Oxford.

emissions of these short-lived warming substances come from outside of the Arctic, non-Arctic state Observers to the Arctic Council are in a crucial position and have contributed substantially to this programme.[39]

Can this current system be amended to create a stronger position for Observer influence, especially from the part of non-Arctic states? Given that the member states have now by consensus revised the rules on the basis of which non-Arctic states can influence the work of the Arctic Council, it does not seem so, at least for the short-term future. Small indigenous peoples organisations have a unique role in the Arctic Council as Permanent Participants, and can wield a lot of influence. Overall, they are satisfied with the system, as the power of the major nation-states and other Observers is now limited, at least to some extent.

However, this does not prevent the active engagement of non-Arctic states in projects undertaken within the subsidiary bodies of the Arctic Council, and some good examples of this have been shown above. Yet, non-Arctic states also face challenges to make their imprint on the work of the Arctic Council, especially when it comes to the more recent activity that has catalysed independent legally binding agreements between the eight Arctic states. Even if the Arctic Council acts only as a platform for negotiating these legally binding agreements, it exerts influence as to who gets to participate in the making of such agreements, and with what status.

The three legally binding agreements that have been concluded under the umbrella of the Arctic Council have been negotiated between the eight Arctic states, and they have become exclusive parties to these agreements. Of interest is that the making of these three negotiations offers a good example of how the region has been built on the basis of the Arctic Eight forming the proper Arctic states, somewhat artificially and forcefully involving Arctic states without Arctic Ocean coastlines. For instance, the first legally binding agreement catalysed by the Arctic Council was the Search and Rescue Agreement,[40] which initially focused only on marine areas. Yet, since it was developed under the task-force of the Arctic Council, it finally included Finland and Sweden as parties, with the idea that they are in charge of search and rescue operations for aircraft accidents in their northern regions. Another interesting example is the second legally binding agreement, the oil spills agreement,[41] which obviously focuses on marine areas. However, this agreement was extended to the north of the Gulf of Bothnia

39 See Arctic Council: "Black Carbon and Methane Expert Group". https://oaarchive.arctic-council.org/handle/11374/1167 (accessed 6 June 2018). See also Arctic Council (2015) "Enhanced Black Carbon and Methane Emissions Reductions: An Arctic Council Framework for Action" in *Annex 4 Iqaluit 2015 SAO Report to Ministers*. https://oaarchive.arctic-council.org/bitstream/handle/11374/610/ACMMCA09_Iqaluit_2015_SAO_Report_Annex_4_TFBCM_Framework_Document.pdf?sequence=1&isAllowed=y (accessed 6 June 2018).

40 Agreement on Cooperation in Aeronautical and Maritime Search and Rescue in the Arctic, signed 12 May 2011 and entered into force 19 January 2013, *International Legal Materials* 50: 1119.

41 Agreement on Cooperation on Marine Oil Pollution Preparedness and Response in the Arctic, signed 15 May 2013 and entered into force 25 March 2016. https://oaarchive.arctic-council.org/handle/11374/529 (accessed 6 June 2018).

of the Baltic Sea, in order to include Finland and Sweden as parties, despite there already being a Nordic treaty regulating oil spill preparedness and response.[42]

From the viewpoint of the non-Arctic states, the most difficult agreement-making process has been that which looked to enhance scientific cooperation, and was signed in May 2017 at the Fairbanks ministerial meeting of the Arctic Council.[43] Despite many nationalities conducting Arctic research, it was the Arctic Eight that wanted to conduct Arctic science between themselves. This was clearly problematic for the many non-Arctic state Observers to the Council, and although they were able to negotiate at least some sort of access to conduct science in the Arctic,[44] there were obviously many questions left hanging in the air.[45] Under Article 17 – "Cooperation with non-Parties" – of the agreement, some sort of access is guaranteed:

1 The Parties may continue to enhance and facilitate cooperation with non-Parties with regard to Arctic science.
2 Parties may in their discretion undertake with non-Parties cooperation described in this Agreement and apply measures consistent with those described in this Agreement in cooperation with non-Parties.
3 Nothing in this Agreement shall affect the rights and obligations of the Parties under agreements with non-Parties, nor preclude cooperation between the Parties and non-Parties.

Yet, even if non-Arctic states were able to negotiate this article into the agreement, the status of their scientists is still in question.

All in all, the non-Arctic states have some rights in the Arctic Council, which enables them to influence the work of the subsidiary bodies. Yet, their role in the agreement making processes has been naturally more limited, especially given that these ultimately become legally binding agreements between the states parties, and are independent of the Arctic Council.

2.4 What is the overall role of non-Arctic actors in Arctic governance?

The discussion of who the Arctic actors are has so far focused mainly on the Arctic Council. This is reasonable, given that it is the Council that is seen as holding the symbolic power to give its seal of approval to those who wish to call themselves Arctic actors. Yet, in reality, Arctic governance is much broader. It is important to understand that general governance processes also influence Arctic

42 See Article 3 on the scope of application of this Agreement.

43 Agreement on Enhancing International Arctic Scientific Cooperation, signed 11 May 2017 and entered into force 23 May 2018. https://oaarchive.arctic-council.org/handle/11374/1916 (accessed 6 June 2018), reproduced in the Appendix of this book.

44 See Chapter 12 by Akiho Shibata in this book.

45 In addition, Permanent Participants were not generally satisfied with the minimalist reference in the agreement on their traditional knowledge.

governance. First, there are processes of global and semi-global governance that tackle issues that influence the Arctic, and even if they do not address the Arctic in particular, they are likely to be extremely influential in the Arctic region.

The most obvious example of these issues is the UN climate change regime, which most recently culminated with the 2015 Paris agreement.[46] The implementation of this agreement in the Arctic is of crucial importance from the viewpoint of what will happen to the Arctic region. The same applies to the UN Sustainable Development Goals that were also adopted in 2015,[47] and also apply to the Arctic region. As current chair of the Arctic Council, Finland has taken the implementation of these two international frameworks as part of its chairmanship priorities.[48] It is also important to keep in mind that all the Arctic states are members of the World Trade Organization and its extensive rules guaranteeing free trade.[49]

Another set of UN related rules that are of vast importance in the Arctic are those enshrined in the UNCLOS (also in its customary international law vis-à-vis the United States), and which sets the ground rules for marine activities in the Arctic waters. The UN Declaration on the Rights of Indigenous Peoples was adopted in 2007, and even if non-legally binding, it does have some legal influence in the Arctic.[50] Other than Russia, all of the other Arctic states have endorsed the Declaration.[51] On a regional level, the work of the United Nations Economic Commission for Europe (UNECE) and its many pollutant conventions

46 Paris Agreement, adopted 12 December 2015 and entered into force 4 November 2016, *United Nations Treaty Collection*, No. 54113.

47 United Nations General Assembly (2015) *Transforming Our World: The 2030 Agenda for Sustainable Development*, UNGA/RES/70/1 (25 September 2015).

48 Arctic Council (2017) "Exploring Common Solutions, Finland's Chairmanship Program for the Arctic Council 2017–2019", at 5, 10–11. https://oaarchive.arctic-council.org/handle/11374/1981 (accessed 6 June 2018)

49 The WTO mandate includes maritime transport services, the negotiation of which is guided by the principles of the General Agreement on Trade in Services. See World Trade Organization webpage: "Maritime transport". www.wto.org/english/tratop_e/serv_e/transport_e/transport_maritime_e.htm (accessed 6 June 2018). See Aldo Chircop (2017) "The IMO, Its Role under UNCLOS and Its Polar Shipping Regulation" *Governance of Arctic Shipping*, *supra* note 3, at 121.

50 See United Nations General Assembly (2007) *Declaration on the Rights of Indigenous Peoples*, UNGA/RES/61/295 (13 September 2007). See also Dorough, *supra* note 19. This declaration is a comprehensive international human rights instrument that affirms the distinct status and human rights of the world's indigenous peoples, including those within the Arctic circumpolar region. According to the International Law Association (ILA) Committee on Rights of Indigenous Peoples and its expert commentary on the UN Declaration, "the relevant areas of indigenous peoples' rights with respect to which the discourse on customary international law arises are self-determination; autonomy or self-government; cultural rights and identity; land rights as well as reparation, redress and remedies". See International Law Association (2010) "Interim Report of the Committee on Rights of Indigenous Peoples" in *Report of the Seventy-Fourth Conference, The Hague*. International Law Association, London: 898.

51 Initially, both the US and Canada voted against the declaration, together with New Zealand and Australia. Gradually, all of these four states have come to endorse the declaration, albeit with some reservations.

is important for the Arctic, given that all eight Arctic states are members of the UNECE.[52] In the future, we may also witness a new implementing agreement to the UNCLOS to govern how biodiversity is managed in areas beyond national jurisdiction, which also means the 2.8 million square kilometre high seas area of the Central Arctic Ocean.[53]

There are also general global conventions, the content of which have been influenced by Arctic Council actors. The Stockholm Convention on Persistent Organic Pollutants (POPs) adopted in 2001 and came into force in May 2004[54] was influenced by Arctic Council actors, as was the Minamata Convention on Mercury, which was adopted in 2013 and came into force in August 2017.[55] In both conventions, the Arctic is specifically mentioned in the Preamble simply because persistent organic pollutants and mercury end up in the Arctic, even if they are not produced there.[56]

Processes of general governance that specifically focus on the Arctic Ocean are largely driven by climate change induced melting of the sea ice. The mandatory Polar Code entered into force at the beginning of 2017. As a Code that applies both in the Arctic and Southern Ocean, it was negotiated in the global International Maritime Organization (IMO).[57] The Arctic Council has undertaken important soft-law work in this process, e.g. by recommending the negotiation of the mandatory Polar Code in the 2009 Arctic Marine Shipping Assessment (AMSA), and also in the follow-up work related to the recommendations issued by the AMSA.[58] Another similar process of governance is the recently adopted

52 See United Nations Economic Commission for Europe webpage. www.unece.org/mission.html (accessed 6 June 2018). See also Finland's Chairmanship Program, Arctic Council (2017), *supra* note 48, at 4: "The work on short-lived climate pollutants could be linked to similar activities under the United Nations Economic Commission for Europe Convention on Long-Range Transboundary Air Pollution".

53 See Molenaar, *supra* note 23, at 25. See also Cymie Payne (2017) "Biodiversity in High Seas Areas: An Integrated Legal Approach" *ASIL Insights* 21–9, 1 September 2017. www.asil.org/insights/volume/21/issue/9/biodiversity-high-seas-areas-integrated-legal-approach (accessed 6 June 2018).

54 *United Nations Treaty Series* 2256: 119. All Arctic states, except United States, have become parties to the Stockholm Convention on POPs.

55 *United Nations Treaty Collection*, No. 54669. All Arctic states, except Russia, have become parties to the Minamata Convention on Mercury.

56 See Oran R. Young (2016) "The Arctic Council at Twenty: How to Remain Effective in a Rapidly Changing Environment" *UC Irvine Law Review* 6–1: 99.

57 IMO (2015) "International Code for Ships Operating in Polar Waters (Polar Code)", MEPC/68/21/Add.1, Annex 10, at 3. www.imo.org/en/MediaCentre/HotTopics/polar/Documents/POLAR%20CODE%20TEXT%20AS%20ADOPTED.pdd (accessed 6 June 2018). The Polar Code addresses marine safety and environmental protection challenges for ships operating in remote, cold environments where marine infrastructure is limited or non-existent. See Chircop, *supra* note 49.

58 See Arctic Council (2009) *Arctic Marine Shipping Assessment 2009 Report.* https://oaarchive.arctic-council.org/handle/11374/54 (accessed 6 June 2018). See also Molenaar, *supra* note 23, at 53–54: "The Arctic council's role in monitoring and assessment is probably what the Council is best known for. … However, the AMSA was in fact more than an assessment as it contained negotiated policy recommendations." See also Arctic Council

agreement to prevent unregulated commercial fishing in the high seas portion of the Central Arctic Ocean.[59] This agreement was concluded between the Arctic Ocean coastal states and four other states (China, Japan, Republic of Korea and Iceland) and the European Union, and is loosely based on the global frameworks of UNCLOS and its implementing of the fish stocks agreement.[60]

Overall, it is obvious that much of the governance of the Arctic is conducted by all the states in the world, and those actors who are active in the relevant decision-making processes. Hence, so-called non-Arctic states can be seen to conduct Arctic governance on a daily basis, simply because many global processes have influence on Arctic governance. The distinction between Arctic and non-Arctic states does not have any practical importance in the cases of the Polar Code and the Central Arctic Ocean fisheries agreement. Many states have influenced how the Polar Code was shaped, based mainly on whether their vessels will access either the Southern or Arctic Oceans. The Central Arctic Ocean fisheries agreement is based on the difference between coastal states and fishing states, as laid down in the fish stocks agreement, and as such, whether one is an Arctic state or not is not of particular relevance.

2.5 Conclusion

When we evaluate the non-Arctic state influence on Arctic legal and policy order, we have to be careful in both delineating who are non-Arctic states and in what context, and also what type of influence they wield in Arctic governance. It is only in terms of the Arctic Council that we can identify who are non-Arctic states, and their associated rights and obligations. Currently, most of those involved seem satisfied with the system, as it gives power of influence to non-Arctic states where most of the work of the Arctic Council (i.e. in the working groups) is carried out.

Since it was the Arctic Council (the Arctic Eight) that became the dominant Arctic inter-governmental forum, rather than the Arctic Five, this has had clear practical consequences. This is manifest for instance in the way that Iceland, Finland and Sweden are now Arctic states, and take part in the work of the standing inter-governmental forum that focuses on the Arctic. Moreover, Finland and

(2015) "Status on the Implementation of the AMSA 2009 Report Recommendations"; and Arctic Council (2017) "Status on Implementation of the AMSA 2009 Report Recommendations: For the period March 2015–March 2017". https://oaarchive.arctic-council.org/handle/11374/415 and https://oaarchive.arctic-council.org/handle/11374/2010 (accessed 6 June 2018).

59 See European Commission (2017): "EU and Arctic Partners agree to prevent unregulated fishing in high seas", 1 December 2017. https://ec.europa.eu/maritimeaffairs/content/eu-and-arctic-partners-agree-prevent-unregulated-fishing-high-seas_en (accessed 6 June 2018). See Chapter 8 by Joji Morishita and Chapter 9 by Erik J. Molenaar in this book. For the text of the agreement, see the Appendix of this book.

60 See the Agreement for the Implementation of the Provisions of the United Nations Convention on the Law of the Sea of 10 December 1982 relating to the Conservation and Management of Straddling Fish Stocks and Highly Migratory Fish Stocks, adopted 4 August 1995 and entered into force 11 December 2001, *United Nations Treaty Series* 2167: 3.

Sweden were integrated into legally binding agreements regarding search and rescue and oil spills, even if somewhat artificially. This shows the power of region-building in the Arctic Council, particularly between the eight Arctic states. But, as also shown, any actor that wants to focus on Arctic governance is bound to file an application to the Arctic Council as the only standing inter-governmental forum focusing on environmental protection and sustainable development in the region. It is hence important for any state or organisation to become an Observer, in order to concretely contribute to Arctic governance.

In the bigger picture, it is obvious that, in one way or another, all states and non-state actors influence Arctic governance, whether they realise it or not, as many of the Arctic issues are regulated via global governance processes. This becomes manifest in the recently released policy document by China,[61] in which China perceives Arctic governance to be mostly part of global governance, and hence the place of China in this governance is significant. Hence, in Arctic legal order-making, all states and other actors are very much a part and parcel of shaping the future of Arctic governance, even if some of the actors take a more active and conscious role in this by being part of the functioning of the Arctic Council.

61 State Council of the People's Republic of China (2018) "China's Arctic Policy", 26 January 2018. http://english.gov.cn/archive/white_paper/2018/01/26/content_281476026660336.htm (accessed 6 June 2018).

3 The rise of Asia and Arctic legal order-making

Political–economic settings

Aki Tonami

3.1 Introduction

The Arctic is changing. In order to cope with and adapt to the quickly transforming Arctic, there have been calls for the creation of a new regime for the Arctic such as a legally binding Arctic Treaty.[1] In 2008, however, in the Ilulissat Declaration the Arctic coastal states, namely Canada, Denmark, Norway, Russia and the United States, formally rejected any "need to develop a new comprehensive international regal regime to govern the Arctic Ocean" similar to the Antarctic Treaty System.[2] It was also an acknowledgement that the existing legal framework created around the 1982 United Nations Law of the Sea Convention (UNCLOS) is sufficient and the Arctic legal order should remain more flexible than rigid, based on "soft-law" instruments and non-binding cooperative frameworks. Indeed, the Arctic Council (AC) is neither an international organisation nor does it have formal law-making capacities.[3] This unique set-up of Arctic governance limits participation of Asian states or actors in the decision-making process since they are, legally speaking, "outsiders". Yet, it allows them to play a different but not insignificant role in developing norms in/about the Arctic. For example, via an Arctic state or a Permanent Participant, they are able to propose projects which reinforce their views on specific issues.[4]

Against this background, this chapter asks the following questions: What are the political and economic contexts that explain the current development? What are the roles that Asian states have played so far in the Arctic legal-order making and the challenges Asian states/actors pose? What are the influences the Asian

1 See, for example, Scott G. Borgers (2008) "Arctic Meltdown: The Economic and Security Implications of Global Warming" *Foreign Affairs* 87–2: 63–77.

2 Christopher R. Rossi (2015) "The Club within the Club: The Challenge of a Soft Law Framework in a Global Arctic Context" *Polar Journal* 5–1: 8–34.

3 Rachael Lorna Johnstone (2016) "Environmental Governance through the Arctic Council: The Arctic Council as Initiator of Norms of International Environmental Law" *Polar Cooperation Research Centre (PCRC) Working Paper* 1: 1–23. www.research.kobe-u.ac.jp/gsics-pcrc/paper.html (accessed 31 January 2019)

4 Heather A. Conley and Matthew Melino (2016) *An Arctic Redesign: Recommendations to Rejuvenate the Arctic Council, A Report of the CSIS Europe Program.* CSIS Center for Strategic & International Studies.

actors have exerted in the past, and can exert today and in future Arctic legal-order making? In answering these questions, I will refer to concepts and theories of international political economy and international relations (IR). The reader should bear in mind that this study is based on mostly Western mainstream IR theories; it is beyond the scope of this chapter to examine a full discussion on non-Western/Asian perspectives on IR theory.[5] This chapter shows that, to maintain international order surrounding the Arctic region, Asian states are realists, placing more priority on the balance of power, diplomacy and the formation of alliances, rather than norm- and rule-making in international institutions. Arctic states would like Asian states to acquire a greater role in the international normative and institutional framework, particularly within already existing forums such as the Arctic Council (or its working groups).[6] However, from the Asian states' point of view, it will be shown that they are only willing to play a role if rule- and norm-making efforts serve their political/economic goals and where they clearly see the value of making mutually acceptable norms and codes of conduct in pursuing their economic security. The "rise" of Asia has taken new challenges to adapt to and to negotiate the Arctic.

3.2 The Arctic, the Arctic Council and the Asian states

Over a period of many decades, the Arctic region has been governed through a multi-layered legal system, which scholars such as Oran Young call an "international regime complex".[7] As more attention is paid to the changing natural environment of the Arctic, however, perhaps the biggest change introduced to the Arctic order-making in the last few years is that this knowledge of a multi-layered legal system is no longer limited to Arctic coastal states. Non-Arctic states/actors are now also aware that Arctic governance consists of arrays of international institutions for developing norms and codes of conduct. In this chapter, however, my primary intention is to discuss Arctic governance and the role of Asian states/actors centring around the Arctic Council. This is because the Arctic Council is not only a "unique intergovernmental forum"[8] but is "the principal institution

5 For a summary of Asian perspectives on international relations theories see, for example, Pichamon Yeophantong (2017) "Asian Perspectives" in *International Relations Theory* edited by Stephen McGlinchey, Rosie Walters and Christian Scheinpflug. E-International Relations Publishing: 117–44.

6 This "requirement" is clearly seen in the Arctic Council Observer Manual, published in 2013, which states that the applicants for Observer status are admitted (only) if "the Council determines (the Observer) can contribute to its work." Once they become Observers they are encouraged to make relevant contributions by participating in working group projects through knowledge sharing or financial support. See Arctic Council (2013) *Arctic Council Observer Manual for Subsidiary Bodies*, as adopted by the Arctic Council at the Eight Arctic Council Ministerial Meeting, Kiruna, Sweden, 15 May 2013. https://oaarchive.arctic-council.org/bitstream/handle/11374/939/EDOCS-3020-v1B-Observer-manualwith-addendum-fi nalized_Oct2016.PDF (accessed 30 August 2018).

7 Oran R. Young (2012) "Building an International Regime Complex for the Arctic: Current Status and next Steps" *Polar Journal* 2: 391–407.

8 Johnstone, *supra* note 3, at 1–23.

for Arctic regional governance" today.[9] It has grown significantly over the two decades since its establishment in 1996 and is now involved in various activities in the Arctic region. Building on its former regime, the 1991 Arctic Environmental Protection Strategy (AEPS), the Arctic Council seeks to tackle (predominantly environmental) problems in the Arctic region through developing Action Plans and its six Working Groups.[10] The Council has become increasingly prominent in the international community; however, it is yet to become an international organisation or adopt any formal law-making powers.[11]

Asian states have also regarded the Arctic Council as the most relevant forum for Arctic governance. Indeed, that is why a number of them applied for Observer status: China in 2006; Republic of Korea in 2008; Japan in 2009; Singapore in early 2012; and India in late 2012.[12] At the May 2013 AC Ministerial Meeting in Kiruna, Sweden, their applications were accepted and they formally became Observers of the Arctic Council. From other parts of Asia, Mongolia also submitted its application for Observer status in 2016, but has yet to be admitted.[13] Since having become Observers, Asian states have applied their rule- and norm-making efforts to the Arctic legal order through attending Ministerial Meetings of the Arctic Council as Observers as well as various Working Groups meeting.[14]

Asian states have also attended meetings that are related but lie outside of the Arctic Council, such as the International Meeting of Representatives of Arctic Council Member States, Observer States and Foreign Scientific Community hosted by the Security Council of Russia[15] or the Conference on Global Leadership in the Arctic: Cooperation, Innovation, Engagement and Resilience (GLACIER) hosted by the Department of State of the United States in 2015.[16] China, Japan and Republic of Korea have been invited to Meetings on High Seas Fisheries

9 Wilfrid Greaves and Daniel Pomerants (2017) " 'Soft Securitization': Unconventional Security Issues and the Arctic Council" *Politik* 3–20: 31–46.

10 Donald R. Rothwell (2014) "The Polar Regions and the Law of the Sea" in *Polar Geopolitics? Knowledges, Resources and Legal Regimes* edited by Richard C. Powell and Klaus Dodds. Edward Elgar, Cheltenham: 19–37.

11 Johnstone, *supra* note 3, at 1–23.

12 Aki Tonami (2016) *Asian Foreign Policy in a Changing Arctic: The Diplomacy of Economy and Science at New Frontiers.* Palgrave Macmillan, London.

13 Yereth Rosen (2016) "How Many Observers Can the Arctic Council Handle?" *The Independent Barents Observer 16 March 2016.* https://thebarentsobserver.com/ru/node/582 (accessed 30 August 2018).

14 See, for example, Sebastian Knecht (2017) "The Politics of Arctic International Cooperation: Introducing a Dataset on Stakeholder Participation in Arctic Council Meetings, 1998–2015" *Cooperation and Conflict* 52-2: 203–223.

15 President of Russia (2017) "Greetings to Participants and Guests of the 7th International Meeting of Representatives of Arctic Council Member States, Observer States and Foreign Scientific Community", 30 August 2017. http://en.kremlin.ru/events/president/news/55462 (accessed 30 August 2018).

16 US Department of State (2015) "Conference on Global Leadership in the Arctic: 30–31 August 2015". https://2009-2017.state.gov/e/oes/glacier/index.htm (accessed 30 August 2018).

in the Central Arctic Ocean since 2015, which eventually led to the Agreement to Prevent Unregulated High Seas Fisheries in the Central Arctic Ocean, an international treaty.[17] Asian states are also parties to the 1982 UN Convention one the Law of the Sea (UNCLOS), which also provides the legal framework to control activities on, over, and beneath the Arctic Ocean. They are members of the International Maritime Organization (IMO), a specialised agency of the United Nations (UN) responsible for regulating international shipping as well. In 2014, the IMO adopted the International Code for Ships Operating in Polar Waters (Polar Code), and it is understood that Asian states (particularly Singapore) have played an active role in the development of the Polar Code.[18]

3.3 The Arctic Council as a liberal institution and Asian states as realists

Asian states have exerted only limited influence over the Arctic legal order-making in the past. This pattern will likely repeat itself as long as the Arctic Council continues to be the principal institution for Arctic governance, as their influence on legal order-making is restrained by the member states of the Council. However, I argue that there is a fundamental difference between the ways in which the existing Arctic states and Asian states/actors see the Arctic and this difference can pose a challenge to the Arctic legal order-making. In the rest of this section, I will pay attention to the behaviour of the states in discussion (the behaviour of existing Arctic states through the development the Arctic Council as well as that of Asian states) in historical context, and use theories of international relations to understand those behaviours.

The Arctic Council was preceded by the Arctic Environmental Protection Strategy (AEPS). AEPS is a multilateral, non-binding agreement by the Arctic states on protecting the Arctic environment. Discussions about AEPS were carried out through a process begun by Finland in 1989. Finland saw that the Arctic environment was in peril and convened the eight circumpolar nations (Canada, Denmark/Greenland, Finland, Iceland, Norway, Russia, Sweden and the United States) to discuss a strategy.[19] In 1989, ministers of the eight Arctic states signed for the first time a common document in Rovaniemi, which became a continuous

17 See Chapter 8 by Joji Morishita and Chapter 9 by Erik J. Molenaar in this book.

18 See for example, Yang Fang (2015) "The Arctic from Singapore's Perspective: A Blessing or a Curse?" in ***International Cooperation in the Development of Russia's Far East and Siberia*** edited by Jing Huang and Alexander Korolev. Palgrave Macmillan, London: 185–201; Ministry of Foreign Affairs of Singapore (2015) "MFA Press Statement: State Visit of His Excellency Ólafur Ragnar Grímsson, President of the Republic of Iceland to Singapore, 11 to 13 November 2015". www.mfa.gov.sg/content/mfa/media_centre/press_room/pr/2015/201511/Press_20151112.printable.html?status=1 (accessed 30 August 2018).

19 Charles Johnson (1997) "The Role of Indigenous Peoples in Forming Environmental Policies" in ***Contested Arctic: Indigenous Peoples, Industrial States, and the Circumpolar Environment*** edited by Erid Alden Smith and Joan McCarter. University of Washington Press, Seattle: 3–12.

process on the Arctic environment called the "Rovaniemi Process".[20] While the process was initiated by Finland, it is noteworthy that the proposal originally came from the Murmansk Initiative in 1987, following the end of the Cold War.[21] The Initiative was introduced in a speech by then-president of the Soviet Union, Mikhail Gorbachev, in Murmansk in 1987 to establish the Arctic as a "zone of peace". The speech included six proposals: the first two on the establishment of a nuclear weapon-free zone in northern Europe, reducing military activities and the stimulation of confidence-building measures in the northern seas; the remaining four concerned civilian, economic cooperation in developing natural resources, coordination of scientific research, cooperation in environmental protection and the opening of the Northern Sea Route (NSR) to international shipping.[22]

In this regard, we can say that the Arctic Council very much reflects the political, economic and environmental background of the period, when much of the world celebrated the end of the Cold War. Indeed, it was symbolic of a renewed attention to liberal institutionalism (or neo-liberal institutionalism) in the early 1990s. During this period, many believed that the dream of world order was possible.[23] Previously, realism had dominated international relations theory since World War II. Realism incorporates five premises.[24] First, that states are the major actors in world affairs. Second, states are severely punished by the international environment if they are unsuccessful in protecting their key interests or pursue objectives beyond their capacity. Third, the motives and acts of states are predominantly shaped by international anarchy. Fourth, states in anarchy are concerned about power and security, are susceptible to conflict and competition, and often fail to cooperate even if they share common interests. Fifth, international institutions' effect on the prospects for cooperation is only marginal.

Different from realism, liberal institutionalists suggest it is no longer states but new actors – such as specialised international agencies and their technical experts – who are the major actors in world affairs.[25] The world has become more pluralistic in terms of actors involved in international relations and these actors have become more dependent on each other.[26] Moreover, in order to achieve peace and prosperity, it is deemed necessary for independent states to gather their

20 Arctic Council website: "Finland", last updated 20 September 2015. www.arctic-council.org/en/about-us/member-states/finland (accessed 30 August 2018).

21 Tonami, *supra* note 12.

22 Lassi Heininen (2011) *Arctic Strategies and Policies: Inventory and Comparative Study*. The Northern Research Forum and the University of Lapland Press, Akureyri.

23 Martin Griffiths, Terry O'Callaghan and Steven C. Roach (2008) *International Relations: The Key Concepts, Second Edition*. Routledge, London: 190–191.

24 Joseph M. Grieco (1988) "Anarchy and the Limits of Cooperation: A Realist Critique of the Newest Liberal Institutionalism" *International Organization* 42–3: 485–507.

25 Ibid.

26 Robert Keohane and Joseph S. Nye (1972) *Transnational Relations and World Politics*. Harvard University Press, Cambridge, MA.

resources and at times surrender some of their sovereignty to create integrated communities to promote economic growth or respond to regional problems. In sum, earlier liberal institutionalists encompassed four propositions. First, states are not the key actors in international relations. Second, states are not unitary or rational agents. Third, states are becoming less concerned about power and security. Fourth, liberal institutionalists believe in international institutions and their ability to promote cooperation.[27] The new liberal institutionalism that appeared in the late 1980s, on the other hand, shares many of the assumptions of (neo-) realism.[28] Neo-liberal institutionalists acknowledge states are indeed key actors in international relations, but not the *only* major actors. States are rational actors, seeking to maximise their interests in all issue areas, but they attempt to do so by cooperation. The greatest obstacle to successful cooperation is non-compliance or cheating by states; although, even if they cooperate, it is never without problems, states will nonetheless allocate loyalty and resources to institutions if they are regarded as mutually beneficial and if they provide states with opportunities to secure their international interests.[29]

Based on the theoretical understanding explained above, I argue that the Arctic Council and surrounding norms and institutions are built predominantly with a liberal or liberal institutionalist point of view.[30] Liberal internationalists support a greater role of international institutions in developing mutually accepted norms and rules of conduct in order to maintain order. Legal order-making in the Arctic, the theme of this book, is understood as an effort to establish and strengthen the international normative and institutional framework so as to bring stability and foreseeability in the future of the Arctic. [31] My argument is that Asian states, on the other hand, take a much more realist view about the governance of the Arctic. In my previous work, I have concluded that various activities conducted by Asian states with regards to the Arctic can be understood as the acts of realist, "developmental" states with a strong element of state-led economic diplomacy.[32] Economic diplomacy in this context is understood in a state-centric realist framework and as "the use of political means as leverage in international negotiations, with the aim of enhancing national economic prosperity, and the use of economic

27 John Baylis, Steve Smith and Patricia Owens (2008) *The Globalization of World Politics: An Introduction to International Relations, Fourth Edition.* Oxford University Press, Oxford.

28 Ibid.

29 Renée Marlin-Bennett (2017) "International Political Economy: Overview and Conceptualization" *Oxford Research Encyclopedia, International Studies.* Oxford University Press, Oxford.

30 For a more on Arctic governance based on IR theories, see Eva Björg Aegisdóttir (2015) *International Governance in the Arctic: The Development of Cooperation, Challenges and Division of Opinions.* Master's thesis submitted to Norwegian University of Science and Technology.

31 Opening Statement by Professor Akiho Shibata, 3rd PCRC Symposium on The Role of Non-Arctic States/Actors in the Arctic Legal Order-making, Kobe, Japan, 7–9 December 2017.

32 Tonami, *supra* note 12.

leverage to increase the political stability of the nation".[33] The state is considered not as the sole main actor but the primary one conducting economic diplomacy, and the purpose of economic diplomacy is the pursuit of economic security – the economic prosperity and political stability of a nation – within an anarchic system. As latecomers to the Western-dominated international system, Asian states have tended towards this use of economic diplomacy. Also in the Arctic, the governments of Asian states have pursued economic diplomacy using a variety of instruments that are relatively more economic or political in character to promote and protect these two types of national interest.

3.4 Asian states and their Arctic engagement

In this section, I will briefly summarise policies (if any) of the five Asian Observer states – namely China, Japan, Republic of Korea, Singapore and India – and their engagement in the Arctic. The section will answer my initial question: what are the political and economic contexts that explain current developments? On the other hand, my discussion on their influence over the Arctic legal order-making in the past is limited, as their ability to do so directly has been strictly restrained by the Arctic states, as we saw in the example of the Observer Manual.[34] Even outside of the Arctic Council, their influence has been subject to the Arctic coastal states. Indeed, China, Japan and Republic of Korea became participants to Meetings on High Seas Fisheries in the Central Arctic Ocean only by invitation of the US. However, this does not mean Asian states will cease their engagement in Arctic affairs in general, using various tools of economic diplomacy described as primarily economic or primarily political in character.

For China, the post-Cold War international environment opened a door to the world, including the Arctic. Rigorous economic reforms in the beginning of the 1990s led to China's rapid economic growth in the latter part of the decade, resulting in a China more confident in demanding a place among the major powers and seeking to extend its reach to regions beyond its immediate neighbourhood. In 1999, China dispatched its first official Arctic expedition and in 2002, then-President Jiang Zemin made the first state visit to Iceland. It can be argued that the Chinese government's emerging Arctic interest during this period was not entirely expected, having previously paid more attention to the Antarctic. Following the financial crisis in 2008 and having managed to escape it reasonably unscathed,

33 Maaike Okano-Heijmans (2013) *Economic Diplomacy: Japan and the Balance of National Interests*. Martinus Nijhoff Publishers, Leiden: 29. Other scholars refer to this as geo-economics, defined as "the use of economic instruments to promote and defend national interests and to produce geopolitical results". See, for example, Jane Golley (2017) "A New Era of Geoeconomics in the Asia-Pacific Region: Will Xi Trump Trump?" in *The Trump Administration's First 100 Days: What Should Asia Do?* ANU College of Asia and the Pacific, Sydney: 22–23.

34 *Arctic Council Observer Manual for Subsidiary Bodies, supra* note 6.

China strengthened its ties to the Arctic states, sometimes using a special relationship with Iceland as a catalyst to navigate through the intricacies of Arctic politics, which in turn has gradually became more crowded and more diplomatically unpredictable.[35] The Chinese government has increased investment in Arctic research and commissioned a second Arctic icebreaker. Large-scale investment deals in oil and gas were concluded at bilateral meetings with Russia. The China Ocean Shipping Company (COSCO) completed the first return trip with a merchant vessel using the NSR, to name a few examples of China's Arctic activities.

What marks China's Arctic engagement is its dualism: the mix of economic and strategic motivations. In terms of the use of natural resources and shipping, two of the three key areas of Arctic governance, China has been one of the most active states among Arctic and non-Arctic states alike by making various types of business agreements. Although there remains a degree of concern about the manner in which Chinese business activities are (or may be) conducted, large-scale investment projects in the Arctic region have been, generally speaking, welcomed, preparing the ground for a truly "win–win" situation, as Chinese Arctic stakeholders contend. It may well be that the Arctic is simply one of numerous destinations for Chinese outward foreign direct investments set by a "Go Out" policy regarding resource development projects and the Belt and Road Initiative. Yet at the same time, China is not entirely explicit in showing its interests in the Arctic to foreign audiences but talks them up to domestic audiences.[36] The 2015 national security law regards activities and assets in the Polar Regions as part of China's national security interests. This dualism is amplified by the low level of transparency more generally in China's policy-making, military planning and strategic thinking. China released its official Arctic policy in January 2018, which listed the following five areas as priorities:[37]

1 Deepening the exploration and understanding of the Arctic
2 Protecting the eco-environment of the Arctic and addressing climate change
3 Utilising Arctic resources in a lawful and rational manner
4 Participating actively in Arctic governance and international cooperation
5 Promoting peace and stability in Arctic cooperation

However, it is not entirely clear what China intends to do in the Arctic due to the general dualism of China's foreign policy and the low transparency of China's policy-making.

Japan was one of the first non-Arctic states (let alone non-Arctic Asian states) to join the International Arctic Science Committee (IASC), establish a national

35 Su Ping and Marc Lanteigne (2015) "China's Developing Arctic Policies: Myths and Misconceptions" *Journal of China and International Relations* 3-1: 1–25.

36 Anne-Marie Brady (2017) *China as a Polar Great Power*. Cambridge University Press, Cambridge, MA: 62–64.

37 State Council of the People's Republic of China (2018) "China's Arctic Policy", 26 January 2018. http://english.gov.cn/archive/white_paper/2018/01/26/content_281476026660336.htm (accessed 30 August 2018).

polar research centre and open a national research station in Ny-Ålesund, Svalbard. Embraced by the Science and Technology Basic Law (1995) that recognised the role of science and technology in renewing the sluggish national economy in the early 1990s, Japan's Arctic engagement has always centred on scientific research. Japan is so far the only Asian state that has its annual Arctic expedition program as well as nation-wide Arctic research programs funded by the government. Members of the Japanese government and scientific community regard the understanding and protection of the natural environment of the Arctic as the most important element of Japan's Arctic engagement. Tackling environmental issues such as climate change is part of Japan's global environmental policy, an area in which Japan has aspired to world leadership since the late 1980s. Hence, it is natural that Japan's approach to legitimise its Arctic engagement is to implement policies to preserve the Arctic environment through better understanding of the region using its science and technology, as specified in the long-awaited Arctic Policy that was released in 2015.[38]

This face of Japan as a humble, technologically advanced and climate-savvy country is the one presented to Arctic states, who would like more stakeholders for environmental protection, one of the three key areas of Arctic governance. However, Japan has a slightly different face regarding management and use of natural sources and shipping, the remaining two key areas of Arctic governance. As one of the world's largest trading nations, securing safe, viable shipping routes is of vital importance for Japan and its businesses, particularly as the Japanese policy-making process is an "iron triangle" made of bureaucracy, politicians and business groups. Japan's business interest groups and public actors conduct small-scale but continuous projects regarding the NSR, making sure they are building an institutional environment that could benefit Japan's interest when and if the NSR eventually becomes a technically and financially viable sea route. Japan's attitude towards Arctic shipping, which can be described as "planting a flag today, to be used tomorrow",[39] is also seen in the management and use of natural resources. Japan is highly dependent on external energy sources and it is evident that the "iron triangle" of bureaucracy, politicians and business groups for energy policy seek to diversify both the supply and the supplier. However, resource development projects in the Arctic are extremely expensive and risky for private entities; therefore, only a semi-public agency company like Japan Oil, Gas and Metals National Corporation (JOGMEC) was able to justify having an interest in large-scale resource development in the Arctic (although JOGMEC announced the cancellation of its Greenlandic project in 2018).

Republic of Korea presents an even more striking example of domestic political factors affecting Arctic policy. Given its relatively recent entry into Arctic-related activities, Republic of Korea has achieved a great deal in its pursuit of further

38 Headquarters for Ocean Policy, Government of Japan (2015) *Japan's Arctic Policy*. www8.cao.go.jp/ocean/english/arctic/pdf/japans_ap_e.pdf (accessed 30 August 2018).

39 Aki Tonami and Stewart Watters (2012) "Japan's Arctic Policy: The Sum of Many Parts" in *Arctic Yearbook 2012*: 93–103.

engagement. Similar to China and Japan, Republic of Korea's Arctic engagement is often interpreted as primarily economic driven, as Republic of Korea too is heavily dependent on foreign energy resources and seeks to diversify energy sources. As a large, maritime trading nation, Republic of Korea has several world-class ports and shipping companies. However, much of Republic of Korea's Arctic engagement is influenced by the Korean decision-makers' shared understanding of the role of "green" in reviving the country's economy after the global financial crisis in 2008, along with a highly centralised government with the President's Office at the centre. The Green Growth concept, introduced by then-President Lee Myung-bak in 2008, regards green technologies as efficient responses in dealing with the negative impacts of climate change; environmental protection and economic growth are not mutually exclusive. The Arctic is regarded as a perfect space to exhibit the potentials of this concept: a prescription to get Republic of Korea's economy back on track as well as to wisely solve environment-related issues in the Arctic with "sustainable Arctic business". This Korean attitude of "killing two birds with one stone" has not changed with the New Northern Policy, announced by the administration of President Moon Jae-in, who was elected in 2017 after the impeachment of Park Geun-hye.[40] The New Northern Policy is a pledge to promote joint economic projects by Republic of Korea and Russia (particularly in the Russian Far East) in various areas, including energy, shipbuilding, fishery and transportation.[41] However, the Policy is not simply about economic cooperation between the two countries; it is designed to bring economic benefits to North Koreans so that they do not have to "resort to nuclear weapons",[42] thereby contributing to a resolution of the problems of the Korean Peninsula.[43]

For Singapore, a small island city-state surrounded by more powerful neighbours, participation in regional or multilateral organisations has been crucial in its foreign policy.[44] While Singapore understands its role as, primarily, a spectator to the changing power patterns of the world, in international or multilateral organisations like the UN even small nations like Singapore can obtain formal equality, potential security of membership and the ability to exert influence beyond their size. Protecting its sovereignty is Singapore's core interest, and as a developmental state whereby the legitimacy of the state is derived from economic growth, advocating the interests of core industries such as shipping, the port sector, and offshore and maritime engineering sector on their behalf has been of vital importance for Singapore. Aside from the conventional tools of balance of power, international institutions such as UNCLOS and IMO offer

40 Yonhap News (2018) "New Northern Policy Seeks to Contribute to Peace on Korean Peninsula" last updated 19 March 2018. http://english.yonhapnews.co.kr/news/2018/03/19/0200000000AEN20180319006600320.html (accessed 30 August 2018).

41 Ibid.

42 Ibid.

43 Jae-Young Lee (2017) "The New Northern Policy and Korean-Russian Cooperation" *Valdai Papers* 76: 2. http://valdaiclub.com/files/16143/ (accessed 30 August 2018).

44 Paragraphs on Singapore and India are largely based on my previous work, Tonami, *supra* note 12, at 93–111.

additional instruments Singapore can manoeuvre within, as shown in Singapore's active participation in the development of the IMO's Polar Code. Singapore's leaders are keenly aware of the need to understand the navigation, energy and environmental dynamics in today's Arctic development in order to guard against Singapore becoming a "global irrelevance" in the way that modern Venice as a port city has become.

What can be said about India's engagement in the Arctic is limited, as it has to date limited its engagement in the region to simply obtaining Observer status. India's engagement is primarily driven by geopolitical concerns, even compared to other Asian states discussed in this chapter. Concerns about climate change aside, India's application for Observer status in the Arctic Council was the result of a pragmatic awareness that India could be losing out to its long-term rival China, as well as a deep desire to gain or regain status in international forums backed by a sense of victimisation under colonialism. In July 2018, India renamed the National Centre for Antarctic and Ocean Research (NCAOR) as the National Centre for Polar and Ocean Research as an indication of the country's intention to be more involved in the Arctic research.[45]

Although non-Arctic and without any formal law-making powers, Asian states interested in the Arctic have established institutions related to Arctic governance. The Asian Forum for Polar Sciences (AFoPS) is a non-governmental organisation established in 2004 as part of an initiative by directors of the polar research institutes of Japan, China and Republic of Korea.[46] The Forum's mandate is to encourage and facilitate cooperation to advance polar sciences among countries in the Asian region.[47] The Forum has five members, which are the national polar research institutions from China, Japan, Republic of Korea, India and Malaysia, with Indonesia, Thailand, Philippines and Vietnam as Observers. China, Japan and Republic of Korea have held a Trilateral High-Level Dialogue on the Arctic on an annual basis since 2016. In the Second Meeting, the three countries adopted a joint statement regarding the Arctic. The statement notes

> the importance of maintaining cooperation based on a rule-based maritime order, further strengthening three countries' contributions to the various international fora over the Arctic and trilateral cooperative projects related to cooperative research for environmental changes and joint observation in the scientific research area over the Arctic.[48]

45 Jacob Koshy (2018) "India to Expand Polar Research to Arctic as Well" *The Hindu*, last updated 19 July 2018. www.thehindu.com/sci-tech/energy-and-environment/india-to-expand-polar-research-to-arctic-as-well/article24463607.ece (accessed 30 August 2018).

46 Kentaro Watanabe et al. (2015) "Special Issue: Asian Forum for Polar Sciences (AFoPS)" *Polar Science* 9–4: 335–400.

47 Asian Forum for Polar Sciences webpage: "Who Are We?" www.afops.org/m11.php (accessed 30 August 2018).

48 Ministry of Foreign Affairs of Japan (2017) "Joint Statement: The Second Trilateral High-Level Dialogue on the Arctic, Tokyo, 8 June 2017" www.mofa.go.jp/files/000263104.pdf (accessed 30 August 2018).

3.5 The rise of Asia and the end of the liberal order in the Arctic?

Asian states have exerted only limited influence over the Arctic legal order-making in the past, partly because their active engagement was institutionally restricted by the Arctic coastal states, which regard the Arctic as "their" regional issue, but not open for Asian "outsiders".[49] In order to overcome this restriction and to increase their general influence on the Arctic affairs, the Asian states have incorporated various tools of economic diplomacy described as primarily economic or primarily political in character. If we go back to the two different schools of IR with regards to regimes – realist and liberal notions – and try to apply them to interpret Asian Arctic policies, realist notions about regimes are much more suitable. For the making of the Arctic legal, political and/or economic order, this fundamental difference between the Asian states and the founding and practical principles of the existing Arctic institutions should be noted.

I argue that this fundamental difference can pose a challenge to the Arctic legal order-making, especially when it is coupled with the rise of Asia (particularly China) and a relative decline of the United States, the principal architect and backer of the liberal world order on which the Arctic legal order is reliant.[50] In order to assess the potential influence of this phenomenon on Arctic governance, a round-table discussion recently published, titled "Rising Powers and the International Order",[51] could be a good starting point and a theoretical reference. G. John Ikenberry and Shiping Tang asserted in an introductory chapter that the cycle of rise and decline of leading states – power transition – was happening again. After seventy years at the top of the global political and economic hierarchy, the United States' grip on leadership is weakening. Meanwhile, a variety of non-Western developing states, China being the primary one, are advancing and seeking to influence global rules and institutions.[52] Tang introduced the view from China on how it sees the current American-led, Western-centric international order, as well as the potential of the "Chinese model" of international order. He summarised that much of China's internal discussion within academic and policymaking circles on international order so far has been "fairly traditional, focusing on (hard) power and money (that is, trade and finance)".[53] These are indeed the two domains where China's ascendency has been most apparent over

49 Per Erik Solli, Elana Wilson Rowe and Wrenn Yennie Lindgren (2013) "Coming into the Cold: Asia's Arctic Interests" *Polar Geography* 36–4: 253–270.

50 Richard N. Haas (2018) "Liberal World Order, R.I.P." *Project Syndicate*, last updated 21 March 2018. www.project-syndicate.org/commentary/end-of-liberal-world-order-by-richard-n—haass-2018–03 (accessed 30 August 2018).

51 G. John Ikenberry and Shiping Tang (eds) (2018) "Special Issue 1 (Rising Powers and the International Order)" *Ethics & International Affairs* 32–1: 1–133.

52 G. John Ikenberry and Shiping Tang (2018) "Introduction" *Ethics & International Affairs* 32–1: 15–16.

53 Shiping Tang (2018) "China and the Future International Order(s)" *Ethics & International Affairs* 32–1: 31–43.

the past four decades, however Chinese academics and policymakers have been largely silent on other international issues that are hugely pertinent to China, such as human rights, refugee flows, environmental protection, antiterrorism and global inequality (except for the Responsibility to Protect doctrine). Tang concluded by saying that even if the post-American and post-Western world comes, any future international order "will still be a rule-based order", but the difference would be that non-Western countries, including rising powers, "will have more input into writing the rules of the future order"; in short, the world is entering a period of "contested multilateralism".[54]

Ikenberry suggested that the liberal international characteristics of order – openness, rules, multilateral cooperation – are likely to persist even if America's hegemony may be diminished.[55] Indeed, the power transition may be taking place, but not as the classical theories predict, where there is a tight link between international order and the rise and fall of great powers and history is a sequence of cycles in which powerful or hegemonic states rise up and build order and dominate the global system until their power declines. Rather, the power transition is more evolutionary; there are lineages and continuity in the modern international order. Conflicts with rising states (led by China) exist over orientations, agendas and leadership, but rising states are not engaged in direct attack on the American-led order because they remain tied to the architecture and principles of a liberal-oriented global order. When states rise, they do not unambiguously confront an American-led order, but they face a wider conglomeration of ordering rules, institutions and arrangement, many of which they have long embraced. The more fundamental the norms and institutions are, the more agreement there is between the US and China as well as other states. Indeed, China and other rising states will have more opportunities to shape the rules and institutions of the existing system; perhaps after all, it may well be that the new constituencies for liberal internationalism are those rising states, while support in the old Western industrial democracies wanes.

Seen the Arctic legal order-making in this light, a liberal order still prevails in the Arctic. The insiders of the Arctic (or those who subscribe to the idea of putting the Arctic Council at the core of the Arctic governance as well as the Arctic regime complex) take a liberal internationalist point of view. Asian states/actors, on the other hand, take a much more realist (if not, neo-liberal institutionalist view at best) view about the governance of the Arctic. A success case where these two different world views have been accommodated and interests met was the Meetings on High Seas Fisheries in the Central Arctic Ocean and the Agreement to Prevent Unregulated High Seas Fisheries in the Central Arctic Ocean, which came as a result of those Meetings. The Meetings took note of the pre-existing international legal framework for fisheries management – such as the 1982 UN

54 Ibid., at 41.
55 G. John Ikenberry (2018) "Why the Liberal World Order Will Survive" *Ethics & International Affairs* 32–1: 17–29.

Convention on the Law of the Sea, the 1995 UN Fish Stocks Agreement and numerous other international instruments – but suggested that there was no international mechanism to "regulate commercial fishing in the high seas area of the central Arctic Ocean, except for the portion of this area that is within the Convention Area of the North-East Atlantic Fisheries Commission".[56] A choice of participants to the Meeting is where power politics is at play. When the first meeting was held in Washington, DC in 2015, delegations were not only limited to the familiar faces of the Arctic states, but also China, the European Union, Japan and Republic of Korea. Given there is as yet very little (or virtually no) cultivatable fisheries stock in the High Seas for the time being, for China, Japan and Republic of Korea, participating in the Meetings and coming to a successful agreement was more about proving legitimacy through rightful membership and rightful conduct.[57]

Against this background, there are various theoretical and policy suggestions in order to accommodate the emergence of Asian states/actors in the Arctic legal order-making. First, traditional Arctic stakeholders such as the Arctic states should – if they would like to maintain and/or improve the existing Arctic legal order – acknowledge that the Asian states will, as they rise politically and economically (and subsequently militarily), inevitably try to shape the rules and institutions of the existing system, even if they may not challenge them directly. In so doing, Asian states' behaviour will be more realist than liberal institutionalist. Their world view is essentially state-centric realist, and their Arctic policies can be understood as the conduct of economic diplomacy, where political means are used as leverage in international negotiations, with the aim of enhancing national economic prosperity, and economic means are used as leverage to increase the political stability of the nation. Arctic governance is facing an era of "contested multinationalism".[58] American hegemony or the world order with the West in the centre may come to an end (or it is transitioning), but the multi-layered, multi-faceted Arctic legal order, as well as the rules and institutions that comprise it, will evolve and last. As an initial step, gaining better knowledge of Asian states, including language skills, by the Arctic states will be a useful start. Likewise, it is essential for Asian states/actors to gain more knowledge of the underlying principles or codes of conduct in the Arctic regime complex. After the end of the Cold War, the members of the Arctic region have carefully crafted a functioning, reasonably conflict-free, multi-layered legal system. There are Arctic "rules of the game".

56 US Department of State (2015) "Chairman's statement on Meeting on High Seas Fisheries in the Central Arctic Ocean, 1–3 December 2015". www.state.gov/e/oes/ocns/fish/regionalorganizations/arctic/statements/279639.htm (accessed 30 August 2018).

57 Ian Clark (2007) *Legitimacy in International Society*. Oxford Scholarship Online: 24.

58 Shiping Tang (2018), *supra* note 53, at 31–43.

3.6 Conclusion

In this chapter, I tried to answer the following questions: What is the political and economic context that explains increased Asian engagement in Arctic affairs? What are the roles that Asian states have played so far in the Arctic legal-order making and what challenges do the Asian states/actors pose? What influence have Asian actors exerted in the past, and will they exert in future Arctic legal-order making? I tried to answer these questions referring to theories of international political economy and international relations. The roles that Asian states have played and their influence in the past in the Arctic legal order-making has been limited, mainly because the Arctic Council has been the principal institution, and as Observers the participation of Asian states has been clearly delineated (restricted) by the Observer Manual. As to challenges, I argue that the fundamental difference between the ways the existing Arctic states and the Asian states/actors see the Arctic can pose a problem; Arctic states take a more liberal internationalist approach, while Asian actors incline to be realists. Arctic states expect Asian states' greater role in international normative and institutional framework, particularly within already existing institutions such as the Arctic Council. However, from the Asian states' point of view, they are only willing to play a role to the extent that the rule- and norm-making efforts serve their political/economic goals, and where they can clearly see the value of making mutually acceptable norms and codes of conduct in pursuing their economic security. The "rise" of Asia has brought new challenges to the Arctic and beyond, and as a result the Arctic legal order has entered a period of contested multilateralism.

4 Japan's role in formation and strengthening of Arctic legal orders

*Keiji Ide**

4.1 Importance of formation and strengthening of legal order

In this chapter, I wish to stress the importance of the whole process of formation and strengthening of legal order in the international community, as we still observe cases where international law and agreements are violated in the real world. Before the formation of legal order, bringing about common understanding among countries is necessary and important as a preparation for the formation of legal orders. The formation of legal orders, such as signing new agreements, is not the end of the story. How to secure their implementation is also very important.

Joseph Nye explains importance of legal order in the international arena as follows: "States have interests in international law for two reasons: predictability and legitimacy."[1] In the Arctic region, we may see more problems, frictions, and even disputes in the future, as economic activities, international trade and investment, and interdependence in the region increase. We should also be mindful of possible tensions in security areas among the major players, which are not necessarily directly related to the Arctic. The protection of the environment in the Arctic region has gained urgency and has become an important task for the international community. Against this background, it is likely that international law and established rules will assist us in dealing with these issues in an unpolitical and predictable manner. The predictability in a wider sense will also be increased by the conscious efforts to promote international cooperation and to create international frameworks to facilitate cooperation in order to avoid problems, frictions and disputes.

* This essay is based on my presentation during the international symposium "The Role of Non-Arctic States/Actors in the Arctic Legal Order-Making" on 7–9 December 2017 at Kobe University, Japan. The opinions expressed in this essay are mine and do not represent those of the Japanese Ministry of Foreign Affairs.

1 Joseph S. Nye Jr. and David A. Welch (2016) *Understanding Global Conflict and Cooperation – An Introduction to Theory and History, Tenth Edition*. Pearson, Harlow: 207.

As Joseph Nye points out, states have interests in international law for legitimacy. In the Arctic region, various states develop their positions in various issues and try to legitimise them referring to international law.

4.2 The world situation and Japan's contribution

Before discussing the particular situation in the Arctic region, I wish to discuss the situation in the world, as issues in the Arctic are a part of or closely related to those of the world. In the world arena, Japan is actively engaging in various challenges and making a contribution to tackling them based on diplomacy and the law.

I wish to take up security issues in a wider sense, with special attention to the issues relating to the sea. There has been a concern that overall tension among the major powers in the recent years may overshadow stability and cooperation in the Arctic region. I am very conscious of this concern. Whenever there is an opportunity to discuss security-related issues in the Arctic context, I try to explain the Japanese government's approach to this issue, that is to continue to promote dialogue with all stakeholders. For example, Russia is one of the key security players in the Arctic region, and Japan recently held a security dialogue of foreign ministers and defense ministers (the so-called "2+2" Ministerial Meeting) with Russia and agreed to promote such dialogue.[2] Japan and Russia are discussing the most sensitive issues, including that of missile defence.

The ocean is very important for Japan in the context of trade routes, sources of various resources (including fish and minerals) and security as a whole. Japan puts her utmost efforts into contributing to the formation and strengthening of legal order related to the sea as a whole. The recently revised Third Basic Plan on Ocean Policy of Japan emphasises that Japan promotes the maintenance and strengthening of international maritime order based on the "rule of law", as the universally recognised standard for all ocean activities.[3] In this context, I wish to mention the great importance the United Nations Convention on the Law of the Sea (UNCLOS) has for its members (currently more than 165 parties) which is the great benefit of predictability and legitimacy. Although the US Senate has not voted with full Senate members to ratify this Convention, previous US governments urged the Senate to approve US accession to the Convention.[4] My understanding of the US government position is that it respects UNCLOS as customary international law. So we can say that the universality of UNCLOS is advancing. On the other hand, however, there are some articles in UNCLOS whose

2 Japan–Russia Foreign and Defence Ministerial Consultation ("2+2" Ministerial Meeting), 31 July 2018. www.mofa.go.jp/erp/rss/northern/page4e_000884.html (accessed 30 August 2018).

3 The Third Basic Plan on Ocean Policy, 15 May 2018. www8.cao.go.jp/ocean/policies/plan/plan03/pdf/plan03.pdf (in Japanese; accessed 30 August 2018).

4 US Department of State website: "The Law of the Sea". www.state.gov/e/oes/lawofthesea/ (accessed 30 August 2018).

meaning is not clear, thus necessitating further elaboration in order for their effective implementation.

As to issues relating to the South China Sea, for example, the government of Japan expressed its position when the Arbitral Tribunal in The Hague issued its judgment (award) in July 2016. The statement by the Japanese foreign minister says: "Japan has consistently advocated the importance of the rule of law and the use of peaceful means, not the use of force or coercion, in seeking settlement of maritime disputes", and "Japan strongly expects that the parties' compliance with this award will eventually lead to the peaceful settlement of disputes in the South China Sea".[5]

The International Maritime Organization (IMO) formulates universal rule for international shipping in order to promote safety of passengers and crews, cooperation in rescue operation, protection of the environment, training of crews, and so on. Japan, as one of the major shipping and shipbuilding countries, actively participates in the making of rules including international agreements in the IMO. Koji Sekimizu, Secretary General of the IMO from 2012 to 2015, explained the IMO's contribution in rule-making related to the Arctic shipping, including the Polar Code.[6]

Japan is promoting cooperation of law-enforcement agencies in the sea both internationally and regionally. Japan hosted the first Coast Guard Global Summit in 2017 in Tokyo with the participation of representatives from 34 countries, one region and three international organisations.[7] Japan is also promoting the North Pacific Coast Guard Forum with the participation of the ocean law-enforcement agencies of six countries, namely Canada, China, Japan, Republic of Korea, Russia and the US.[8] Personally, I believe that some synergy or cooperation might be pursued in the future between Japan and the Arctic Coast Guard Forum (ACGF), which is organised by eight Arctic countries since 2015, so that the expertise of both sides would be shared.

Another example of Japan's contribution is to create a legal framework to promote international cooperation to combat piracy in Asia. With the Japanese initiative, countries that suffer piracy in Asia started negotiations to create a new international agreement and, in November 2004, the Regional Cooperation

5 Statement by the Japanese Foreign Minister Fumio Kishida on the Arbitration between the Republic of the Philippines and the People's Republic of China regarding the South China Sea (Final Award by the Arbitral Tribunal), 12 July 2016. www.mofa.go.jp/press/release/press4e_001204.html (accessed 30 August 2018).

6 Keynote speech by Koji Sekimizu, "Polar Code and the Contribution of Non-Arctic States in its Formation and Implementation", at International Symposium on the Role of Non-Arctic States/Actors in the Arctic Legal Order-making, 7–9 December 2017, Kobe, Japan.

7 Chairman's Summary of the Coast Guard Global Summit, Tokyo, Japan, 14 September 2017. www.kaiho.mlit.go.jp/info/kouhou/h29/k20170914/k170914-2.pdf (both in Japanese and English; accessed 30 August 2018).

8 Japan's Coast Guard website: "North Pacific Coast Guard Forum". www.kaiho.mlit.go.jp/mission/kokusai/kitataiheiyou.html (in Japanese; accessed 30 August 2018).

Agreement on Combating Piracy and Armed Robbery against Ships in Asia (ReCAAP) was adopted and came into effect in September 2006.[9]

4.3 The situation in the Arctic region and Japan's efforts

4.3.1 Japan's Arctic policy and the rule of law in the Arctic

Japan's Arctic policy is firmly embedded within these broader efforts of Japan to promote cooperation in the ocean and strengthen the rule of law in the international community. Japan's Arctic Policy adopted on 16 October 2015 states clearly that Japan will "ensure the rule of law, and promote international cooperation in a peaceful and orderly manner" in its endeavours to be an important player that contributes to the international community through its actions relating to Arctic issues.[10] It also states that "[t]here is a need for Japan to be involved appropriately in formulating international agreements and rules regarding the Arctic".[11] The third revised Basic Plan on Ocean Policy of May 2018 has one chapter on Japan's Arctic policy and reiterates the importance of "rule of law" in the oceans, including the Arctic Ocean.[12]

Japan also promotes the rule of law, or a rule-based legal order, in the Arctic through trilateral high-level dialogues on the Arctic between Japan, China and Republic of Korea. At the second meeting hosted by Japan in 2017, the joint statement stated that "it is indispensable for the international community to ensure the protection and preservation of the fragile marine environment of the Arctic Ocean, and maintain peace, stability and constructive cooperation based on a rule-based maritime order".[13] The joint statement for the third dialogue, hosted by China, reaffirmed "the importance for the international community to maintain peace, stability and constructive cooperation in a rule-based manner".[14]

4.3.2 International agreements negotiated under the Arctic Council and Japan

Under the auspices of the Arctic Council (AC), three legally binding international agreements have been negotiated so far. These are: (a) Agreement on

9 Japanese Ministry of Foreign Affairs website. www.mofa.go.jp/mofaj/gaiko/kaiyo/kaizoku_gai.html (in Japanese; accessed 30 August 2018). ReCAAP website. www.recaap.org/about_ReCAAP-ISC (accessed 30 August 2018).

10 The Headquarters for Ocean Policy, Government of Japan (2015) *Japan's Arctic Policy.* www8.cao.go.jp/ocean/english/arctic/pdf/japans_ap_e.pdf (accessed 30 August 2018).

11 Ibid.

12 The Third Basic Plan on Ocean Policy, *supra* note 3.

13 Paragraph 1 of Joint Statement of the Second Trilateral High-Level Dialogue on the Arctic, Tokyo, 8 June 2017. www.mofa.go.jp/files/000263104.pdf (accessed 30 August 2018).

14 Paragraph 3 of Joint Statement of the Third Trilateral High-Level Dialogue on the Arctic, Shanghai, 8 June 2018. www.fmprc.gov.cn/mfa_eng//wjdt_665385/2649_665393/t1567103.shtml (accessed 30 August 2018).

Cooperation on Aeronautical and Maritime Search and Rescue in the Arctic (signed 2011); (b) Agreement on Cooperation on Marine Oil Pollution Preparedness and Response in the Arctic (signed 2013); and (c) Agreement on Enhancing International Arctic Scientific Cooperation (signed 2017). The signatories to these three agreements are the eight Arctic states, who are also the members of the AC. Non-Arctic states, including Japan, cannot become signatories or accede later to the agreements. However, as an Observer of the meeting without decision-making powers, Japan sent the scientist Dr Hiroyuki Enomoto, Vice Director of NIPR, to its earlier meetings, and the international law specialist Professor Akiho Shibata to its later meetings on the negotiations of the Agreement on Enhancing International Arctic Scientific Cooperation.[15] Japan expressed her readiness to promote actual cooperation in the Arctic region either within the framework of these three agreements or out of such framework.

4.3.2.1 Agreement on Cooperation on Marine Oil Pollution Preparedness and Response in the Arctic

I myself had the honour of explaining Japan's position at the Senior Arctic Officials (SAO) Meeting on 25 and 26 October 2017 in Oulu, Finland, when we discussed implementation of the Agreement on Cooperation on Marine Oil Pollution Preparedness and Response in the Arctic. I explained that Japan will contribute to the prevention of pollution in the Arctic in the following five areas.

First, Japan continues to actively participate in Working Groups of the AC, such as the AMAP, PAME, SDWG, CAFF and EGBCM.

Second, Article 17 of the Agreement stipulates cooperation with non-Parties. This article has not been invoked so far, but if this article is invoked in the future, Japan will be ready to contribute as much as possible. In fact, Japan has experience of international cooperation in the field of oil pollution. Japan dispatched the Japan Disaster Relief Expert Team composed of specialists in prevention of oil pollution to the Philippines in 2006 and 2013. Also, the Japan Coast Guard cooperated with its Republic of Korea's counterpart in this regard in 2007.

Third, Japan contributes to solve problems in the Arctic region through international/universal cooperation, such as the IMO (to combat the oil pollution problem), UNEP (World Mercury Assessment and efforts to reduce Short-Lived Climate Pollution (SLCP) emissions), OECD (to cope with chemical materials) and Minamata Convention on Mercury.

Fourth, Japan promotes bilateral cooperation with Arctic countries. Japan respects the environment protection policy of Finland, the chair country of the AC, and Japan's National Institute for Environmental Studies and Finish Environment Institute (SYKE) concluded the Memorandum of Cooperation in July 2017. Japan's National Institute of Polar Research (NIPR) concluded the Memorandum of Cooperation with Russia's Arctic and Antarctic Institute

15 For details of the negotiations on this agreement, see Chapter 12 by Akiho Shibata in this book.

in August 2017. Black carbon is one of most important issues for international cooperation. Japan and Russia started to prepare for joint monitoring of black carbon in the Arctic region. Although the Asian countries do not have an obligation to report the emission volume of black carbon, Japan will do her best to do so.

Finally, Japan promotes cooperation with the business community, which is expected to pay more attention to the protection of the environment and prevention of pollution in the Arctic region. More active communication and cooperation among all stakeholders are encouraged in Japan. The Japanese delegation listened carefully to the opinion expressed by indigenous people in SDWG to introduce high-quality drainage and garbage disposal system.

4.3.2.2 Agreement on Enhancing International Arctic Scientific Cooperation

I had the honour of explaining Japan's policy to actively promote international Arctic scientific cooperation at the round table organised by the Norwegian foreign ministry in the framework of the Arctic Frontier on 22 January 2018 at Tromso, Norway.[16]

Arctic scientific research is very important for the world, but there are big challenges as we have gaps in data and discrepancy in data formulation. Therefore, international Arctic scientific cooperation should be further promoted. The Agreement on Enhancing International Arctic Scientific Cooperation should function effectively, first of all among the eight signatory countries, but AC Observer countries, including Japan, should not be excluded from the scope of cooperation set by the Agreement. My expectation is that this Agreement will give a strong positive impetus to cooperation in the other international fora and in bilateral settings.

Specifically, I highly appreciate paragraph 11 of the preamble of the Agreement, which recognises the significant scientific expertise and invaluable contribution to scientific activities made by AC Observers. My understanding about "Participants" in Article 1 is that they may include researchers and scientific institutions from AC Observer countries. Actual implementation of this article including the Participants from non-Arctic states will greatly assist in promoting our cooperation. I also appreciate that in Article 1 "scientific activities" are defined broadly. As to Article 9 on the importance of cooperation with holders of traditional and local knowledge, Japanese scientists and researchers have been cooperating in their scientific activities with such indigenous peoples as Greenlanders and Yakut Sakha people. Japan expects that Article 17 (cooperation with non-Parties) will be actively utilised. Japan will be ready to join the work to evaluate this agreement

16 I would like to express my deepest gratitude to Professor Akiho Shibata, Kobe University, and Dr Hiroyuki Enomoto, Vice Director of NIPR, Japan, for their valuable advice on preparing my presentation.

in the future. I also explained many possibilities to promote scientific cooperation in other international multilateral fora[17] and in bilateral frameworks.[18]

4.3.3 Agreement on central Arctic Ocean fisheries

In November 2017, a basic agreement was achieved to ban unregulated fishing in the High Seas of the central Arctic Ocean. Ten parties (nine countries and the EU), including Japan, had actively engaged in discussion and negotiations to produce the draft Agreement to Prevent Unregulated High Seas Fisheries in the Central Arctic Ocean.[19] The protection of fishery resources and the environment is a challenge not only for Arctic states, but also for other interested states in the world. I am happy that Japan contributes to that end. It is also very important to promote international cooperation in the research of fishery resources in the Arctic Ocean.

4.4 Conclusion

Japan has been contributing to the formation and strengthening of legal order in the international community, and these efforts have had a positive impact on the formation and strengthening of the Arctic legal orders. Japan's efforts to deepen dialogue and to improve relations with relevant countries in order to improve the difficult security environment play an important part in working towards this end. The challenges that the Arctic is facing today are very wide and deep rooted; Arctic states alone cannot solve them. Non-Arctic states should also put their utmost efforts into promoting cooperation. Japan will further put their efforts into contributing to the formation and strengthening of Arctic legal orders, playing an active part not only in the AC, but also in other international organisations and fora, as well as in bilateral settings.

17 I mentioned the following important efforts and projects, of which Japan has high expectations: IASC (International Arctic Science Committee); SAON (Sustainable Arctic Observation Network); GEO (Global Earth Observation) and its Cold Region Initiative, Arctic GEO; MOSAiC (Multidisciplinary drifting Observatory for the Study of Arctic Climate); PAG (Pacific Arctic Group); and the Arctic Science Minsiters Meeting (ASM).

18 I explained Japan–Russia scientific cooperation, which relates to cooperation in the Arctic, as one of examples. For example, Japan–Russian Science and Technology Cooperation Agreement, signed and came into effect in 2000; Cooperation Memorandum between Japanese Ministry of Education, Culture, Sports, Science and Techonology (MEXT) and Russian Ministry of Education and Science on Japan-Russia Science and Technology Joint Project, signed in September 2017; and Cooperation memorandum between Japanese NiPR and Russian Arctic and Antarctic Institute, concluded in 2017. In the MEXT memorandum, it is mentioned that rational utilisation of nature including research of the Arctic, is one of the priority areas in Japan–Russian cooperation.

19 See Chapter 8 by Joji Morishita in this book on Japan's contribution to this agreement.

5 China's Arctic policy white paper and its influence on the future of Arctic legal developments

Egill Thor Nielsson and Bjarni Már Magnússon

5.1 Introduction

China introduced its long-awaited first Arctic policy white paper on 26 January 2018 at a press conference in Beijing.[1] The white paper was published by the State Council Information Office of the People's Republic of China[2] and jointly introduced by Hu Kaihong, Spokesperson of the State Council Information Office of China, and Kong Xuanyou, Vice Minister of China's Ministry of Foreign Affairs, with a live 40-minute session simultaneously interpreted into English for an international audience. With the release of its Arctic policy white paper, the government of China followed the two other East Asian countries that were accepted as Arctic Council Observers in May 2013, namely Republic of Korea and Japan who had published their first Arctic policy papers in 2013[3] and 2015,[4] respectively.

The three East Asian countries have common interests in Arctic affairs as was evident at the Third Trilateral High-Level Dialogue on the Arctic taking place on 8 June 2018 in Shanghai, which concluded with a joint statement signed by Gao Feng, Special Representative for Arctic Affairs of the Ministry of Foreign Affairs of People's Republic of China, Kang Jeong-sik, Ambassador for Arctic Affairs of the Ministry of Foreign Affairs of Republic of Korea, and Eiji Yamamoto, Ambassador in charge of Arctic Affairs of the Ministry of Foreign Affairs of Japan, as the heads of delegations. The statement "reaffirmed the importance to promote

1 State Council Information Office of China (2018) *SCIO Briefing on China's Policy on the Arctic*, Beijing, China, 26 January 2018. www.scio.gov.cn/32618/Document/1618357/1618357.htm (accessed 26 January 2018).
2 State Council Information Office of the People's Republic of China (2018) "China's Arctic Policy", 26 January 2018. http://english.gov.cn/archive/white_paper/2018/01/26/content_281476026660336.htm (accessed 26 January 2018).
3 Government of Republic of Korea (2013) *Arctic Policy of the Republic of Korea*. http://library.arcticportal.org/1902/1/Arctic_Policy_of_the_Republic_of_Korea.pdf (accessed 2 May 2018).
4 Headquarters for Ocean Policy, Government of Japan (2015) *Japan's Arctic Policy*. www8.cao.go.jp/ocean/english/arctic/pdf/japans_ap_e.pdf (accessed 2 May 2018).

trilateral cooperation on the Arctic, especially in the area of scientific research",[5] and further signified the importance of what has been called the "Global Arctic".[6] This is especially evident under Article 3 of the trilateral joint statement:

> The three [heads of delegations] recognised that the changing Arctic brings about opportunities and challenges with global implications and international impacts, and reaffirmed the importance for the international community to maintain peace, stability and constructive cooperation in a rule-based manner. Through this Dialogue, the People's Republic of China, Japan and the Republic of Korea addressed common challenges over the Arctic, from the perspective of East Asian countries, and reiterated their intention to make contributions to promoting peace, stability and sustainable development in the Arctic.[7]

The growing interest in Arctic affairs of these three East Asian countries, guided by the challenges of climate change on the one hand and the many complementarities between Arctic and Asian economies on the other, are evident throughout "China's Arctic Policy" white paper. The document reflects China's will for further engagement in the Arctic region with a wide-ranging overview of its Arctic responsibilities and opportunities in accordance to international law. This includes an important historical context of China's participation in Arctic cooperation, as a state party to the Spitsbergen treaty from 1925, and a strong focus on scientific research including China's membership in the International Arctic Science Committee since 1996, the organisation of nine Chinese National Arctic Research Expeditions (CHINAREs) since 1999, and the establishment of the Arctic Yellow River Station in Ny Ålesund in the Spitsbergen Archipelago in 2004.[8]

Furthermore, the Polar Research Institute of China (PRIC) was established in 1989 with China's natural scientific investigations primarily being focused on the Antarctic, with 34 Chinese National Antarctic Research Expeditions taking place (as of June 2018) and the construction of the fifth Antarctic research station under way.[9] However, the first Chinese-constructed icebreaker, R/V *Xuelong II*, will ensure the possibility of annual Arctic research expeditions from the

5 Ministry of Foreign Affairs of the People's Republic of China (2018) *Joint Statement: The Third Trilateral High-Level Dialogue on the Arctic*, Shanghai, China, 8 June 2018. www.fmprc.gov.cn/mfa_eng/wjbxw/t1567103.shtml (accessed 11 June 2018).

6 Lassi Heininen and Matthias Finger (2018) "The 'Global Arctic' as a New Geopolitical Context and Method" *Journal of Borderlands Studies* 33–2: 199–202.

7 *Joint Statement, supra* note 5.

8 China's Arctic Policy, *supra* note 2.

9 People's Daily (2018) "China's 5th Antarctic research station to begin construction on Inexpressible Island", 18 January 2018. http://en.people.cn/n3/2018/0118/c90000-9316930.html (accessed 27 April 2018).

year 2019.[10] The Arctic is perhaps the region in the world where science has the greatest sway in policy and industry, as the Arctic Council, the primary intergovernmental forum for cooperation on Arctic affairs, was established in 1996 to build amongst other things on the scientific work of the Arctic Environmental Protection Strategy.[11]

The scientific and historical aspects of China's Arctic engagement highlighted in the white paper thus provide an important backdrop for China's political and economic Arctic ambitions of "pledging cooperative governance and elaborating a vision of the 'Polar Silk Road' ",[12] signifying a comprehensive long-term commitment towards Arctic affairs in terms of science, economy and governance.

5.2 China's Arctic policy white paper

The main features of the white paper are more or less in accordance to earlier statements, most noticeably a keynote speech delivered by Vice Foreign Minister Zhang Ming at the China Country Session of the Third Arctic Circle Assembly in Reykjavik, Iceland, October 2015, titled "China in the Arctic: Practices and Policies".[13] Zhang outlined three principles of China's contribution, as a near-Arctic state, for Arctic cooperation: "[1] respect, [2] cooperation, and [3] win-win", with a list of six main fields for Chinese Arctic engagement:

(1) Further explore and understand the Arctic;
(2) Protect and rationally use the Arctic;
(3) Respect the inherent rights of Arctic countries and the indigenous people;
(4) Respect the rights of non-Arctic countries and the overall interests of the international community;
(5) Build a multi-tiered Arctic cooperation framework for win-win results; and
(6) Uphold the Arctic governance system based on existing international law.[14]

10 China Daily (2017) "China's first home-built icebreaker named Snow Dragon 2", 27 September 2017. www.chinadaily.com.cn/china/2017-09/27/content_32544019.htm (accessed 27 April 2018); The State Council Information Office of China (2017) *China's Arctic Expeditions Increase to Once a Year*, 11 October 2017. www.scio.gov.cn/32618/Document/1565665/1565665.htm (accessed 27 April 2018).

11 *Ottawa Declaration on the Establishment of the Arctic Council*, 19 September 1996. https://oaarchive.arctic-council.org/bitstream/handle/11374/85/EDOCS-1752-v2-ACMMCA00_Ottawa_1996_Founding_Declaration.PDF?sequence=5&isAllowed=y (accessed 1 May 2018).

12 State Council Information Office of the People's Republic of China (2018) *China Publishes Arctic Policy, Eyeing Vision of 'Polar Silk Road'*, Beijing, China, 26 January 2018. www.scio.gov.cn/32618/Document/1618210/1618210.htm (accessed 26 January 2018).

13 Embassy of the People's Republic of China in the Republic of Iceland (2017) *China in the Arctic: Practices and Policies*, Keynote Speech by Vice Foreign Minister Zhang Ming at the China Country Session of the Third Arctic Circle Assembly, Reykjavik, Iceland 17 October 2017. http://is.china-embassy.org/eng/xwdt/t1307016.htm (accessed 2 May 2018).

14 Ibid.

A fourth principle of sustainability was added to the white paper in January 2018, whereas the specific fields of Arctic engagement were reduced to five with the more specific wording on China's actual contributions in the Arctic, including a broader global focus and more elaborate goals within each field and a perspective of safeguarding "the common interests of all countries and the international community in the Arctic".[15] However, it is suggested that in order to realise the above-mentioned policy goals, China will have to participate in Arctic affairs through cooperation and peaceful measures to reach mutually beneficial goals with local partners. The white paper reaffirms China as a "near-Arctic State" – a phrase that has been used within the Chinese Arctic community for several years,[16] underpinning the importance of the region to Chinese interests.

In the white paper, it is also stated that China supports platforms such as "The Arctic: Territory of Dialogue", "The Arctic Circle", "Arctic Frontiers" and "The China–Nordic Arctic Research Center" (CNARC) in promoting exchanges and cooperation among the stakeholders. These events have been important in order to introduce China's Arctic engagement, whereas the government is furthermore "supporting the participation of research institutions and enterprises in Arctic governance with their own expertise put to good use".[17] This is encouraging to international research collaboration, while supporting "enterprises to participate in the commercial development and utilization of the Arctic in a lawful and orderly manner".[18]

Chinese participation in international Arctic fora has significantly increased in the past few years, most noticeably with contributions at the annual Arctic Circle Assemblies in Iceland, where high-level delegations have every year introduced China's policy, scientific and commercial engagement in Arctic affairs since 2013. The assemblies are also where, for example, representatives from state-owned enterprises such as China COSCO Shipping, China National Petroleum Corporation (CNPC) and Sinopec have introduced projects concerning transportation and energy. Moreover, researchers from PRIC and the Shanghai Institutes of International Studies have introduced scientific collaboration including the joint China–Iceland Aurora Observatory (CIAO),[19] CHINAREs and CNARC.[20]

The Arctic: Territory of Dialogue[21] forum in Arkhangelsk, Russia, is where China sent its highest-level Arctic delegation to date in March 2017, led by

15 China's Arctic Policy, *supra* note 2.

16 SIPRI (2012) *China Defines Itself as a 'Near-Arctic State', says SIPRI*, 10 May 2012. www.sipri.org/media/press-release/2012/china-defines-itself-near-arctic-state-says-sipri (accessed 3 May 2018).

17 China's Arctic Policy, *supra* note 2.

18 Ibid.

19 Further information on CIAO is available at its official website: https://karholl.is/en/ (accessed 2 May 2018).

20 Further information on the program of each Arctic Circle Assembly is available at its official website: http://arcticcircle.org/ (accessed 3 May 2018).

21 Further information on The Arctic: Territory Dialogue is available at its official website: http://forumarctica.ru/en/ (accessed 6 May 2018).

Wang Yang, then Vice Premier and currently a member of the Politburo, which holds great significance as the seven-member standing committee now includes a member with extensive hands-on knowledge of Arctic affairs. Wang's message of China's willingness to participate more deeply in the peaceful and sustainable development of the Arctic was reflected by *China Daily*'s headline "Beijing aspires to bigger Arctic role",[22] according to the four principles of China's Arctic engagement.[23]

The establishment of CNARC in December 2013 by four Chinese and six Nordic research institutes with capacities to influence and coordinate Arctic research has also provided an important platform for enhanced Arctic cooperation, having hosted six China–Nordic Arctic Cooperation Symposiums to date, provided fellowship exchanges of Nordic and Chinese scholars, and interlinked researchers, policy-makers and industry leaders in CNARC Round-table dialogues on themes such as Arctic shipping, Arctic tourism and Arctic fisheries to improve joint understanding and promote information exchange between international Arctic stakeholders.[24]

However, what is of particular interest in "China's Arctic Policy" white paper is the new aspect of a "Polar Silk Road", advancing "Arctic-related cooperation under the Belt and Road Initiative"; with the Belt representing a land-based "Silk Road Economic Belt" and the Road representing "the 21st-century Maritime Silk Road".[25] Launched in September 2013, the Belt and Road Initiative is the initiative of China's President Xi Jinping to enhance the prosperity of China and Belt and Road Initiative partner countries based on five pillars: (a) policy coordination, (b) infrastructure connectivity, (c) unimpeded trade, (d) financial integration and (e) closer people-to-people ties.[26]

China has already showcased capabilities in Arctic economic development based on the intersection between research, policy and industry, becoming a leader in Arctic shipping, as icebreaker R/V *Xuelong* became the first vessel to transit all three Arctic seaways. During CHINARE-5 in 2012, it was the first Chinese-flagged vessel to transit an Arctic seaway, sailing from Qingdao to Reykjavik

22 China Daily (2017) "Beijing Aspires to Bigger Arctic Role", 1 April 2017. www.chinadaily.com.cn/china/2017-04/01/content_28764725.htm (accessed 6 May 2018).

23 Ministry of Foreign Affairs of the People's Republic of China (2017) *Wang Yang: China Upholds Three Major Policy Principles of Respect, Cooperation and Sustainability to Participate in Arctic Affairs*, 29 March 2017. www.fmprc.gov.cn/mfa_eng/zxxx_662805/t1450508.shtml (accessed 6 May 2018).

24 See Jian Yang (2017) "Four Impacts from the China–Nordic Arctic Research Center" in *The Arctic in World Affairs: A North Pacific Dialogue on Building Capacity for a Sustainable Arctic in a Changing Global Order* edited by Robert W. Corell, Jong Deog Kim, Yoon Hyung Kim and Oran R. Young. Korea Maritime Institute, Busan and East–West Center, Honolulu: 291–299. Further information on CNARC is available at its official website: www.cnarc.info/ (accessed 2 May 2018).

25 China's Arctic Policy, *supra* note 2.

26 State Council of the People's Republic of China (2015) *Action Plan on the Belt and Road Initiative*, 30 March 2015. http://english.gov.cn/archive/publications/2015/03/30/content_281475080249035.htm (accessed 28 April 2018).

through the Northeast Passage by the coast of Russia, and back to Shanghai from Akureyri, Iceland, through the Transpolar Passage.[27] For CHINARE-8 in 2017, *Xuelong* transited the Arctic Ocean through the high end of the North East Passage, between the Transpolar Passage and the Northern Sea Route, with large parts of the voyage outside of any exclusive economic zone, and the Northwest Passage by the coast of Canada on its way back to Shanghai, thus concluding a full Arctic Rim expedition.[28] Following *Xuelong*'s Northeast Passage journey in 2012, China COSCO Shipping undertook its first commercial Arctic shipping voyage in 2013 and by March 2018 the company had concluded a total of 14 Northeast Passage transits. It has become the first international shipping company to offer regular services through the passage with aims to further increase its commercial Arctic shipping.[29] In 2018 alone COSCO has planned for ten Northeast Passage commercial transits.[30] An outside stakeholder has arguably taken the lead ahead of Arctic nations in Arctic shipping, and the "Polar Silk Road" signals a will for further infrastructure and trade engagement.

5.3 The "Polar Silk Road" and international reactions

Although the "Polar Silk Road" was first formally announced in the Arctic policy white paper, Arctic-based projects had been included into the Belt and Road Initiative earlier. A very significant step in regards to the Belt and Road Initiative's further expansion into the Arctic was taken in June 2017 with the "Vision for Maritime Cooperation under the Belt and Road Initiative" document, issued jointly by the National Development and Reform Commission and the State Oceanic Administration, "to synchronize development plans and promote joint actions among countries along the 21st Century Maritime Silk Road".[31]

The document highlights that "China will strive to designate three 'blue economic passages' – the China–Indian Ocean–Africa–Mediterranean Sea Blue Economic Passage; the China–Oceania–South Pacific Blue Economic Passage; and one that will lead to Europe via the Arctic Ocean".[32] The fact that the Arctic sea

27 Further information on CHINARE-5 is available at an Arctic Portal hosted website: www.chinare5.com/ (accessed 2 May 2018).

28 China Daily (2017) "Science Vessel Returns from Arctic", 11 October 2017. http://usa.chinadaily.com.cn/2017-10/11/content_33135400.htm (accessed 6 May 2018).

29 Global Times (2018) "Chinese Commercial Ships Explore Arctic Routes Amid 'Polar Silk Road' Ambitions", 8 February 2018. www.globaltimes.cn/content/1088825.shtml (accessed 27 April 2018).

30 Arctic Today (2018) "Chinese Shipper on Path to 'Normalize' Polar Shipping", 26 June 2018. www.arctictoday.com/chinese-shipper-path-normalize-polar-shipping/ (accessed 26 June 2018).

31 State Council of the People's Republic of China (2017) *Vision for Maritime Cooperation under the Belt and Road Initiative*, 20 June 2017. http://english.gov.cn/archive/publications/2017/06/20/content_281475691873460.htm (accessed 28 April 2018).

32 State Council of the People's Republic of China (2017) *3 Sea Routes Planned for Belt & Road Initiative*, 21 June 2017. http://english.gov.cn/state_council/ministries/2017/06/21/content_281475692760102.htm (accessed 28 April 2018).

lanes are highlighted with two of the world's most active seaway trade routes is of great significance for the future importance of Arctic shipping. China's main Arctic partner to date has been Russia, the only Arctic state that had joined the Belt and Road Initiative by July 2018, and China's main projects in the Arctic for energy production and transportation have been firmly based on cooperation with Russian partners.

The Belt and Road Initiative has in practical terms been active in the Arctic since 2015 with a 9.9 per cent stake investment of the Silk Road Fund into the $27 billion Yamal LNG project in Russia.[33] CNPC furthermore holds a 20 per cent stake in Yamal LNG, and since 2016 the Russian operator Novatek with a 50.1 per cent stake has had a credit line extension of $12 billion with two Chinese policy banks, China Development Bank and Export–Import Bank of China.[34] The development of the "Silk Road on Ice" with Russian partners is furthermore the basis for the proposed international "Polar Silk Road". The Arctic region has become a significant part of the strategic relationship of China and Russia, with Arctic shipping featured in the two countries' bilateral strategic accord.[35]

Russia's Arctic basin port activity has increased significantly the past couple of years with terminals handling 49.7 million tons of cargo (+40.6 per cent, year on year) in 2016. Terminals handled 74.2 million tons of cargo (+49.1 per cent, year on year) in 2017, with the Port of Sabetta, servicing the Yamal LNG project, handling 7.99 million tons (up in 2.8 times) in 2017.[36] The growth is expected to continue, as the Yamal–Nenets Autonomous Region is the world's largest natural gas producing area, accounting for approximately 80 per cent of Russia's natural gas production and approximately 16 per cent of the world's gas production. A new project, Arctic LNG 2, also operated by Novatek, is already attracting potential Chinese partners with a memorandum of understanding signed between Novatek with China Development Bank for the implementation of the project,[37] a strategic cooperation agreement with the

33 Novatek website: "NOVATEK and the Silk Road Fund conclude framework agreement on acquisition of stake in Yamal LNG", 3 September 2015. www.novatek.ru/en/press/releases/index.php?id_4=984 (accessed 27 April 2018).

34 Reuters (2016) "China lenders provide $12 bln loan for Russia's Yamal LNG project-sources", 29 April 2016. https://uk.reuters.com/article/russia-china-yamal/china-lenders-provide-12-bln-loan-for-russias-yamal-lng-project-sources-idUKL2N17V2MI (accessed 27 April 2018).

35 Belt and Road Portal: "A look at the Ice Silk Road", 14 July 2017. https://eng.yidaiyilu.gov.cn/qwyw/rdxw/19745.htm (accessed 27 April 2018).

36 Avelana website: "Total throughput and container volume of Russian seaports in 2016", January 2017. http://avelana.ru/en/total-throughput-and-container-volume-of-russian-seaports-in-2016/ (accessed 21 November 2017); Avelana website: "Total throughput and container volume of Russian seaports in 2017", 12 January 2018. http://avelana.ru/en/total-throughput-and-container-volume-of-russian-seaports-in-2017/ (accessed 21 April 2018).

37 Novatek website: "NOVATEK signed MOU with China Development Bank", 1 November 2017. www.novatek.ru/en/press/releases/index.php?id_4=1950 (accessed 27 April 2018).

CNPC[38] and a statement on expanded Arctic transportation collaboration with China COSCO Shipping.[39] Previously, to facilitate upcoming growth in Western parts of the Russian Arctic, China COSCO Shipping with other Chinese corporations, including Poly Group, China Marine Fuel Service Corporation and the Export–Import Bank of China, have confirmed their interest in Arctic infrastructure build-up in the Arkhangelsk Port and the connected Belkomur railway project.[40] These examples showcase the growth of China–Russia Arctic cooperation, which has developed into large-scale projects.

China has now proposed Belt and Road memorandums of understanding to the Nordic countries linking the Eurasian continent in a more comprehensive way with infrastructure build-up for expanding trade links and investments. These agreements include ones with Iceland,[41] which is the only Arctic state to have a Framework Agreement on Arctic Cooperation (2012)[42] and Free Trade Agreement (2013)[43] with China. Finland, however, has been the most active of the Nordic countries in economic cooperation with China, having launched the first China–Finland train connection in November 2017,[44] and China has in recent years become one of Finland's most important trade and investment partners.[45] Two railway projects connecting Finland to the Baltics (Helsinki to Tallinn tunnel) and Norway (the Rovaniemi to Kirkenes railway line, or Arctic

38 Novatek website: "NOVATEK signed Strategic Cooperation Agreement with CNPC", 1 November 2017. www.novatek.ru/en/press/releases/index.php?id_4=1951 (accessed 27 April 2018).

39 Novatek website: "NOVATEK and COSCO SHIPPING to Expand Arctic Transportation Collaboration", 27 March 2018. www.novatek.ru/en/press/releases/index.php?id_4=2330 (accessed 27 April 2018).

40 See, e.g., reporting on this from TASS (2017) "Potential investor of Russia's Belkomur railway to attend Arctic Forum", 9 March 2017. http://tass.com/economy/934559 (accessed 27 April 2018); Barents Observer (2017) "Chinese company COSCO confirms interest in trans-Arctic shipping to Arkhangelsk", 26 September 2017. https://thebarentsobserver.com/en/arctic/2017/09/chinese-company-cosco-confirms-interest-trans-arctic-shipping-arkhangelsk (accessed 27 April 2018).

41 Embassy of the People's Republic of China in the Republic of Iceland (2018) *Remarks by H.E. Ambassador JIN Zhijian at the Reception Upon Assuming the Post and Celebrations of Chinese New Year*, 22 February 2018. http://is.china-embassy.org/eng/xwdt/t1536495.htm (accessed 2 May 2018).

42 Embassy of the People's Republic of China in the Republic of Iceland (2012) *Chinese Premier Wen Jiabao Pays Official Visit to Iceland*, 25 April 2012. http://is.china-embassy.org/eng/xwdt/t926273.htm (accessed 2 May 2018).

43 Ministry of Commerce of the People's Republic of China (2013) *China–Iceland FTA*. http://fta.mofcom.gov.cn/topic/eniceland.shtml (accessed 2 May 2018).

44 China Daily (2017) "First China-Finland Train Connection Launched", 11 November 2017. www.chinadaily.com.cn/world/2017-11/11/content_34404277.htm (accessed 27 April 2018).

45 Finnish Business Council Shanghai (2017) *China Is Finland's Most Important Trading Partner*, 22 September 2017. https://fbcs.fi/news/china-finlands-most-important-trading-partner (accessed 27 April 2018).

Corridor) have been named as potential Belt and Road Initiative investments.[46] Furthermore, Arctic affairs featured in the Joint Declaration Between the Republic of Finland and the People's Republic of China on Establishing and Promoting the Future-oriented New-type Cooperative Partnership, signed at the occasion of President Xi Jinping's state visit to Finland in April 2017.[47] Norway has increased Arctic cooperation with China since the normalisation of relations between the two countries in December 2016,[48] and the aforementioned joint Finnish–Norwegian Arctic Corridor railway project is undergoing a feasibility study between the two countries' ministries of transportation,[49] which places the Port of Kirkenes as one of the potential Northeast Passage transhipment hubs connecting East Asian and European markets.[50]

The Kingdom of Denmark is the only Nordic state to have a comprehensive strategic partnership with China (2008), but the Arctic is not explicitly featured in the China–Denmark joint work programme 2017–2020.[51] However, there are two references to Greenland in regards to natural resources (geological surveys) and the environment (groundwater). The issue of China–Denmark Arctic cooperation has largely been focused on security issues concerning Greenland,[52] whereas the Premier of Greenland made a visit to China in 2017 to promote relations in fields such as trade and tourism.[53] Sweden has, however, largely focused on issues other than the Arctic in its cooperation with China, while the Nordic Council of

46 China Daily (2018) "Finland touts 'Arctic Corridor' tunnel", 2 March 2018. www.chinadaily.com.cn/a/201803/02/WS5a984a41a3106e7dcc13efe8.html (accessed 27 April 2018).

47 Office of the President of the Republic of Finland (2017) *Joint Declaration between the Republic of Finland and the People's Republic of China on Establishing and Promoting the Future-oriented New-type Cooperative Partnership*, 3 May 2017. www.tpk.fi/public/default.aspx?contentid=360378&culture=en-US (accessed 27 April 2018).

48 Office of Prime Minister of Norway (2016) *Statement of the Government of the People's Republic of China and the Government of the Kingdom of Norway on Normalization of Bilateral Relations*, 19 December 2016. www.regjeringen.no/globalassets/departementene/ud/vedlegg/statement_kina.pdf (accessed 5 May 2018).

49 Ministry of Transport and Communications of Finland (2018) *Study on the Arctic Rail Line Completed: Kirkenes Routing to be Examined Further*, 9 March 2018. www.lvm.fi/-/study-on-the-arctic-rail-line-completed-kirkenes-routing-to-be-examined-further-968073 (accessed 27 April 2018).

50 Barents Observer (2018) "Finland says new Arctic railway should lead to Kirkenes", 9 March 2018. https://thebarentsobserver.com/en/arctic/2018/03/finland-says-new-arctic-railway-should-lead-kirkenes (accessed 27 April 2018).

51 Ministry of Foreign Affairs of Denmark (2017) *China–Denmark Joint Work Programme (2017–2020)*, 3 May 2017. www.fmprc.gov.cn/mfa_eng/wjdt_665385/wjzcs/P020170504665552423685.pdf (accessed 27 April 2018).

52 Reuters (2018) "Greenland's courting of China for airport projects worries Denmark", 22 March 2018. www.reuters.com/article/china-arctic-greenland/greenlands-courting-of-china-for-airport-projects-worries-denmark-idUSL4N1QP346 (accessed 2 May 2018).

53 Embassy of the People's Republic of China in the Kingdom of Denmark (2017) *Ambassador Deng Ying Meets Premier of Greenland Self-Government*, 31 October 2017. www.fmprc.gov.cn/ce/cedk/eng/zgxw/t1506254.htm (accessed 2 May 2018).

Ministers and the Chinese Ministry of Foreign Affairs published a "Joint Press Release [on] Strengthening Sino-Nordic Cooperation" in May 2017 that mentioned Arctic cooperation within the fields of science, research and education.[54]

It will be of great interest to see how discussions progress in regards to the Nordic countries potentially becoming members of the Belt and Road Initiative, having all participated as founding members of the Asian Infrastructure Investment Bank[55] and engaged in a deeper dialogue with China on Arctic-related issues both bilaterally and regionally. The internationalisation and implementation of the "Polar Silk Road" in the Eurasian Arctic arguably depends on collaboration with Nordic partners in order to extend from bilateral cooperation with Russia.

In the American Arctic, Canada and the United States have shown little interest in considering participation in the Belt and Road Initiative, focusing rather on the security and global governance issues that the Belt and Road Initiative may entail for their positions in the world. There have, however, been regional initiatives promoting cooperation with China, most noticeably from the State of Alaska, with cooperation agreements signed amongst other things on LNG at the occasion of the visit of President Xi Jinping in April 2017.[56]

It is safe to say that there was no lack of coverage and commentary on "China's Arctic Policy" from international and local media and researchers. As could be expected, the main focus is on the introduction of the "Polar Silk Road", which made up for the headlines for the coverage of international newspapers such as the *Financial Times* ("China Reveals Arctic Ambitions with Plan for 'Polar Silk Road' "),[57] Reuters ("China Unveils Vision for 'Polar Silk Road' across Arctic)[58] and Bloomberg ("Don't Fear China's Arctic Takeover: It's Natural that China Wants to Stake a Claim at the Top of the World").[59] The reports were generally rather neutral in their stance, placing the "Polar Silk Road" in a larger context of global affairs.

54 Ministry of Foreign Affairs of the People's Republic of China (2017) *Joint Press Release Strengthening Sino-Nordic Cooperation*, 25 May 2017. www.fmprc.gov.cn/mfa_eng/wjbxw/t1465224.shtml (accessed 2 May 2018).

55 Asian Infrastructure Investment Bank website: "Members and Prospective Members of the Bank, 2018". www.aiib.org/en/about-aiib/governance/members-of-bank/index.html (accessed 8 May 2018).

56 Anchorage Daily News (2017) "Governor details China–Alaska LNG deal, but skeptics still have questions", 23 November 2017. www.adn.com/business-economy/energy/2017/11/22/governor-reveals-china-alaska-lng-deal-but-skeptics-still-have-questions/ (accessed 6 May 2018).

57 Financial Times (2018) "China reveals Arctic ambitions with plan for 'Polar Silk Road' ", 26 January 2018. www.ft.com/content/c7bd5258-0293-11e8-9650-9c0ad2d7c5b5 (accessed 5 May 2018).

58 Reuters (2018) "China unveils vision for 'Polar Silk Road' across Arctic", 26 January 2018. www.reuters.com/article/us-china-arctic/china-unveils-vision-for-polar-silk-road-across-arctic-idUSKBN1FF0J8 (accessed 5 May 2018).

59 Bloomberg (2018) "Don't fear China's Arctic takeover", 30 January 2018. www.bloomberg.com/view/articles/2018-01-30/don-t-fear-china-s-arctic-takeover (accessed 5 May 2018).

Although other reports downplayed the commercial feasibility of the "Polar Silk Road", *Forbes* used the headline "Even China's 'Polar Silk Road' Can't Change the Inconvenient Map of Eurasia"[60] and placed security issues concerning the American Arctic at the foreground.[61] Moreover, Danish journalist Martin Breum rightly points out that "the real question on China's new Arctic policy will be how the Arctic responds".[62] On this note, various reports have been produced placing China's Arctic policy within the context of specific countries, including the "China's Arctic Dream" report by Heather A. Conley at the Center for Strategic and International Studies[63] and the policy briefing "China as an Arctic Great Power: Potential Implications for Greenland and the Danish Realm"[64] by Camilla T. N. Sørensen's at the Institute for Strategy at the Royal Danish Defence College. Both reports showcased the need for balanced analyses in assessing how the "China's Arctic Policy" white paper can influence Arctic affairs, focusing on what it can mean in actual terms and evaluating the proposition it holds from an Arctic perspective.

It is safe to say that China's Arctic policy white paper has received more attention in international media and policy circles than similar policy papers from any other country. This is especially interesting when comparing China's Arctic policy with other non-Arctic states, including the aforementioned East Asian countries of Japan and Republic of Korea, as well as European non-Arctic countries such as the United Kingdom[65] and Germany,[66] which have all published Arctic policy papers that are along similar lines, focused on shouldering responsibility in regards to climate change while promoting opportunities in the Arctic, without

60 Forbes (2018) "Even China's 'Polar Silk Road' can't change the inconvenient map of Eurasia", 29 January 2018. www.forbes.com/sites/salvatorebabones/2018/01/29/even-chinas-polar-silk-road-cant-change-the-inconvenient-map-of-eurasia/#2ba2d185c2bf (accessed 5 May 2018).

61 CBC (2018) "What does China's new Arctic policy mean for Canada?", 27 January 2018. www.cbc.ca/news/canada/north/what-does-china-s-new-arctic-policy-mean-for-canada-1.4506754 (accessed 5 May 2018).

62 Arctic Today (2018) "The real question on China's new Arctic policy will be how the Arctic responds", 31 January 2018. www.arctictoday.com/real-question-chinas-new-arctic-policy-will-arctic-responds/ (accessed 5 May 2018).

63 Heather A. Conley (2018) *China's Arctic Dream*. Center for Strategic and International Studies (CSIS). https://csis-prod.s3.amazonaws.com/s3fs-public/publication/180220_Conley_ChinasArcticDream_Web.pdf?3tqVgNHyjBBkt.p_sNnwuOxHDXs.ip36 (accessed 1 March 2018).

64 Camilla T. N. Sørensen (2018) *China as an Arctic Great Power, Policy Brief*. Royal Danish Defence College. www.fak.dk/publikationer/Documents/Policy%20Brief%202018%2001%20februar%20UK.pdf (accessed 1 March 2018).

65 Government of the United Kingdom (2018) *Beyond the Ice: UK Policy towards the Arctic*, 4 April 2018. https://assets.publishing.service.gov.uk/government/uploads/system/uploads/attachment_data/file/697251/beyond-the-ice-uk-policy-towards-the-arctic.pdf (accessed 2 May 2018).

66 Federal Foreign Office of Germany (2013) *Germany's Arctic Policy Guidelines*, November 2013. www.bmel.de/SharedDocs/Downloads/EN/International/Leitlinien-Arktispolitik.pdf?__blob=publicationFile (accessed 2 May 2018).

headline-grabbing terms such as the "Polar Silk Road". The economic sway of China as the world's largest trader and second largest economy, alongside its tangible commitment in the Yamal LNG project, Arctic shipping and scientific achievements, already makes it a significant stakeholder in terms of Arctic affairs. Openly stating interests and commitments, as is done in China's Arctic policy white paper, is an important step towards further collaborative efforts between Arctic and non-Arctic partners, for all levels of collaboration. The fact that the two most mentioned words in the white paper are "cooperation", 46 times, and "research", 41 times, is an indicator that knowledge and mutual benefits are at the centre of China's Arctic engagement.[67]

5.4 The legal framework

The biggest political and legal significance of China's white paper is the reaffirmation of its international legal commitments towards the Arctic. If one wants to summarise the main international law aspects of China's policy, the terms "law-based governance" and "international cooperation" come to mind. The paper recognises the sovereignty of the Arctic states while referring to third-party rights, such as the freedom of navigation, and the rights of the international community in the Arctic, mainly concerning the International Seabed Area. Kamrul Hossain pointed out that the paper "is probably best read as a policy declaration reaffirming China's adherence to pre-existing legal frameworks governing the Arctic region".[68]

Some commentators have expressed their surprise that international law is a core element of China's white paper because China is a powerful state which does not have to rely as much on international law as small states. This mindset seems to view international law and geopolitics as a clashing phenomenon. To the contrary, international law does not outlaw geopolitical struggles between states. International law creates a pathway for states to seek their national interests in a way considered acceptable by the international community. The role of international law in the context of geopolitics is "to pronounce on the legality of particular conducts forming part of the broader agenda of geopolitical expansion and counter-expansion, as opposed to judging the propriety of broader geopolitical interests".[69] What China is doing in the white paper is employing international law to strengthen its perceived position in the Arctic as a key player and downplaying its secondary status as an observer in the main intergovernmental forum

67 Barents Observer (2018) "These are China's top 10 keywords for the Arctic", 30 January 2018. https://thebarentsobserver.com/en/arctic/2018/01/these-are-chinas-top-keywords-arctic (accessed 5 May 2018).

68 Kamrul Hossain (2018) "China's White Paper on the Arctic: Legal Status under International Law", *ASIL Insight* 22–7. www.asil.org/insights/volume/22/issue/7/chinas-white-paper-arctic-legal-status-under-international-law (accessed 11 June 2018).

69 Alexander Orakhelashvili (2008) "International Law and Geopolitics: One Object, Conflicting Legitimacies" *Netherlands Yearbook of International Law* 39: 155.

in the Arctic, the Arctic Council. In this context it must kept in mind that the Arctic is neither the Wild West of the nineteenth-century American frontier nor is it the twenty-first-century South China Sea. As elsewhere, international law places power struggles in the region within structural limits that states generally respect.

Early in the paper, China's view of the overall legal framework in the Arctic is explained. It rightly points out that "there is no single comprehensive treaty for all Arctic affairs".[70] Furthermore, it states that "the Charter of the United Nations, the United Nations Convention on the Law of the Sea (UNCLOS), the Spitsbergen Treaty and other treaties and general international law govern Arctic affairs at present".[71] Later in the paper, "treaties on climate change and the environment, and relevant rules of the International Maritime Organization"[72] are added to the list.

China's commitment to the international legal framework extends to all major issues that concern the Arctic such as shipping and shipping routes, climate change, oil and gas exploitation and gas exploitation. China calls for stronger environmental management and cooperation in the Arctic and supports a legally binding treaty on fisheries management in the high seas portion of the central Arctic Ocean. One thing must be noted; given how much emphasis is placed on respecting the international legal commitments relevant for the Arctic and how cleverly the white paper is structured, it is rather odd that it refers not to indigenous peoples' guaranteed rights under treaty law but notes that all states should "respect the tradition and culture of the indigenous peoples".[73] Whether this is a mistake or done on purpose is difficult to tell.

The policy paper makes strong references to UNCLOS and the UN Charter. The references to UNCLOS, the main treaty concerning ocean affairs globally, is no surprise. One of the central purposes of UNCLOS is to define various maritime zones, their extents and limits. It also lays out the principles and rules for navigation, including provisions on transit passage through straits used for international navigation. The strong reference to the UN Charter was, however, rather surprising. China refers to its permanent member position in the UN Security Council (UNSC) where it "shoulders the important mission of jointly promoting peace and security in the Arctic".[74] China notes also that it "upholds the current Arctic governance system with the UN Charter and the UNCLOS as its core".[75]

70 China's Arctic Policy, *supra* note 2.

71 Ibid. China is party to the three treaties as well as to other important treaties that govern the Arctic. Charter of the United Nations, *United Nations Treaty Series* 1: xvi; United Nations Convention on the Law of the Sea, *United Nations Treaty Series* 1822: 396; Treaty between Norway, The United States of America, Denmark, France, Italy, Japan, the Netherlands, Great Britain and Ireland and the British overseas Dominions and Sweden concerning Spitsbergen, *League of Nations Treaty Series* 2: 7.

72 China's Arctic Policy, *supra* note 2.

73 Ibid.

74 Ibid.

75 Ibid.

Furthermore, China states that it "supports the peaceful settlement of disputes over territory and maritime rights and interests by all parties concerned in accordance with such treaties as the UN Charter and the UNCLOS and general international law".[76] In this context, China makes an interesting reference to one of the key concepts of international relations, reciprocity,[77] when it states that " 'respect' is the key basis for China's participation in Arctic affairs. Respect should be reciprocal. It means all States should abide by international treaties such as the UN Charter and the UNCLOS, as well as general international law".[78]

Although China gives credit to the Arctic Council, on the regional level, as the "main intergovernmental forum on issues regarding the environment and sustainable development of the Arctic", the focus of the policy is on the global legal framework where China plays a greater role, especially in matters concerning peace and security. In this context it should be kept in mind that a footnote to the Ottawa declaration, the founding document of the Arctic Council, states clearly that the "Arctic Council should not deal with matters related to military security". As is well known, traditionally and perhaps unfortunately, considerations concerning military security have been prioritised higher than considerations concerning the environment and sustainable development in international politics.

Timo Koivurova has pointed out that as a state without an Arctic coastline, "it's valuable for China to invoke a framework of rules that strongly emphasizes China's role in Arctic governance".[79] Koivurova also notes that in the Arctic Council "China is only an observer, a status lower than the small Indigenous Peoples' organizations that would normally be dubbed as non-governmental organizations in other intergovernmental bodies or treaty negotiations".[80] By referring to "the entire framework of international law, China places itself in the drivers' seat".[81]

It must be asked whether the strong emphasis on the UN Charter and China's permanent member status in the UNSC has consequences on future legal developments and what those consequences might be. Within the UN, the UNSC has the primary responsibility for the maintenance of international peace and security.[82] One could argue that this emphasis is an example of the rhetoric of militarisation of the Arctic. Such a conclusion would be misguided, not only because China's white paper does not have a direct effect on the fact that the Arctic Ocean has been for decades an important region for the deployment of nuclear missile submarines for Russia and NATO but also because referring to the broader

76 Ibid.

77 Ibid.

78 Ibid.

79 Timo Koivurova (2018) "China & the Arctic: Why the focus on international law matters", *ArCticles – Arctic Centre Papers*. www.arcticcentre.org/blogs/China—the-Arctic-Why-the-focus-on-international-law-matters/ne2t4glg/cb324fd9-7981-4181-85a4-b9f583822512 (accessed 11 June 2018).

80 Ibid.

81 Ibid.

82 Article 24(1) of the UN Charter.

international law framework could be seen as an effort to halt the development of regional international law in the Arctic. Another view is that China's reference to general international law is to underline that China is a big actor in world politics and performs an important role in various crucial treaty regimes for the Arctic. There is a wide scope for speculation.

5.5 Third-party rights and the interests of the international community

It is self-evident that China is a not a coastal state to the Arctic Ocean. Consequently, China does not enjoy the same rights under international law as the coastal states do. On the other hand, China and other non-coastal states enjoy various rights in the Arctic Ocean, as clearly expressed in the policy:

> States from outside the Arctic region do not have territorial sovereignty in the Arctic, but they do have rights in respect of scientific research, navigation, overflight, fishing, laying of submarine cables and pipelines in the high seas and other relevant sea areas[83] in the Arctic Ocean, and rights to resource exploration and exploitation in the Area, pursuant to treaties such as UNCLOS and general international law. In addition, Contracting Parties to the Spitsbergen Treaty enjoy the liberty of access and entry to certain areas of the Arctic, the right under conditions of equality and, in accordance with law, to the exercise and practice of scientific research, production and commercial activities such as hunting, fishing, and mining in these areas.[84]

This is rather straightforward and in line with well-established international norms. What is not as straightforward is the references to the interests of the international community. The white paper justifies various actions China has taken in the Arctic with the end goal that they "safeguard the common interests of all countries and the international community in the Arctic".[85] The international community has certain rights in the central Arctic Ocean in the international seabed area,[86] which UNCLOS defines as the common heritage of mankind.[87]

Another related aspect of the white paper is that no direct mention is made of the delineation of the outer limits of the continental shelf beyond 200 nautical miles, the issue that put the Arctic into the global spotlight, often labelled as

83 Mainly the Exclusive Economic Zone, see Article 58(1)(2) of UNCLOS.

84 China's Arctic Policy, *supra* note 2.

85 Ibid.

86 The international seabed area is usually referred to as the Area. Article 1(1) of UNCLOS defines the Area as "the seabed and ocean floor and subsoil thereof, beyond the limits of national jurisdiction".

87 Article 136 of UNCLOS. The Authority acts on the behalf of mankind in whom the resources of the Area are vested. See UNCLOS article 137(2).

the "scramble for the Arctic".[88] In a statement given in Svalbard in June 2009, Hu Zhengyue, a Chinese assistant minster of foreign affairs, stated:

> When determining the delimitation of outer continental shelves, the Arctic states need to not only properly handle relationships among themselves, but must also consider the relationship between the outer continental shelf and the international submarine area that is the common human heritage, to ensure a balance of coastal countries' interests and the common interests of the international community.[89]

Stockholm International Peace Research Institute's policy paper on China's Arctic aspirations from 2012 states that "many Chinese scholars believe that UNCLOS does not entirely safeguard China's perceived Arctic interests" concerning the continental shelf beyond 200 nautical miles.[90] These considerations are, intentionally or unintentionally, hidden in the white paper as references to the international seabed area and the interest of the international community in the Arctic. When a coastal state establishes the outer limits of its continental shelf beyond 200 nautical miles (in most instances on the basis of the recommendations of the Commission on the Limits of the Continental Shelf),[91] it is not only deciding the jurisdiction and sovereign rights it enjoys in the continental shelf

88 Al Jazeera (2010) "A Scramble for the Arctic", 8 December 2010. www.aljazeera.com/indepth/features/2010/11/20101130181427770987.html (accessed 8 June 2018); New York Times (2015) "U.S. is Playing Catch-Up with Russia in Scramble for the Arctic", 29 August 2015. www.nytimes.com/2015/08/30/world/united-states-russia-arctic-exploration.html?_r=0 (accessed 11 June 2018).

89 Linda Jakobson (2010) "China Prepares for an Ice-Free Arctic" *SIPRI Insights on Peace and Stability* 2/2010: 10. http://books.sipri.org/files/insight/SIPRIInsight1002.pdf (accessed 15 June 2015). China has also made references to the International Seabed Area when addressing other parts of the oceans. See *Note Verbale of the Permanent Mission of the People's Republic of China to the Secretary General of the United Nations*, 6 February 2009, Doc. CML/2/2009. www.un.org/depts/los/clcs_new/submissions_files/jpn08/chn_6feb09_e.pdf (accessed 11 June 2018).

90 Linda Jakobson and Jingchao Peng (2012) "China's Arctic Aspiration"' *SIPRI Policy Paper* 34: 18. www.sipri.org/sites/default/files/files/PP/SIPRIPP34.pdf (accessed 11 June 2018).

91 Three recent articles address the primary issues thoroughly: Viatcheslav V. Gavrilov (2016) "The LOSC and the Delimitation of the Continental Shelf in the Arctic Ocean" *The International Journal of Marine and Coastal Law* 31: 315–338; Øystein Jensen (2016) "Russia's Revised Arctic Seabed Submission" *Ocean Development and International Law* 47: 72–88; Bjørn Kunoy (2017) "Assertions of Entitlement to the Outer Continental Shelf in the Central Arctic Ocean" *International and Comparative Law Quarterly* 66: 367–409. See generally about the establishment of the outer limits of the continental shelf beyond 200 nm in Suzette Suarez (2008) *The Outer Limits of the Continental Shelf*. Springer, Heidelberg; Øystein Jensen (2014) *The Commission on the Limits of the Continental Shelf*. Brill, Leiden; Bjarni Már Magnússon (2015) *The Continental Shelf beyond 200 Nautical Miles*. Brill, Leiden; Signe Veierud Busch (2016) *Establishing the Continental Shelf Beyond 200 Nautical Miles by the Coastal State*. Brill, Leiden.

but also the boundary line between the continental shelf and the international sea bed area.[92] Although most outer limits in the central Arctic Ocean have or will be decided bilaterally or even trilaterally, there will remain areas of deep ocean floor that are part of the international seabed area and that are beyond national jurisdiction. The language used in the white paper leaves room for China to react in response to actions taken by coastal states in the Arctic Ocean concerning the establishment of the outer limits of the continental shelf beyond 200 nautical miles without directly stating so.[93]

5.6 Conclusion

The Arctic policy white paper first and foremost reaffirms China's interest in Arctic affairs and collaborative efforts with Arctic partners to understand and develop the region. The white paper reaffirms China's international legal commitments while employing arguments based on international law to strengthen its position in the Arctic. The influence on future Arctic legal developments might thus lie in how global governance impacts the Arctic region, which has seen stable conditions despite sanctions between Russia and the seven other Arctic states following the annexation of Crimea. Arctic cooperation has been built largely on important scientific collaboration and sustainable development with mutual benefits for outside partners. The white paper presents a balanced view of the responsibilities and opportunities that the Arctic region has to offer for Chinese enterprises implementing the "Polar Silk Road" with a win–win proposition to enhance connectivity with Arctic economies. At the same time, it includes a strong emphasis of the importance of protecting fragile environments and addressing climate change. In sum, the white paper articulates China's current and potential Arctic engagement, but what actually happens depends much on the response from Arctic countries.

92 The definition of the Area is a negative one "for in order to know the exact extent of the Area, one needs to know up to where exactly coastal states have extended their national jurisdiction at sea". Erik Franckx (2010) "The International Seabed Authority and the Common Heritage of Mankind: The need for States to Establish the Outer Limits of their Continental Shelf" *International Journal of Marine and Coastal Law* 25: 543, 552.

93 Bjarni Már Magnússon (2015) "China as the Guardian of the International Seabed Area in the Central Arctic Ocean" *Yearbook of Polar Law* 7: 83.

Part II

People(s) in the Arctic

6 Our homeland

Arctic indigenous peoples' perspectives on non-Arctic states

Dalee Sambo Dorough

6.1 Introduction

> Our language contains the memory of four thousand years of human survival through the conservation and good managing of our Arctic wealth.
>
> Ours is the language of the very environment that challenges the environmental safety of existing offshore technology.
>
> Our language contains the intricate knowledge of the ice that we have seen no others demonstrate. Without our central involvement, there can be no safe and responsible Arctic resource development.
>
> We Inupiat live under four of the five flags of the Arctic coast. One of those four flags is badly missed here today ... it is generally agreed that we enjoy certain aboriginal legal rights as indigenous people of the Arctic. It is important that our governments agree about the status of these rights if they are to be uniformly respected.[1]
>
> (Eben Hopson, Founder Inuit Circumpolar Council)

> Drastic changes are occurring within our world. We are on the forefront of these changes. We have lived here for millennia and have grown and changed with all that is around us. All that is around us physically and spiritually nourishes us, and our culture reflects the Arctic because we are part of this ecosystem.[2]
>
> (Food Security Report, ICC)

Any discussion of legal order in the Arctic must recognise the status and rights of Arctic indigenous peoples throughout their circumpolar homeland, including the Inuit of the Russian Far East, Alaska, Canada and Greenland, the Sámi of northern Norway, Sweden, Finland and Russia as well as the various indigenous peoples and nations throughout the whole of the Russian Arctic territory. Indeed,

1 Eben Hopson (1977) "Welcoming Speech", 13 June 1977, Barrow, Alaska on the occasion of the first Inuit Circumpolar Conference.

2 ICC-Alaska (2015) *Alaska Inuit Food Security Conceptual Framework: How to Assess the Arctic from an Inuit Perspective*, Technical Report. ICC, Alaska: 4.

the states that have grown up around these long-standing, unique indigenous peoples, were all once "non-Arctic". In fact, the earliest expeditions by non-Arctic explorers were plagued by failure and near-death experience, their success only ensured by the knowledge, capacity and compassion of Inuit hunters.[3] Even the Vikings, facing grave difficulties and harsh conditions, retreated. Significantly, despite random and strange contact with Arctic explorers, Inuit homelands have largely remained our own domain. However, with time, technology and present global environmental conditions, we are now faced with dramatic change, including in the realm of political reality and legal orders.

Nevertheless, since first contact, Inuit have been generally successful at not only defining, but continuously re-defining our relations with others and working to maintain our cultural integrity as well as our blood relations across imposed national borders and an increasingly volatile political, economic, social and cultural milieu.

It is crucial to underscore that the Inuit worldview of the circumpolar Arctic region is expansive and inclusive of both *terra firma* and *marinus*. Inuit are a maritime people with an ancient history of reliance upon both the marine and terrestrial environment. Therefore, this chapter will emphasise the perspectives of Inuit largely due to their status and rights as a maritime Arctic people and the fact that the author is of Inuit descent.

This chapter will briefly cover the background and current work of Inuit political organisation, engagement in the United Nations and regional work of the Arctic Council, Inuit rights and status in the Arctic legal order, and conclude with some recommendations for non-Arctic states in this regard.

6.2 Inuit Circumpolar Council

Though a 1973 Arctic Peoples Conference was hosted by the International Work Group for Indigenous Affairs in Copenhagen, the first formal meeting of the Inuit took place in June 1977 at Barrow, Alaska. At the invitation of then Mayor Eben Hopson of the North Slope Borough, Inuit leaders from throughout Alaska, Canada and Greenland gathered in the Barrow High school gymnasium. An invitation was extended to the Siberian Yup'ik of the Soviet Union, but in the midst of the Cold War they were denied participation. The first conference resulted in a commitment to establish an official trans-Arctic Inuit organisation. In addition, numerous resolutions were adopted concerning the priorities of the day, ranging from safeguarding Inuit whaling rights to peaceful use of the Arctic to Arctic Policy and Land Claims to Education and Village Technology.[4]

3 Adriana Craciun (2016) *Writing Arctic Disaster: Authorship and Exploration*. Cambridge University Press, Cambridge.

4 Inuit Circumpolar Conference (1977) *Summary and Resolutions*, Barrow, Alaska, 13–19 June 1977. www.inuitcircumpolar.com/resolutions6.html (accessed 4 April 2018).

Resolution 77–01 provided the pathway towards future organisation by affirming that:

> Whereas, the Inuit of Greenland, Alaska and Canada are one indivisible people with a common language, culture, environment and concerns; Whereas, the Inuit of the circumpolar regions declare the oneness of its culture, environment and land and the wholeness of the homeland and that it is only the boundaries of certain nation states that separate us; ... Whereas, we wish to reaffirm our right to self-determination; and Whereas, there is a need for an international organization of Inuit to study, discuss, represent, lobby and protect our interests on the international level; ... That this Charter be so drafted as to include, but not be limited to the following areas of concern namely:

a) the safeguard and protection of the resources of the Inuit homeland;
b) the preservation, retention and further development of Inuit language and culture in all their aspects;
c) the development and improvement of adequate and safe transportation and communication systems for the Inuit homeland;
d) the Inuit be adequately consulted and take part in any and all discussions affecting their homeland which may have potential significant impact;
e) the development of proper and adequate game management systems for our homeland;
f) the development of mutual exchange in areas of improving all aspects of living conditions;
g) the development of a meaningful Arctic policy;
h) the establishment of funding sources to permit the operation and future existence of this international Inuit body.[5]

At the subsequent 1980 conference in Nuuk, Greenland, the ICC was crystallised as the "transnational organization in the Inuit homeland to serve these people in the circumpolar region".[6] As articulated in its Charter, the principal goals of ICC are to: a) strengthen unity among Inuit of the circumpolar region; b) promote Inuit rights and interests on an international level; c) develop and encourage long-term policies that safeguard the Arctic environment; and d) seek full and active partnership in the political, economic, and social development of circumpolar regions.

In 1977, the objective of "the development of a meaningful Arctic policy" was expressed and took shape throughout the various ICC General Assemblies and

5 ICC Resolution 77–01, 15 June 1977. www.inuitcircumpolar.com/iccs-beginning.html (accessed 4 April 2018).

6 ICC Resolution 79–01, 17 July 1979. www.inuitcircumpolar.com/resolutions6.html (accessed 4 April 2018).

recently updated in 2010. One of the key objectives of the ICC Principles and Elements for a Comprehensive Arctic Policy[7] is respect for and recognition of the rights of Inuit, which transcend international boundaries. In addition, the ICC Arctic Policy principles seek to gain coherence and coordination in relation to indigenous rights. The recognition and treatment of Inuit rights by both Arctic and non-Arctic states has been uneven at best and misunderstood or unacknowledged at worst.

Another crucial theme is the need for the full, effective and direct role of Inuit in promoting and protecting our distinct culture, our unique environment, and our traditions and values at all decision-making levels, from local to regional to national and international. As the title suggests, the ICC's Arctic Policy document is comprehensive, addressing issues ranging from the right of self-determination to peace and security and scientific research to environmental protection to Inuit elders and youth. These Arctic policy principles and elements have ultimately influenced numerous other developments, including the Arctic Council, the UN Declaration on the Rights of Indigenous Peoples,[8] the ILO revision of the Convention on Indigenous and Tribal Peoples, 1957[9] (which resulted in ILO C169),[10] the IUCN's World Conservation Strategy and other international developments. To a large extent, non-Arctic actors have remained uninformed and ignorant of the substance of the distinct human rights of Inuit despite the fact that many non-Arctic states have engaged in the international human rights standard-setting process for decades.

The ICC gained non-governmental organisation (NGO) status from the UN Economic and Social Council (ECOSOC) in 1983, which has provided access to a wide range of UN specialised agencies, organs and bodies. At that time, there were only 12 indigenous peoples' organisations that held such "consultative status" with the United Nations.[11] In 1986, the Siberian Yup'ik of the Russian Far East were able to join the ICC and actively engage in their work. Presently, the organisation represents approximately 165,000 Inuit through Inuit Nunaat, the traditional Inuit homeland. In addition, the ICC was one of the framers of the Ottawa Declaration and an original Permanent Participant to the Arctic

7 Inuit Circumpolar Conference/Centre for Northern Studies and Research (1992) ***Principles and Elements for a Comprehensive Arctic Policy.*** http://arctic.gordonfoundation.ca/sites/default/files/ICC_Principles_and_Elements_for_a_Comprehensive_Policy_PART_1.pdf (accessed 7 August 2018). The initial draft was prepared in 1983 and refined through Inuit debate and dialogue until its final adoption at the 1992 ICC General Assembly held in Inuvik, NWT, Canada.

8 United Nations Declaration on the Rights of Indigenous Peoples (2007), UNGA/RES/61/295, Annex, 13 September 2007.

9 Indigenous and Tribal Populations Convention, International Labour Organization C107, adopted 26 June 1957 and entered into force 2 June 1959.

10 Indigenous and Tribal Peoples Convention, International Labour Organization C169, adopted 27 June 1989 and entered into force 5 September 1991.

11 See generally Jens Dahl (2012) *The Indigenous Space and Marginalized Peoples in the United Nations.* Palgrave Macmillan, London: 37–38.

Council (to be discussed below) when this intergovernmental forum was established in 1996. In addition, the ICC leadership and representatives substantively influenced the Arctic Council Rules of Procedure, including the emphasis upon consensus decision-making as well as other procedural rules. One of the key Inuk diplomats involved in these organisational discussions was then ICC President Mary Simon, who later became the Canadian Ambassador for Circumpolar Affairs.

ICC holds a major General Assembly every four years wherein Inuit delegates from across the circumpolar region elect a new Chair and an Executive Council, develop policies, and adopt resolutions that will guide the activities of the organisation for the coming term. The General Assembly is the heart of the organisation, providing an opportunity for sharing information, discussing common concerns, debating issues, and strengthening the bonds between all Inuit, and significant cultural celebration.

Over its four decades, it is safe to say that the ICC has garnered a solid reputation for Inuit diplomacy.[12] ICC's work has substantially increased Arctic knowledge, political leadership and important insights into the lives, conditions and concerns of Arctic peoples generally and Arctic indigenous peoples specifically.

6.3 Intertwining national and international developments

In a global sense, the intersection of Inuit aspirations and international relations have afforded Inuit the opportunity to raise awareness about the issues facing our peoples and to demonstrate the legitimacy of Inuit perspectives in the context of international human rights law and a wide range of other issues.

Simultaneous with the ICC's preparation of the Arctic Policy, the UN took on the initiative of preparing a declaration on the rights of indigenous peoples, initiated in 1982 by five independent human rights experts of the UN Working Group on Indigenous Populations (WGIP). Due to these concurrent debates and dialogue, we were able to intensify or amplify our fundamental organisational objectives as well as influence many provisions of the UN Declaration's final texts adopted by the UN General Assembly in 2007.[13]

12 See generally Frances Abele and Thierry Rodon (2007) "Inuit Diplomacy in the Global Era: The Strengths of Multilateral Internationalism" *Canadian Foreign Policy* 13–3: 45–63; Gary Wilson (2007) "Inuit Diplomacy in the Circumpolar North" *Canadian Foreign Policy* 13–3: 65–80.

13 From 1982 to 2007, the ICC participated in the Working Group on Indigenous Populations (WGIP), which forwarded their text to the then Sub-Commission on Prevention of Discrimination and Protection of Minorities, which subsequently adopted the draft UN Declaration in Resolution 1994/45 of 26 August 1994 as an annex. U.N. Doc. E/CN.4/1995/2, E/CN.4/Sub.2/1994/56 (1994), 105. The text was then transmitted to the Commission on Human Rights and subsequently to its successor, the Human Rights Council. The ICC maintained its participation throughout the HRC consideration as well as in the Third Committee and, finally, the General Assembly.

In this regard, there were and continue to be conditions within the Arctic region that are dramatically distinct from those facing indigenous peoples in other parts of the world. For example, the remote, cold climate conditions as well as the heavy reliance upon the coastal seas and Arctic Ocean for survival and sustenance. Such living conditions have always been the hallmark of Inuit and their profound relationship with the Arctic environment. This is in dramatic contrast to indigenous peoples in milder, temperate or equatorial climates.

Among other articles, an explicit example of Inuit engagement was inclusion of the term 'sea-ice' in the original article 26 of the WGIP draft UN Declaration.[14] Despite the overall cost to participate throughout all of the UN human rights standard-setting sessions, the ICC recognised the importance of the UN Declaration as a tool to advance our concerns within our particular geopolitical region and beyond. Therefore, we maintained our constant presence and participation in all relevant human rights standard-setting sessions of the UN.[15] It is important to underscore the fact that UN member states from across the globe also played a direct role in this standard-setting exercise, ranging from Japan to India to France and the United Kingdom. So the constant chore of the ICC and other indigenous NGOs was to educate and influence such member states to ensure that the individual and collective rights related to our distinct status were safeguarded.

Aside from the adverse impacts of the Cold War, throughout the elaboration of the UN Declaration, a wide range of developments within the Arctic were happening at a very fast pace. Threats to Inuit whaling activities[16] emerged within the context of the International Whaling Commission; low-level test flights[17] were being initiated throughout the Canadian Arctic and sub-Arctic; a mass drowning of thousands of caribou in Northern Quebec[18] (later attributed – but still disputed – to flooding initiated by Hydro Quebec and their massive, complex hydroelectric system affecting the Caniapiscau River); the 1986 Chernobyl disaster; offshore lease sales in the Chukchi and Beaufort Seas; and dumping of radioactive waste into the Arctic Ocean by the former USSR just to name a few.

14 Article 26 of WGIP *draft* UN Declaration: "Indigenous peoples have the right to own, develop, control and use the lands and territories, including the total environment of the lands, air, waters, coastal seas, sea-ice, flora and fauna and other resources which they have traditionally owned or otherwise occupied or used. This includes the right to the full recognition of their laws, traditions and customs, land-tenure systems and institutions for the development and management of resources, and the right to effective measures by States to prevent any interference with, alienation of or encroachment upon these rights." Unfortunately, this term has been removed in the final text of the Declaration.

15 In addition to the UN Declaration work, the ICC participated in the 1988 and 1989 revision process of the ILO's Convention on Indigenous and Tribal Populations, No. 107.

16 In the mid-1970s, the International Whaling Commission extended its regulations to Inuit whaling activity in Alaska and voted to ban the subsistence take of whales by the Inuit of Alaska's north and northwest coast.

17 A 1983 agreement between Canada and the United States allowed cruise missile low-level test flights to take place over certain corridors throughout Northern Canada, including Goose Bay, Northwest Territories and Labrador.

18 Sports Illustrated (1984) "Letter from the Publisher", 15 October 1984. New York Times (1992) "Power Struggle", 12 January 1992.

More significantly, the growth and strengthening of Inuit political leadership and institutions as well as the recognition of Inuit rights to lands, territories and resources through national law in the United States; the comprehensive Inuit land claims agreements in Canada; and the status of the Greenland Government in the Danish realm all have a direct bearing upon the Arctic legal order.

By virtue of the Alaska Native Claims Settlement Act of 1971 (ANCSA)[19] adopted by the US Congress and signed into law by President Nixon, the Inuit of Alaska collectively hold right and title to nearly 16 million acres, including surface and subsurface rights at both the regional and village corporation level. In addition, two regions – North Slope and Northwest Arctic – have organised state-chartered Borough governments that provide local control and capture revenue from developments on their respective lands.

In Canada, the James Bay and Northern Québec Agreement of 1975[20] is regarded as "the first major agreement between the Crown and the native people in Canada since the numbered treaties of the 19th and early 20th centuries".[21] The agreement was triggered by the 1971 announcement of the mega project to build a complex system of hydroelectric dams throughout the territory of the Cree and Inuit of Northern Quebec. The Agreement provided for 8,151 square kilometres for the Inuit. The provisions also affirm exclusive harvesting rights throughout the lands transferred as well as over an additional 15,000 square kilometres of land. More recently, discussions over the Nunavik Self-Government Political Accord (the Accord)[22] have been agreed upon, providing for a measure of self-government and self-determination.

Just to the east of Alaska, the Inuvialuit Final Agreement (IFA),[23] the subject of one of the 1977 ICC resolutions, was finally adopted between the Inuvialuit and the Crown in 1984. The Agreement provided for 90,600 square kilometres of land, including 12,980 square kilometres of subsurface mineral rights and $152 million. In addition to hunting and fishing rights secured by the Agreement, the Inuvialuit have co-management roles in matters related to fisheries, wildlife, and environmental impact through various joint boards and councils. As one might guess, self-determination and self-government were not addressed and the corporate model of ANCSA was generally replicated in the Inuvialuit context. However, the major distinctions between the Inuvialuit and ANCSA are that

19 The Alaska Native Claims Settlement Act of 1971, Pub. L. No.92–203, 85 Stat. 688, 43 U.S.C.A. §§1601 et seq.

20 The James Bay and Northern Quebec Agreement, signed on 11 November 1975. www.gcc.ca/pdf/LEG000000006.pdf (accessed 21 August 2018).

21 See John A. Price and Brian Craik (2011, 2015) "James Bay and Northern Québec Agreement" *The Canadian Encyclopedia*. www.thecanadianencyclopedia.ca/en/article/james-bay-and-northern-quebec-agreement/ (accessed 21 August 2018).

22 Political Accord between the Nunavik Party, the Government of Québec and the Federal Government for the Examination of a Form of Government in Nunavik through the Establishment of a Nunavik Commission, 5 November 1999. www.autochtones.gouv.qc.ca/relations_autochtones/ententes/inuits/19991105_en.htm (accessed 21 August 2018).

23 Inuvialuit Final Agreement, 5 June 1984. www.irc.inuvialuit.com/sites/default/files/Inuvialuit%20Final%20Agreement%202005.pdf (accessed 21 August 2018).

the Inuvialuit included negotiated provisions (rather than an Act of Congress or Parliament); a full and formal referendum allowing for free, prior and informed consent; and an agreement, rather than a "settlement". It also entrenched hunting, fishing and gathering rights as well as joint management.

Significantly, the Nunavut Land Claims Agreement of 1993[24] is the largest Aboriginal land claim settlement in Canadian history. When the Agreement was signed, legislation was also passed leading to the creation of a new Canadian territory called Nunavut on 1 April 1999. The new territory is a public government serving both Inuit and non-Inuit in the form of a unicameral legislative assembly. However, provisions for a form of self-government for the Nunavut Inuit were included in the agreement. Inuit have title to approximately 350,000 square kilometres of land and of this about 35,000 square kilometres include mineral rights. Inuit and government are represented equally in matters concerning wildlife management, resource management and environmental boards. Inuit rights to harvest wildlife on lands and waters throughout the Nunavut settlement area were secured. A scheduled distribution of compensation over a 14-year period totals approximately $1.161 billion as well as revenue sharing from royalties generated by oil, gas and mineral development on Crown lands.

In contrast to being used as "human flag poles" to advance the interests of the government of Canada,[25] the reality and terms of Nunavut as an autonomous territory is a significant development for Inuit, which certainly figures into the issue of Canadian Arctic sovereignty and the Northwest Passage. The combination of public government and provision for possible distinct Inuit government have led some to believe that "devolution" of control to Nunavut will enhance Canada's assertion of sovereignty over the internal waters of the Canadian high Arctic.[26]

Interestingly, when the Inuit Circumpolar Conference General Assembly in Barrow, Alaska, was being organised, the Labrador Inuit were preparing to pursue a land claims agreement with the Canadian government. After 27 years of effort,

24 Nunavut Land Claims Agreement Act, S.C. 1993, C.29, signed on 25 May 1993. www.gov.nu.ca/sites/default/files/Nunavut_Land_Claims_Agreement.pdf (accessed 21 August 2018).

25 See generally Shelagh D. Grant (2016) *Errors Exposed: Inuit Relocations to the High Arctic, 1953–1960.* Centre for Military, Security and Strategic Studies, Centre on Foreign Policy and Federalism & Arctic Institute of North America. http://pubs.aina.ucalgary.ca/dcass/82785.pdf (accessed 9 August 2018). More recently, CTV News (2018) "Ottawa sorry for using Inuit as 'human flagpoles'", 18 August 2018, covering Canadian government apology to Inuit forcibly relocated in 1953: "As a side benefit, having Canadian civilians living in an otherwise unoccupied area bolstered Canadian sovereignty at a time when other nations, especially the United States, were expressing increasing interest in the Arctic as a possible front in the Cold War with the Soviet Union." www.ctvnews.ca/ottawa-sorry-for-using-inuit-as-human-flagpoles-1.543546 (accessed 9 August 2018).

26 See generally Samantha Arnold (2008) "Nelvana of the North, Traditional Knowledge, and the Northern Dimension of Canadian Foreign Policy" *Canadian Foreign Policy Journal* 14–2: 95–107; Samantha L. Arnold and Stéphane Roussel (2009) "Expanding the Canada–US security regime to the North?", paper presented at the Academic Roundtable "Security Prospects in the High North: Geostrategic Thaw or Freeze?", 29–30 January 2009, Reykjavík, Iceland.

the Labrador Inuit Land Claims Agreement[27] was adopted by referendum of the Labrador Inuit in December 2004. The Labrador Inuit now own 15,800 square kilometres of land as well as traditional use rights (including hunting, fishing, harvesting and social and ceremonial use) to 72,500 square kilometres of land and 48,690 square kilometres of sea.

This agreement specifies Aboriginal self-government and like other Canadian Inuit agreements provides for a co-management role for Labrador Inuit. More significantly, the provisions explicitly address the off-shore areas in terms of water rights and the adjacent ocean zone extending to the limit of Canada's territorial sea consistent with the UN Convention on the Law of the Sea. In addition, Inuit self-government, rather than merely public government or a corporate structure, is affirmed.

Significantly, each of these four agreements are considered modern-day treaties in Canadian law and their status as such is explicitly protected within the context of section 35 of the Canada's 1982 Constitution Act:[28] (1) The existing aboriginal and treaty rights of the aboriginal peoples of Canada are hereby recognised and affirmed; (2) in this Act, "aboriginal peoples of Canada" includes the Indian, Inuit and Métis peoples of Canada; (3) for greater certainty, in subsection (1) "treaty rights" includes rights that now exist by way of land claims agreements or may be so acquired; and (4) notwithstanding any other provision of this Act, the aboriginal and treaty rights referred to in subsection (1) are guaranteed equally to male and female persons.[29]

Canada declared in its November 2010 endorsement of the UN Declaration: "We are now confident that Canada can interpret the principles expressed in the Declaration in a manner that is consistent with our Constitution and legal framework."[30] On 16 December 2010, the last objecting state – the United States – reversed its position.[31] Thus, the UN Declaration is now a consensus international human rights instrument.

In September 2017, Prime Minster Trudeau addressed the UN General Assembly affirming that the government of Canada supports the UN Declaration

27 Labrador Inuit Land Claims Agreement, signed on 22 January 2005. www.aadnc-aandc.gc.ca/eng/1293647179208/1293647660333 (accessed 21 August 2018).

28 Constitution Act, 1982. http://laws-lois.justice.gc.ca/eng/Const/page-15.html#h-38 (accessed 21 August 2018).

29 Section 35.1 was added by the Constitution Amendment Proclamation, 1983 (see SI/84–102). http://laws-lois.justice.gc.ca/eng/Const/page-16.html (accessed 4 April 2018).

30 Canada (2010) "Canada's Statement of Support on the United Nations Declaration on the Rights of Indigenous Peoples", 12 November 2010. www.aadnc-aandc.gc.ca/eng/1309374239861 (accessed 9 August 2018).

31 United States (Barack Obama) (2010) "Remarks by the President at the White House Tribal Nations Conference", The White House, Office of the Press Secretary, Washington, DC, 16 December 2010: "(I)n April, we announced that we were reviewing our position on the U.N. Declaration on the Rights of Indigenous Peoples. And today I can announce that the United States is lending its support to this declaration." www.whitehouse.gov/the-press-office/2010/12/16/remarks-president-white-house-tribal-nations-conference (accessed 9 August 2018).

without qualification and will fully implement it at the domestic level.[32] In addition, he has initiated two highly important policies. The first is in the form of his mandate letters to a number of ministers, including Minister of Crown – Indigenous Relations and Northern Affairs, Carolyn Bennett, whose mandate letter states: "No relationship is more important to me and to Canada than the one with Indigenous Peoples. It is time for a renewed, nation-to-nation relationship with Indigenous Peoples, based on recognition of rights, respect, co-operation, and partnership."[33] Also, on 9 February 2017, both Prime Minister Justin Trudeau and Inuit leadership from all four land claims agreement areas and the national Inuit leader of Inuit Tapiriit Kanatami (ITK – a national organisation representing Canadian Inuit) signed the Inuit–Crown Partnership Declaration.[34] The Declaration is a commitment made by the federal government and Inuit leadership to work in partnership on shared priorities through an Inuit–Crown Partnership Committee.

The Declaration is a non-binding symbol of goodwill and partnership that does not replace or infringe upon existing legal agreements, working relationships, or responsibilities between Inuit throughout Canada and the Crown. Since its signing, there have been at least two Partnership Committee meetings and priority issues that have been identified include funding for housing; elimination of tuberculosis by 2030; early learning and child care; an Arctic Policy Framework that outlines infrastructure needs; and ensuring Inuit residents and Inuit governments are "at the forefront of decisions about the future of their region".[35]

32 Prime Minister Justin Trudeau's Address to the 72th Session of the United Nations General Assembly, 21 September 2017. https://pm.gc.ca/eng/news/2017/09/21/prime-minister-justin-trudeaus-address-72th-session-united-nations-general-assembly (accessed 9 August 2018).

33 Minister of Crown-Indigenous Relations and Northern Affairs Mandate Letter, 4 October 2017. https://pm.gc.ca/eng/minister-crown-indigenous-relations-and-northern-affairs-mandate-letter (accessed 4 April 2018).

34 Prime Minister of Canada and President of Inuit Tapiriit Kanatami announce the Inuit–Crown Partnership Committee. The Rt. Hon. Justin Trudeau, Prime Minister of Canada: "Last December, I promised that federal ministers and Inuit leaders would meet regularly to tackle important issues. Today, we're making good on that pledge by signing the Inuit Nunangat Declaration with our Inuit partners. While much remains to be done to address the unique social, cultural, economic, and environmental issues that Inuit face every day, we will move forward together, based on a respectful, renewed Inuit–Crown relationship, for the benefit of all Canadians." *Natan Obed, President of Inuit Tapiriit Kanatami*: "The Inuit–Crown Partnership Committee will play an important role as we take action on the priorities that matter to Inuit and Canadians. This committee will enhance cooperation between Inuit Tapiriit Kanatami and the federal government, allowing us to continue renewing the relationship between Inuit and the Crown in a sustainable and positive way." https://pm.gc.ca/eng/news/2017/02/09/prime-minister-canada-and-president-inuit-tapiriit-kanatami-announce-inuit-crown (accessed 4 April 2018).

35 Justin Trudeau, Prime Minister of Canada (2018) "Inuit–Crown Partnership Committee makes progress on shared priorities", Ottawa, Ontario, 29 March 2018. https://pm.gc.ca/eng/news/2018/03/29/inuit-crown-partnership-committee-makes-progress-shared-priorities (accessed 4 April 2018).

Similar to the heightened political and legal developments amongst Inuit elsewhere, the 1979 establishment of the Home Rule Government in Greenland is another example where Inuit prompted re-definition of relations with others. Enacting the Greenland Home Rule Act,[36] the Kingdom of Denmark did in fact recognise Greenland as a distinct community within its "realm". The Act provided for both legislative and executive branches of home rule government in Greenland, with powers to administer domestic affairs and a range of international affairs with the exception of foreign relations and defence or national security. However, Greenland Government has the latitude to advance their own interests within the European Community.

One clear example of such a matter is the 2004 revised Agreement between US and Denmark,[37] including Home Rule Government of Greenland, to amend the 1951 Agreement pursuant to the North Atlantic Treaty concerning the defence of Greenland.[38] The Agreement focuses on the strategic role of Thule Air Base, defence areas in Greenland, and the need for cooperation within NATO in ensuring North Atlantic security. The Agreement references the need to "ensure due protection of the environment and hunting areas in Greenland"[39] as well as the need to consult with the Home Rule Government regarding "any significant changes to United States military operations or facilities in Greenland".[40] Finally, the Home Rule Government "may appoint a representative with whom the U.S. commanding officer at Thule Air Base will consult on local affairs that affect the Home Rule Government of Greenland".[41] Another example of the

36 The Greenland Home Rule Act, Act No.577 of 29 November 1978. www.stm.dk/_p_12712.html (accessed 21 August 2018).

37 Agreement between the Government of the United States of America and the Government of the Kingdom of Denmark, including the Home Rule Government of Greenland, to amend and supplement the Agreement of April 27, 1951, as amended, pursuant to the North Atlantic Treaty between the Government of the United States of America and the Government of the Kingdom of Denmark Concerning the Defense of Greenland (Defense Agreement) including relevant subsequent Agreements related thereto, signed at Igaliku 6 August 2004 and entered into force 6 August 2004. With related joint declarations on environmental cooperation in Greenland; and economic and technical cooperation also signed in Iqaliku (Greenland) by the same three parties. www.nanoq.gl (accessed 21 August 2018).

38 Defense of Greenland: Agreement Between the United States and the Kingdom of Denmark, 27 April 1951.

39 Article 3(1)(b): "In the exceptional case of planned landings of military aircraft in Greenland outside airports, the Government of the United States consults with and informs the government of the Kingdom of Denmark, including the Home Rule Government of Greenland, in order to ensure due protection of the environment and hunting areas in Greenland."

40 Article 3(1)(c): "Consistent with the Defense Agreement, as amended herein, and the Memorandum of Understanding of March 13, 1991, and without prejudice to other relevant agreements and arrangements between the Parties, the Government of the United States will consult with and inform the Government of the Kingdom of Denmark, including the Home Rule Government of Greenland, prior to the implementation of any significant changes to United States military operations or facilities in Greenland."

41 Article 3(2)(a): "The Home Rule Government of Greenland may appoint a representative with whom the U.S. commanding officer at Thule Air Base will consult on local affairs that affect the Home rule Government of Greenland ...".

extent of authority that the Greenland Government enjoys is the EU Partnership Agreement.[42]

In 2006 Greenland and the EU agreed on a comprehensive partnership for the sustainable development of Greenland. The Partnership Agreement is a political Declaration stating the parties' intentions to continue and expand their cooperation within various areas. The Declaration was made in recognition of the close historical, political, economic and cultural ties between Greenland and the EU. Essentially, the agreement provides Greenland with approximately 25 million euros to support Greenland Education in exchange for fishing rights for the EU.

Dramatic news included the 25 November 2008 referendum wherein 75.5 per cent of the Greenlandic electorate voted "yes" to the question of pursuing independence and nationhood. The 2008 referendum was the result of comprehensive review and study by the Commission on Self-Government established by the Parliament in 2002. There is no doubt that the Greenland Government, through its establishment of the Commission on Self-Government, reviewed all developments in international law concerning the right of self-determination and the UN Declaration text well before pursuing this referendum. This is a significant example of how Inuit have and will benefit from the reality of the UN Declaration. The future efforts of the Greenlandic Inuit to re-define and re-conceptualise their relations with others, in this case initially through self-government but potentially through actual sovereignty and independence, can clearly be traced not only to their own political aspirations, but also to the work of Inuit (and all indigenous peoples) at the international level.[43]

Another significant example of recognition of the distinct status and rights of Inuit and other Arctic indigenous peoples emerged in the dialogue that resulted in the creation of the Arctic Council. The 1996 Ottawa Declaration affirmed that:

> Out of a total of 4 million inhabitants of the Arctic, approximately 500,000 belong to indigenous peoples. Indigenous peoples' organizations have been granted Permanent Participants status in the Arctic Council. The Permanent Participants have full consultation rights in connection with the Council's negotiations and decisions. The Permanent Participants represent a unique feature of the Arctic Council, and they make valuable contributions to its activities in all areas.[44]

42 Council Decision 2014/137/EU of 14 March 2014 on relations between the European Community on the one hand, and Greenland and the Kingdom of Denmark on the other, OJ L 76, 15.3.2014: 1–5.

43 Act on Greenland Self-Government, Act no. 473 of 12 June 2009 (English translation). https://naalakkersuisut.gl/~/media/Nanoq/Files/Attached%20Files/Engelske-tekster/Act%20on%20Greenland.pdf (accessed 5 October 2018).

44 *Ottawa Declaration on the Establishment of the Arctic Council*, 19 September 1996. https://oaarchive.arctic-council.org/bitstream/handle/11374/85/EDOCS-1752-v2-ACMMCA00_Ottawa_1996_Founding_Declaration.PDF?sequence=5&isAllowed=y (accessed 31 July 2018).

The Ottawa Declaration foresaw the status of Permanent Participants for Arctic indigenous peoples and their original organisations: Inuit Circumpolar Council (ICC); the Russian Arctic Indigenous Peoples of the North (RAIPON); and the Saami Council (SC). Later, the Arctic Athabaskan Council (AAC); the Aleut International Association (AIA); and the Gwich'in Council International (GGI) were welcomed. Since that time, these organisations have had an important and influential role in the work of the Arctic Council, both at the senior level and within the flurry of Working Groups that have since been established.

As reflected by these remarkable political and legal developments as well as the existing and emerging adverse environmental, social and cultural impacts upon Inuit communities and their homelands, the benefits that could be derived from an international human rights framework to address the fundamental rights Inuit can be easily identified. Hence, the importance of the UN Declaration and the norms affirmed in this unique international human rights instrument. Clearly, the procedural and substantive work to gain from the UN Declaration did in fact counterbalance the asymmetrical nature of negotiations over land claims provisions otherwise shaped by colonisation and the imposition of Western legal perspectives. Now, this counterbalance of international legal weight is sorely needed in the context of indigenous peoples and their efforts to promote and protect their rights in the face of the rapid and radical change taking place in the Arctic.

The objective of the UN Declaration process was to help reverse the tide of colonisation. One of the other important features of the UN Declaration is the fact that it is universal and ensures the expression of our distinct cultural context. Indeed, the concept of cultural context[45] is significant in order to reinforce the positive purposes of international human rights instruments. Our Arctic regional and cultural particularities and conditions require the manifestation of every right in a fashion unique to our circumstances. The UN Charter itself recognises that regional organs and arrangements were anticipated by the United Nations in order to accommodate regional differences.[46] This sentiment is also captured by one of the preambular paragraphs of the UN Declaration which recognises different circumstances and national and regional particularities.[47]

45 American Anthropological Association (1947) "Statement on Human Rights" *Amer. Anthropologist* 49–4: 539, 542–543: "Today the problem is complicated by the fact that the UN Declaration must be of worldwide applicability. It must embrace and recognize the validity of many different ways of life."

46 Charter of the United Nations, Chapter VIII.

47 New preambular paragraph: "*Recognizing* also that the situation of indigenous peoples varies from region to region and from country to country and that the significance of national and regional particularities and various historical and cultural backgrounds should be taken into consideration." This is a major improvement over the text originally circulated in the Commission on Human Rights Working Group on the Draft Declaration (CHR-WGDD). This new language allows for the play of the important principle of universality of human rights and the significance of international law.

Again, it is important to underscore the role that all UN member states played in the drafting and negotiation of the UN Declaration, including both the Arctic eight states and non-Arctic states, ultimately in favour of Inuit and other indigenous peoples of the Arctic.

It is crucial for both Arctic and non-Arctic states to understand not only the concerns of Arctic indigenous peoples, but also their human rights as distinct peoples. As noted above, the late Eben Hopson articulated this need over 40 years ago and identified the importance of our distinct rights to be "uniformly respected". In regard to the drafting and negotiation of the UN Declaration, Inuit played an active and influential role. In addition, the ICC has been active within the International Labor Organization; the Organization of American States; the World Intellectual Property Organization; and numerous other international fora.

6.4 Significance of international human rights law

Like the Universal Declaration of Human Rights, the UN Declaration provides a comprehensive human rights framework for indigenous human rights. Therefore, it is important to recognise that human rights are interrelated, indivisible and interdependent; and they are inalienable, cannot be destroyed or extinguished. The UN Declaration is also complemented by two other indigenous specific international instruments, namely the ILO Convention on Indigenous and Tribal Peoples No. 169 (1989)[48] and the American Declaration on the Rights of Indigenous Peoples[49] adopted by the OAS in 2016. The UN Declaration does not create any new rights, but more specifically it provides the cultural context necessary for the international human rights regime to be responsive to the distinct status and rights of indigenous peoples both collectively and as individuals.

After nearly 25 years in the making the UN Declaration affirms that indigenous peoples have the right to self-determination. The right enunciated in the UN Declaration[50] is the same right as that articulated in the legally binding International Covenant on Civil and Political Rights[51] and the International Covenant on Economic, Social and Cultural Rights[52] of 1966 and specifically article 1, which affirms that:

1 All peoples have the right of self-determination. By virtue of that right they freely determine their political status and freely pursue their economic, social and cultural development.

48 ILO C169, *supra* note 10.

49 American Declaration on the Rights of Indigenous Peoples, AG/RES.2888 (XLVI-O/16) (15 June 2016).

50 Article 3, UN Declaration, *supra* note 8.

51 International Covenant on Civil and Political Rights (ICCPR), adopted 16 December 1966 and entered into force 23 March 1976.

52 International Covenant on Economic, Social and Cultural Rights (ICESCR), adopted 16 December 1966 and entered into force 3 January 1976.

2 All peoples may, for their own ends, freely dispose of their natural wealth and resources without prejudice to any obligations arising out of international economic co-operation, based upon the principle of mutual benefit, and international law. In no case may a people be deprived of its own means of subsistence.

Article 3 of the UN Declaration states that: "Indigenous peoples have the right to self-determination. By virtue of that right they freely determine their political status and freely pursue their economic, social and cultural development."[53] Furthermore, the UN Declaration affirms the rights of indigenous peoples to lands, *territories* and resources; the right to free, prior and informed consent in regard to a range of matters; the right to participation in decision-making; protection from destruction of their culture; and the right to security, including food security and cultural security. Indeed, the UN Declaration is the longest discussed and negotiated human rights instrument in UN history. It also was the first time that the *subjects* of the instrument – in this case, indigenous peoples – participated extensively along with states in its formulation. This process set an important benchmark for indigenous peoples' democratic participation in UN standard-setting.

The UN Declaration continues to grow in significance. Regional[54] and domestic[55] courts and commissions are increasingly relying on it. Notably, many are

53 Article 3, UN Declaration, *supra* note 8.

54 In the Inter-American human rights system, see, e.g., *Case of the Kaliña and Lokono Peoples* v. *Suriname (Merits, Reparations and Costs)*, I/A Court H.R., Series C No. 309 (Judgment) 25 November 2015, para. 122; *Case of the Community Garifuna Triunfo de la Cruz & its members* v. *Honduras (Merits, Reparations and Costs)*, I/A Court H.R., Series C No. 305 (Judgment) 8 October 2015, para. 51; *Case of the Kuna Indigenous People of Madungandí and the Emberá Indigenous People of Bayano and their Members* v. *Panama*, I/A Court H.R. Series C No. 284, Preliminary objections, merits, reparations and costs (Judgment) 14 October 2014, para. 118. In Africa, see, e.g., *African Commission on Human and Peoples' Rights* v. *Republic of Kenya*, Application No. 006/2012, African Court on Human and Peoples' Rights, Judgment, 26 May 2017, paras. 131, 181, n. 53, and 209; *Centre for Minority Rights Development (Kenya) and Minority Rights Group International on behalf of Endorois Welfare Council* v *Kenya*, African Commission on Human and Peoples' Rights, Communication No. 276/2003, Twenty-Seventh Activity Report, 2009, Annex 5, para. 204.

55 In Belize, see *Cal et al. v. Attorney General of Belize* and *Minister of Natural Resources and Environment*, Claim No. 171, and *Coy et al. v. Attorney General of Belize* and *Minister of Natural Resources and Environment*, Claim No. 172, Consolidated Claims, Supreme Court of Belize, judgment rendered on 18 October 2007 by the Hon. Abdulai Conteh, Chief Justice. Affirmed on appeal in *Attorney-General of Belize et al.* v. *Maya Leaders Alliance et al.*, Belize Court of Appeal, Civil Appeal No. 27 of 2010, judgment rendered on 25 July 2013. See also *Sarstoon Temash Institute for Indigenous Management* [SATIIM] v. *Attorney General of Belize*, Claim No. 394 of 2013, Supreme Court of Belize, decision rendered by the Hon. Michelle Arana, 3 April 2014. In New Zealand, see *Paki and other v. Attorney-General, [2014] NZSC 118*; *Takamore* v. *Clarke*, [2011] NZCA 587, *per* Glazebrook and Wild JJ, (appeal denied [2012] NZSC 116), para. 250, n. 259. In Australia, see *Aurukun Shire Council & Anor v. CEO Office of Liquor Gaming and Racing in the Department of Treasury*, [2010] QCA 37, Supreme Ct. Queensland, paras. 33–35.

non-Arctic state institutions, such as the courts and commissions of the Organization of American States and the African Commission on Human and Peoples Rights. Also, a "system-wide action plan"[56] has recently been devised within the UN with international and national dimensions. The action plan has the ultimate goal of implementing, with the effective participation of indigenous peoples, the UN Declaration at all levels.

In addition to the UN Declaration, numerous other important international developments are directly relevant. As noted above, the ILO C169 is vital for two reasons: 1) Norway and Denmark have ratified ILO 169; and 2) the UN Declaration and ILO 169 are mutually reinforcing and compatible.[57] Therefore, UN member states must be mindful of the interrelated, interdependent and indivisible nature of the rights enunciated in all international human rights instruments as well as how they can potentially be reinforced by other human rights jurisprudence and developments. Also, the recently adopted OAS American Declaration on the Rights of Indigenous Peoples[58] is relevant and substantively enhances the overall indigenous-specific international human rights framework. There are differences between these instruments and one must be cognisant of which instrument affirms the highest standard.

The synergy created by the negotiation of the UN Declaration also triggered significant consideration of indigenous human rights and perspectives in numerous intergovernmental bodies ranging from the IUCN to the International Whaling Commission or the World Bank and the recently adopted Paris Agreement on Climate Change and the 2030 Sustainable Development Goals. Numerous other standards have been developed or are emerging in relevant international fora nearly every day and corresponding jurisprudence at the local, national and international level is also contributing to greater understanding of the content of indigenous human rights.

International human rights instruments largely focus on individual rights. By affirming for the most part indigenous peoples' *collective* rights, the UN Declaration fills an important gap in the international system. In this regard, the International Law Association (ILA) completed the task of an expert commentary on the

56 Permanent Forum on Indigenous Issues (2016) "System-wide action plan for ensuring a coherent approach to achieving the ends of the United Nations Declaration on the Rights of Indigenous Peoples", UN Doc. E/C.19/2016/5 (19 February 2016).

57 See, for example, the UN–Indigenous Peoples' Partnership (UNIPP) (2010) "For democratic governance, human rights and equality", Multi-Donor Trust Fund, Terms of Reference ILO, OHCHR, UNDP, Framework Document, 15 February 2010: 4: "With the adoption of the *UN Declaration*, the international normative framework regulating the protection of the rights of indigenous peoples has been firmly strengthened. The [*Indigenous and Tribal Peoples Convention, 1989*] is fully compatible with the *UN Declaration* on the Rights of Indigenous Peoples and the two instruments are mutually reinforcing." mptf.undp.org/document/download/4144 (accessed 5 October 2018).

58 American Declaration on the Rights of Indigenous Peoples, AG/RES.2888 (XLVI-O/16) (15 June 2016).

UN Declaration and arrived at the conclusion that though the whole of the UN Declaration is not legally binding, key provisions are in the realm of customary international law and thereby, binding upon UN member states, both Arctic and non-Arctic as well as those that presently do not have indigenous peoples within their borders.

The ILA Committee on the Rights of Indigenous Peoples' 2010 Interim Report updated the search for state practice and *opinio juris* and independently reached, with ever more examples of domestic and international practice, many of the results arrived at earlier, including the finding of customary international law including the right to the recognition and preservation of cultural identity; the right to traditional lands and natural resources; and the right to reparation and redress for the wrongs suffered.[59] That research was completed and brought up to date in the Final Report of the ILA as submitted to the 75th ILA Biennial Meeting in Sofia, Bulgaria.[60]

The existing and future discussion by all actors, Arctic and non-Arctic, will have to take all of these developments into account as they begin to engage and potentially influence the overall Arctic legal order. This is especially true in the face of the adverse impacts of climate change, such as changing ice conditions and disappearance of sea ice; coastal erosion; dramatic weather changes; greater risk in unknown and fast changing conditions; and reduced biodiversity and invasion of species – each of these dynamics can be devastating for Arctic indigenous peoples not to mention their cumulative impacts.

Furthermore, with the changing sea-ice conditions the impacts of increased Arctic shipping activity will occur. Many of the following impacts have been witnessed by Inuit coastal communities and they will likely become greater threats to the overall environmental integrity of the Arctic and the cultural integrity of the Inuit and their food security in particular:

- changing ice conditions due to fracturing of sea ice
- coastal erosion generated by increased waves
- vessel noise and disruption
- disruption of marine mammal habitat and migration routes

59 For detailed research, see the chapter by the Committee's Rapporteur, University of Siena Professor Federico Lenzerini (2010, 2012) "The Rights of Indigenous Peoples under Customary International Law", 2010 ILA Interim Report: 43–52; and 2012 ILA Final Report: 28–29.

60 The Rapporteur integrated work done at an intersessional workshop at the European University Institute in Florence, Italy, and combined subcommittee reports in a 52-page interim report for the ILA's 74th Biennial Meeting in The Hague. After another intersessional meeting conducted at the University of Anchorage in Alaska in August 2011, at the invitation of Inuit Committee member Dalee Sambo Dorough, the final report of the committee and a resolution for the ILA's 75th Biennial Meeting in Sofia was prepared. The final report supplemented the interim report of 2010.

- increased potential for contamination due to waste; ballast water; petroleum, oil and lubricants (POLs), including heavy fuel oil
- increased potential for major oil spills and similar disasters
- invasive species
- increased marine traffic
- increased militarisation
- construction of ports and breakwaters
- vessel collisions and accidents that communities are unprepared for

The pressures by both Arctic and non-Arctic states are already being felt. For these and many other reasons, to date, Arctic Council Permanent Participants have varying opinions on the admission of new Observers,[61] be they NGOs, intergovernmental organisations (IGOs) or non-Arctic states. For example, the ICC objected to Observer status of the European Union due to their damaging policy of fur seal bans – largely driven by animal rights organisations based in Europe – that devastated the economic vitality of many Canadian Arctic Inuit communities.

6.5 Recommendations to non-Arctic actors

As noted at the outset of this chapter, indigenous peoples and UN member states worked for over 25 years to achieve the UN Declaration. Too often, UN member states forget their solemn obligations in the field of human rights, too focused upon national security, economic development and other national interests. There appears to be a consistent tendency to behave as though international obligations or commitments made in one realm have no relevance within another or they take the view that some other government department is responsible for the rights, concerns and interests of indigenous peoples when in fact, the whole of government, the overall nation-state, holds these responsibilities and obligations. More troubling is the dynamic of governments both ignoring their commitments and actively working to undermine or diminish such obligations within another intergovernmental organisation.[62]

61 Present Observers to the Arctic Council: France – Barrow Ministerial meeting, 2000; Germany – Iqaluit Ministerial meeting, 1998; Italian Republic – Kiruna Ministerial meeting, 2013; Japan – Kiruna Ministerial meeting, 2013; The Netherlands – Iqaluit Ministerial meeting, 1998; People's Republic of China – Kiruna Ministerial meeting, 2013; Poland – Iqaluit Ministerial meeting, 1998; Republic of India - Kiruna Ministerial meeting, 2013; Republic of Korea – Kiruna Ministerial meeting, 2013; Republic of Singapore – Kiruna Ministerial meeting, 2013; Spain – Salekhard Ministerial meeting, 2006; Switzerland – Fairbanks Ministerial meeting, 2017; United Kingdom – Iqaluit Ministerial meeting, 1998; and 13 IGOs and 13 NGOs.

62 Permanent Forum on Indigenous Issues (2016) "Study on how States exploit weak procedural rules in international organisations to devalue the United Nations Declaration on the Rights of Indigenous Peoples and other international human rights law", UN Doc. E/C.19/2016/4 (9 May 2016). https://undocs.org/E/C.19/2016/4 (accessed 21 August 2018).

Indeed, the phenomenon of "rights ritualism" is far too common among many UN member states, especially in relation to indigenous peoples and their distinct human rights. Hilary Charlesworth describes the condition thusly:

> Ritualism is a technique of embracing the language of human rights precisely to deflect human rights scrutiny and to avoid accountability for human rights abuses, while at the same time gaining the positive reputational benefits or legitimacy associated with human rights commitments.[63]

Many have heard the Chinese and other non-Arctic state governments affirm their concern for the "interests and concerns"[64] of Arctic indigenous peoples at various venues, but refusal to acknowledge the substance of such interests, concerns or rights within other venues or domestically. Furthermore, for those seeking admission as an Observer, the Arctic Council will "take into account the extent to which observers ... [r]espect the values, interests, culture and traditions of Arctic indigenous peoples".[65] Both Arctic and non-Arctic states express such a pathology and whether or not non-Arctic states will do so in the context of recognising and respecting the status, rights and role of Arctic indigenous peoples remains to be seen.

In order for the Arctic legal order to develop in a comprehensive, coherent and socially just fashion, it is crucial for non-Arctic states to acknowledge and recognise that though they are not Arctic states, they remain subject to the commitments that they have made at the international level in relation to indigenous peoples and especially Arctic indigenous peoples as they endeavour to have a place and role in the Arctic legal order. To do so, they must work to:

- Educate themselves, identify individuals that are or can become experts in the field of Arctic indigenous peoples and human rights
- Engage at the community level of Arctic indigenous peoples

63 Hilary Charlesworth (2017) "A Regulatory Perspective on the International Human Rights System" in *Regulatory Theory: Foundations and Applications* edited by Peter Drahos. ANU Press, Acton ACT, Australia: 357–374. www.jstor.org/stable/j.ctt1q1crtm.31 (accessed 21 August 2018).

64 Jia Guide, Deputy Director General of the Department of Treaty and Law (Ministry of Foreign Affairs, People's Republic of China) spoke on China–Nordic Arctic Cooperation at the 2014 Arctic Circle Assembly at Harpa Conference Center in Reykjavik, Iceland, stated: "To build a strong and broad-based social foundation for Arctic cooperation we should continue to enhance the interaction and exchanges between research institutions, enterprises and civil societies. The Chinese government will guide its private sector to follow the domestic laws of Arctic countries concerned and relevant international treaties in conducting Arctic activities, taking fully into account the ecological environment, *the interests and concerns of the indigenous people* and combining its economic interests with the welfare of the local community." Video recording last accessed on 8 August 2018 at: https://vimeo.com/111294770.

65 See Arctic Council website: "Criteria for Admitting Observers". https://arctic-council.org/index.php/en/about-us/arctic-council/observers (accessed 21 August 2018).

- Engage with Arctic indigenous peoples outside the formal halls of the Arctic Council and other inter-governmental fora
- Engage in outreach to indigenous peoples' organisations and especially the Permanent Participants
- Meet to discuss real potential for genuine collaboration or at a minimum to identify areas of mutual interest and dialogue both within and external to the Arctic Council
- Be clear, specific and straightforward about their Arctic specific interests, objectives, initiatives and projects
- Consider ways and means to advance research in the field of social sciences and other areas of concern to Arctic indigenous peoples

6.6 Conclusion

There are a multitude of Arctic initiatives and entities emerging. As Mayor Harry Brower of the North Slope Borough recently stated in his welcoming remarks at the Inuit Circumpolar Council 13th General Assembly:

> We have lived in the Arctic for thousands of years. It is our home. In Alaska, we have been reacting to others who wander into our region since 1854 … I am tired of asking for a seat at someone else's table…Our country is just realizing it is an arctic nation. Over 59 new non-profit organizations have been established since we met last to debate Arctic policy. They are spending millions of dollars considering what the rest of the world should do with the Arctic. Our Vision of The Arctic We Want should be their Guide; they should be asking us for a seat at our table.[66]

His views are shared by those Inuit diplomats and statesmen of the past and they are shared by those of the present. It is crucial that the rights and role of Arctic indigenous peoples be recognised and respected. This chapter has endeavoured to address our background and history as a people that have chosen to unite and organise ourselves in the face of change that we knew would come. Our current work as an Inuit political organisation has been successful on many levels, from engagement in the United Nations to the regional work of the Arctic Council. We have now set our sights on a host of other initiatives that require our attention. However, one issue that has remained constant is the central need for all others to respect and recognise Inuit rights and status and, in particular, within the new Arctic legal order that non-Arctic states are working to conceptualise and realise. Again, the Arctic is our homeland.

We are focused upon our efforts to shape all of these new, different and emerging issues from our point of view – like the theme of the ICC 13th General Assembly – we seek to define the Arctic that we want. In relation to the Arctic

66 Harry K. Brower, Mayor of the North Slope Borough (2018) "Welcoming Remarks: Our Vision of the Arctic", ICC General Assembly, 16 July 2018.

that we want, in September 2015, the UN General Assembly adopted by consensus a key instrument for achieving sustainable development globally – *Transforming Our World: The 2030 Agenda for Sustainable Development.*[67] In particular, states resolved:

> between now and 2030, to *end poverty and hunger everywhere*; to combat inequalities …; to *protect human rights* and *promote gender equality and the empowerment of women and girls*; and to *ensure the lasting protection of the planet and its natural resources.*[68]

Therefore, it is essential to underscore that in 2012, in *The Future We Want*, the Rio+20 UN Commission on Sustainable Development recognised "the importance of the United Nations Declaration … in the context of *global, regional, national and subnational implementation* of sustainable development strategies".[69] We regard these not as hollow aspirations and goals. The world community and especially UN member states within the Arctic region should be working to identify, in collaboration with Inuit and other Arctic indigenous peoples, the future we want in the Arctic. At least one Arctic state has made explicit, verbal commitments to be responsive to the aspirations of the Inuit.

The approach taken by the government of Canada has built upon the Inuit comprehensive land claims agreements, which were negotiated (not a unilateral act of Congress or Parliament like Alaska) over years. They began with an Agreement in Principle, norms that couldn't be retreated from by either side. Following negotiation, they were adopted by referendum of the eligible Inuit individuals that would be affected – an act of consent on the basis of the Agreement interpreted into their Inuit dialects. In addition, they receive Constitutional section 35 protection.

These modern-day treaties affirm Inuit rights to lands, territories and resources; rights to manage and co-manage their resources; and again, the Labrador Inuit Land Claims Agreement affirms Inuit rights to the 12-mile territorial sea consistent with the UN Convention on the Law of the Sea. Though they are not perfect, they are significant and substantive in contrast to conditions faced by indigenous peoples in other regions of the world.

Canadian Prime Minister Trudeau has made a solemn commitments to implement the UN Declaration at the national level. He also set out important directives to his entire Cabinet through his Mandate letters specifically underscoring

67 UN General Assembly (2015) *Transforming Our World: The 2030 Agenda for Sustainable Development*, UNGA/RES/70/1, 25 September 2015 (adopted without a vote).

68 Ibid., para. 3 (emphasis added). On 1 January 2016, the 17 Sustainable Development Goals of the 2030 Agenda for Sustainable Development came into effect. Along with such Goals, there are 169 associated targets.

69 Rio+20 United Nations Commission on Sustainable Development (2012) *The Future We Want*, Rio de Janeiro, Brazil, 20–22 June 2012, UN Doc. A/CONF.216/L.1 (19 June 2012), para. 49 (emphasis added); endorsed by General Assembly (2012) *The Future We Want*, UNGA/RES/66/288, 27 July 2012 (without vote).

the important relationship between the federal government and the indigenous peoples of Canada. Not to mention the fact that his new Attorney General is an indigenous woman. Furthermore, in February 2017, Trudeau mandated a new Working Group of Ministers – chaired by the Minister of Justice – to review relevant federal laws, policies, and operational practices. The purpose is not only to ensure the Crown is "meeting its constitutional obligations with respect to Aboriginal and treaty rights", but also "adhering to international human rights standards, including the United Nations Declaration".[70] In addition, the Trudeau administration signed the 2017 Inuit Crown Partnership Agreement with the national Inuit Tapiriit Kanatami, the national Inuit organisation, which established a Committee of national and regional leadership. Again, this bilateral mechanism establishes priorities, for example the crisis of suicide, and helps to maintain a dialogue between Inuit and the national government.

Though Inuit remain watchful and await full delivery on such promises, these are significant steps for an Arctic UN member state to initiate. For all other Arctic and non-Arctic states, the time for governments to work with Inuit and all other Arctic indigenous peoples to effectively realise the UN Declaration across our homelands is past due. This chapter has attempted to illustrate the central nature of Inuit status and rights within the legal order of the Arctic. It should be apparent that through our direct participation in all Arctic related matters, states and others can make a significant contribution to the security and sustainability of the Arctic for all of humankind. We will be final arbitrators of whether or not our relations will result in a win–win for all concerned, but in particular for ourselves as the real people of the Arctic.

70 Justin Trudeau, Prime Minister of Canada (2017) "Prime Minister announces Working Group of Ministers on the Review of Laws and Policies Related to Indigenous Peoples", 22 February 2017. http://pm.gc.ca/eng/news/2017/02/22/prime-minister-announces-working-group-ministers-review-laws-and-policies-related (accessed 21 August 2018).

7 Sustaining a conservationist agenda?

NGO influence on Arctic sealing, whaling and hydrocarbon regimes

Marzia Scopelliti and Nikolas Sellheim

7.1 Introduction

The richness in natural resources in the Arctic and the opening of shipping routes[1] are but a few reasons that have spurred increased international attention towards the Arctic region. As a consequence, an increasing number of non-Arctic stakeholders now claim a voice in circumpolar governance.[2] Amongst these are organisations that have emerged independently from national governments – non-governmental organisations (NGOs). In particular, the effective regulation of multifaceted environmental issues that are at the core of Arctic governance (e.g. climate change, sustainable development of resources, pollution, conservation and animal welfare) ranges high on their agenda.

International law-making is a state-driven process. Notwithstanding, especially in the context of transnational environmental issues, the contributions of NGOs have shown most prominently. In order to tackle environmental problems that are global in scope and nature, nation states have relied on the contributions of NGOs as a means to achieve effective policy- and law-making. While the legitimacy and accountability of these organisations are contentious,[3] their participation in the law-making process has in many instances become an institutionalised practice, often acknowledged as bringing transparency, knowledge and expertise to intergovernmental negotiations.[4] The Arctic Council (AC) is no exception

1 An overview of natural resources exploitation opportunities in the Arctic is provided by Timo Koivurova (2016) "Arctic Resources: Exploitation of Natural Resources in the Arctic from the Perspective of International Law" in *Research Handbook in International Law and Natural Resources* edited by Elisa Morgera and Kati Kulovesi. Edward Elgar, Cheltenham: 349–366.

2 Suffice as an example the great number of non-Arctic stakeholders that have applied for the Observer status to the Arctic Council from 2009 onwards.

3 See, e.g., Anne Peters, Lucy Koechlin, Till Förster and Gretta Fenner Zinkernagel (2009) *Non-State Actors as Standard Setters*. Cambridge University Press, Cambridge; Alan Boyle and Christine Chinkin (2007) *The Making of International Law*. Oxford University Press, Oxford.

4 Sebastian Oberthür, Matthias Buck, Sebastian Müller et al. (2002) *Participation of Non-Governmental Organisations in International Environmental Governance: Legal Basis and Practical Experience*. Ecologic, Berlin: 40.

here and organisations such as the International Union for the Conservation of Nature (IUCN) or the World Wildlife Fund for Nature (WWF) are Observers to the AC.[5] Yet, it is less clear to which degree these non-state actors influence the deliberative processes. For example, which normative implications have, if any, the narratives told and what are the advocacy strategies used by different environmental NGOs?

The influence of environmental NGOs on the Arctic legal order has received relatively little attention in legal scholarship, especially if compared with the state of research on the role and interests of non-Arctic states in circumpolar affairs.[6] Most academic work has concentrated on NGOs who are Observers to the AC.[7] Against this backdrop, this chapter instead examines the influence of conservationist NGOs that, outside of the AC, have been able to directly or indirectly influence the Arctic legal order. By choosing contentious and emotional issues under international law – marine mammal and hydrocarbon exploitation – we demonstrate how conservationist narratives of NGOs have directly impacted on the Arctic legal environment.

7.2 NGOs in international (environmental) law

This chapter focuses on globally operating organisations of civil origin that have been established independently from a nation state, referred to as NGOs. These organisations commonly follow normative sets of goals – such as the improvement of human rights, environmental protection or animal rights – and are, by definition, not profit-seeking. Members of an NGO retain their status voluntarily due to shared interests or the pursuance of common goals. With a strong and solvent membership the organisation tries – with varying success – to make its voice heard and to exercise its moral authority.[8]

Especially with the dawn of the "environmental awakening" in the 1960s, spurred by the publication of Rachel Carson's *Silent Spring*[9] in 1962, the number of non-state, or transnational, actors has risen dramatically: while at

5 See also Chapter 2 by Timo Koivurova in this book.

6 See, e.g., Andrew Chater (2016) "Explaining Non-Arctic States in the Arctic Council" *Strategic Analysis* 40–3: 173–184; Olav S. Stokke (2014) "Asian Stakes and Arctic Governance" *Strategic Analysis* 38–6: 770–783; and Chapter 13 by Knecht and Spence in this book.

7 See, e.g., Dorothea Wehrmann (2017) "Non-State Actors in Arctic Council Governance" in *Governing Arctic Change. Global Perspectives* edited by Kathrin Keil and Sebastian Knecht. Palgrave Macmillan, London: 187–206; Dorothea Wehrmann (2016) "The Polar Regions as 'Barometers' in the Anthropocene: Towards a New Significance of Non-State Actors in International Cooperation?" *Polar Journal* 6–2: 379–397; Sébastien Duyck (2015) "Polar Environmental Governance and Nonstate Actors" in *Diplomacy on Ice: Energy and the Environment in the Arctic and Antarctic* edited by Rebecca Pincus and Saleem H. Ali. Yale University Press, Yale: 13–40.

8 Steve Charnovitz (2006) "Nongovernmental Organizations and International Law" *American Journal of International Law* 100: 348–372, at 348.

9 Rachel Carson (1962) *Silent Spring*. Houghton Mifflin, Boston.

the UN Conference on the Human Environment in 1972 170 NGOs were accredited, in 2012 9,856 NGOs attended the Rio+20 Summit.[10] While this number does not differentiate between different types of organisations, we consider NGOs that are based on specific values, shared ideas and specific philosophical approaches concerning human–environment interaction.[11] They therefore do not necessarily correspond to Haas's definition of "epistemic communities" which is a "network of professionals with recognised expertise and competences in a particular domain and an authoritative claim to policy-relevant knowledge within that domain or issue-area".[12] Instead, these NGOs exert influence based on specific views on how humans are to interact with the natural environment.

Even though NGOs are not formal subjects in international law they are crucial for its agenda-setting stage, its interpretation, implementation and further development.[13] Several strategies allow them to do so, which have generally been grouped under the categories of "inside advocacy" or "outside advocacy" strategies.[14] The first approach denotes the direct flow and transmission of information, that is direct access, to decision-makers. For instance, an NGO exercises inside advocacy by being observer to or participant in international diplomacy, where it seeks to directly influence decision-makers and to shape ideas and norms relevant for the outcome of the respective meeting.[15] Thus, while direct participation in the law-making process can be a more effective strategy,[16] some NGOs may not be able to directly influence law-making and therefore lobby through external channels.

In such a context, outside advocacy refers to the targeted influencing and shaping of public opinion. Seeking to exert pressure from the outside, NGOs influence public opinion, which in turn might increase domestic public pressure on national governments. The staging of demonstrations and protests or organising side events and manifestations are but a few examples of outside advocacy

10 Christian Downie (2016) "Transnational Actors: Nongovernmental Organizations, Civil Society and Individual" in *Routledge Handbook of Global Environmental Politics* edited by Paul G. Harris. Routledge, Abingdon: 176–186, at 176.

11 For a brief overview, see Elli Louka (2006) *International Environmental Law. Fairness, Effectiveness, and World Order.* Cambridge University Press, Cambridge: 16–21.

12 Peter Haas (1992) "Introduction: Epistemic Communities and International Policy Coordination" *International Organization* 46: 1–35, at 3.

13 Charnovitz (2006), *supra* note 8.

14 Carola Betzold (2013) "Business Insiders and Environmental Outsiders? Advocacy Strategies in International Climate Change Negotiations" *Interest Groups & Advocacy* 2–3: 302–322, at 305.

15 See, e.g., Radoslav S. Dimitrov (2016) "Environmental Diplomacy: International Conferences and Negotiations" in Paul G. Harris, *supra* note 10, at 263–264.

16 Variations in the effectiveness of inside advocacy are also dependent on factors such as: responsiveness of the lobbied government or delegation, and NGO influence which, in turn, is determined by resources (financial and human) and by the structure of negotiations. See Carola Betzold (2014) "Responsiveness or Influence? Whom to Lobby in International Climate Change Negotiations" *International Negotiations* 19: 35–61.

exercised by NGOs which, being otherwise unable to influence the negotiation process, become external advocates.

Although the belonging and moving of an NGO from one advocacy strategy to another is not always clear-cut, the classification of "inside and outside advocacy" seems broad enough to identify the range of activities that most environmentalist NGOs choose to influence law(s) that are also relevant for the Arctic region.[17]

7.3 The Arctic legal order and conservationist NGOs

Governance of the Arctic is built on multi-layered systems of national regulation, regional and international agreements, complemented by soft law instruments, all of which see different levels of influence of non-governmental actors.[18] Even though the AC and the Law of the Sea (LOS) Convention are central in this regard as the primary mechanism for circumpolar governance, they are not the only ones. To this end, this chapter to a large extent focuses on the influence that specific conservationist NGOs have had on outside legal orders *affecting* and *being relevant for* the Arctic.

In recent years the development of Arctic law has been subject to centripetal and centrifugal forces. On the one hand, the adoption of three regional agreements under the auspices of the AC[19] has contributed to its function in a norm-building process and likewise opened the debate on its institutional reform and future legal status.[20] For the purposes of this chapter, the influence of NGOs on this process will not be addressed. On the other hand, the number of Arctic-relevant law-making forums, for example in the European Union (EU), within the International Whaling Commission (IWC) or generally within the purview of the United Nations has increased, while different developments have taken place outside the structure of the AC which have included a range of non-Arctic

17 See, for example, on the whaling regime Charlotte Epstein (2008) *The Power of Words in International Relations. Birth of an Anti-Whaling Discourse.* MIT Press, Cambridge, MA. See also Michele M. Betsill and Elisabeth Correll (eds) (2008) *NGO Diplomacy: The Influence of Nongovernmental Organizations in International Environmental Negotiations.* MIT Press, Cambridge, MA. On CITES and the UNFCCC, see Sebastian Oberthür, Matthias Buck, Sebastian Müller et al. (2002), *supra* note 4.

18 Waliul Hasanat (2012) *Soft-law Cooperation in International Law: The Arctic Council's Efforts to Address Climate Change.* Doctoral dissertation, Lapland University Press.

19 Agreement on Cooperation on Aeronautical and Maritime Search and Rescue in the Arctic (SAR), signed 12 May 2011 and entered into force 19 January 2013. https://oaarchive.arctic-council.org/handle/11374/531 (accessed 9 August 2018); Agreement on Cooperation on Marine Oil Pollution Preparedness and Response in the Arctic (OPPRA), signed 15 May 2013 and entered into force 25 March 2016. https://oaarchive.arctic-council.org/handle/11374/529 (accessed 9 August 2018); Agreement on Enhancing International Arctic Scientific Cooperation, signed 11 May 2017 and entered into force 23 May 2018. https://oaarchive.arctic-council.org/handle/11374/1916 (accessed 9 August 2018), reproduced in the Appendix of this Book.

20 See, e.g., Svein V. Rottem (2016) *The Arctic Council: Vision, Structure and Participation.* Fridtjof Nansen Institute, Norway: 1–13.

actors.[21] This is not only the case of the law that is expressly developed for the Arctic, as in the case of the Polar Code or the Central Arctic Ocean Fisheries Agreement,[22] but also for those international or regional regimes developed to tackle a wide range of environmental issues, including the exploitation of marine and energy resources. In such a hybrid, multilevel and multi-stakeholder legal structure, manifold possibilities for direct or indirect non-governmental influence exist.

To exemplify the influence of conservationist NGOs on the Arctic-*relevant* legal order being negotiated, decided upon and implemented outside of the Arctic, we now turn to their role in the shaping of laws and policies pertaining to the hunt for marine mammals. Particularly the European bans on trade in seal products as well as Aboriginal Subsistence Whaling (ASW) under the International Convention for the Regulation of Whaling (ICRW)[23] are taken up as case studies on how conservationist agendas have impacted this Arctic-relevant legal order. The final section of the chapter takes a closer look at the case of Greenpeace as an influential advocate in the Arctic region.

7.3.1 NGOs and the European seal trade

Up to this day the trade in seal products has been an integral part of Arctic traditional economies and culture.[24] This notwithstanding, in the late 1960s international protests against the seal hunt, directed specifically against the large-scale, non-indigenous "commercial" hunts in Atlantic Canada, grew. Crucial in this regard was the work of Brian Davies who formed the International Fund for Animal Welfare (IFAW) in 1968, now one of the leading NGOs opposing the seal hunt.[25]

As part of a systemic and successful campaign to end the seal hunt, Davies invited journalists from all over the world to document it, boosting donations to several million dollars. With this financial backing, paired with campaigns with high visibility, the anti-sealing movement was able to initiate worldwide campaigns against Canadian sealing.[26]

21 This is the case of the *International Code for Ships Operating in Polar Waters*, adopted by the International Maritime Organisation in 2014; of the *Agreement on unregulated fishing in the Arctic Ocean*, negotiated among the five Arctic coastal States, the European Union, Iceland and three East Asian states; and the *Agreement on "Biodiversity Beyond National Jurisdictions"*, currently under negotiation in a UN framework.

22 See both Chapter 8 by Joji Morishita and Chapter 9 by Erik J. Molenaar in this book.

23 International Convention for the Regulation of Whaling, adopted on 2 December 1946 and entered into force 10 November 1948, 161 UNTS 72.

24 See, e.g., Nikolas Sellheim (2018) *The Seal Hunt: Economies, Cultures and Legal Regimes*. Brill, Leiden.

25 Donald Barry (2005) *Icy Battleground: Canada, the International Fund for Animal Welfare, and the Seal Hunt*. Breakwater Books, St. John's.

26 Janice S. Henke (1985) *Seal Wars! An American Viewpoint*. Breakwater Books, St. John's: 70–71.

In 1977 IFAW started campaigns in Europe – Britain, West Germany, Italy, Netherlands and France – in order to achieve consumer boycotts of seal pelts. Additionally, a new and controversial report[27] brought animal welfare aspects of the seal hunt onto the public's agenda, furthermore fuelling European protests. The first direct consequence for the Arctic-relevant legal order occurred in June 1978 when Italy banned the import of furs of seal pups, included those hunted by Arctic indigenous peoples. Italy was thus the first European country to establish a legal barrier for the importation of seal products due to NGO outside advocacy. One year later, also the Dutch government declared its intention to formalise an import ban.[28]

As a result of campaigns and public pressure, on 28 March 1983 the European Communities (EC) adopted the so-called "Seal Pups Directive",[29] which banned the trade in products stemming from harp and hooded seal pups. Even though the ban was not Arctic-specific, given the fact that harp seals (*Pagophilus groenlandicus*) and hooded seals (*Cystophora cristata*) were exclusively hunted in the Arctic, the directive directly impacted socio-economic conditions in Arctic seal-hunting communities. While the directive was to be in place only for two years, in 1985 it was extended until 1989 and indefinitely thereafter. By then, however, outside advocacy of NGOs had become inside advocacy, or even consultancy: Brian Davies was advisor on seal issues to the Council of the European Communities during the adoption process of the Seal Pups Directive.[30] Even though the seal hunt was legal in Canada, the EC had legally shamed and outlawed it. At the same time it aimed to recognise the socio-economic importance of subsistence hunting for the Inuit and thus the directive provides for an exemption for Inuit communities from any trade barrier – the so-called "Inuit exemption".[31]

Since the EC was a major market for seal products at that time, in the wake of the Seal Pups Directive, due to an absent labelling scheme and thus uncertainty as to whether specific seal products were legal or not, fur traders abstained from buying all seal products – also from Inuit communities – rendering the Inuit exemption toothless. As a result, Inuit hunters lost an important part of their income,[32] causing significant resentment within Inuit (and non-Inuit) sealing communities towards the EC. Dropping revenues led to a higher dependency on wage employment and transfer payments, in turn leading to advancing dissolution

27 William Jordan (1978) *The Killing of Harp Seal Pups: Report for Royal Society for the Prevention of Cruelty to Animals*. Royal Society for the Prevention of Cruelty to Animals.

28 Barry (2005), *supra* note 25, at 54–56.

29 Council of the European Union (1983) "Council Directive 83/129/EEC of 28 March 1983 concerning the importation into Member States of skins of certain seal pups and products derived therefrom" Brussels: Official Journal of the European Communities (OJ L 91, 9.4.1983, pp. 30–31).

30 Alan Herscovici (1985) *Second Nature. The Animal-Rights Controversy*. CBC Enterprises, Toronto: 84.

31 Council of the European Union (1983), *supra* note 29, article 3.

32 Albert H. Malouf (1987) *Royal Commission on Seals and the Sealing Industry in Canada report*. Vol. 2. Supply and Services Canada: 225–226.

of traditional Inuit cultural and social practices.[33] The change in a non-Arctic legal order affecting the Arctic, which was caused by outside advocacy, thus directly translated into effects on traditional social orders. It does not come as a surprise that the term "Greenpeace" stands synonymous with outsiders causing negative effects on Arctic livelihoods.[34]

The European Union – formally established in 1992 – went further than its predecessor and adopted a total ban on seal products in 2009.[35] Since the EU has significant legal competences in the Arctic[36] and EU-internal legislation such as the trade bans on seal products directly affect Arctic seal hunts on the ground, we consider parts of EU law relevant components of the Arctic legal order. Throughout the *travaux préparatoires* of the regime, NGOs were an integral part of the consultation process while they were also exercising outside advocacy. Most notably, in order to analyse animal welfare aspects of the Canadian seal hunts, material produced by the Humane Society International (HSI) as well as IFAW were used and were also part of preparatory meetings.[37] At the same time, People for the Ethical Treatment of Animals (PETA) and the HSI organised protests against the hunt in Strasbourg and Brussels and distributed attitude-influencing materials before the different votes in the European Parliament.[38] Not surprisingly, the European Parliament voted with an overwhelming majority for a total ban on trade in seal products. Although once again the ban held an exemption for indigenous peoples, its effects were drastic, particularly because of the interwoven trade pathways of Inuit and non-Inuit seal products.[39]

7.3.2 NGOs and Arctic whaling

As is the case with EU law, the international legal order can also directly affect Arctic local practices. One example is the international whaling regime. As with sealing, whaling has been an important element of the past and present socioeconomy in the Arctic.[40] For almost 90 states, whaling is regulated by the ICRW

33 George Wenzel (1991) *Animal Rights, Human Rights: Ecology, Economy and Ideology in the Canadian Arctic.* University of Toronto Press, Toronto: 123–132.

34 As observed by Sellheim in Nunavut in 2012.

35 European Union (2009) "Regulation (EC) No 1007/2009 of the European Parliament and of the Council of 16 September 2009 on Trade in Seal Products" Brussels: Official Journal of the European Union (OJ L 286, 31.10.2009, pp. 36–39), as amended.

36 Timo Koivurova, Kai Kokko, Sebastian Duyck et al. (2012) "The Present and Future Competence of the European Union in the Arctic" *Polar Record* 48–4: 361–371.

37 Nikolas Sellheim (2015) "Policies and Influence: Tracing and Locating the EU Seal Products Trade Regulation" *International Community Law Review* 17: 3–36.

38 Nikolas Sellheim (2013) "The Neglected Tradition? The Genesis of the EU Seal Product Trade Ban and Commercial Sealing" *Yearbook of Polar Law* 5: 417–450.

39 Government of Nunavut (2012) *Report on the Impacts of the European Union Seal Ban, (EC) NO 1007/2009, in Nunavut.* Department of the Environment, Iqaluit.

40 See, e.g., Johan N. Tønnessen and Arne O. Johnsen (1982) *The History of Modern Whaling.* C. Hurst & Company, London.

and administered by the IWC. Since the season of 1985/86 a moratorium on commercial whaling has been in place which,[41] to a large degree, had been put in place because of the dominant non-utilitarian discourse that has accompanied whaling at least since the early 1970s, largely caused by NGOs.[42] Notably, these same NGOs have been observers to the IWC since the 1960s. Greenpeace received observer status only in 1978 and became one of the most vocal anti-whaling NGOs in the commission.[43]

Due to the ICRW's "opting out" provisions, aboriginal and scientific whaling, as well as the complex histories of past and present whaling nations under the regime, NGO activities to impact whaling have followed a twofold approach. For example, Greenpeace has applied tactics of "shaming and blaming" *inter alia* by initiating boycotts on Norwegian fish in the late 1980s. Norway, a whaling nation, had opted out of the moratorium and was therefore legally capable to continue commercial whaling.[44] On the other hand, the direct-action-oriented Sea Shepherd (Conservation Society) (SSCS) considers itself an enforcer of the whaling moratorium.[45] SSCS directly impacted Arctic whaling in 1986 when SSCS members sank two whaling vessels in Reykjavík harbour while damaging Iceland's only whale processing plant. The organisation also attacked Norwegian whalers which spurred pro-whaling sentiments in Norway.[46] These actions were publicly justified as a means to enforce the whaling moratorium. Iceland, at that time, had not opted out from but circumvented the moratorium by intensifying its scientific whaling programme.[47] As a result of the incidents in Iceland, the IWC revoked the observer accreditation of SSCS in 1987 and the relationship between the two organisations remains strained.[48]

By influencing public opinion worldwide and by contributing to a discourse of a "superwhale",[49] environmental NGOs have contributed to the IWC becoming an organisation whose majority supports a whaling moratorium.[50] Much to their dismay, however, whaling in the Arctic has not ceased: whaling nations such as

41 See, e.g., Alexander Gillespie (2005) *Whaling Diplomacy: Defining Issues in International Environmental Law*. Edward Elgar, Cheltenham.

42 Epstein (2008), *supra* note 17.

43 Steinar Andresen and Tora Skodvin (2008) "Non-state Influence in the International Whaling Commission, 1970 to 2006" in Betsill and Correll, *supra* note 17, at 119–147.

44 Ibid.

45 Avelie Stuart, Emma F. Thomas, Ngaire Donaghue et al. (2013) " 'We may be pirates, but we are not protesters': Identity in the Sea Shepherd Conservation Society" *Political Psychology* 34–5: 753–777.

46 Andresen and Skodvin (2008), *supra* note 43, at 137.

47 Malgosia Fitzmaurice (2015) *Whaling and International Law*. Cambridge University Press, Cambridge: 73; Iceland officially left the IWC in 1992 due to the moratorium, but rejoined in 2001 albeit with a reservation towards the moratorium.

48 IWC (2008) "Statement on Safety at Sea". Press Release of March 2008. https://iwc.int/intersession08#safety (accessed 9 August 2018).

49 A merger of anthropomorphised attributes of all whale species, making the "superwhale" endangered, social, intelligent, etc. See Arne Kalland (2011) *Unveiling the Whale: Discourses on Whales and Whaling*. Berghahn Books, New York: 28–46.

50 Epstein (2008), *supra* note 17.

Iceland and Norway – Canada withdrew from the IWC in 1983 – continue to hunt whales while Arctic indigenous peoples of IWC members, for example in Greenland, Chukotka and Alaska, maintain their whale hunts.

The whaling regime grants Aboriginal Subsistence Whaling a special place and from the outset "aborigines" were exempted from bans on the killing of grey and right whales, if carried out for local consumption. This is also the case in the context of the whaling moratorium which does not apply to aboriginal whalers to fulfil their subsistence needs.[51] NGO-perception of ASW is not clear-cut, however: (1) IWC observer organisations, for example IFAW, do not officially oppose ASW.[52] However, to our knowledge there is no official statement that openly protects – or even supports – ASW in order to follow international standards pertaining to indigenous rights. (2) Whale and Dolphin Conservation (WDC), on the other hand, notes that "certain aboriginal subsistence whaling communities have abused the definition by allowing whale meat to enter the commercial exchange chain".[53] Also the HSI maintains this approach.[54] In other words, WDC and HSI limit their acceptance of ASW to a strictly non-commercial, local, "hand-to-mouth" sphere of exchange. It is noteworthy that some observer NGOs challenge contemporary ASW – even though it is legal under the prevailing regime – and thereby compromise the allocation of quotas through their influence on delegations.[55] The failure of allocating Greenland its ASW bowhead whale quota exemplifies this. This failure prompted some hunters to take bowhead whales irrespective of the absence of a quota, causing discussions on a possible infraction of the ICRW, for example at the 2016 meeting of the IWC.[56] (3) Non-observer organisations such as SSCS do not maintain a particular stance on ASW. It appears, however, that subsistence whaling is equally opposed as any other whaling. For example, a young Yup'ik hunter who killed a bowhead whale and posted this on social media received death threats from members of SSCS as a response.[57] SSCS's founder and Executive Director Paul Watson publicly stated: "I have no apologies for my anger. It enraged me to see this kid bragging about

51 In order to obtain a quota, national governments, on behalf of their aboriginal people are to produce a Needs Statement which "details the cultural, subsistence and nutritional aspects of the hunt, products and distribution". See Fitzmaurice (2015), *supra* note 47, at 248.

52 IFAW: "Is IFAW against all forms of whaling?" www.ifaw.org/united-states/node/1941 (accessed 9 August 2018).

53 WDC: "Aboriginal Subsistence Whaling". http://uk.whales.org/issues/aboriginal-subsistence-whaling (accessed 9 August 2018).

54 HIS: "Humane Society International Calls on the International Whaling Commission to Curb Violations of Global Moratorium" last modified 11 September 2014. www.hsi.org/news/press_releases/2014/09/iwc-65-091114.html (accessed 9 August 2018).

55 See, e.g., Animal Welfare Institute: "Aboriginal Subsistence Whaling". https://awionline.org/content/subsistence-whaling (accessed 9 August 2018).

56 IWC, Infractions Sub-Committee: "Summary of Infractions Reports received by the Commission for 2014 and 2015", IWC/66/INF04 Rev (2016). https://archive.iwc.int/?r=6262&k=c53dfd1fdc (accessed 9 August 2018).

57 Indian County Today: "Yupik Teen Hunter Receives Death Threats" last modified 30 August 2017. https://indiancountrymedianetwork.com/culture/social-issues/yupik-teen-hunter-receives-death-threats/ (accessed 9 August 2018).

snuffing out the life of a Bowhead whale that was over 240 years old."[58] Watson also considers hunting whales for subsistence purposes "cetacide" – murder.[59]

7.3.3 Rebutting conservationist pressure – an Arctic response

Even though the international legal order pertaining to whaling and sealing affected the Arctic dramatically, Arctic governments have acted as active agents to improve their conditions and to invoke their rights as sovereigns. Canada, for one, left the IWC in 1983 after the moratorium on whaling had been decided upon. This reaction was prompted due to the constitutional provisions to protect native peoples' rights to hunt wildlife.[60] Moreover, Canada and Norway – unsuccessfully – used the dispute settlement regime under the World Trade Organization (WTO) to overthrow the 2009 EU Seal Regime.[61]

However, also sub-national regions – Greenland and the Faroe Islands – together with Norway and Iceland responded to these developments and countered international legal and discursive developments: in 1992 they formed the North Atlantic Marine Mammal Commission (NAMMCO). Based on the Agreement on Cooperation in Research, Conservation and Management of Marine Mammals in the North Atlantic,[62] NAMMCO is to "to contribute through regional consultation and cooperation to the conservation, rational management and study of marine mammals in the North Atlantic".[63] This means, even though powerful entities such as the EC/EU and other non-Arctic states within the IWC have made use of the no-use narrative of international NGOs, Arctic states and peoples have made use of the provisions under the UNCLOS to rebut this development.[64] Even though the Faroe Islands and Greenland are dependencies of the

58 Paul Watson: Facebook page, 14 August 2017. www.facebook.com/captpaulwatson/posts/10155320358970932 (accessed 9 August 2018).

59 Ibid.

60 Robert L. Friedheim (2001) "The IWC as a Contested Regime" in *Toward a Sustainable Whaling Regime* edited by Robert L. Friedheim. University of Washington Press, Seattle: 3–48.

61 Sellheim (2018), *supra* note 24.

62 Agreement on Cooperation in Research, Conservation and Management of Marine Mammals in the North Atlantic, adopted on 9 April 1992 and entered into force on 8 July 1992. nammco.wpengine.com/wp-content/uploads/2016/10/nammco-agreement-with-signatures-and-logo.pdf (accessed 1 December 2018).

63 Ibid., Article 2; The possibility to establish and organisation for the management of marine mammals follows article 65 of the UNCLOS which sets out that "states shall co-operate with a view to the conservation of marine mammals and in the case of cetaceans shall in particular work through the appropriate international organizations for their conservation, management, and study". Even though the IWC was the primary body for marine mammal management at the time of conclusion of UNCLOS, the article does not prevent the establishment of other "appropriate" organisations to manage marine mammals.

64 The formation of other organisations for the management of marine mammals is explicitly referred to in UNCLOS article 65, which requires states to "cooperate with a view to the conservation of marine mammals and in the case of cetaceans [...] in particular [to] work through the appropriate international organizations for their conservation, management and study".

Kingdom of Denmark, the Danish government did not object to (or control) the formation of NAMMCO. This is noteworthy since under the IWC the Faroe Islands and Greenland do not represent themselves in their own capacity, but are formally represented by Denmark.

NAMMCO allows for the participation of observers – NGOs, IGOs and non-member governments. Notably, Denmark is such an observer. Once an organisation has received observer status it retains this position as long as there is consensus amongst NAMMCO members. Generally, observers are not permitted to the meetings of NAMMCO committees. As of 2018, ten NGOs are accredited observers most of which are Arctic indigenous and pro-sustainable use organisations.[65] Organisations opposing the hunt for marine mammals are not observers and have never applied for observership to Council meetings. However, some attended workshops on killing methods that were open to the public.[66]

The establishment of NAMMCO has impacted on the legal order in the Arctic pertaining to the management of marine mammals. Some commentators saw the IWC undermined by the establishment of NAMMCO.[67] Despite these fears, NAMMCO and the IWC cooperate closely and both organisations are observers to each other. Even though NAMMCO's membership is significantly smaller than that of the IWC, its mandate is broader and includes small cetaceans and pinnipeds. While the IWC can impose decisions on its members due to a majority-based voting structure, binding decisions in NAMMCO are made by consensus and the committees work by recommendation only. We argue, therefore, that this reflects the importance for its member states to effectively counter the international no-use trend and to re-establish the marine mammal hunt as an activity of Arctic socio-economic relevance.

NAMMCO's purpose is to counter the limits and dysfunctionality of the IWC and to bring together like-minded countries and organisations regarding the management and utilisation of marine mammals. In this sense, the influence of NGOs on the IWC and the establishment of the whaling moratorium backfired: NAMMCO is strictly science-based and has revitalised the debate on sustainable utilisation of marine mammals for *all* communities – and not just aboriginal – depending on them.[68] Given its consensus-based decision-making, clear mission and small membership, NAMMCO is an important role model for other regional wildlife management organisations.[69]

65 NAMMCO (2016): "Procedures & Rules for Observers Attending NAMMCO Meetings". https://nammco.no/wp-content/uploads/2018/03/nammco_guidelines-observers-2016_list-obs-feb2018.pdf (accessed 9 August 2018).

66 NAMMCO Secretariat, personal communication, email, 19 April 2018.

67 Kaye Anable (1993) "NAMMCO Defies the International Whaling Commission's Ban on Commercial Whaling: Are Whales in Danger Once Again?" *Global Business & Development Law Journal* 6–2: 637–651.

68 NAMMCO Agreement, Chapeau.

69 Brettny Hardy (2006) "A Regional Approach to Whaling: How the North Atlantic Marine Mammal Commission is Shifting the Tides for Whale Management" *Duke Journal of Comparative & International Law* 17: 169–198.

While the mission of anti-sealing and anti-whaling NGOs was successful in the sense that it spurred hunting and trade moratoria, the situation in the Arctic and the negative effects of these bans have prompted Arctic governments to launch cooperative efforts for putting the sustainable utilisation and management of marine mammals back on the international agenda. Even though NGOs have contributed to the altering of the legal order affecting the Arctic – exemplified in this case by the ICRW and the EU ban on trade in seal products – the establishment of NAMMCO could mean a normative shift back to the science-based management and utilisation of wild fauna in the Arctic and in the world. In this sense, NAMMCO member states are altering the legal order away from a normative opposition to knowledge-based decision-making.[70]

7.4 The case of Greenpeace

When looking at the legal order affecting the Arctic and the different players within it, one organisation stands out: Greenpeace. Greenpeace has a long history of involvement in the Arctic where the organisation's founders planned to sail a boat to stop nuclear bomb testing already in 1971. The NGO was founded as an independent campaigning organisation committed to non-violence and creative confrontation that today operates in over 55 countries and with the support of roughly 3 million members.[71] Since the Arctic is the region where many of Greenpeace's causes coalesce (e.g. marine mammal hunting, climate change, oil and gas exploitation), it is no surprise that the NGO strategically aims to influence Arctic governance and law.

When the campaign "Save the Arctic" was launched in 2012, Greenpeace's far-reaching Arctic objectives became public: (1) the creation of a global sanctuary in the international waters around the North Pole, banning oil drilling and fishing; (2) the defence of Arctic wildlife; and (3) coalition with local communities and Arctic IPs.[72] Concerning (1), at least in part, this proposal opposes the AC criteria for admitting Observers, which require *inter alia* the recognition of Arctic states' sovereignty, sovereign rights and jurisdiction in the Arctic.[73] Moreover, due

70 See also Lars C. Blichner (2015) "Epistemic Dependence and the EU Seal Ban Debate" *Politics and Governance* 3–1: 49–60.

71 Greenpeace International: "Amchitka: the Founding Voyage". www.greenpeace.org/archive-international/en/about/history/amchitka-hunter/ (accessed 9 August 2018).

72 Notwithstanding Greenpeace opposition to the commercial whaling industry, there is also evidence of its support for aboriginal practices as early as 1997, when the environmental NGO was heavily criticised by more extremist animal rights groups, such as the Sea Shepherd Society. See, Nunatsiaq News: "Greenpeace under attack for helping Inuit whalers" last modified 10 October 1997. http://nunatsiaq.com/stories/article/greenpeace_under_attack_for_helping_inuit_whalers/ (accessed 10 April 2018)

73 Piotr Graczyk and Timo Koivurova (2014) "A New Era in the Arctic Council's External Relations? Broader Consequences of the Nuuk Observer Rules for Arctic Governance" *Polar Record* 50–254: 225–236, at 233. Moreover, commercial fisheries will be banned in the Central Arctic Ocean for at least the next 16 years. See Chapter 8 by Joji Morishita and Chapter 9 Erik J. Molenaar in this book.

to its anti-sealing history, the organisation maintains a controversial relationship with Arctic peoples – indigenous and non-indigenous alike. In light of this – and arguably also to gain legitimacy amongst Arctic peoples – Greenpeace Canada issued an official apology in 2014 in which the organisation also expressed respect towards Inuit livelihoods and highlighted the common interests of Inuit and Greenpeace in protecting the Arctic environment.[74] Notwithstanding, calls for a compensation scheme for the economic loss and deprivation of property caused by anti-sealing campaigns have been uttered.[75]

In the AC the organisation has faced resistance. Greenpeace first attempted to become an AC Observer in 2013. Its request was denied, however, since only applications submitted by nation states were considered. In 2014, Greenpeace unsuccessfully repeated its application. Official statements and information on the reasons for excluding Greenpeace are not available since decisions on new Observers take place in closed meetings.[76] We speculate that in light of the large number of applications by major political state actors paired with the council's institutional reform, Greenpeace's application is particularly contentious to address and consensus difficult to reach among Member States and Permanent Participants (PPs). In other words, even if all but one member state or PP were in favour of Greenpeace's application, its request would still fail. In light of the organisation's difficult Arctic history, it appears unlikely that resistance is going to wane in the future. As a result, at the time of writing, Greenpeace has never been able to access AC meetings or subsidiary bodies and thus lacks socialisation, sense of community and recognition of common values with the AC.[77] Consequently, Greenpeace has thus far not been considered an insider advocate,[78] but rather remains an activist outsider relying on outside advocacy strategies. In other words, the organisation has thus far failed to directly

74 Greenpeace: "Greenpeace apology to Inuit for impacts of seal campaign" last modified 25 June 2014. www.greenpeace.org/canada/en/blog/Blogentry/greenpeace-to-canadasab original-peoples-work/blog/53339/ (accessed 19 April 2018).

75 CBC News: "Greenpeace should compensate Inuit for effects of anti-sealing campaign, says activist" last modified 1 December 2016. www.cbc.ca/news/canada/north/greenpeace should-compensate-over-anti-sealing-campaign-says-activist-1.3875701 (accessed 19 April 2018).

76 No information on this issue appears in the Arctic Council minutes but Koivurova and Knecht report on this. See Timo Koivurova (2013) "Multipolar and Multilevel Governance in the Arctic and Antarctic" *Proceedings of the Annual Meeting of American Society of International Law* 107: 443–446; Sebastian Knecht (2015) "New Observers Queuing Up: Why the Arctic Council should expand – and expel" *The Arctic Institute*: www.thearcticinstitute.org/new-observers-queuing-up/ (accessed 9 August 2018).

77 Socialisation has been used as a criterion to assess how different Observers to the AC have internalised the norms established within Arctic regional cooperation. See Piotr Graczyk, Małgorzata Smieszek, Timo Koivurova et al. (2017) "Preparing for the Global Rush: the Arctic Council, Institutional Norms, and Socialisation of Observer Behaviour" in Kathrin Keil and Sebastian Knecht, *supra* note 7, at 121–139.

78 On the contrary, the WWF, for example, is highly visible in the AC and involved in the work of different subsidiary bodies and Task Forces. See Wehrmann (2017) *supra* note 7, at 193.

influence the law emerging from the Arctic itself and has been forced to focus on those legal orders affecting the Arctic.

Greenpeace has not shied away from further challenging the Arctic legal order that applies to the use of natural resources, particularly in domestic settings: one of the most visible actions undertaken by Greenpeace has been the protest against drilling operations in the Russian Prirazlomnaya oil rig, known as the *Arctic Sunrise Case*. Named after the vessel flying Dutch flag that carried 30 activists into the Russian EEZ in 2013, the seizing of *Arctic Sunrise* and the arrest of its crew by Russian authorities prompted the reaction of the Netherlands, who initiated an arbitration against the same year under the dispute settlement mechanism of UNCLOS, including a request for provisional measures before the International Tribunal for the Law of the Sea (ITLOS). Apart from its legal elements, the case "allowed Greenpeace to present itself as an innocent victim of a State that was flouting the law"[79] even though Russia had plausible reasons to prosecute the organisation.[80] Following the arrest of the crew and the accusation of piracy as per articles 100–107 and 110 of the LOS Convention, a petition to free the 30 activists was launched, giving international publicity and support to Greenpeace's actions and causes. A strictly legal case – the results of which,[81] we contend, did not come as a surprise to Greenpeace – was thus turned into a campaign of public pressure, both challenging Russian oil activities in the Arctic and the prevailing legal order as set out in the LOS Convention. Thus, without direct access to the AC or other means of inside advocacy, Greenpeace has taken a – legally speaking – domestic issue of Russian oil drilling in Russian waters to the international stage. The end result would presumably be to gather sufficient outside pressure that force Russia to abandon its Arctic oil-drilling operations.

Similarly, in 2014 Greenpeace launched a petition in support of the Inuit community of Clyde River, Nunavut, which protested against a decision to allow a five-year seismic blasting project. After a social media campaign that gave international attention to the case, the Supreme Court of Canada ruled in favour of the community in 2017,[82] also marking a victory for Greenpeace. The case is notable since it signals an improvement in the relationship between Arctic local communities and Greenpeace and that, after the organisation's official apology for its anti-seal-hunt campaign, new opportunities for partnerships between the organisation and indigenous communities are slowly emerging.[83]

79 Alex O. Elferink (2014) "The Arctic Sunrise Incident and the International Law of the Sea" *The JCLOS Blog*: http://site.uit.no/jclos/2014/02/28/hello-world/ (accessed 9 August 2018).

80 Ibid.

81 Although Russia did not recognise the ITLOS ruling, *Arctic Sunrise* and its crew were released in 2014 having been granted amnesty by the State Duma. In 2015, the country was ordered by the Permanent Court of Arbitration to pay a compensation to the Netherlands. Whether this payment has ever occurred cannot be ascertained at the time of writing.

82 Supreme Court of Canada, *Clyde River (Hamlet) v. Petroleum Geo-Services Inc.* (Judgement). [2017] 1 SCR 1069, 26 July 2017.

83 See Arctic Deeply: "Environmental NGOs Team Up with Inuit", last modified 20 May 2016. www.newsdeeply.com/arctic/community/2016/05/19/undrip-reconciliation-not-litigation-is-the-key (accessed August 2018).

In 2017, Greenpeace Norway launched legal proceedings against the Norwegian government in *The People v. Arctic Oil*[84] in which the organisation challenged the Norwegian government over the issuance of new licences for oil exploitation in the Barents Sea. Following the wave of climate litigation that arose in Europe since the success of the *Urgenda Case*,[85] Greenpeace Norway and other local NGOs alleged that granting new licences was in breach of art. 112 of the Norwegian Constitution and in opposition to the *spirit* of the Paris Agreement, ratified by Norway shortly before the licences were issued. From a legal perspective, the latter case is innovative since it resorts to climate litigation as a means of judicial governance against climate change.[86] Although a final decision on the case is still pending,[87] Greenpeace has tried to directly influence public policy and decision-making by obtaining an enforceable court order. Moreover, and in the context of Greenpeace's campaign against oil drilling, the suit added a legal element to be considered by states and oil companies when assessing the profitability of oil exploitation in the Arctic: threatened by the possibility of having their profits delayed due to legal actions, oil companies may be discouraged from operating in these already hostile and climatically challenging areas. Nevertheless, considering the close ties existing between the state and the civil society in Norway[88] and the country's reliance on extractive industry to finance its welfare model, it is doubtful that the case has helped Greenpeace Norway in the long term to acquire more backing in the country.

As the above demonstrates, and because the maintenance of a pristine Arctic environment as bolstered in the campaign "Save the Arctic" coalesces and reflects most of its environmental objectives, Greenpeace is an active outside advocate in the region. By creating outside pressure through the mobilisation of public opinion for a specific cause, the organisation has ensured that its voice is being heard in the making of Arctic law(s) and governance – outside of the primary body of Arctic governance, the AC. By reverting to legal proceedings before domestic courts, the organisation has furthermore directly engaged in the formulation and interpretation of applicable national laws. Although Greenpeace's campaigns

84 Oslo Tingrett (2018) *Föreningen Greenpeace Norden & Natur og Ungdom vs Staten ved Olje- og energidepartementet*, 16–166674TVI-OTIR/06 (Judgement), 4 January 2018.

85 See, e.g., Pau de Vilchez Moragues (2016) "Broadening the Scope: The Urgenda Case, the Oslo Principles and the Role of National Courts in Advancing Environmental Protection Concerning Climate Change" *Spanish Yearbook of International Law* 20: 71–92.

86 On judicial governance and the functions of litigation in the context of climate change, see Daniel Bodansky, Jutta Brunnée and Lavanya Rajamani (2017) *International Climate Change Law*. Oxford University Press, Oxford: 283.

87 At the time of writing, an appeal has been filed by Nature and Youth/Young FoE Norway and Greenpeace Norway to the Norwegian Supreme Court, after the Oslo District Court has ruled in favour of the Norwegian government. See Friends of the Earth Europe: "YFoE Norway takes government to supreme court over arctic oil" last modified 5 February 2018. www.foeeurope.org/yfoee/yfoe-norway-takes-government-supreme-court-050218 (accessed 9 August 2018).

88 See Kristin Strømsnes, Per Selle and Gunnar Grendstad (2009) "Environmentalism between State and Local Community: Why Greenpeace Has Failed in Norway" *Environmental Politics* 18–3: 391–407.

have not always had a tangible impact on the legal order governing the Arctic, the NGO's narrative of saving the Arctic as a centrepiece in the world's climate, it has nevertheless gained international attention. This, in turn, has been instrumental for Greenpeace to secure international support, membership and organisational survival,[89] something that will likely foster its influence on the shaping of the legal order(s) emerging in the Arctic and certainly in the legal order(s) relevant for and applicable in the Arctic.

7.5 Conclusion

The influences of non-governmental organisations on the Arctic legal order are manifold and have emerged out of a growing trend of civil society to become part of the state-centred law-making and decision-making process of international law. Especially as regards the environment, the involvement of NGOs has increased dramatically since the 1960s and they have become an important means to influence policy results by impacting on domestic and international public opinion and by becoming inside advocates.

As demonstrated in the case of sealing and whaling, NGOs have played an important role in the adjustment of the legal regimes directly applicable *in* the Arctic (the ICRW) and relevant *for* the Arctic (EU Seal Regime). This combination has created a legal environment framed by no-use narratives of marine mammals. *Prima facie* a success for NGOs, this has prompted some Arctic peoples and states to respond either by legal means or by the formation of a new body – NAMMCO. The protests of NGOs have thus brought those Arctic states closer together in which marine mammal hunts still play an important socio-economic role.

The analysis of Greenpeace showed that, although the organisation remains formally excluded from the AC and does not directly contribute to its work nor to its quasi-normative function, this has not diminished its capacity to influence or challenge the general legal orders that are also relevant to the Arctic, such as climate change and oil and gas developments. This reaffirms the polycentric nature of Arctic governance and allows us to assume that non-governmental influence on the Arctic legal order will likely continue in the future.

In conclusion, environmental NGOs exert an influence on the Arctic legal order. They do so by directly challenging, even altering, the prevailing legal order in the region or when, to the contrary, their advocacy results in Arctic actors producing a new body of law *in* or *for* the Arctic.

89 This is fundamental for an organisation that, like Greenpeace, resorts on individual donations and claims to raise funds independently from the public and business sectors. See on this, ibid.

Part III

Arctic marine legal order-making

8 The Arctic Five-plus-Five process on central Arctic Ocean fisheries negotiations

Reflecting the interests of Arctic and non-Arctic actors

Joji Morishita

8.1 Introduction

Responding to the reduction of sea ice coverage in the Arctic Ocean caused by climate change (see Figure 8.1), the international community expressed its hope that fisheries could be initiated in the high seas area of the central Arctic Ocean (CAO)[1] in summer. Along with this hope arose concerns that unregulated fisheries could emerge. The "Arctic Five", the five coastal states of the CAO, namely Canada, Denmark (on behalf of the Faroe Islands and Greenland), Norway, the Russian Federation and the United States, convened a series of intergovernmental and scientific meetings to discuss this issue. On 16 July 2015, the Arctic Five adopted the Declaration concerning the Prevention of Unregulated High Seas Fishing in the Central Arctic Ocean in Oslo, Norway (the Oslo Declaration).[2]

Following the initiative by the United States, the Arctic Five-plus-Five (Arctic 5-plus-5) meeting was convened in Washington, DC in December 2015, to which China, the European Union (EU), Iceland, Japan and Republic of Korea in addition to the Arctic Five were invited. The "plus 5" states were identified, presumably through the Arctic Five consultation process for adopting the Oslo Declaration, as those with potential capacity to conduct fishing operations in the high seas area of the CAO. The meeting expanded the scope of participation from that of the Oslo Declaration and aimed at establishing a legally binding agreement on the issue. After six meetings in two years, a legally binding international instrument – Agreement to Prevent Unregulated High Seas Fisheries in the Central Arctic Ocean – was concluded by the Arctic 5 plus 5 on 30

1 In this chapter, the CAO includes both high seas and EEZs. When the high seas are discussed, it will be stated as "the high sea of the CAO". The Arctic Ocean (AO) is the seas generally within the Arctic Circle and the CAO is a part of AO surrounded by the five central Arctic Ocean coastal states.

2 *Declaration concerning the Prevention of Unregulated High Seas Fishing in the Central Arctic Ocean*, 16 July 2015, Oslo, Norway. www.regjeringen.no/globalassets/departementene/ud/vedlegg/folkerett/declaration-on-arctic-fisheries-16-july-2015.pdf (accessed 18 July 2018).

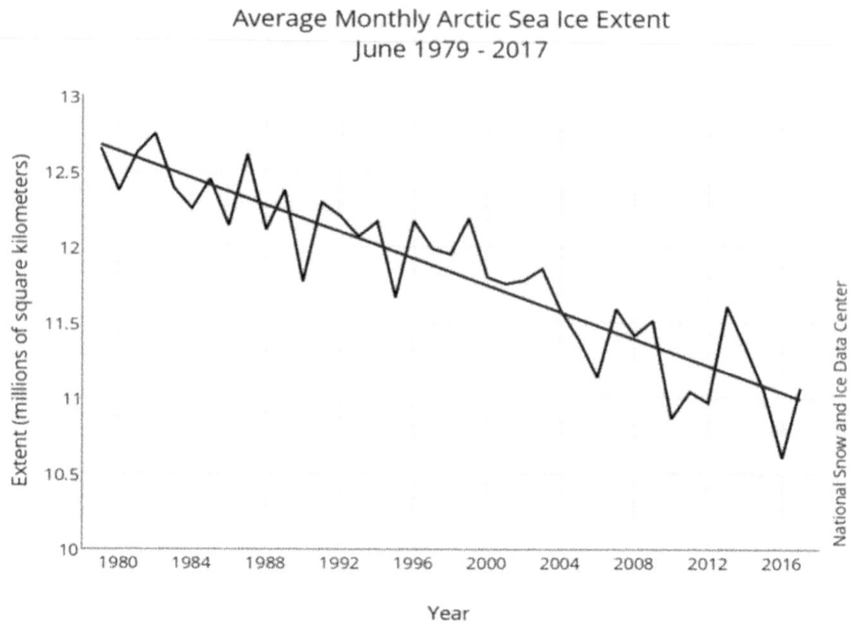

Figure 8.1 Decreasing sea ice coverage in the Arctic Ocean

Source: National Snow and Ice Data Center (NSIDC): http://nsidc.org/arcticseaicenews/2017/07/arctic-ice-extent-near-levels-recorded-in-2012/ (accessed 18 July 2018)

November 2017 in Washington, DC.[3] This chapter analyses the 5-plus-5 process leading to the Agreement.[4]

8.2 Background and chronology of negotiations

The CAO is surrounded by the five coastal states – Canada, Denmark (on behalf of Greenland), Norway, the Russian Federation, and the United States – and its central part including the North Pole is enclosed by the exclusive economic zones (EEZs) (or a Fisheries Protection Zone around Svalbard) of these five states.

The CAO is mostly icebound in winter and ice-free waters occur in summer. In the EEZs of the five coastal states, indigenous and coastal peoples have been fishing the abundant fish species for centuries or more. FAO data show that currently there is not much commercial fishery in the Arctic Ocean, indicating no

3 Agreement to Prevent Unregulated High Seas Fisheries in the Central Arctic Ocean, signed 3 October 2018. The text of the agreement is available in the Appendix of this book and from: https://eur-lex.europa.eu/resource.html?uri=cellar:2554f475-6e25-11e8-9483-01aa75ed71a1.0001.02/DOC_1&format=PDF (accessed 10 October 2018).

4 Since I represented the government of Japan in the Arctic 5-plus-5 meetings, this chapter is based on my own personal views and understanding. The content of this chapter does not represent the positions and views of the government of Japan and I am wholly responsible for its content, including any errors.

Table 8.1 Chronology of main meetings on Central Arctic Ocean fisheries

	Arctic 5 meetings	*Arctic 5 plus 5 meetings*	*Scientific meetings*
2010	June, Oslo		
2011			June, Anchorage
2013	April-May, Washington, D.C.		
			October, Tromso
2014	24–26 February, Nuuk		
2015			14–16 April, Seattle
	16 July, Oslo, Declaration concerning the Prevention of Unregulated High Seas Fishing in the Central Arctic Ocean		
		1–3 December, Washington, D.C.	
2016		19–21 April, Washington, D.C.	
		6–8 July, Iqaluit, Nunavut, Canada	
			26–28 September, Tromso
		29 November-1 December, Torshavn, the Faroe Island	
2017		15–18 March, Reykjavik	
		28–30 November, Washington, D.C.	

immediate interest from the Arctic coastal states in Arctic fisheries.[5] This lack of interest may stem from the fact that the seemingly perpetual sea ice cover of the CAO was considered an obstacle to commercial fisheries. However, decreasing sea ice particularly in the summer, caused by climate change and associated rising temperatures, changes in wind patterns and ocean currents, has created an ice-free area even in the high seas portion of the CAO. Additionally, climate change brings about changes in the marine ecosystem leading to a potential of commercially viable fishery resources emerging in or migrating into the high seas of the CAO.

The new emerging situations in the CAO triggered a series of international meetings (Table 8.1). It should be noted that political and scientific processes have been concurrently progressing in a coordinated fashion.

5 FAO (2016) "World Capture Production by Marine Fishing Areas, 18 Arctic Sea" *FAO Yearbook of Fishery and Aquaculture Statistics 2016*. Food and Agriculture Organization: 8, A-1 (a).

8.3 Discussions at political processes

The process regarding the future management of the Arctic Ocean started with a meeting in Oslo in June 2010 where officials of the Arctic Five met. They agree to link political and scientific processes regarding CAO fisheries. Two meetings of scientists (Anchorage in June 2011 and Tromsø in October 2013) considered the conditions of the Arctic Ocean and its marine ecosystem, reviewed available scientific information, and discussed future possible cooperation. The second meeting was held in Washington, DC in April/May 2013 and confirmed the leading role of the Arctic Five in conserving and managing the living marine resources of the Arctic Ocean.[6]

The following sections review the discussions in the political processes starting from the 2014 Arctic 5 meeting in Nuuk, Greenland which prepared the basis for the Oslo Declaration.

8.3.1 The Arctic Five meeting in Nuuk, Greenland[7]

The Arctic Five met in Nuuk, Greenland, from 24 to 26 February 2014. The main purpose of the meeting was to continue discussions surrounding the development of interim measures to prevent unregulated fishing in the CAO and to continue discussions on related scientific matters. At the meeting, it was reaffirmed that, based on available scientific information, commercial fishing in the high seas area of the CAO is unlikely to occur in the near future and, therefore, there is no need to develop any additional regional fisheries management organisation or arrangement (RFMO/As) for this area.

The Arctic Five also agreed on the desirability of developing appropriate interim measures to deter future unregulated fishing in the high seas of the CAO. The participating states agreed to commit themselves, as interim measures, to (i) authorise their vessels to conduct commercial fishing in the high seas area only pursuant to one or more RFMO/As that are or may be established; (ii) establish a joint program of scientific research; and (iii) coordinate their monitoring, control and surveillance activities, among others. Based on this, the Nuuk meeting agreed to develop a Ministerial Declaration for signature or adoption by the five states based on the provisions described above. This led to the adoption of the Oslo Declaration in July 2015.

It is important to note that the meeting decided to invite other states than the Arctic Five that may have an interest in fishing in the high seas of the CAO. The purpose of the broader process was to develop a set of interim measures, compatible with the Ministerial Declaration, that would include commitments by additional states through a legally binding international agreement.

6 Njord Wegge (2015) "The Emerging Politics of the Arctic Ocean: Future Management of the Living Marine Resources" *Marine Policy* 51: 331–338.

7 Chairman's Statement, Meeting on Arctic Fisheries, Nuuk, Greenland, 24–26 February 2014. www.afsc.noaa.gov/Arctic_fish_stocks_third_meeting/Arctic Fisheries Nuuk Chairmans and ToR for 3rd Meeting.pdf (accessed 18 July 2018).

8.3.2 The Oslo Declaration

One and a half years after the Nuuk meeting, the Arctic Five adopted the Declaration concerning the Prevention of Unregulated High Seas Fishing in the Central Arctic Ocean (Oslo Declaration) on 16 July 2015[8] in a legally non-binding form.

In its preamble, the Oslo Declaration acknowledges the changes in the marine ecosystems of the Arctic Ocean due to climate change and recognises that commercial fishing in the high seas portion of the CAO is unlikely to occur in the near future. Consequently, there is no need at present to establish any additional RFMO/As for this area. Following the precautionary approach, the Oslo Declaration, however, expresses desire for implementing interim measures to deter unregulated fishing in the future.

The operative part of the Oslo Declaration also reflects the conclusions of the Nuuk meeting by agreeing to (i) authorise vessels to conduct commercial fishing in the high seas area only pursuant to one or more RFMO/As; (ii) establish a joint program of scientific research with the aim of improving understanding of the ecosystems of this area; and (iii) promote compliance by coordinating monitoring, control and surveillance activities. Finally, the Oslo Declaration acknowledges the interest of other states in the following terms:

> We acknowledge the interest of other States in preventing unregulated high seas fisheries in the central Arctic Ocean and look forward to working with them in a broader process to develop measures consistent with this Declaration that would include commitments by all interested States.

8.3.3 The Arctic Five-plus-Five negotiations

8.3.3.1 First Meeting, December 2015[9]

In order to initiate the "broader process", the first Meeting on High Seas Fisheries in the Central Arctic Ocean hosted by the United States in Washington, DC from 1 to 3 December 2015 saw delegations from the People's Republic of China, the EU, Iceland, Japan and Republic of Korea, in addition to the Arctic Five. Because the meeting was the first opportunity for the Arctic 5 plus 5 to discuss the Arctic high seas fishing issue, it was exploratory in nature. Furthermore, a number of delegations made clear that they did not have a mandate to negotiate any particular instrument relating to the topic and, therefore, the meeting was conducted on a non-committal basis.

In order to provide the scientific basis for the meeting, the outcomes of the third Meeting of Scientific Experts on Fish Stocks in the Central Arctic Ocean, which was held in Seattle on 14–16 April 2015 was reported. The scientific meeting was joined by scientists from the "plus 5" and expressed the desire to cooperate in advancing scientific research and monitoring. The meeting discussed the

8 Oslo Declaration, *supra* note 2.

9 Chairman's Statement, Washington, D.C., 1–3 December 2015. www.state.gov/e/oes/ocns/fish/regionalorganizations/arctic/statements/279639.htm (accessed 18 July 2018).

important questions of "whether and when there might exist a stock or stocks of fish sufficient to support a sustainable commercial fishery in the high seas area of the CAO and the effects of any such fishery on the ecosystems".[10] Based on the report from scientists, the first Arctic 5 plus 5 meeting reaffirmed that it is unlikely that there will be a possibility for a sustainable commercial fishery in that area in the near future. The meeting, however, recognised that changes in the Arctic region were happening so rapidly that predictions were accompanied by uncertainties and that, therefore, a precautionary approach was needed. The meeting also expressed an interest in strengthening international scientific collaboration, given the very limited scientific information.

While the meeting was conducted on a non-committal basis, the United States presented a proposal for an international agreement to implement the Oslo Declaration. The agreement would commit its parties to, among others, (i) authorise their vessels to conduct commercial fishing in this high seas area only pursuant to one or more RFMO/As that are or may be established; and (ii) establish a joint programme of scientific research with the aim of informing future fisheries management decisions and improving understanding of the ecosystems of this area.

The US proposal received preliminary reactions from some delegations including suggestions to strengthen or clarify languages of the proposal. However, the discussions and reactions were mainly conceptual in nature.

8.3.3.2 The Second Meeting, April 2016[11]

The second Meeting of Arctic 5 plus 5 was held again in Washington, DC from 19 to 21 April 2016, less than five months after the first Meeting, also hosted by the United States. This considerable speed for hosting meetings that discuss a possible international agreement probably reflects a political need in the United States, as will be explained later. Some delegations attended the second meeting with a mandate to negotiate a legally binding instrument on this topic.

A possible instrument was regarded to be interim in nature and, therefore, would be reviewed periodically. The instrument would include a commitment to keep the question of whether to establish one or more additional RFMO/As for the CAO with the long-term objective of promoting conservation and sustainable use of living marine resources in the Arctic under regular review. One of the reasons why the possible instrument was regarded as an interim measure was that many delegations supported the principle of sustainable use of marine living resources and they thought an instrument only preventing unregulated high seas fishing would be inconsistent with this principle. In other words, even if commercial fishing in the high seas is unlikely to be viable in the near future, it was necessary for them to indicate their commitment as a policy to establish a system

10 Ibid.

11 Chairman's Statement, Washington, DC, 19–21 April 2016. www.afsc.noaa.gov/Arctic_fish_stocks_fourth_meeting/pdfs/Chairman's_Statement_from_Washington_Meeting_April_2016-2.pdf (accessed 18 July 2018).

for conservation and management of fisheries resources sometime in the future based on the sustainable use principle.

While suggestions and comments for further improving the US draft were presented at the second meeting, some key issues remained for discussion in future meetings, including the "stepwise approach", the relationship between the instrument and other international agreements or organisations, the joint programme of scientific research and decision-making.

The "stepwise approach" requires some explanation and could include the following steps which are not mutually exclusive:

- adjusting the Oslo Declaration with input from the plus 5 such that a new, broader non-binding statement could be adopted;
- negotiating a binding international agreement of the kind proposed by the United States; and
- negotiating in the foreseeable future an agreement or agreements to establish one or more additional RFMO/As for the area.

8.3.3.3 Third Meeting, July 2016[12]

The third meeting was held in Iqaluit, Nunavut, Canada from 6 to 8 July 2016 and made substantial progress in many of the main issues discussed towards resolutions in differences of views among delegations. Delegations generally believed that there was a possibility of successful conclusion of this process in the near future even though different proposals for a new declaration or a legally binding agreement were tabled.

In addition to the issue of the legal format of the instrument, remaining issues for further discussions included the conditions under which a decision might be made to commence negotiations on an agreement to establish one or more additional RFMO/As and decision-making procedures. The "conditions" or triggers for commencing negotiations to establish one or more additional RFMO/As could include, for example, a stock level of marine living resources to be targeted for fishing. In other words, if/when the estimated stock biomass of a potential commercial fishing species reaches XX tons, negotiations for establishing one or more additional RFMO/As will begin.

One of the key elements that was raised during the meeting was the importance of indigenous and local knowledge, particularly concerning their role in the joint programme of scientific research and monitoring. This is understandable as indigenous and local communities have been harvesting marine living resources and observing marine environment/ecosystem for millennia. Their accumulated knowledge, while it could be anecdotal rather than scientific, is indispensable for the conservation and management of marine living resources especially when scientific baseline data is inadequate.

12 Chairman's Statement, Iqaluit, Nunavut, Canada, 6–8 July 2016. www.state.gov/e/oes/ocns/fish/regionalorganizations/arctic/statements/279641.htm (accessed 18 July 2018).

8.3.3.4 Fourth Meeting, November/December 2016[13]

The fourth meeting was held in Tórshavn, the Faroe Island, from 29 November to 1 December 2016 and was conducted on the basis of a Chairman's Text circulated in October 2016 in the format of a legally binding agreement. The Chairman's Text included the outcomes of the Fourth Meeting of Scientific Experts on Fish Stocks in the Central Arctic Ocean, which was held in Tromsø on 26–28 September 2016. Delegations felt that they made good progress in resolving differences of view on a number of the main issues under discussion and that the discussions could be concluded in the near future. However, some key points remained unresolved. Of particular concern were:

- the manner in which the agreement addresses exploratory fishing;
- the conditions under which a decision might be made to commence negotiations on an agreement to establish one or more additional regional fisheries management organisations or arrangements for the CAO;
- decision-making procedures.

The negotiating states were not able to find an agreement on these issues and were forced to postpone further discussions to the next meeting.

8.3.3.5 Fifth Meeting, March 2017[14]

Considerable progress was made at the fifth meeting held in Reykjavik from 15 to 18 March 2017 in resolving differences of views on many issues under discussion in the draft agreement concerning: (i) the use of terms; (ii) its objective; (iii) many of the measures that would be applied under the draft agreement; (iv) all provisions relating to a Joint Program of Scientific Research and Monitoring; (v) the value of incorporating local and indigenous knowledge; (vi) all provisions relating to exploratory fishing; (vii) dispute settlement; and (viii) most provisions concerning signature, accession, entry into force, withdrawal and relation to other agreements.

Remaining issues included (a) a description or definition of the Agreement Area; (b) the conditions under which a decision might be made to commence negotiations for establishing one or more RFMO/As; (c) the possibility to adopt other conservation and management measures that could apply after such negotiations have commenced; and (d) decision-making procedures. Details for these issues will be elaborated in the sections below.

13 Chairman's Statement, Tórshavn, The Faroe Islands, 29 November–1 December 2016. www.state.gov/e/oes/ocns/fish/regionalorganizations/arctic/statements/279642.htm (accessed 18 July 2018).

14 Chairman's Statement, Reykjavik, Iceland, 15–18 March 2017. www.state.gov/e/oes/ocns/fish/regionalorganizations/arctic/statements/279643.htm (accessed 18 July 2018).

At the close of the fifth meeting, the Chairman offered to circulate within a week his recommendations for resolving the remaining issues under negotiation. His intention was that if all delegations can accept those recommendations within two months, there will be no need for another round of negotiations. Eventually, some delegations could not accept those recommendations, especially regarding decision-making procedures. Another round of negotiations became necessary to finalise the text.

8.3.3.6 Sixth and final meeting, November 2017[15]

The final meeting was held in Washington, DC from 28 to 30 November 2017. The Chairman's Statement at the close of the meeting declared that the meeting "successfully concluded negotiations on the draft *Agreement to Prevent Unregulated High Seas Fisheries in the Central Arctic Ocean*".[16] While there was no explanation on how the remaining issues were resolved, the Statement describes the achievements of the 5-plus-5 process in the following manner.

> The Agreement will prevent unregulated commercial fishing in the high seas portion of the central Arctic Ocean, an area that is roughly 2.8 million square kilometers in size, roughly the size of the Mediterranean Sea. Commercial fishing has never been known to occur in this area, nor is it likely to occur in the near future. However, given the changing conditions of the Arctic Ocean, the governments in question developed this Agreement in accordance with the precautionary approach to fisheries management.
>
> The Agreement will establish and operate a Joint Program of Scientific Research and Monitoring with the aim of improving the understanding of the ecosystem(s) of this area and, in particular, of determining whether fish stocks might exist in this area that could be harvested on a sustainable basis. The Agreement envisions the possibility that one or more additional regional fisheries management organizations or arrangements may be established for this area in the future.

The Agreement is unique as it was concluded even before problems such as unregulated fisheries and overharvesting actually materialise. It is also unique as it is an interim agreement that incorporates a "stepwise approach" and has a clear "shelf life". This is reasonable because changes in the CAO are under way in an unprecedented pace and there are great uncertainties in the direction/scale/nature of the future changes. The Agreement has some ambiguities such as a "trigger" for moving to a next step of negotiating establishment of one or more RFMO/As. In a sense, the Agreement made some important decisions

15 Chairman's Statement, Washington, DC, 28–30 November 2017. www.state.gov/e/oes/ocns/fish/regionalorganizations/arctic/statements/281792.htm (accessed 18 July 2018).
16 Ibid.

for future considerations. Conclusion of negotiations is in fact a beginning of a new stage. We have to observe future developments regarding the CAO fisheries issues very closely.

8.4 Interests of the players

8.4.1 Overview

The negotiations for the high seas fishery in the CAO was triggered by the rapid disappearance of sea ice in the Arctic Ocean caused by the climate change. At the same time, it should be noted that goals for the negotiations and focal points during the negotiations varied among the players: they also shifted and evolved through the course of the negotiations. While the Arctic 5-plus-5 negotiations started because of the adoption of the Oslo Declaration in July 2015, this chapter does not analyse the process that had led to the Declaration in detail since its main purpose is the analysis of the Arctic 5-plus-5 process. However, it is noteworthy that the entire process was led by the initiative of the United States, which was the chair of the Arctic Council from 24 April 2015 to 11 May 2017, during the period of the negotiations. Moreover, even though the Oslo Declaration was adopted as a non-binding document, it was originally contemplated as a legally binding agreement, which was primarily opposed by Russia. These factors cannot be neglected when scrutinising the Arctic 5-plus-5 negotiations.

When concluding the negotiations on the draft Agreement to Prevent Unregulated High Seas Fisheries in the Central Arctic Ocean in November 2017, the United States delegation and many other delegations noted that the Agreement was unique and unprecedented as it was concluded in a precautionary manner. Many fisheries agreements were negotiated only as a response to serious problems, such as overfishing. What made the conclusion of this unique and unprecedented agreement possible? Was there any sense of urgency among delegations that made the conclusion of the Agreement in relatively short two years possible? Can the varied interests of the players in the negotiations explain the uniqueness of the Agreement?

From publicly available information, it would be safe to assume that the Arctic Five discussions had started because of the concerns that some fisheries resources could appear in the high seas portion of the CAO as a result of the rapidly melting sea ice; that commercial fisheries could begin without any international regulations; and that the fisheries resources and the Arctic marine ecosystem could be seriously damaged. These are indeed legitimate concerns.

However, the first Meeting of Scientific Experts on Fish Stocks in the Central Arctic Ocean held in June 2011 in Anchorage, Alaska, in accordance with the instructions from the Arctic Five, concluded that there was no urgency. At the same time, they recognised that knowledge was limited and it was necessary to establish baseline data. This conclusion was reconfirmed by the second Scientific Committee held in October 2013 in Tromsø, Norway. They concluded that there were no prospects in the near future for commercial concentrations of fish in the high seas area. However, they also agreed that there remained a need to know more about fish stocks with the potential to be harvested in the high seas.

Despite the agreed views of scientists that there were no near-future prospects for commercial concentrations of fish in the high seas area of the CAO, the Oslo Declaration was adopted two years after the second scientific meeting. Furthermore, the draft Agreement to Prevent Unregulated High Seas Fisheries in the Central Arctic Ocean was concluded in November 2017. What was the motivation for pushing the "unprecedented" negotiations forward? Where did the energy come from to keep the negotiations running?

8.4.2 The players

8.4.2.1 United States

The United States played a key role as a locomotive of the negotiations. While international discussions regarding the changing Arctic Ocean and a possible need for a fisheries management had emerged long before going into the Arctic 5-plus-5 negotiations, the negotiation period coincides with the "legacy" building period of then-president Barack Obama who was scheduled to leave the White House in January 2017. As many of the past presidents did, Obama was keen to add a "legacy" to his achievements as the president of the United States. In August 2016, President Obama established the Papahānaumokuākea Marine National Monument in Hawaii. The Monument was then the largest Marine Protected Area (MPA) in the world.[17] On 20 December 2016, President Obama made a decision that permanently prohibited development of new oil and natural gas excavation sites in some locations in the Arctic Ocean and the Atlantic Ocean for the protection of the environment and marine life.[18] As he was interested in the protection of the marine environment and Arctic issues, it would be safe to assume that an international agreement for preventing illegal fisheries in the high seas of the CAO was an ideal candidate for his legacy. A source in the US delegation to the Arctic 5-plus-5 negotiations referred to strong instructions from a high level for early conclusion of the negotiations. The fact that the United States hosted three Arctic 5-plus-5 meetings out of the total of six and that they also provided ambassador David Balton, deputy assistant Secretary of State, as the chair of the meeting demonstrates the strong commitment and high-level energy of the United States government for the early conclusion of the negotiations.

17 NOAA National Marine Sanctuaries website: "Papahānaumokuākea Expands, Now Largest Conservation Area on Earth". https://sanctuaries.noaa.gov/news/aug16/president-announced-expansion-of-papahanaumokuakea-marine-national-monument.html (accessed 16 August 2018).

18 Fortune (2016) "Obama Bans New Oil and Gas Drilling Off Alaska and Part of the Atlantic", 21 December 2016. http://fortune.com/2016/12/21/barack-obama-oil-gas-drilling-ban-arctic-alaska-atlantic-coast/ (accessed 17 August 2018).

It is without a doubt that the well-experienced and well-respected ambassador Balton played an important role, as a chair, for the successful conclusion of the Arctic 5-plus-5 negotiations. He had chaired and represented the United States at numerous negotiations including the UN Fish Stock Agreement and establishment of different RFMOs. Furthermore, the Arctic issues attract his attention and he has been very active in the field, including as the Chair of the Arctic Council during the US Chairmanship from 2015 to 2017.

8.4.2.2 Russia

The negotiations would not have been concluded only with the political will of the United States and a capable chair. We must remember that US–Russia relations were extremely difficult at the time of the Arctic 5-plus-5 negotiations in light of the US sanctions against Russia as a response to the Russian annexation of Crimea.[19] It was difficult for the United States and Russia to have a positive dialogue especially through their capitals. Geopolitically as well as geographically, the Arctic 5-plus-5 negotiations would have never been successful without cooperation with Russia whose EEZ occupies a large part of the CAO. In the early stage of the negotiations, Russia was reluctant to have a legally binding agreement, but eventually supported the Agreement that was proposed and promoted by the United States. What was Russia's reason to change its view on the agreement?

Historically, Russia viewed itself as having to defend its domain on three fronts: the western side facing Europe; the southern side extending from national borders with China to Kazakhstan and the Middle East; and the eastern side facing the United States over the Bering Strait. Since the Russian shoreline comprises roughly one-third of the Arctic coastline, the Arctic Ocean can be considered Russia's backyard and, relatively speaking, has been under its control. Additionally, the Arctic Ocean remains a strategically highly sensitive area where various military and intelligence operations have been conducted by countries concerned.

However, melting ice in the Arctic Ocean opened up this backyard and created opportunities as well as risks such as increased maritime traffic through the Arctic sea routes, development of energy resources and the possibility of commercial fisheries in the high seas. For Russia, these could be matters of concern that could make the Arctic Ocean the fourth and new front. On the other hand, Russia can expect substantial economic benefits from development and export of natural gas from the Yamal Peninsula, user fees for the Northern Sea Route, among others. It seems fair to say that Russia has somewhat competing interests of maximising economic benefits from the Arctic Ocean while preventing other countries from disturbing its backyard.

19 Jon Rahbek-Clemmensen (2017) "The Ukraine Crisis Moves North: Is Arctic Conflict Spill-Over Driven by Material Interests?" *Polar Record* 53–1: 1–15.

In the early stage of the Arctic 5-plus-5 negotiations, Russia took a position against a legally binding agreement and kept a low profile during the negotiations without commenting much on the draft agreement document tabled by the United States. In the latter part of the negotiations, however, Russia actively engaged in the discussions regarding the draft agreement document and submitted a series of proposals to amend the document. Is this a clear change of positions on the side of the Russian delegation? Or had they just observed the development in the early stage of the negotiations and decided to join the discussion later? Unfortunately, we have no material to answer these questions.

From my own observations it is noteworthy that the composition of the Russian delegation had changed during the negotiations in terms of the levels of representation and organisations they represented. This may or may not have something to do with their position at the negotiations. We also know that in the latter part of the negotiations the United States engaged in dialogue with Russia more actively. This may or may not have something to do with the change of the US presidency from Obama to Trump.

8.4.2.3 China and Republic of Korea

Both China and Republic of Korea were taking a relatively flexible position throughout the negotiations and actively participated in the discussions. Their basic position was the sustainable use of fisheries resources in case such resources become available in future in the high seas of the CAO. However, their enthusiasm for establishing fishing interests and securing fishing possibilities in the high seas area does not seem to be as strong as that at other fisheries meetings.

China was notably flexible in the discussions on specific wordings for provisions of the draft Agreement. This was a mild surprise for those who know China's often strong and rigid arguments in other fisheries related meetings such as the Commission for the Conservation of Antarctic Marine Living Resources (CCAMLR). This contrast could be explained simply by the difference between the Antarctic Ocean where substantial fisheries interests already exist now and in future and the high seas portion of the CAO where no near future prospects for commercial fisheries exists.

Needless to say, both China and Republic of Korea are interested in the development potential of the Arctic Ocean as a whole, not just limited to fisheries. They have been investing and participating in the Yamal natural gas and other Arctic projects; they have been expanding their scientific research capacity, including ice-breaker research vessels, in the Arctic Ocean; and they have been participating in the Arctic Council as Observer and promoting their presence in many of its subsidiary meetings. Arguably, therefore, the Arctic 5-plus-5 negotiations for the fisheries agreement can be interpreted as part of a larger strategy of their involvement in the Arctic affairs, rather than for the purpose of seeking short-term and real economic benefits in the field of fisheries.

8.4.2.4 Canada and Denmark (Greenland and the Faroe Islands)

Canada and Denmark, the latter on behalf of Greenland and the Faroe Islands, promoted the rights and interests of indigenous peoples in the Arctic area on many occasions during the Arctic 5-plus-5 negotiations and, recognising the risk of over-simplification, acted more actively in promoting indigenous rights and interests. Norway, Russia and the United States also have indigenous peoples in their Arctic territories who are engaged in fisheries in their coastal waters. Yet, even though the US delegation, for example, did include a representative of their indigenous communities, the US was not a spearhead in promoting indigenous rights in the negotiations possibly because of their overall low-profile[20] approach in the negotiations. Naturally, the motivation of states to promote indigenous issues varies from country to country, depending on a plethora of issues such as the sizes of the indigenous populations, their history, and their current economic and political status in the country, to say the least.

Fisheries conducted by the indigenous peoples of the Arctic coastal states are small scale as well as subsistence fisheries within the EEZs of each state. Furthermore, at least the United States has prohibited commercial fisheries in its Arctic EEZ waters since 2009. As long as available scientific and fisheries data show, it seems that target species of the indigenous fisheries have no high commercial values. Therefore, concern of the Arctic coastal states, especially for Canada and Denmark/Greenland/Faroe Islands, has been possible adverse effects of potential commercial fisheries in the high seas of the CAO.

Naturally there was no opposition to include due considerations to indigenous peoples in the Agreement and it duly reflected this aspect: the Preamble dedicates three paragraphs to recognise the rights of indigenous peoples, their interests in the conservation and management of living marine resources, and potential contribution of indigenous and local knowledge; Article 4.2 prescribes that the Join Program of Scientific Research and Monitoring, to be established by the Agreement, shall take into account indigenous and local knowledge; Article 5.2 also provides indigenous peoples with a mechanism to participate in the implementation of the Agreement through "committees or similar bodies in which representatives of Arctic communities, including Arctic indigenous peoples, can participate".

The manner in which indigenous interests are reflected in the Agreement is consistent with that of the Arctic Council and, therefore, it can be understood that Canada and Denmark succeeded in reflecting their main interests in the Agreement. While indigenous peoples are not explicitly provided with special status as in the case of the Arctic Council, their special interests are well recognised;

20 Dirk Zeller et al. (2011) "Arctic Fisheries Catches in Russia, USA, and Canada: Baseline for Neglected Ecosystems" *Polar Biology* 34–7: 955–973; Report of 2nd Scientific Meeting on Arctic Fish Stocks, Tromsø 28–31 October 2013. www.afsc.noaa.gov/Arctic_fish_stocks_third_meeting/Report%20of%202nd%20Scientific%20Meeting%20on%20Arctic%20Fish%20Stocks%2028%2031%20October%202013.pdf (accessed 20 August 2018).

participation in committees or similar bodies to be formed for the implementation of the Agreement (Article 5.2), and references to their rights, interests and knowledge (preambles).

8.4.2.5 Iceland

Iceland is a member of the Arctic Council. However, it was not a part of the Arctic Five consultations because its EEZ does not face the high seas portion of the CAO. Iceland was not invited to the Arctic Five meetings because, while it is an Arctic state, it is not a coastal state of the "central" Arctic Ocean including the high seas subject to the Arctic 5-plus-5 negotiations. Iceland was not happy with this and there was some tension, although not evident, during the Arctic 5-plus-5 process.[21]

Differences of interpretation of the Svalbard Treaty[22] between Norway and other parties to the Treaty, including Iceland,[23] which ratified the Treaty in 1994, also had some influences on the negotiations, especially in defining the agreement area in the Agreement. The agreement area is defined in Article 1 (a) as a provision of "Use of Terms" rather than an independent article. This was an attempt to play down the issue of the agreement area. The wording of the provision was also selected because of the differences of interpretation regarding the boundary separating the high seas and the area subject to the Svalbard Treaty and the legal character of jurisdiction exercised by Norway. Article 1 (a) defines the high seas area as "surrounded by waters within which" coastal states "exercise fisheries jurisdiction", not national jurisdiction.

While Iceland could take a position as a coastal country of the Arctic Ocean at the Arctic 5- plus-5 negotiations, they acted as a fishing country supporting the sustainable use of fisheries resources. This is not surprising as Iceland is a major fishing country but the situations above, especially the difference of positions regarding the interpretation of the Svalbard Treaty, might have prompted Iceland to be on the same side with the fishing countries rather than with the coastal countries of the Arctic Ocean.

8.4.2.6 The European Union

At international meetings concerning fisheries and oceans, the European Union (EU) is often oriented towards protecting the marine environment and strictly

21 Eilís Quinn (2015) "Iceland Blasts Arctic Five for Exclusion from Fishing Agreement" Eye on the Arctic website. www.rcinet.ca/eye-on-the-arctic/2015/07/30/iceland-blasts-arctic-five-for-exclusion-from-fishing-agreement/ (accessed 18 July 2018).

22 Treaty between Norway, the USA, Denmark, France, Italy, Japan, the Netherlands, Great Britain and Ireland and the British Overseas Dominions and Sweden with regard to the Archipelago of Spitsbergen, signed 9 February 1920 and entered into force 14 August 1925, *League of Nations Treaties Series* 2: 7.

23 Erik J. Molenaar (2012) "Fisheries Regulation in the Maritime Zones of Svalbard" *The International Journal of Marine and Coastal Law* 27: 3–58.

regulating fishing activities. For example, the EU is a keen supporter of the introduction of Marine Protected Areas (MPAs) and Environmental Impact Assessments (EIAs) in the United Nations BBNJ (marine biological diversity of areas beyond national jurisdiction) discussions. While there should be and there is no inconsistency between environmental protection and sustainable use of fisheries resources, the EU took the position during the negotiations that if/when commercial fisheries resources become available in the high seas portion of the CAO, the agreement should not just prohibit unregulated fisheries but reflect the principle of the sustainable use. The EU delegation, including the head of delegation, mainly consisted of officials from the European Commission's Directorate General (DG) Maritime Affairs and Fisheries (DG MARE) responsible for EU policies concerning maritime affairs and fisheries. Notably, it was not the DG Environment, whose mandate is to implement policies on environmental protection. This could explain the EU's positions at the Arctic 5-plus-5 process, but we have no bases to explain why the EU sent the mainly DG MARE delegation. In light of the EU's general interests in protecting and conserving the Arctic environment, it would not have been surprising had it sent a delegation centring around DG Environment representatives.

It is also noteworthy that only a few national representatives, including Spain and the Netherlands, joined the EU delegation, apart from local embassy staff of other EU Members when meetings were held. Spain has generally strong interests in fisheries. Combined with the DG MARE representation, this limited national representation could be another factor that formed the character of the EU delegation.

8.4.2.7 Japan

Japan, as one of the non-coastal members of the Arctic 5-plus-5 process, has two main areas of interests in the fisheries negotiations: first, its aspiration to maintain and strengthen Japan's role and presence in the Arctic affairs; second, its general interests in fisheries and sustainable use of marine living resources.

Japan's involvement in the Arctic affairs started mainly from scientific research. Japan's latest Arctic Policy, established on 16 October 2015, also states that Japan's objective is "to play a leading role for sustainable development in the Arctic in the international community, with foresight and policy based on science and technology that Japan has advantage in order to achieve sustainable development".[24] It should be noted that Japan aims to play a leading role in the international community regarding Arctic affairs and obviously the Arctic Council is the main forum for promoting Japan's presence. However, as a non-Arctic state, Japan is merely an Observer at the Arctic Council. For Japan, therefore, the

24 Headquarters for Ocean Policy, Government of Japan (2015) *Japan's Arctic Policy.* www8.cao.go.jp/ocean/english/arctic/pdf/japans_ap_e.pdf (accessed 18 July 2018).

Arctic 5-plus-5 process is a place where Japan can enhance its presence in the Arctic affairs with its expertise in fisheries and science. Moreover, we can argue that in this process Japan tries to compensate its "inferior" status in the Arctic Council. In other words, Japan could not accept any arrangement that reinforces its inferior status by recognising any superior status of the Arctic coastal states in the Agreement. In the latter half of the negotiations, the status issue, including decision-making mechanism and entry into force requirements, were the main interests of the Japanese delegation.

The other aspect that Japan is naturally interested in is the sustainable use of marine living resources in the Arctic area. Sustainable use of the resources based on scientific evidence is Japan's consistent and global policy.[25] However, fishing industries in Japan do not have any interest in conducting fisheries operations in the high seas of the CAO because of the low prospect of emergence of commercial fisheries stocks and the declined motivation of Japan's fishing industries to expand their operations outside the current fishing grounds. In other words, Japan's position to promote the stepwise approach was mainly based on its sustainable use policy rather than real economic interests.

However, Japan is interested in the science of the Arctic environment and its marine living resources. The unprecedented changes in the Arctic and general lack of baseline data in the area are attracting strong interests from scientists in many different fields. The Agreement and its provision for scientific cooperation (Article 4) would provide a very useful platform for Japan to promote its scientific activities in the Arctic. Japan's challenge is how to take advantage of the Agreement to play a leading role in the science of the Arctic.

8.5 Main items of interests at the Negotiations

8.5.1 Framework of the agreement: legally binding or not

At the first meeting of the Arctic 5-plus-5 process, the United States submitted a draft agreement that generally follows the content of the Oslo Declaration. The purpose of this proposal was to establish a legally binding framework through the Arctic 5-plus-5 process. In order to reach the overarching objective of the Oslo Declaration – prevention of illegal fishing – it was more desirable and effective to have a legally binding agreement. Since the plus 5 members at present essentially include all players who have the capacity to conduct fishing operations in the central Arctic high seas, a legally binding agreement would be more efficient to attain the goal of the Oslo Declaration. Also for building a legacy for outgoing President Obama, it would have been more desirable to conclude a legally binding agreement.

25 See, e.g., Atsushi Sunami, Tomoko Hamachi, and Shigeru Kitaba (2013) "The Rise of Science and Technology Diplomacy in Japan" *Science & Diplomacy* 2–1. www.sciencediplomacy.org/article/2013/rise-science-and-technology-diplomacy-in-japan (accessed 19 July 2018).

At the first Arctic 5-plus-5 meeting in December 2015, many of the participating members were in an "observing mode" and did not have mandates to negotiate a legally binding instrument. At the second meeting in April 2016, many members came with the mandate to negotiate a legally binding instrument, and negotiations for such an instrument had in effect started. Russia, on the other hand, kept its original position that it would be enough to expand the scope of the Oslo Declaration by inviting the plus 5 to join the declaration. It should be noted, however, that Chair Balton did not hurry in making a conclusion about the legal character of the instrument, respecting the Russian position.

Eventually Russia agreed to a legally binding agreement. Once the Russian delegation became active in the negotiations towards a legally binding instrument, one of their main targets was to secure a certain superiority of Arctic littoral states in the decision-making mechanism. For Russia, it seems, the reflection of coastal countries' superiority in the Agreement was an essential condition to accept a legally binding instrument. Since it was agreed that decision-making of the Agreement was consensus based (Article 6), coastal countries' superiority was not achieved in that respect since coastal countries and *all other members* of the Agreement have veto rights under the consensus system. The only place where coastal states' interests are explicitly considered is the Preamble where "the special responsibilities and special interests of the central Arctic Ocean coastal States" are recognised "in relation to the conservation and sustainable management of fish stocks in the central Arctic Ocean".

8.5.2 *Stepwise approach*

At the beginning of the Arctic 5-plus-5 process, the main theme of the negotiations was to prevent illegal fishing in the high seas portion of the CAO and to promote scientific research and the collection of scientific information, reflecting the content of the Oslo Declaration. However, the plus-5 members, mainly Japan and the EU, argued that it was not desirable to conclude an agreement only to prohibit the utilisation of marine living resources even if there is little prospect of viable commercial fisheries in the high seas area in the near future. They requested the agreement to include a provision which, in case fisheries resources become available in future in the high seas portion of the CAO, enables the sustainable use of the resources by establishing a RFMO/A. This argument was supported by other members, including China and Korea.

Accordingly, the Arctic 5-plus-5 negotiations accepted the concept of a stepwise approach where the Agreement is an interim one and the first step towards the possibility of establishing a RFMO/A in the future. Article 5, paragraph 1 (c) describes this process and is one of the core provisions of the Agreement:

> Article 5 paragraph (1)(c)
>
> The Parties shall, inter alia:
>
> 1.
>   a. ....
>   b. ....
>   c. on the basis of the scientific information derived from the Joint Program of Scientific Research and Monitoring, from the national scientific programs, and from other relevant sources, and taking into account relevant fisheries management and ecosystem considerations, including the precautionary approach and potential adverse impacts of fishing on the ecosystems, consider, *inter alia*, whether the distribution, migration and abundance of fish in the Agreement Area would support a sustainable commercial fishery and, on that basis, determine:
>   (i) whether to commence negotiations to establish one or more additional regional or subregional fisheries management organizations or arrangements for managing fishing in the Agreement Area; and
>   (ii) whether, once negotiations have commenced pursuant to subparagraph (i) above and once the Parties have agreed on mechanisms to ensure the sustainability of fish stocks, to establish additional or different interim conservation and management measures in respect of those stocks in the Agreement Area.

This concept might not have been the best approach for the Arctic Five. They, arguably, felt more comfortable with maintaining the status quo rather than with the emergence of commercial fisheries in the high seas area adjacent to their EEZs. However, the stepwise concept was accepted with no obvious objection. This could be because of the desire of the United States to conclude the Agreement in time so that it could be added as a legacy of President Obama. Also, it should be noted that the common understanding of the Arctic 5-plus-5 is that there would be no emergence of commercially viable fisheries resources in the high seas area of the CAO in the near future anyway. Practically speaking, the next step on this stepwise approach could be a long time into the future – if it ever comes.

Although a stepwise approach received a wide support, this may not work unless there is common understanding as to when and how, in terms of a decision-making system, a negotiation for the establishment of a RFMO/A could be initiated. Therefore, the Arctic 5-plus-5 negotiations spent substantial time in discussing what should be a "trigger" for starting these negotiations and what kind of a decision-making system would be appropriate.[26] An example for such trigger could be an increase of a target fisheries resource above a certain level. However, we do not have enough information as to what species of fish could emerge in the high seas portion of the CAO in the future since scientific data are limited.[27] This particular trigger would not be practical, at least at present. Another trigger or criterion could be the ever more reduction of sea ice coverage. However, even though sea-ice coverage has certain annual fluctuations, the decreasing trend is clear. Furthermore, decreasing ice coverage does not directly lead to emergence of fisheries resources. Consequently, this trigger would also present some practical problems.

A proposal was tabled to initiate negotiations for the establishment of a RFMO/A after a pre-determined period of time following the entry into force of the first step and irrespective of the situation/emergence of fisheries resources. While there is no scientific basis for this idea, a certainty was introduced as to when in the future the Parties would initiate the next step. This was a desirable arrangement for those who support the stepwise approach. Eventually, it was agreed that this Agreement has a "shelf life" of 16 years and its members must make a decision whether to negotiate a new agreement or to simply extend the Agreement. The "shelf life" provision, Article 13, was included to secure progress in the stepwise approach.

8.5.3 Joint programme of scientific research

The promotion of scientific cooperation among members was already one of the main points of the Oslo Declaration. This was necessary and important because: (i) there was strong interests in the possibility of commercially viable fisheries resources emerging in the high seas area of the CAO as a result of the decreasing sea ice coverage; (ii) there were inadequate scientific data and analysis regarding fisheries resources in the high seas area, including baseline data of the current status of the resources; and (iii) there are pure scientific interests in the rapidly changing Arctic environment in general. No one country can conduct all the necessary research and analyses and, therefore, international cooperation is a logical and desirable approach.

Due to the effects of the climate change, the Arctic Ocean and the entire Arctic region are facing rapid changes that have never been experienced in human history. From pure scientific viewpoint, scientists cannot and should not miss this subject for research and study. There are, of course, limits in scientific capacity, in any one country to conduct scientific research to cover the whole Arctic Ocean. Furthermore, a large part of the Arctic Ocean belongs to the EEZs of the five

26 It should be noted that a decision-making system would also be applied to other issues requiring a decision.

27 Arctic Council (2013) *Arctic Biodiversity Assessment: Status and Trends in Arctic Biodiversity.* Conservation of Arctic Flora and Fauna (CAFF): 213, 214.

coastal countries. In conducting scientific analysis, it is important to consider the interaction between the land areas and the ocean to understand the whole picture of the Arctic. All those conditions make scientific cooperation imperative.[28]

For the plus-5 members, a joint programme of scientific research in the Arctic Ocean is indeed quite an attractive proposition. They also recognised their responsibility for conducting research as countries capable of carrying out commercial fisheries in the high seas area. Many of them, therefore, expressed interest in and support for a joint programme of scientific research throughout the Arctic 5-plus-5 process. It should be noted, however, that fishing industries of the members have not expressed any interest in beginning fisheries operations at present due to the uncertain prospects concerning the emergence of commercially viable fisheries resources. This situation makes the joint programme of scientific research for the sake of science practically the only merit of joining the negotiations.

The scientific meetings, which were attended by both Arctic Five and plus 5 scientists, were held concurrently with, yet somewhat independently from, the Arctic 5-plus-5 negotiations: the actual management of the scientific meetings was entrusted to the scientists, and participation of non-coastal members to the scientific meetings predated the Arctic 5-plus-5 meetings. This is noteworthy since the terms of reference of the scientific meetings were adopted by the Arctic 5-plus-5 meetings, and the results of the scientific meetings have been presented to the Arctic 5-plus-5 meetings. The Agreement places the scientific meetings as a part of its system and the joint programme of scientific research will be established (Article 4.1) and implemented within the framework of the Agreement (Article 4).

Scientific meetings will be held "at least every two years and at least two months in advance of the meetings of the Parties" and terms of reference and other procedures for the functioning of the joint scientific meetings shall be adopted "within two years of the entry into force of this Agreement" (Article 4.4). Article 4.3 is also important for the promotion of scientific activities as it requires the adoption of a data sharing protocol among the Parties.

However, the scientific meeting under the Agreement might keep its independent nature for the time being because of: (i) its historic development and management as somewhat independent entity from the negotiations; (ii) recognition of many of the participating scientists regarding the scientific meeting as a part of Arctic science in general rather than a subsidiary body of the Arctic 5-plus-5 process; and (iii) no urgency of providing scientific advices to fisheries management by a RFMO/S as its subsidiary body.

8.5.4 Decision-making

Decision-making was the last remaining issue in the negotiation process. During the negotiations, there were no substantial differences between the Arctic

28 On Arctic Science Cooperation Agreement concluded in 2017 by the eight Arctic states, see Chapter 12 by Akiho Shibata of this book.

littoral and the non-littoral states regarding items such as the objectives of the Agreement and specific approaches for implementing the objectives. However, regarding a decision-making system, there were clear differences of positions and approaches. Coastal states, notably Russia and Canada, argued for the priority, special interests and rights of coastal states. Non-coastal states, notably Japan and the EU, had concerns regarding the possibility of a creeping jurisdiction by coastal states adjacent to the high seas area and of effects to the power balance between the Arctic members and the Observers at the Arctic Council. Again, the United States was relatively flexible and kept a low profile in the discussion regarding this issue.

Various ideas were proposed as to a decision-making system including a super-majority voting system, some form of requirement of consent from coastal states and/or a right of veto by coastal states. Eventually a consensus system was adopted for all decision-making including the condition for entry into force of the Agreement as provided by Articles 6 and 11.

The Arctic 5-plus-5 process, however, selected a decision-making method that addresses the interests of both coastal and non-coastal members: while coastal states can prevent any decision they consider adversarial to their own interests, for non-coastal states consensus is the equal footing method that creates no grouping or priority status among the parties to the Agreement.

Naturally, there is the risk that one member with a different opinion from the rest could veto a decision. In fact, in the beginning of the Arctic 5-plus-5 negotiations, several members expressed their concerns regarding this aspect. However, they made a choice that could lead to practical difficulties in decision-making in order to satisfy the interests of both coastal and non-coastal members.

However, even though the Arctic Five and the plus 5 follow substantially different interests, there is no need to be too pessimistic about the consensus system. This is because: (i) all Arctic 5-plus-5 members essentially share the same objectives regarding the management of the high seas of the CAO (i.e. prevention of unregulated fisheries); (ii) at present, at least, there is no prospect of a situation arising that could bring about serious conflicts between the members; and (iii) there are good examples for consensus-building on difficult issues, for example in the CCAMLR. The CCAMLR's example is encouraging as its membership includes a wide range of representations in terms of, for instance, economic development, geography, interests in Antarctic affairs, and territorial interests. Still, consensus decisions are made and implemented.

8.6 Conclusion: the future of the Arctic Five-plus-Five process

Many international fisheries agreements have been created in response to conflicts among countries over fisheries resources and challenges regarding overfishing situations. In some cases, negotiations started only when the problem had become critically serious. On the other hand, the new Agreement for the high seas area of the CAO was created, involving almost all players concerned, in a very short time of two years even before fisheries resources emerge in the high seas area and even before any illegal and unregulated fisheries have started. Thus, the Agreement is uniquely precautionary. We need some time before we see how this unique agreement develops or evolves towards a next step. At present, however, the Agreement can be and should be regarded as a success by the international diplomatic community.

At the same time, the members of the Agreement should actively create values from this unique international instrument, rather than just waiting for some values to emerge. If there is no prospect in the near future for commercial fisheries in the high seas area of the CAO, the immediate value would be the joint programme of scientific research and other scientific cooperation among the members.

9 Participation in the Central Arctic Ocean Fisheries Agreement

*Erik J. Molenaar**

9.1 Introduction

The negotiations on the Agreement to Prevent Unregulated High Seas Fisheries in the Central Arctic Ocean (CAOF Agreement)[1] were successfully concluded on 30 November 2017 in Washington, DC at the end of the sixth meeting, almost exactly two years after the negotiations began.[2] On 7 February 2018, a Legal and Technical Review took place in Washington, DC and a final English text was subsequently circulated among the delegations on 23 February 2018.[3] The ceremony of signature was held in Ilulissat, Greenland, on 3 October 2018. Until the last minute, it seemed that the Russian Federation (Russia) would not send a representative to this ceremony to sign the CAOF Agreement, but the Agreement was finally signed by all ten parties.[4]

* Writing this chapter was made possible by funding from the Netherlands Polar Programme. The author participated in all except the first of the six rounds of negotiations on the CAOF Agreement; some as the representative of the Netherlands in the delegation of the European Union (EU); some as a legal expert of the European Commission in the delegation of the EU. The views in this chapter are those of the author and not necessarily those of the Netherlands government or the European Commission. The author is very grateful for comments received from David Balton on an earlier version.

1 Agreement to Prevent Unregulated High Seas Fisheries in the Central Arctic Ocean, signed 3 October 2018 not in force, European Commission, Doc. COM (2018) 453 final, Annex (12 June 2018).

2 See Chapter 8 by Joji Morishita in this book for a detailed account of the negotiations. The Chairman's Statements of all six meetings can be found at www.state.gov/e/oes/ocns/fish/regionalorganizations/arctic/statements/index.htm. For an analysis of the first meeting see Erik J. Molenaar (2016) "The December 2015 Washington Meeting on High Seas Fishing in the Central Arctic Ocean" *The JCLOS Blog*, 5 February 2016. http://site.uit.no/jclos/2016/02/05/the-december-2015-washington-meeting-on-high-seas-fishing-in-the-central-arctic-ocean/ (accessed 10 October 2018).

3 The intention was for the English text to be translated into the three other official languages of the CAOF Agreement – Chinese, French and Russian – to be followed by a verification of the accuracy of these translations, and acceptance by all delegations of the final texts in these other official languages.

4 The EU signed the CAOF Agreement on 26 October 2018 and the other nine participants on 3 October 2018. Denmark signed in respect of the Faroe Islands and Greenland (cf. signed version of the CAOF Agreement on file with author).

The negotiations on the CAOF Agreement have also become known as the so-called "Five-plus-Five process", as the ten participants consisted of the five central Arctic Ocean coastal states (Canada, Denmark in respect of the Faroe Islands and Greenland, Norway, Russia and the United States; also: the "Arctic Five") and five other states and entities: China, the European Union (EU), Iceland, Japan and Republic of Korea (also: "the Other Five"). The Five-plus-Five process builds on a *de facto* preparatory process among the Arctic Five (further: "Arctic Five process"), which culminated in the adoption of the Declaration concerning the Prevention of Unregulated High Seas Fishing in the Central Arctic Ocean (Oslo Declaration).[5] Both processes took place outside the scope of the Arctic Council or any other intergovernmental body.

The main drivers for both processes were the receding sea ice in the Arctic Ocean[6] as well as spatial shifts in the distributional ranges of many fish stocks from tropical regions towards the polar regions,[7] against a background of increasing global demand in fish and a deteriorating overall status of global fish stocks.[8] At the time of writing, however, there was no fishing in the high seas portion of the central Arctic Ocean[9] at all, and practically no large-scale commercial fisheries in the portions of the coastal state maritime zones (e.g. territorial seas and exclusive economic zones (EEZs)) that are adjacent to this high seas area. From a normative perspective, therefore, the aforementioned processes were above all aimed at pursuing precautionary, science-based and ecosystem approaches to fisheries management, and avoiding unregulated high seas fishing by ensuring full high seas coverage with regional fisheries management organisations (RFMOs).[10]

5 *Declaration concerning the Prevention of Unregulated High Seas Fishing in the Central Arctic Ocean*, 16 July 2015, Oslo, Norway. www.regjeringen.no/globalassets/departementene/ud/vedlegg/folkerett/declaration-on-arctic-fisheries-16-july-2015.pdf (accessed 10 October 2018). See also Erik J. Molenaar (2016) "International Regulation of Central Arctic Ocean Fisheries" in *Challenges of the Changing Arctic: Continental Shelf, Navigation, and Fisheries* edited by Myron H. Nordquist, John N. Moore and Ronan Long. Brill, Leiden: 429–463.

6 See, for instance, AMAP (2017) "Snow, Water, Ice and Permafrost in the Arctic (SWIPA)". www.amap.no/documents/doc/Snow-Water-Ice-and-Permafrost-in-the-Arctic-SWIPA-2017/1610 (accessed 6 June 2018).This Report notes that "The Arctic's climate is shifting to a new state" and the "Arctic Ocean could be largely free of sea ice in summer as early as the late 2030s".

7 See, e.g., Tore Haug et al. (2017) "Future Harvest of Living Resources in the Arctic Ocean North of the Nordic and Barents Seas: A Review of Possibilities and Constraints" *Fisheries Research* 188: 38–57. *Reports of the Third (April 2015), Fourth (September 2016) and Fifth (October 2017) Meetings of Scientific Experts on Fish Stocks in the Central Arctic Ocean (FiS-CAO Meetings)*. www.afsc.noaa.gov/Arctic_fish_stocks_fifth_meeting/ (accessed 10 October 2018).

8 See FAO (2018) *The State of World Fisheries and Aquaculture 2018*: 6. www.fao.org/fishery/sofia/en (accessed 10 October 2018).

9 See section 9.2 for clarification of geographical terminology.

10 See Art. 2 of the CAOF Agreement. For an explanation of the concept of an RFMO see subsection 9.4.2.

Uncertainties on the future of fisheries in the (central) Arctic Ocean nevertheless abound, for instance due to the potential impacts of increased fresh-water inflow and pollution – in particular from Russian rivers – as well as ocean acidification. These could reduce or eliminate any new fishing opportunities that may arise in this area.[11] Sea-ice regression in the Arctic means at any rate that the North Pacific and the North Atlantic Oceans will become increasingly connected.[12] Together with merchant shipping, this creates a pathway for the introduction of invasive species. One of these pathways has facilitated the settlement and rapid increase in the abundance of snow crab (*Chionoecetes opilio*) in the Barents Sea in recent years.[13]

As reflected in its title, the focus of this chapter is on participation in the COAF Agreement; covering the Five-plus-Five process as well as the CAOF Agreement. The analysis is undertaken in the context of the domains of international fisheries law, the international law of the sea and the international law relating to the Arctic. As will become clear, however, these are not clearly demarcated or distinct domains of international law, and they frequently overlap.

The chapter's structure is as follows: section 9.2 discusses "Geographical Definitions and the Status of Participants in the Five-Plus-Five Process" and section 9.3 "The Interests of Participants in the Five-Plus-Five Process". This is followed by a concise overview of international fisheries law in section 9.4, which also devotes special attention to aspects relating to participation in RFMOs. Section 9.5 then focuses on "The CAOF Agreement", with subsections devoted to its structure and institutions, Agreement Area, key interim measures, decision-making, entry into force and duration, the nature of the Agreement, a more in-depth analysis on participation in the Five-plus-Five process and the (future) CAOF Agreement, also in comparison with selected RFMOs and, finally, the role of the Arctic Five. The chapter ends with section 9.6 "Conclusions".

11 See Haug et al., *supra* note 7. See also Jørgen S. Christiansen, Catherine W. Mecklenburg and Oleg V. Karamushko (2014) "Arctic Marine Fishes and their Fisheries in Light of Global Change" *Global Change Biology* 20: 352–359; Vicky W.Y. Lam, William W.L. Cheung and U. Rashid Sumaila (2016) "Marine Capture Fisheries in the Arctic: Winners or Losers under Climate Change and Ocean Acidification?" *Fish and Fisheries* 17: 335–357; Miranda C. Jones and William W.L. Cheung (2014) "Multi-model Ensemble Projections of Climate Change Effects on Global Marine Biodiversity" *ICES Journal of Marine Science* 72–3: 741–752; CAFF (2013) *Arctic Biodiversity Assessmen: Status and Trends in Arctic Biodiversity*: Ch. 1, pp. 22–23. www.caff.is (accessed 10 October 2018).

12 Mary S. Wisz et al. (2015) "Arctic Warming Will Promote Atlantic-Pacific Fish Interchange" *Nature Climate Change* 5–3: 1–5.

13 Jan H. Sundet and Sergey Bakanev (2014) "Snow crab (*Chionoecetes opilio*) – a new invasive crab species becoming an important player in the Barents Sea ecosystem" *Doc. ICES CM 2014/F:04*. www.ices.dk/sites/pub/CM%20Doccuments/CM-2014/Theme%20Session%20F%20contributions/F0414.pdf (accessed 31 January 2019). This has, *inter alia*, led to a dispute between Norway and the European Union (EU) on the applicability of the Spitsbergen Treaty to the continental shelf below the Fisheries Protection Zone (FPZ) established by Norway off Svalbard. See, e.g., European Parliament (2017) "Parliamentary Question No. O-000077/2017 on EU–Norway dispute on snow crab fisheries in Svalbard", 11 October 2017. Treaty between Norway, the USA, Denmark, France, Italy, Japan, the Netherlands, Great Britain and Ireland and the British Overseas Dominions and Sweden with regard to the Archipelago of Spitsbergen, signed 9 February 1920 and entered into force 14 August 1925, *League of Nations Treaties Series* 2: 7.

9.2 Geographical definitions and the status of participants in the Five-plus-Five process

At present, there are no generally accepted geographical definitions for the terms "Arctic", "marine Arctic", "Arctic Ocean" and "central Arctic Ocean". For the purpose of this chapter, the term "marine Arctic" corresponds to the marine waters included within the boundary agreed by the Arctic Council's Conservation of Arctic Flora and Fauna (CAFF) working group (see Figure 9.1).

As Iceland is located in the marine Arctic as defined above, it qualifies at any rate as an "Arctic coastal state". The Arctic Five obviously also qualify as such. These six states plus Finland and Sweden are "Arctic states" on account of their membership of the Arctic Council and its precursor, the Arctic Environmental

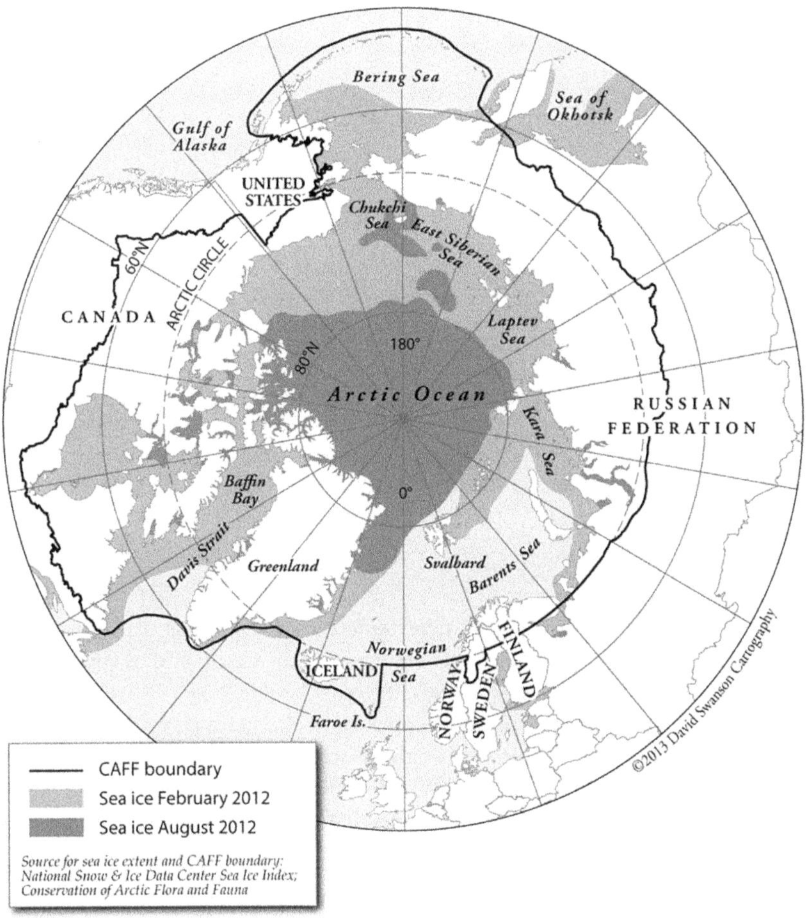

Figure 9.1 The Arctic region: general overview

Source: Map prepared by David Swanson and reproduced here with his permission.

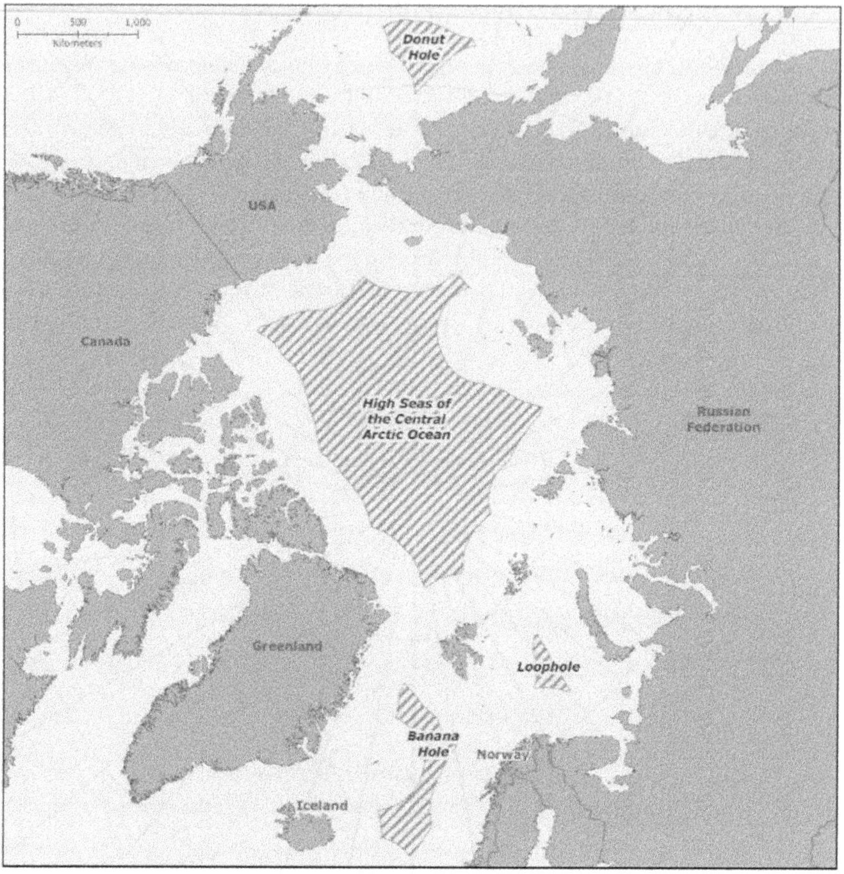

Figure 9.2 High seas pockets in the marine Arctic

Source: Map used with permission of the Pew Charitable Trusts.

Protection Strategy (AEPS).[14] The determination of the status of Arctic state is therefore above all an agreement between these eight states, and as such in principle not opposable to third states and entities.

Figure 9.2 shows the four high seas pockets of the marine Arctic, namely the so-called "Banana Hole" in the Norwegian Sea, the so-called "Loophole" in the Barents Sea, the so-called "Donut Hole" in the central Bering Sea and the so-called "high seas (portion) of the central Arctic Ocean". The last is approximately 2.8 million square kilometres in size, roughly the size of the Mediterranean Sea.[15]

14 Arctic Environmental Protection Strategy (AEPS), 14 June 1991, *International Legal Materials* 30: 1624–1669.

15 Chairman's Statement, sixth meeting, *supra* note 2.

The CAOF Agreement uses the terms "Arctic Ocean" and "central Arctic Ocean" without defining them. They appear above all in a context of broader ecosystems and their marine living resources as well as related scientific research and monitoring.[16] The term "high seas portion of the central Arctic Ocean" appears in the definitions of the geographical scope of the Oslo Declaration and the CAOF Agreement (see subsection 9.5.2). Its consistent use implies two agreements. First, the central Arctic Ocean consists of a high seas portion as well as adjacent coastal state maritime zones. Second, the "broader" Arctic Ocean consists of the central Arctic Ocean as well as some undefined adjacent waters.[17] These agreements provide comfort to Iceland, which regards itself as an Arctic Ocean coastal state and repeatedly requested to join the Arctic Five process.[18] These issues have some similarity with the issue of the non-opposability of the status of Arctic state referred to above. All this notwithstanding, the participants in the Five-plus-Five process agreed that only the Arctic Five are central Arctic Ocean coastal states.

While Denmark is an Arctic state, it did not have a single status in the Arctic Five and Five-plus-Five processes. The Kingdom of Denmark consists of three parts: "mainland" Denmark, the Faroe Islands and Greenland. The Kingdom is a central Arctic Ocean coastal state exclusively on account of Greenland, and an Arctic (Ocean) coastal state on account of the Faroe Islands. The Kingdom's EU membership only applies to mainland Denmark. Due to the EU's exclusive competence in "the conservation of marine biological resources under the common fisheries policy",[19] it represents mainland Denmark at the external level, including in the Five-plus-Five process.[20] The hybrid status of Denmark in the Arctic Five process is also reflected in the fact that it signed the Oslo Declaration only in respect of Greenland, and not also in respect of the Faroe Islands.[21]

China, Japan and Republic of Korea have the same status in the Five-plus-Five process: all of them are non-Arctic States as well as high seas fishing states. The status of the EU in the Five-plus-Five process is even more complex than

16 See in particular the Preamble and Art. 4(1). Exceptions are Art. 3(6), which is explained by its focus on the issue of compatibility in the context of Art. 7 of the Fish Stocks Agreement; and Art. 14(2), which should be understood in the context of the dispute on the geographical scope of the Spitsbergen Treaty. For the Fish Stock Agreement, see Agreement for the Implementation of the Provisions of the United Nations Convention on the Law of the Sea of 10 December 1982 relating to the Conservation and Management of Straddling Fish Stocks and Highly Migratory Fish Stocks (Fish Stocks Agreement), adopted 4 August 1995 and entered into force 11 December 2001, *United Nations Treaty Series* 2167: 3.

17 See also the use of "Central Arctic Ocean" in the context of the OSPAR Commission's consideration of an "Arctic Ice High Seas MPA". See Summary Record of the 16th OSPAR Commission Meeting, Doc. OSPAR 16/20/1-E (2016), at para. 6.27(c).

18 See Molenaar, *supra* note 5, at 447.

19 Art. 3(1)(d) of the Treaty on the Functioning of the European Union (TFEU). http://eur-lex.europa.eu/collection/eu-law/treaties.html (consolidated version) (accessed 10 October 2018).

20 See Molenaar, *supra* note 5, at 432–433 for some additional observations.

21 Signed version of the 2015 Oslo Declaration (on file with author).

that of Denmark. First of all, the EU is not a state but an intergovernmental organisation *sui generis*, as it is an economic and political union between 28 European states. The international community's recognition of the EU and its predecessors as a full participant in international fisheries law – as well as the international law of the sea more in general – materialised during the third United Nations Conference on the Law of the Sea (UNCLOS III) and was laid down in the United Nations Convention on the Law of the Sea (LOS Convention).[22] In the domain of international fisheries law, the EU commonly has the status of regional economic integration organisation (REIO).[23] When this chapter uses the phrase "states and entities", this is intended to capture the EU as well as Taiwan (Chinese Taipei). Once Taiwan's significant role in international marine capture fisheries became generally accepted, the international community's recognition of its status was enshrined in the Fish Stocks Agreement.[24] The EU and Taiwan are the two exceptions to the general rule that the status of full participant in intergovernmental fisheries bodies is reserved exclusively for states.

In the Five-plus-Five process, the EU represented all its member states, including mainland Denmark, Finland and Sweden. The latter three are all Arctic states, but not Arctic coastal states. The EU therefore acted in a *de facto* capacity as high seas fishing State, with three of the 28 member states represented by it being Arctic states. Finally, it should be noted that China, Japan and Republic of Korea were granted Observer status in the Arctic Council in 2013, while the EU could be said to have been granted such a *de facto* Observer status then as well.[25] As noted in subsection 9.5.6.1, however, having this status does not seem to have been a significant consideration – or at all – for inviting them to participate in the Five-plus-Five process.

The seabed of the Banana Hole, Loophole and Donut Hole consists entirely of so-called "outer continental shelves" of coastal states. While most of the seabed "underlying" the high seas portion of the central Arctic Ocean will consist of outer continental shelves, there will be one or more pockets of the Area – the deep seabed beyond the continental shelves of coastal states.[26] More clarity on this will take a considerable number of years, *inter alia* due to the heavy workload of the Commission on the Limits of the Continental Shelf (CLCS) in processing submissions by coastal states.

22 United Nations Convention on the Law of the Sea, Montego Bay, adopted 10 December 1982 and entered into force 16 November 1994, *United Nations Treaty Series* 1833: 396 (LOS Convention); Art. 305(1)(f) and Annex IX.

23 As regards "entity", see Art. 1(2)(b) of the Fish Stocks Agreement.

24 Ibid., at Arts 1(3) and 17(3).

25 *Kiruna Declaration on the occasion of the Eighth Ministerial Meeting of the Arctic Council*, 15 May 2013, Kiruna, Sweden.

26 Art. 1(1)(1) of the LOS Convention.

9.3 The interests of participants in the Five-plus-Five process

The interests of the participants in the Five-plus-Five process are quite unique and hardly comparable with the interests of participants in most other intergovernmental negotiations on high seas fishing. This is above all caused by the fact that no high seas fishing ever took place in the central Arctic Ocean before. Rather than a scenario where a need has arisen to regulate an existing high seas fishery because it has led to over-exploitation of target species or undesirable impacts on non-target species or the broader ecosystem, the Five-plus-Five therefore had the opportunity to determine the conditions under which a future high seas fishery would be allowed to commence.

Only the negotiators of the Convention on the Conservation and Management of Pollock Resources in the Central Bering Sea (CBS Convention)[27] and the Convention on the Conservation of Antarctic Marine Living Resources (CAMLR Convention)[28] had been in a somewhat similar position. Negotiations on the former commenced after the high seas pollock stock had fully collapsed. There has been no recommencement of fishing for pollock in the Donut Hole since the entry into force of the CBS Convention, as the substantive and procedural conditions for this have not been satisfied.[29]

Negotiations on the CAMLR Convention commenced in anticipation of large-scale fishing for krill in the waters adjacent to the Antarctic continent, consisting of coastal state maritime zones as well as areas of the high seas and the Area (i.e. areas beyond national jurisdiction (ABNJ)); both *de jure* and *de facto*.[30] While "boom and bust" fisheries had already occurred in these waters before the negotiations, and fisheries were ongoing when the CAMLR Convention entered into force, its decision-making body – the Commission for the Conservation of Antarctic Marine Living Resources (CCAMLR) – subjected these fisheries to increasingly more stringent regulations. CCAMLR's pioneering role in regulating new and exploratory fisheries eventually found its way in Article 6(6) of the Fish Stocks Agreement, and thereby became an international minimum standard.[31] Reference should also be made to the International Whaling Commission

27 Convention on the Conservation and Management of Pollock Resources in the Central Bering Sea, adopted 16 June 1994 and entered into force 8 December 1995, *International Legal Materials* 34: 67.

28 Convention on the Conservation of Antarctic Marine Living Resources, adopted 20 May 1980 and entered into force 7 April 1982, *United Nations Treaty Series* 1329: 47.

29 See Arts IV(1)(a) and VII and Part 1 of the Annex of the CBS Convention.

30 The *de facto* status of ABNJ is a consequence of the agreement to disagree on the question of territorial sovereignty over the Antarctic continent, and the resulting absence of universally recognised coastal states.

31 See Richard Caddell (2018) "Precautionary Management and the Development of Future Fishing Opportunities: The International Regulation of New and Exploratory Fisheries" *International Journal of Marine and Coastal Law* 33: 199–260.

(IWC)'s adoption of a non-time bound moratorium on commercial whaling in 1982 – which became effective in the season 1985–86 – and its decision to lift the moratorium only once substantive and procedural conditions had been met. This moratorium remains in effect until today.

The Arctic Five had set forth the conditions under which their vessels would be allowed to commence a future fishery by means of their non-legally binding Oslo Declaration, thereby acting upon the stewardship role claimed by them in the 2008 Ilulissat Declaration.[32] In their position as initiators of the Five-plus-Five process, they were subsequently able to use the Oslo Declaration as the basis for the initial draft text in a legally binding format used in the Five-plus-Five process. Two key elements of the Oslo Declaration are of crucial importance in this regard: its geographical scope – the high seas portion of the central Arctic Ocean – and its qualified abstention from commercial high seas fishing.[33] The Other Five agreed to use these two key elements as a point of departure and they were eventually also laid down in the CAOF Agreement (see subsections 9.5.2 and 9.5.3). While the Other Five managed to include a reference to the notion of compatibility in Article 3(6) of the CAOF Agreement,[34] this provision relates exclusively to transboundary fish stocks and will therefore only trigger constraints on fishing by the Arctic Five in their maritime zones adjacent to the CAOF Agreement Area sometime in the future, once the northward migration of fish stocks reaches the high seas portion of the central Arctic Ocean (see further below).

It is submitted that these two key elements create a fundamental difference between the central Arctic Ocean fisheries interests of the Arctic Five on the one hand, and those of the Other Five on the other hand.[35] The fisheries interests of the Arctic Five are derived from their sovereignty, sovereign rights and jurisdiction over fisheries resources in their adjacent coastal state maritime zones[36] as well as from their right to fish on the high seas.[37] Conversely, the fisheries interests of the Other Five are solely derived from their right to fish on the high seas. This essentially

32 The Ilulissat Declaration, Arctic Ocean Conference of 28 May 2008, *International Legal Materials* 48: 362.

33 Cf. the fifth preambular paragraph and its first interim measure, Oslo Declaration, *supra* note 5.

34 Art. 3(6) reads: "Consistent with Article 7 of the 1995 Agreement, coastal States Parties and other Parties shall cooperate to ensure the compatibility of conservation and management measures for fish stocks that occur in areas both within and beyond national jurisdiction in the central Arctic Ocean in order to ensure conservation and management of those stocks in their entirety."

35 The ensuing observations are not immediately applicable to Denmark in respect of the Faroe Islands and Greenland, whose hybrid status in the negotiations means it has a much more complex set of interests.

36 Arts 2(1), 49(1), 56(1)(a) and 77(4) of the LOS Convention.

37 Art. 116 of the LOS Convention. The flag State entitlement to the surplus of the total allowable catch (TAC) pursuant to Art. 62(2) of the LOS Convention did not play a role in the Five-plus-Five process, mainly because Canada and the United States do not provide foreign vessels with fisheries access to their maritime zones; save for some minor exceptions.

means that, while there will be different scenarios leading to the occurrence of a fish stock in the high seas portion of the central Arctic Ocean that would allow for the commencement of a commercially viable fishery, the Other Five can be expected to be overall more inclined to vote in favour of a commencement of high seas fishing than the Arctic Five. The Arctic Five may only be supportive of such a commencement if they intend to participate in the fishery themselves or, if they do not intend to do so, if this would not significantly conflict with their coastal state interests.

These coastal state interests could be predominantly utilisation-oriented or conservation-oriented. Conflict with utilisation-oriented coastal state interests of the Arctic Five could for instance arise in case of a so-called "straddling fish stock", which is a fish stock occurring in one or more EEZs and the adjacent high seas. Those of the Arctic Five that would allow fishing for such a stock in their own maritime zones adjacent to the CAOF Agreement Area have a clear interest to withhold support for the commencement of fishing for the high seas "component" of the stock. The high seas would then act as a *de facto* reserve for the replenishment of the stock's coastal component. Moreover, before a northward expansion of a fish stock reaches the high seas portion of the central Arctic Ocean, the stock will first have to "traverse" the adjacent coastal state maritime zones. The Arctic Five could therefore be in a position to stifle this northward expansion by increasing fishing effort in their own maritime zones.[38]

Conflict with conservation-oriented coastal State interests of the Arctic Five could also arise in relation to a straddling fish stock. Those of the Arctic Five that would prohibit fishing for such a stock in their own maritime zones adjacent to the CAOF Agreement Area – for whatever reason – are unlikely to support the commencement of fishing for the high seas component. Moreover, those of the Arctic Five that would prohibit fishing more generally in their own maritime zones may also be hesitant to support the commencement of fishing in the high seas for stocks that do not also occur in their own maritime zones. They could, for instance, be concerned about the broader ecosystem effects that high seas fishing might have on ecosystems in their own maritime zones.

The Arctic Five also have utilisation-oriented as well as conservation-oriented interests in relation to the natural resources of their outer continental shelves underlying the high seas portion of the central Arctic Ocean. First of all, sedentary species (e.g. snow crab) are not covered by the CAOF Agreement due to their exclusion from the definition of "fish".[39] Second, the Arctic Five are entitled to impose restrictions on high seas bottom fisheries that have significant adverse impacts on these sedentary species or other benthic organisms (e.g. sponge beds or cold-water coral reefs), provided that the exercise of this entitlement does not

38 See also Leilei Zou and Henry P. Huntington (2018) "Implications of the Convention on the Conservation and Management of Pollock Resources in the Central Bering Sea for the Management of Fisheries in the Central Arctic Ocean" *Marine Policy* 88: 135.

39 Art. 1(b) of the CAOF Agreement reads: " 'fish' means species of fish, molluscs and crustaceans except those belonging to sedentary species as defined in Article 77 of the [LOS Convention]".

infringe or result in any unjustifiable interference with the right to fish on the high seas.[40] Third, even in case fishing does not target sedentary species on the outer continental shelf and also does not make direct physical contact with sedentary species or the seabed, a coastal state could still be concerned about potential predator–prey relationships between non-sedentary species targeted by high seas fisheries on the one hand, and sedentary species and other benthic organisms belonging to its continental shelf on the other hand.

At least as important as these "fisheries interests" of the participants in the Five-plus-Five process in relation to the central Arctic Ocean are their broader interests in the domains of international fisheries law, the international law of the sea and the international law relating to the Arctic. It is important to emphasise here that a state often acts in multiple capacities. As regards the domain of international fisheries law, it acts as a coastal state in its own region but may act as a distant water fishing state in other regions. Depending on the circumstances, a state may decide that its interests in one capacity prevail over its interests in another capacity. This could even lead to a scenario where, in its capacity as a distant water fishing state it could agree to concessions to coastal states in their region, and use these concessions – in its capacity as a coastal state – as a precedent for similar concessions in its own region.

The phenomenon of "creeping coastal state jurisdiction" has been one of the principal drivers in the development of the international law of the sea. Before World War II, this domain was largely built on the freedom of the high seas and the associated primacy of flag state jurisdiction postulated by Grotius. Soon after World War II, however, technological developments in offshore hydrocarbon exploitation and marine capture fisheries led coastal states to claim exclusive access and jurisdiction over living and non-living resources in increasingly broader maritime zones adjacent to their coasts.[41] The LOS Convention's recognition of the sovereignty, sovereign rights and jurisdiction of coastal states in their broader and new maritime zones was very successful in bringing an end to unilateral coastal state claims to new maritime zones; the principal exception being Chile's *Mar Presencial*.[42] There have nevertheless been various occasions where coastal states have contemplated further extending their jurisdiction. Calls to that effect arose for instance within the United States and the Soviet Union in response to the over-exploitation of pollock in the Donut Hole towards the end of the 1980s.[43] Another example are the calls

40 Arts 77(1) and 78(2) of the LOS Convention.

41 See Robert Y. Jennings (1972) "A Changing International Law of the Sea" *Cambridge Law Journal* 31: 34–36; Bernard H. Oxman (2006) "The Territorial Temptation: A Siren Song at Sea" *American Journal of International Law* 100: 830–851.

42 See Erik J. Molenaar (2015) "New Maritime Zones and the Law of the Sea" in *Jurisdiction over Ships – Post-UNCLOS Developments in the Law of the Sea* edited by Henrik Ringbom. Brill, Leiden: 267–271.

43 David Balton (2001) "The Bering Sea Doughnut Hole Convention: Regional Solution, Global Implications" in *Governing High Seas Fisheries: The Interplay of Global and Regional Regimes* edited by Olav Schramm Stokke. Oxford University Press, Oxford: 150–151.

within Canada in the mid-2000s to claim so-called "custodial management" over fisheries resources on the nose and tail of the Grand Banks of Newfoundland and the Flemish Cap.[44] Canada eventually decided to focus its efforts instead on modernising the Convention on Future Multilateral Cooperation in the Northwest Atlantic Fisheries (NAFO Convention).[45] However, Canada had shown to be prepared to unilaterally claim extended coastal state jurisdiction in the past, for instance by means of its 1970 Arctic Waters Pollution Prevention Act[46] and its legislation authorising at-sea high seas enforcement action against foreign vessels, which led to the famous arrest of the Spanish-flagged fishing vessel *Estai* in 1995.

In situations where coastal states regard unilateral extensions of coastal state jurisdiction – whether individually or acting in concert – as undesirable, they can still exert significant control over fishing in adjacent ABNJ by exercising the port and coastal state jurisdiction that is already available to them under existing international law. Access to their ports and fishing access to their maritime zones could, for instance, be made conditional on not fishing in adjacent areas of high seas. All or some of these approaches are, for instance, pursued by Chile in relation to its *Mar Presencial*,[47] by Norway and the Russian Federation in relation to the Loophole,[48] and by the parties to the Nauru Agreement[49] in relation to certain high seas pockets in the Western and Central Pacific.[50] In fact, most RFMOs also pursue some or all of these approaches, and some of these consist entirely or mainly of coastal states (see subsection 9.5.6.3).

Creeping coastal state jurisdiction continues to be relevant today. Rather than unilateral action by a single state or several states acting in concert, however, it occurs predominantly at the multilateral level through intergovernmental organisations pursuant to their mandate as "competent international organizations" under the LOS Convention. A good example in this regard is the so-called "cooperative legislative competence" between the International Maritime Organization (IMO) and its members acting in their capacity of coastal states. The LOS Convention explicitly provides for this in relation to the designation

44 See Molenaar, *supra* note 42, at 252.

45 Convention on Future Multilateral Cooperation in the Northwest Atlantic Fisheries (NAFO Convention), signed 24 October 1978 and entered into force 1 January 1979, *United Nations Treaties Series* 1135: 369, as amended. www.nafo.int (consolidated version) (accessed 10 October 2018). At present it is named "Convention on Cooperation in the Northwest Atlantic Fisheries".

46 Act of 26 June 1970, as amended; currently R.S.C., 1985, c. A-12. laws-lois.justice.gc.ca (accessed 10 October 2018).

47 See Molenaar, *supra* note 42, at 270.

48 See Molenaar, *supra* note 5, at 429.

49 Agreement concerning Cooperation in the Management of Fisheries of Common Interest, Nauru, signed 11 February 1982 and entered into force 2 December 1982, as amended in April 2010. www.pnatuna.com (consolidated text) (accessed 10 October 2018).

50 See Art. I(3), A Third Arrangement Implementing the Nauru Agreement Setting Forth Additional Terms and Conditions of Access to the Fisheries Zones of the Parties, signed 16 May 2008, as amended. www.pnatuna.com (consolidated text) (accessed 10 October 2018).

of sea lanes and traffic separation schemes in straits used for international navigation and archipelagic waters.[51] However, IMO also developed similar mechanisms under the SOLAS Convention[52] for mandatory ships' routeing measures and ship reporting systems beyond the territorial sea without an explicit basis in the LOS Convention,[53] thereby amounting to a manifestation of multilateral creeping coastal state jurisdiction.

Other examples are the coastal state jurisdiction beyond the outer limit of the territorial sea relating to underwater cultural heritage created by the UCH Convention,[54] and relating to the removal of wrecks created by the Wreck Removal Convention.[55] It should be noted, however, that the latter two do not enjoy a comparable extent of acceptance as the coastal state jurisdiction created under the SOLAS Convention. At the time of writing, the status of participation in the SOLAS Convention (164) exceeded that of the UCH Convention (56) and the Wreck Removal Convention (41) by far.[56] While the UCH Convention was controversial and adopted by a vote – with four against and 15 abstentions[57] – the Wreck Removal Convention was adopted by consensus. The relatively low status of participation in the Wreck Removal Convention could be mainly explained by a lack of interest among coastal states in the new coastal state jurisdiction it offers, for instance because only a few are confronted with the kinds of problems with wrecks addressed by the Convention.

Some states are concerned about the potential of multilateral creeping coastal state jurisdiction in the currently ongoing negotiation process on an "International legally binding instrument under the LOS Convention on the conservation and sustainable use of marine biological diversity of areas beyond national jurisdiction" (BBNJ process).[58] These concerns are above all based on coastal state assertions of their special roles, interests or rights in ABNJ adjacent to their maritime zones, in particular in relation to the identification and designation of

51 Arts 41(4) and 53(9) of the LOS Convention.

52 International Convention for the Safety of Life at Sea, London, adopted 1 November 1974 and entered into force 25 May 1980, *United Nations Treaty Series* 1184: 277, with protocols and regularly amended.

53 Erik J. Molenaar (1998) *Coastal State Jurisdiction over Vessel-Source Pollution*. Kluwer Law International, The Hague: 527.

54 Convention on the Protection of the Underwater Cultural Heritage, adopted 1 November 2001 and entered into force 2 January 2009, *United Nations Treaty Series* 2562: 3. See in particular Arts 9 and 10.

55 Nairobi International Convention on the Removal of Wrecks, Nairobi, adopted 18 May 2007 and entered into force 14 April 2015, IMO Doc. LEG/CONF.16/19 (23 May 2007). See Arts 8–10.

56 Based on information available from: www.imo.org and www.unesco.org/eri/la/convention.asp?KO=13520&language=E&order=alpha (accessed 30 August 2018).

57 Mariano J. Aznar (2014) "The Contiguous Zone as an Archaeological Maritime Zone" *International Journal of Marine and Coastal Law* 29: 1–51, fn. 48.

58 UNGA/RES/72/249 (24 December 2017).

area-based management tools – including marine protected areas – and environmental impact assessments.[59]

Some of these concerned states also participated – or were represented – in the Five-plus-Five process and were determined to avoid a scenario where successful assertions of special roles, interests or rights of "adjacent coastal states" in the Five-plus-Five process would be used as a precedent in the BBNJ process. The concerns of these states were in part also based on the Arctic Five's assertion in the 2008 Ilulissat Declaration that they are in "a unique position" in relation to the central Arctic Ocean more in general. At their second ministerial (Foreign Affairs) meeting in 2010, the Arctic Five also specifically asserted "a unique role and interest" in the conservation and management of central Arctic Ocean fisheries.[60] It is acknowledged that while these assertions certainly have merit in view of their coastal state maritime zones in the central Arctic Ocean, this is less obvious in the context of the Arctic Five and Five-plus-Five processes, as they were spatially confined to the high seas portion of the central Arctic Ocean. This means that both high seas fishing states and coastal states have roles, interests and rights. It should be noted that the three other Arctic states strongly criticised the Arctic Five ministerial (Foreign Affairs) meetings in 2008 and 2010 on the ground that these undermined the Arctic Council. Of these three, only Iceland participated in its own right in the Five-plus-Five process.

The preceding discussion on the linkages between the BBNJ process and the Five-plus-Five process also serves to illustrate the overlap between the domains of the international law of the sea and the international law relating to the Arctic. It is submitted that the interests of the participants in the Five-plus-Five process in the latter domain are – in one way or another – all related to the Arctic Council, which is at present generally accepted to be the principal forum for intergovernmental cooperation in relation to the Arctic. As observed in section 9.2, the Arctic Five and Iceland are Members of the Arctic Council, and mainland Denmark, Finland and Sweden were represented by the EU in the Five-plus-Five process. China, Japan, Republic of Korea and the EU have *de jure* or *de facto* Observer status with the Arctic Council. The fact that membership of the Arctic Council is limited to the eight Arctic states is not inconsistent with general international law. The situation would, for example, be different if the Council were to engage in regulation that interferes with rights of third states or entities (e.g. the freedoms

59 See the multiple references to "adjacent coastal States" in the Report of the PrepCom, UN Doc. A/AC.287/2017/PC.4/2 (31 July 2017). See also Alex G. Oude Elferink (2018) "Coastal States and MPAs in ABNJ: Ensuring Consistency with the LOSC" *International Journal of Marine and Coastal Law* 33–3: 437–466. The notion of adjacency should in this context be interpreted broadly and also comprises the scenario of areas of high seas lying above continental shelves.

60 Cf. the Chair's Summary of the Arctic Five's meeting in Chelsea, Canada, in March 2010. www.mid.ru/en/foreign_policy/news/-/asset_publisher/cKNonkJE02Bw/content/id/257162.

of fishing and navigation on the high seas) in a manner that would be inconsistent with the *pacta tertiis* principle (e.g. by means of at-sea high seas enforcement).[61]

The balance between the rights and obligations of Arctic Council Observers – in particular non-Arctic states and the EU – has been a sensitive issue for many years. This may in part be caused by insufficient awareness among non-Arctic state Observers that general international law does not at present provide them with a clearly applicable and unqualified entitlement to participate in the Council; let alone a right to become a member. At any rate, some non-Arctic state Observers are dissatisfied with their limited rights and the rather broad and cumulative admission criteria,[62] and often find their inferior participatory status difficult to accept. This is particularly striking during formal meetings of the Council, when their delegations sit at the back, and the delegations of members and permanent participants sit at the main table.

The inferior participatory status of non-Arctic state Observers in the Arctic Council can also be illustrated by means of the three treaties that have been negotiated under the auspices of the Arctic Council so far; namely the Arctic SAR Agreement,[63] the Arctic MOSPA[64] and the Arctic Scientific Cooperation Agreement[65]. As argued by this author elsewhere, these three treaties and their Meetings of the Parties (MOPs) are – together with the Arctic Council's constitutive instrument, its Ministerial Declarations, other instruments and its institutional structure – part of the so-called "Arctic Council System".[66] None of these three treaties provide for accession by non-Arctic states and entities, regardless of their having Observer status. As regards the Arctic SAR Agreement and the Arctic MOSPA this is also understandable, as an entitlement under international law for them to accede cannot be readily identified. The Arctic Scientific Cooperation Agreement is a somewhat different case due to the entitlements of all states on marine scientific research pursuant to the LOS Convention.[67]

61 See Erik J. Molenaar (2012) "Current and Prospective Roles of the Arctic Council System within the Context of the Law of the Sea" *International Journal of Marine and Coastal Law* 27: 565–568.

62 See Rules 37 and 38, and para. 6 of Annex 2, *Arctic Council Rules of Procedure,* most recent version adopted by the Kiruna Ministerial Meeting, 2013. www.arctic-council.org.

63 Agreement on Cooperation in Aeronautical and Maritime Search and Rescue in the Arctic, signed 12 May 2011 and entered into force 19 January 2013, *International Legal Materials* 50: 1119.

64 Agreement on Cooperation on Marine Oil Pollution Preparedness and Response in the Arctic, signed 15 May 2013 and entered into force 25 March 2016. https://oaarchive.arctic-council.org/handle/11374/529

65 Agreement on Enhancing International Arctic Scientific Cooperation, signed 11 May 2017 and entered into force 23 May 2018. https://oaarchive.arctic-council.org/handle/11374/1916 (accessed 6 June 2018), reproduced in the Appendix of this book.

66 See Molenaar, *supra* note 61.

67 Cf. the Preamble and Art. 6(2) of the Agreement, and the frequent references to consistency with international law in Arts 6(1), 10 and 16. The Preamble also recognises "the significant scientific expertise and invaluable contributions to scientific activities being made by non-Parties and specifically by the Arctic Council Permanent Participants and Arctic Council Observers". Art. 17 of the Agreement is also very different from the virtually identical

However, as the geographical scope of the Arctic Scientific Cooperation Agreement is not limited to ABNJ but also covers land territory and coastal state maritime zones,[68] it is still understandable that participation is limited to Arctic states.[69]

This distinction between the Arctic SAR Agreement and the Arctic MOSPA on the one hand, and the Arctic Scientific Cooperation Agreement on the other, may also explain – in part – why the former's negotiation processes did not involve non-Arctic state Observers – even though some explicitly requested this[70] – while the latter's negotiation process was open to all categories of Observers, and several non-Arctic states also exercised this entitlement. But broader support for transparency and inclusiveness is likely to have been another reason for the broader participation in the third negotiation process. Finally, it should be mentioned that none of the new, more peripheral Arctic bodies established in 2014 and 2015 entitle non-Arctic states to become (full) members.[71]

In light of the inferior participatory status of non-Arctic states and entities in the Arctic Council, the Arctic Council System, and the new, more peripheral Arctic bodies, it is therefore understandable that China, the EU, Japan and Republic of Korea welcomed the opportunity to participate on an equal footing with Arctic states in the Five-plus-Five process. Similarly, these three states and the EU shared a clear interest in bringing the Five-plus-Five process to a successful conclusion, as that would offer the prospect of obtaining an equal participatory status as Arctic states in a legally binding Arctic governance instrument and its decision-making body. As the Five-plus-Five process took place outside the scope of the Arctic Council, there would not be a formal hierarchical relationship with the Council either. In fact, as the CAOF Agreement is a legally binding instrument and its MOP (see subsection 9.5.1) competent to adopt legally binding decisions, an international lawyer would regard it as superior to the Arctic Council, which is "merely" a high-level intergovernmental forum without the competence to adopt legally binding decisions.

As a final note, it is important to highlight that the successful conclusion of the Five-plus-Five demonstrates that, irrespective of their different interests and positions, the participants also share many interests.

provisions included in Art. 18 of the Arctic SAR Agreement and Art. 17 of the Arctic MOSPA. Earlier drafts of the former were amended in response to interventions from category (a) Observers. The final version contains the phrase "obligations of the Parties under agreements with non-Parties" and thereby implicitly the rights of non-Parties.

68 Annex 1 to the Arctic Scientific Cooperation Agreement.

69 See Chapter 12 by Akiho Shibata in this book. See also Akiho Shibata and Maiko Raita (2016) "An Agreement on Enhancing International Arctic Scientific Cooperation: Only for the Eight Arctic States and Their Scientists?" *The Yearbook of Polar Law* 8: 129–162.

70 See Molenaar, *supra* note 61, at 575–577.

71 See, for example, Arctic Economic Council, established in 2016; Arctic Offshore Regulators Forum, established in 2016; and Arctic Coast Guard Forum, established in 2015. See Erik J. Molenaar (2017), "The Arctic, the Arctic Council, and the Law of the Sea" in Robert C. Beckman, Tore Henriksen, Kristine Dalaker Kraabel, Erik J. Molenaar and J. Ashley Roach (eds) (2017) *Governance of Arctic Shipping: Balancing Rights and Interests of Arctic States and User States.* Brill, Leiden: 53 and 57–59.

9.4 International fisheries law

9.4.1 Introduction

International fisheries law is the domain (or: "rule-complex") of international law that relates specifically to the conservation, management and/or development of marine capture fisheries. It consists of substantive norms (e.g. rights, obligations and objectives), substantive fisheries standards (e.g. catch restrictions) as well as institutional rules and arrangements (e.g. mandates and decision-making procedures). International fisheries law is part of public international law and can also be seen as a branch or part of the domain of the international law of the sea.

The global component of international fisheries law applies to the marine Arctic and the (central) Arctic Ocean, however defined. The cornerstone in the global jurisdictional framework for marine capture fisheries is provided by the LOS Convention, which provides for the division of seas and oceans in maritime zones and specifies the basic rights and obligations of states therein. The LOS Convention regulates the exercise of entitlements to fishing that states have in their capacities as coastal or flag states through various key obligations. Whereas coastal states have exclusive access and jurisdiction over fisheries resources in essentially all their maritime zones,[72] the two main entitlements of flag states are their right to fish on the high seas, and access to the surplus of the total allowable catch (TAC) in EEZs of coastal states.[73]

The general obligations included in the LOS Convention have been built upon by a suite of global fisheries instruments, in particular the Fish Stocks Agreement, several legally binding and non-legally binding instruments adopted by the United Nations Food and Agriculture Organization (FAO) as well as certain (parts of) United Nations General Assembly (UNGA) Resolutions. As a result, these key obligations have gradually developed into the following:

1 to avoid over-exploitation of target species by means of setting a science-based TAC, which strives for maximum sustainable yield (MSY) as qualified by the precautionary approach;
2 to strive for the optimum utilisation of target species within the EEZ by providing other states with access to the surplus of the TAC;
3 to pursue an ecosystem approach to fisheries (EAF), which often focuses in particular on (a) predator-prey relationships; (b) impacts of fisheries on non-target species and the ecosystem as a whole; and (c) impacts of oceanographic or climate processes, or pollution, on fish stocks;
4 to cooperate in relation to transboundary fish stocks and fish stocks that occur exclusively on the high seas (further: "discrete high seas fish stocks"); and
5 to exercise effective jurisdiction and control over a state's own vessels.

72 Arts 2(1), 49(1), 56(1)(a) and 77(4) of the LOS Convention.
73 Arts 62(2) and 116 of the LOS Convention.

The LOS Convention, the Fish Stocks Agreement and FAO's fisheries instruments are primarily concerned with establishing the jurisdictional framework. They do not contain substantive fisheries standards such as catch restrictions through TACs, allocations of fishing opportunities through national quotas, gear restrictions or temporal/seasonal or spatial measures (e.g. closed areas). Actual fisheries regulation is conducted by states individually or collectively. The primary means for collective regulation is through RFMOs, which have the mandate to impose legally binding fisheries conservation and management measures on their members. The Fish Stocks Agreement designates RFMOs as the preferred vehicles for the conservation and management of straddling fish stocks (i.e. stocks occurring within the maritime zones of one or more coastal states and on the high seas) and highly migratory fish stocks (e.g. tuna).

9.4.2 RFMO/As

There are at present no generally accepted definitions for the concepts of an RFMO or a regional fisheries management arrangement (RFMA). While no definitions are included in the LOS Convention for either concept, Article 1(1)(d) of the Fish Stocks Agreement nevertheless defines an RFMA as

> a cooperative mechanism established in accordance with the [LOS] Convention and this Agreement by two or more States for the purpose, *inter alia*, of establishing conservation and management measures in a subregion or region for one or more straddling fish stocks or highly migratory fish stocks.

A noteworthy feature of this definition is that an RFMA can also have just two participating states (or entities), and does not necessarily have to be established pursuant to a legally binding instrument. Moreover, the concepts of an RFMO and an RFMA are not exclusively used in relation to straddling and highly migratory fish stocks, but also for other categories of fish stocks, such as anadromous, shared and discrete high seas fish stocks.[74]

In view of this chapter's focus on participation, attention is only devoted to RFMO/As whose regulatory areas include areas of high seas or consist entirely of high seas. As determined by this author elsewhere,[75] there are at present five "tuna RFMOs" and 11 "non-tuna RFMO/As" – which manage straddling fish stocks and discrete high seas fish stocks – as listed in Table 9.1. As the CAOF Agreement is arguably an RFMA (see subsection 9.5.5), it is included in Table 9.1 as well, even though it had not yet entered into force by the time of writing. Four of the 11 non-tuna RFMO/As are regarded as RFMAs, including the CAOF Agreement. One of these has a Conference of the Parties (COP), and two a MOP as the main

74 See Molenaar, *supra* note 5, at 441–445 for a more comprehensive discussion.

75 Erik J. Molenaar (2019) "Participation in Regional Fisheries Management Organizations", in *Strengthening International Fisheries Law in an Era of Changing Oceans* edited by Richard Caddell and Erik J. Molenaar. Hart Publishing, Oxford: pp. 103–129.

Table 9.1 Selected RFMOs and RFMAs

Acronym	*Name in full*	*Constitutive instrument*
Tuna RFMOs		
CCSBT	Commission for the Conservation of Southern Bluefin Tuna	CCSBT Convention
IATTC	Inter-American Tropical Tuna Commission	IATTC Convention
ICCAT	International Commission on the Conservation of Atlantic Tunas	ICCAT Convention
IOTC	Indian Ocean Tuna Commission	IOTC Agreement
WCPFC	Western and Central Pacific Fisheries Commission	WCPF Convention
Non-Tuna RFMOs		
CCAMLR	Commission for the Conservation of Antarctic Marine Living Resources	CAMLR Convention
GFCM	General Fisheries Commission for the Mediterranean	GFCM Agreement
NAFO	Northwest Atlantic Fisheries Organization	NAFO Convention
NEAFC	North-East Atlantic Fisheries Commission	NEAFC Convention
NPFC	North Pacific Fisheries Commission	NPFC Convention
SEAFO	South East Atlantic Fisheries Organization	SEAFO Convention
SPRFMO	South Pacific Regional Fisheries Management Organization	SPRFMO Convention
Non-Tuna RFMAs		
CAOF Agreement	Agreement to Prevent Unregulated High Seas Fisheries in the Central Arctic Ocean (MOP)	CAOF Agreement
CBS Convention	Convention on the Conservation and Management of Pollock Resources in the Central Bering Sea (COP)	CBS Convention
JNRFC	Joint Norwegian Russian Fisheries Commission	JNRFC Agreement
SIOFA	Southern Indian Ocean Fisheries Agreement (MOP)	SIOFA

decision-making body. The fourth – JNRFC – seems to be regarded as an RFMA by its two Members, even though they named it a “Commission”.[76]

For the remainder of this chapter, references to RFMOs are meant to include RFMAs, unless indicated otherwise.

76 Molenaar, *supra* note 5, at 443.

9.4.3 Aspects relating to participation in RFMOs

Neither the LOS Convention nor the 1958 High Seas Fisheries Convention[77] explicitly mention a right of states – whether in their capacity as coastal states, states fishing on the high seas, or otherwise – to participate in existing regional fisheries bodies. As regards the LOS Convention, however, such a right could to some extent be inferred from various provisions.[78]

Article 8(3) of the Fish Stocks Agreement contains an explicit right for "States having a real interest in the fisheries concerned" to become members of an existing RFMO. As this right is preceded in the same paragraph by an obligation for "States fishing for the stocks on the high seas and relevant coastal States' to become members of such RFMOs, these states can be presumed to have a real interest. It seems reasonable to assume that the decision to include the requirement of a real interest was motivated by a desire to exclude states without it. This might have been inspired by the lack of any substantive restrictions on membership of the IWC,[79] which has resulted in a situation where whaling states are often outnumbered by "non-user States".[80] In the context of this chapter on marine capture fisheries, non-user states refer to states that are mainly concerned with strengthening an RFMO's performance on conservation in general, or minimising the impacts of fishing on (iconic) non-target species or ecosystems in particular. Another category of states that existing members of RFMOs can be expected to be inclined to exclude are so-called "new entrants", namely states that are not presently fishing but would like to do so.[81]

Whereas Article 8(3) applies to existing RFMOs, Articles 8(5) and 9(2) of the Fish Stocks Agreement apply to the establishment of new RFMOs. In case of a "particular straddling fish stock or highly migratory fish stock" for which no existing RFMO can establish conservation and management measures, Article 8(5) requires "relevant coastal States and States fishing on the high seas" to cooperate to establish such an RFMO. Once these states have commenced such cooperation, they are required pursuant to Article 9(2) to "inform other States which they are aware have a real interest in the work of the proposed [RFMO] of such cooperation". While this could mean non-user states or new entrants, it may also relate to coastal states and states fishing on the high seas that are not yet involved in the negotiations. Attention should finally be drawn to the words

77 Convention on the High Seas, Geneva, adopted 29 April 1958 and entered into force 30 September 1962, *United Nations Treaty Series* 450: 11.

78 E.g. based on the phrase "with participation by all States concerned" included in Arts 61(5) and 119(2).

79 Arts III(1) and X(2) of the International Convention for the Regulation of Whaling (ICRW) adopted 2 December 1946 and entered into force 10 November 1948, *United Nations Treaty Series* 161: 72, as amended; consolidated version available at iwc.int.

80 Erik J. Molenaar (2000) "The Concept of 'Real Interest' and Other Aspects of Co-operation through Regional Fisheries Management Mechanisms" *International Journal of Marine and Coastal Law* 15: 475–531, at 496.

81 Ibid. On new entrants more in general, see Andrew Serdy (2015) *The New Entrants Problem in International Fisheries Law*. Cambridge University Press, Cambridge.

"inform" and "in the work of", which were apparently preferred above an invitation to participate in the (negotiation of) the establishment of the RFMO.[82]

As the Fish Stocks Agreement's inclusion of the requirement of a real interest constrains the freedom of high seas fishing, this raises the question as to whether this is consistent with the LOS Convention, as required by Article 4 of the Fish Stocks Agreement. Moreover, even though the Fish Stocks Agreement does not explicitly give RFMOs competence to determine whether or not an applicant for membership meets the requirement of real interest,[83] the constitutive instruments of several RFMOs that were already in existence during the negotiation of the Fish Stocks Agreement contained restrictions on membership and gave these RFMOs competence to approve or reject (further: approval role) applications for accession and/or membership.[84] It would therefore not have been difficult to imagine that new RFMOs would follow in their footsteps – if only due to overlaps in participation – and impose similar restrictions on membership and/or claim such an approval role. Furthermore, as the Fish Stocks Agreement lacks a definition of the requirement of real interest and any guidance as to how it should be applied, it is not able to ensure some level of inter-regional uniformity. So far, the (Resumed) Fish Stocks Agreement Review Conferences have not been used for this purpose either.[85]

9.5 The CAOF Agreement

9.5.1 Structure and institutions

As shown in Table 9.2, the CAOF Agreement is a relatively short treaty and consists of a Preamble, 15 articles and the usual wording on the date of signature and official languages.[86] The titles of the 15 articles reveal that only the first four articles are really substantive. Articles 5 and 6 could be categorised as procedural/institutional, and Articles 9–15 are in many treaties often grouped together as "Final Provisions".

The principal decision-making body under the CAOF Agreement is the MOP, which shall be held at least once every two years.[87] At least two months before

82 See also Molenaar, *supra* note 80, at 495–496, 513 and 522.

83 Art. 11 of the Fish Stocks Agreement does not deal with membership of RFMOs as such, but only with the "nature and extent of participatory rights'.

84 E.g. Art. 20(4) of Convention on Future Multilateral Cooperation in the North-East Atlantic Fisheries (NEAFC Convention), signed 18 November 1980 and entered into force 17 March 1982, *United Nations Treaties Series* 1285: 129, as amended; consolidated version available at www.neafc.org. Pursuant to the predecessor of the current NAFO Convention (*supra* note 45) – any state could accede (cf. Art. XXII(4)) but membership of the Fisheries Commission – then also the main management body under the NAFO Convention – was reserved to Contracting Parties already participating in the fisheries or those that have provided satisfactory evidence that they expect to participate in the fisheries within a certain time (Art. XIII(1)).

85 See www.un.org/depts/los/convention_agreements/review_conf_fish_stocks.htm.

86 On the official languages, see *supra* note 3 and accompanying text.

87 Art. 5(1).

Table 9.2 Structure of the CAOF Agreement

	Preamble
Art. 1	Use of Terms
Art. 2	Objective of this Agreement
Art. 3	Interim Conservation and Management Measures Concerning Fishing
Art. 4	Joint Program of Scientific Research and Monitoring
Art. 5	Review and Further Implementation
Art. 6	Decision-Making
Art. 7	Dispute Settlement
Art. 8	Non-Parties
Art. 9	Signature
Art. 10	Accession
Art. 11	Entry into Force
Art. 12	Withdrawal
Art. 13	Duration of this Agreement
Art. 14	Relation to Other Agreements
Art. 15	Depositary
	Date of signature and authentic texts

MOPs, the parties will convene "joint scientific meetings",[88] which will formalise the FiSCAO meetings that have been held so far.[89] Furthermore, MOPs may "form committees or similar bodies in which representatives of Arctic communities, including Arctic indigenous peoples, may participate".[90]

9.5.2 CAOF Agreement Area

A definition of the geographical scope of the CAOF Agreement was regarded as necessary during the Five-plus-Five process; above all to clarify that the three other high seas pockets in the marine Arctic (see section 9.2) are not included. The Oslo Declaration defines its geographical scope as:

> the single high seas portion of the central Arctic Ocean that is entirely surrounded by waters under the fisheries jurisdiction of Canada, the Kingdom of Denmark in respect of Greenland, the Kingdom of Norway, the Russian Federation and the United States of America

The delegations in the Five-plus-Five eventually agreed to include a definition in Article 1 entitled "Use of terms". The chapeau to this provision reads "For the purposes of this Agreement" and is followed by:

> (a) "Agreement Area" means the single high seas portion of the central Arctic Ocean that is surrounded by waters within which Canada, the Kingdom of

88 Art. 4(6).
89 See *supra* note 7.
90 Art. 5(2).

Denmark in respect of Greenland, the Kingdom of Norway, the Russian Federation and the United States of America exercise fisheries jurisdiction;

While there are similarities between the two definitions, there are also differences. Both definitions combine the clarification of the geographical scope of the CAOF Agreement with compromise wording that safeguards positions held by states in relation to the unresolved dispute on the spatial scope of the Spitsbergen Treaty.[91] A proposal by one of the Other Five which would have avoided all sensitive terminology related to this dispute entirely – namely: "The single high seas portion of the central Arctic Ocean that surrounds the geographical North Pole" – did not secure sufficient support. This may be because some of the Arctic Five wanted to be specifically mentioned, and their status as central Arctic Ocean coastal states thereby explicitly highlighted and recognised.

The Arctic Five eventually agreed to include the wording "waters under the fisheries jurisdiction" in the Oslo Declaration to safeguard their positions on the dispute on the spatial scope of the Spitsbergen Treaty. This wording could not be agreed in the subsequent Five-plus-Five process as it was not acceptable to one of the Other Five and no longer acceptable to one of the Arctic Five. Moving the definition from a separate provision to the list of definitions – thereby limiting its application exclusively to the CAOF Agreement – and including a broad non-prejudice clause in Article 14(2) of the CAOF Agreement[92] were insufficient to persuade them. One possible explanation is that (parts of) the current administrations of these two states take the view that Norway cannot exercise any coastal state jurisdiction seaward of the outer limit of its territorial sea around Svalbard. If so, they would regard these waters and their underlying seabed as high seas and the Area, whereas Norway has established a Fisheries Protection Zone (FPZ) beyond its territorial sea around Svalbard and treats the seabed as part of its continental shelf. It is submitted, however, that the wording eventually agreed on – "waters within which [...] exercise fisheries jurisdiction" – does not necessarily strengthen the positions of these states – or weaken Norway's position – in comparison with the wording of the Oslo Declaration.

As shown in Figure 9.3, the geographical scope of the Oslo Declaration as well as the CAOF Agreement create a geographical overlap with the Convention Area of the North-East Atlantic Fisheries Commission (NEAFC).[93] The overlap was discussed during the early stages of the Five-plus-Five process, but no delegation felt strongly about avoiding it.

91 See *supra* note 13. For a discussion see Erik J. Molenaar (2012) "Fisheries Regulation in the Maritime Zones of Svalbard" *The International Journal of Marine and Coastal Law* 27: 3–58.

92 Which reads: "Nothing in this Agreement shall prejudice the positions of any Party with respect to its rights and obligations under international agreements and its positions with respect to any question relating to the law of the sea, including with respect to any position relating to the exercise of rights and jurisdiction in the Arctic Ocean."

93 Art. 1(a) of the NEAFC Convention, *supra* note 84.

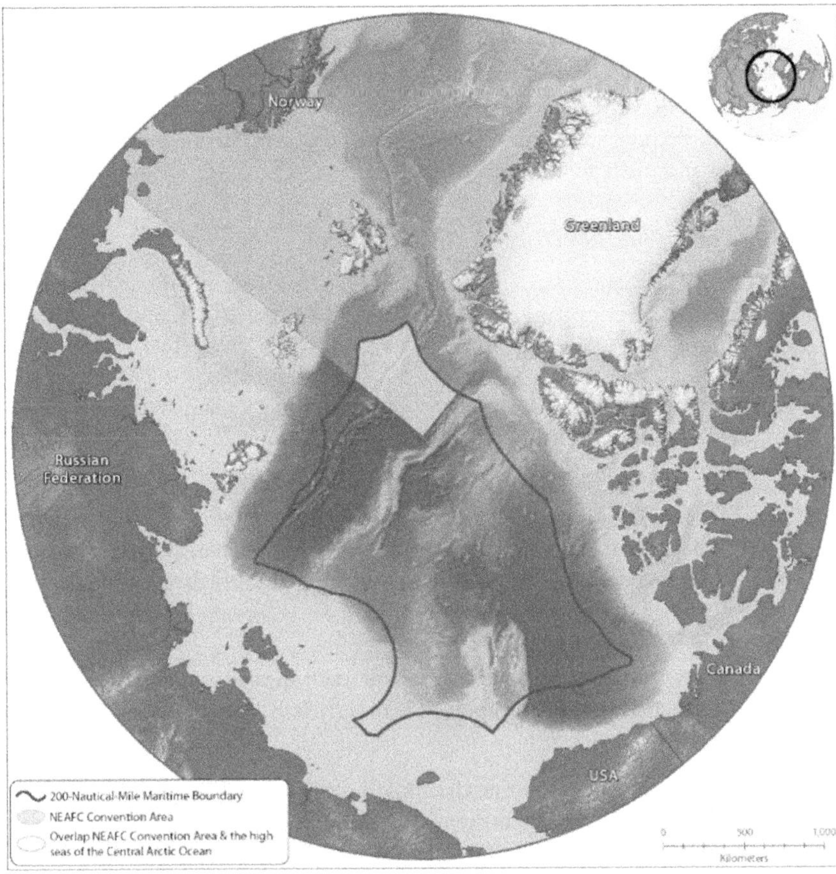

Figure 9.3 The high seas portion of the central Arctic Ocean and the NEAFC Convention Area

Source: Map used with permission of the Pew Charitable Trusts.

From the perspective of substantive fisheries regulation, a geographical overlap with the NEAFC Convention Area nevertheless poses a risk of inconsistencies between, on the one hand, the NEAFC Convention and NEAFC's recommendations and other decisions, and, on the other hand, the CAOF Agreement and the MOP's conservation and management measures, and other decisions. Examples in this regard are commercial and exploratory fishing pursuant to Article 3(1)(b) and (3) of the CAOF Agreement (see next subsection) in the "NEAFC/CAOF overlap area". If such fishing would be conducted by vessels flying the flag of a state that is not a NEAFC member and also does not have the status of Cooperating Non-Contracting Party with NEAFC, this would be "presumed to be undermining the effectiveness of" NEAFC Recommendations, resulting in the vessels being placed on NEAFC's Illegal, Unreported and Unregulated (IUU)

Vessel List.[94] It is worth emphasising that this is not a hypothetical issue as overlap areas between RFMO/As are by no means unique and have also caused actual problems.[95] Whereas Article 14(4) of the CAOF Agreement contains a conflict cause that also applies to the relationship between the CAOF Agreement and the NEAFC Convention,[96] it may be opportune for the MOP under the CAOF Agreement to exclude the "NEAFC/CAOF overlap area" from some or all of its conservation and management measures.

9.5.3 Key interim measures

The CAOF Agreement's key interim fisheries conservation and management measures are included in paragraphs (1) and (3) of Article 3,[97] and are formulated as follows:

> 1. Each Party shall authorize vessels entitled to fly its flag to conduct commercial fishing in the Agreement Area only pursuant to:
>
>   (a) conservation and management measures for the sustainable management of fish stocks adopted by one or more regional or subregional fisheries management organizations or arrangements, that have been or may be established and are operated in accordance with international law to manage such fishing in accordance with recognized international standards, or
>   (b) interim conservation and management measures that may be established by the Parties pursuant to Article 5, paragraph 1(c)(ii).
>
>   [....]
>
> 3. A Party may authorize vessels entitled to fly its flag to carry out exploratory fishing in the Agreement Area only pursuant to conservation and management measures established by the Parties on the basis of Article 5, paragraph 1(d).

Commercial fishing[98] is therefore governed by paragraph (1) and exploratory fishing[99] by paragraph (3). Paragraph (1)(a) – which is modelled on similar text included

94 Cf. Art. 44 of the NEAFC Scheme of Control and Enforcement 2018.
95 Examples in this regard are the IATTC-WCPFC overlap area and the even larger but undefined geographical overlap between CCAMLR and CCSBT due to the latter not having a geographically defined mandate (for a discussion see Rosemary Rayfuse (2019) "Climate Change and International Fisheries" in *Strengthening International Fisheries Law in an Era of Changing Oceans*, *supra* note 75 pp. 247–268.
96 It reads: "This Agreement shall not alter the rights and obligations of any Party that arise from other agreements compatible with this Agreement and that do not affect the enjoyment by other Parties of their rights or the performance of their obligations under this Agreement. This Agreement shall neither undermine nor conflict with the role and mandate of any existing international mechanism relating to fisheries management."
97 Para. (4) deals with "scientific research activities involving the catching of fish".
98 Defined in Art. 1(d) as "fishing for commercial purposes".
99 Defined in Art. 1(e) as "fishing for the purpose of assessing the sustainability and feasibility of future commercial fisheries by contributing to scientific data relating to such fisheries".

in the Oslo Declaration – and paragraph (1)(b) do not establish a general ban, moratorium or freeze of fishing effort, but a qualified abstention from commercial fishing on the high seas portion of the central Arctic Ocean. There are three exceptions to this abstention. The first concerns commercial fishing pursuant to existing RFMO/As. While there was consensus among the Five-plus-Five that NEAFC qualifies as an RFMO, some delegations were not convinced that Joint Norwegian Russian Fisheries Commission (JNRFC)[100] also qualifies as an RFMO or RFMA. The phrase "established and are operated in accordance with international law" was proposed by these delegations in furtherance of their positions and their associated concern that fishing by Norwegian and Russian vessels under the auspices of JNRFC in the high seas portion of the central Arctic Ocean would constitute an exception from the abstention.[101]

The second exception relates to commercial fishing under the auspices of future RFMO/As. This is a reflection of the so-called "stepwise" approach, according to which the CAOF Agreement has in principle an interim nature and is intended to be replaced by one or more RFMO/As sometime in the future. The stepwise approach is also reflected in Article 2 "Objective of this Agreement"[102] and various other provisions.[103] The establishment of one or more of such RFMO/As would then lead to a complete or partial termination (or "lifting") of the abstention, or the termination of the CAOF Agreement in its entirety, either by not extending its duration or otherwise.[104]

The third exception relates to commercial fishing under the auspices of the MOP under the CAOF Agreement. Once the MOP has agreed to commence negotiations to establish one or more RFMO/As, Articles 3(1)(b) and 5(1)(c)(ii) authorise it to adopt interim conservation and management measures on commercial fishing. This recognises that it may take a considerable number of years to conclude before negotiations to establish an RFMO/A are concluded and the RFMO/A is also formally established.

As regards exploratory fishing, paragraph (3) of Article 3 entitles parties to authorise their vessels to conduct such fishing, provided this occurs "pursuant to" conservation and management measures adopted by the MOP on the basis of Article 5(1)(d). These measures – which are to be adopted within three years of the entry into force of the CAOF Agreement – must meet various conditions (e.g. that "exploratory fishing shall be limited in duration, scope and scale to minimize impacts on fish stocks and ecosystems"[105]). Article 5(1)

100 Agreement between the Government of the Kingdom of Norway and the Government of the Union of Soviet Socialist Republics on Co-operation in the Fishing Industry (JNRFC), signed and entered into force 11 April 1975, *United Nations Treaty Series* 983: 7.

101 Note also that the preambular paragraph starting with "Underlining the importance" explicitly mentions NEAFC but not JNRFC or any other regional fisheries bodies, and also contains the phrase "established [...] international law".

102 Which reads: "The objective of this Agreement is to prevent unregulated fishing in the high seas portion of the central Arctic Ocean through the application of precautionary conservation and management measures as part of a long-term strategy to safeguard healthy marine ecosystems and to ensure the conservation and sustainable use of fish stocks."

103 In particular Arts 5(1)(c) and 14(3).

104 See paras (2) and (3) of Art. 13.

105 Art. 5(1)(d)(ii).

(d)(ii) stipulates that "a Party may authorize exploratory fishing only after it has notified the other Parties of its plans for such fishing and it has provided other Parties an opportunity to comment on those plans". Instead of this duty of notification combined with limited review, some delegations proposed that specific authorisations on exploratory fishing would need prior approval by the MOP. This proposal failed to attract sufficient support, however.

9.5.4 Decision-making, entry into force and duration

It is submitted that the Chairman's Compromise Proposal of 23 March 2017[106] following the fifth meeting sought to offer a package-deal on three key unresolved issues: the CAOF Agreement Area, decision-making and the Agreement's entry into force. While the first issue – discussed in subsection 9.5.2 – largely stands by itself, the latter two are interconnected as both mainly revolve around the role of the Arctic Five.

As regards decision-making, the negotiations had converged to multiple decision-making procedures towards the end of the fifth meeting. Decisions on questions of substance would, in the absence of consensus, be made by a three-quarters majority including at least three of the Arctic Five. A separate decision-making procedure would be applied to the scenario of commercial fishing once the parties had decided to commence negotiations to establish one or more RFMO/As (see previous subsection). In such a scenario, the commencement of commercial fishing could be delayed for a period of up to two years at the request of a particularly affected coastal state. As became clear very early on during the sixth meeting, however, these arrangements no longer enjoyed sufficient support, as one of the Arctic Five demanded a veto for the Arctic Five and some of the Other Five rejected any special role of the Arctic Five in decision-making whatsoever, among other things in light of their concerns on creeping coastal state jurisdiction (see section 9.3). During the last hours of the sixth meeting, the delegations agreed on one single decision-making procedure for all matters of substance – i.e. consensus decision-making – as part of a package deal on decision-making, entry into force and the Agreement's duration. The package deal's element on decision-making is laid down in Article 6 of the CAOF Agreement.

As regards entry into force, at the end of the fifth meeting almost all delegations were prepared to accept that entry into force would not only require formal adherence – encompassing ratification, acceptance, approval or accession – by a qualified majority of all the participants, but also by a certain number of the Arctic Five. Some of the Arctic Five nevertheless insisted that the CAOF Agreement could not enter into force without formal adherence by all of the Arctic Five; thereby granting each of them a *de facto* veto on entry into force. At the fifth meeting, one of the Other Five proposed a compromise that would have given the Arctic Five a period of six years from the ceremony of signature to formally adhere. If not all had done so by then, only the requirement of a qualified majority among all participants would remain.[107] As some of the Arctic Five continued

106 On file with author.

107 Similar arrangements are included in Art. 38 of the Convention on the Conservation and Management of High Seas Fishery Resources in the South Pacific Ocean (SPRFMO Convention),

to insist on having a *de facto* veto on entry into force until the very final stages of the sixth meeting, and some of the Other Five could not accept this due to their concerns on creeping coastal state jurisdiction, one of the Other Five suggested that a compromise proposal could be to require formal adherence by all participants before the Agreement could enter into force. While making this suggestion, that delegation nevertheless made it clear that it preferred its previous compromise proposal. In the end, however, the delegations opted for the latter suggestion as part of the package deal on decision-making, entry into force and the Agreement's duration. The package deal's element on entry into force is laid down in Article 11(1) of the CAOF Agreement.

It is worth highlighting that the CAOF Agreement's requirement on entry into force is quite exceptional in the domain of international fisheries law. Of the 15 other RFMO/As listed in subsection 9.4.2, only two have the same requirement; namely CCSBT and JNRFC.[108] However, as the negotiations to establish these RFMO/As involved only three and two states respectively, such a requirement is also understandable. The requirements on entry into force did not prove difficult to satisfy for CCSBT and JNRFC, but this may well be different for the CAOF Agreement due to the much larger number of instruments of formal adherences needed. The CAOF Agreement's entry into force could not just take a considerable period of time, but a scenario of non-entry into force should not be ruled out either. This scenario eventually materialised in the case of the controversial Galapagos Agreement[109] – negotiated by Chile, Colombia, Ecuador and Peru – and eventually led to the negotiation and establishment of SPRFMO.[110] It is finally worth emphasising that while the three treaties negotiated under the auspices of the Arctic Council[111] all require formal adherence by all participants as a condition for entry into force, this was not used as a source of inspiration for the EU's proposal during the Five-plus-Five process.

The idea of having a "sunset clause" or some other limitation on the duration of the CAOF Agreement had been floated in advance of the sixth meeting. As all delegations in the Five-plus-Five process were fully aware that the landmark adoption of the Ross Sea region marine protected area within CCAMLR in October 2016 was to a significant extent attributable to its period of designation,[112]

---

signed 14 November 2009 and entered into force 24 August 2012, www.sprfmo.int; and Art. 36 of the Convention on the Conservation and Management of Highly Migratory Fish Stocks in the Western and Central Pacific Ocean (WCPFC Convention), signed 5 September 2000 and entered into force 19 June 2004, *United Nations Treaty Series* 2275: 43.

108 See Art. 17(2) of the Convention for the Conservation of Southern Bluefin Tuna (CCBST Convention), signed 10 May 1993 and entered into force 20 May 1994, *United Nations Treaty Series* 1819: 360; and Art. VI of the JNRFC Agreement, *supra* note 100.

109 Framework Agreement for the Conservation of the Living Marine Resources on the High Seas of the Southeast Pacific, signed 14 August 2000, not in force, *Law of the Sea Bulletin* 45 (2001): 70–78.

110 See Erik J. Molenaar (2005) "Addressing Regulatory Gaps in High Seas Fisheries" *International Journal of Marine and Coastal Law* 20: 543–544 and 547 (in particular fn. 60).

111 See *supra* notes 63–65.

112 See CCAMLR Conservation Measure 91–05 (2016), at paras 20 and 21. www.ccamlr.org/en/measure-91-05-2016

there can be no doubt that it also contributed to floating a similar idea in the Five-plus-Five process. Experience with the substantive and procedural conditions for re-commencing fishing for pollock in the Donut Hole (see section 9.3) are certain to have been in the minds of the participants of the Five-plus-Five process as well; and possibly even the experience with the substantive and procedural conditions for re-commencing commercial whaling.

Support for some sort of sunset clause quickly spread at the sixth meeting once progress on decision-making stalled. Discussion centred above all on the length of the initial period of duration and the procedure by which duration could be extended. Proposals on the initial period of duration ranged from 10 to 30 years. The delegations that favoured a longer initial period were eventually prepared to settle for 16 years once agreement had in principle been reached on the requirements for entry into force. Their assumption was that as the CAOF Agreement's entry into force would take a considerable period of time, this amounted to a *de facto* extension of the initial period of duration.

As regards the procedure for extension, the main proposals were: (a) extension by means of a consensus decision; (b) automatic extension unless a qualified majority supports the termination of the Agreement; and (c) automatic extension unless any party formally objects. Option (b) would have enabled a minority – presumably from the Arctic Five – to extend the Agreement indefinitely, and was therefore unacceptable to the Other Five. The difference between options (a) and (c) may perhaps appear cosmetic at first sight. However, as option (a) is framed as a group decision but option (c) as an individual decision, the latter was less attractive to the delegations of the Other Five because they anticipated that they would be more likely to support discontinuing extension at some time in the future than the Arctic Five. Blocking extension of an exceptionally precautionary fisheries agreement such as the CAOF Agreement will not be an easy step to take as it will not be received well by the international community generally and by environmental NGOs in particular. As part of the above-mentioned package deal, however, the delegations agreed on option (c) with five-year extension period(s) and an initial period of duration of 16 years following the Agreement's entry into force. This element of the package deal is included in Article 13 of the Agreement. Finally, reference should be made to Article 12 of the Agreement, which contains each party's right to withdraw from the Agreement by means of a written notification to the depositary.

9.5.5 *Nature of the Agreement*

The "nature" of the CAOF Agreement can be understood in different ways. First, in terms of its legal status under international law, it is clear that the CAOF Agreement is a legally binding instrument. Consensus on the legal status of the outcome of the Five-plus-Five process only materialised at the last meeting.[113]

113 See, for instance, the phrase "in the format of a legally binding agreement" in the Chairman's Statements of the fourth and fifth Meetings.

Up until then, Russia consistently emphasised that it did not necessarily prefer a legally binding outcome above a non-legally binding outcome. One would have thought that the package deal of the Chairman's Compromise Proposal of 23 March 2017 – namely: abstention from commercial high seas fishing for what could be presumed to be a considerable number of years, and without any real restrictions on fishing in coastal state maritime zones – would have been a very successful result for Russia. However, after three delegations had formally accepted the Compromise Proposal, the ambiguous response by Russia was interpreted as a rejection by other delegations, thus making a further round of negotiations inevitable.

The successful conclusion of the negotiations at the sixth meeting with substantive agreement among all delegations on a text of a legally binding instrument puts things in a different perspective; at least for the time being. It suggests that Russia pursued a deliberate negotiation strategy aimed at maximising concessions from other delegations as these were aware that non-participation in a future CAOF Agreement by the "largest" central Arctic Ocean coastal state – measured by the size of adjacent coastal state maritime zones – would be highly problematic in terms of the Agreement's effectiveness and legitimacy. On the other hand, Russia may also have realised that its non-participation in an exceptionally precautionary fisheries agreement would reflect unfavourably on its reputation, and would have barred it from having any control on individual decisions of the MOP as well as the wider evolution of the CAOF Agreement.

As alluded to already, however, words of caution are in order, as some time will pass until the full extent of Russia's support for the CAOF Agreement can be ascertained. Although Russia signed the CAOF Agreement on 3 October 2018, it remains to be seen if Russia actually ratifies or accedes to the Agreement. As explained in the previous subsection, the significance of this is difficult to downplay because the CAOF Agreement can only enter into force once all the Five-plus-Five formally adhere to it. Ultimately, therefore, only the entry into force of the CAOF Agreement can dismiss speculations about Russia's preference for a role of JNRFC in the high seas portion of the central Arctic Ocean, or its fundamental objections to granting non-Arctic states and entities a role in Arctic governance that is formally equal to the role of Arctic states.

The nature of the CAOF Agreement can also be characterised in terms of its restrictions on high seas fishing. As argued in subsection 9.5.3, the CAOF Agreement should be regarded as a qualified abstention from high seas fishing, rather than a general ban, moratorium or freeze of fishing effort. In light of the exceptions to the abstention from commercial fishing, the ability to engage in exploratory fishing pursuant to the MOP's conservation and management measures – provided there is consensus to adopt these, despite the three-year timeframe stipulated in Article 5(1)(d) – and the complex arrangements on the duration of the Agreement, it is not possible to classify the abstention as entirely indefinite or entirely temporary. However, as extension of duration can be discontinued by one single party, it is more convincing to classify it as temporary. This view is supported by the stepwise approach reflected in the CAOF Agreement, according to which the Agreement has in principle an interim nature and is intended to be replaced by one or more RFMO/As sometime in the future.[114]

The fact that the abstention is best regarded as qualified and temporary does not diminish its significance for the legal regime of the high seas, however. Making the commencement of commercial and exploratory fishing on the high seas portion of the central Arctic Ocean conditional on obtaining prior approval by the MOP can be regarded as an important step in the post-World War II process of the gradual transformation of the freedom of the high seas as originally postulated by Grotius, into an increasingly conditional freedom. Important other recent steps in this process are the restrictions on bottom fishing on the high seas – in particular in areas that have not been subjected to bottom fishing before[115] – and the inclusion of environmental impact assessments among the agreed topics of the BBNJ process.[116] While the CAOF Agreement could be regarded as an implementation of the rationale of the obligations on new and exploratory fisheries included in Article 6(6) of the Fish Stocks Agreement – the origins of which can be traced back to CCAMLR at the end of the 1980s[117] – the scale and manner in which the CAOF Agreement does so are unparalleled and could not possibly have been contemplated during the negotiations of the Fish Stocks Agreement.

Finally, even though the Five-plus-Five did not intend to establish an RFMA and may also not regard the CAOF Agreement as such at present, there are nevertheless good arguments for categorising the CAOF Agreement as an RFMA within the meaning of the Fish Stocks Agreement. First of all, the restrictions imposed on exploratory fishing pursuant to Articles 3(3) and 5(1)(d) of the CAOF Agreement qualify as "conservation and management measures" pursuant to the definition in Article 1(1)(b) of the Fish Stocks Agreement. Second, Article 10(2) of the CAOF Agreement contains the requirement of real interest as the only substantive condition for accession (see subsection 9.5.6.1), which thereby directly implements Article 8(3) of the Fish Stocks Agreement. Third, and more importantly, in light of, *inter alia*, its Objective in Article 2, its qualified and temporary abstention from commercial high seas fishing, and its Joint Program of Scientific Research and Monitoring, the CAOF Agreement as a whole should be regarded as a "cautious conservation and management measure" in the context of the obligations in Article 6(6) of the Fish Stocks Agreement just mentioned above.

9.5.6 Participation

9.5.6.1 Participation in the Five-plus-Five process

The ten participants in the Five-plus-Five process are listed at the outset of this chapter. While the process was formally initiated by the Arctic Five – outside the

114 See *supra* note 103 and accompanying text.

115 A landmark in this regard is UNGA Resolution on Sustainable fisheries, including through the 1995 Agreement for the Implementation of the Provisions of the United Nations Convention on the Law of the Sea of 10 December 1982 relating to the Conservation and Management of Straddling Fish Stocks and Highly Migratory Fish Stocks, and related instruments, UNGA/RES/59/25 (17 November 2004), paras 57 and 66–71.

116 See *supra* note 59 and accompanying text.

117 See Caddell, *supra* note 31, at 207.

scope of the Arctic Council or another existing intergovernmental body – the leadership and perseverance of its Chair – United States Ambassador David Balton, who also chaired the Arctic Five process – played a critical role as well. Based on the Arctic Five's discussions in Nuuk in February 2014 on what was then called the "broader process", the United States invited the four other central Arctic Ocean coastal states and the Other Five to participate in what would become known as the Five-plus-Five process.

No change in participation was made since then. Apart from the EU, no other non-state actors – i.e. other intergovernmental organisations, (representatives of) Arctic indigenous peoples, or non-governmental organisations (NGOs) – participated in their own right. However, at all meetings of the Five-plus-Five process the delegations of Canada, Denmark (in respect of the Faroe Islands and Greenland) and the United States included members from the Arctic indigenous communities in those respective states. In addition, the United States delegation included a representative of the United States fishing industry and a representative of the United States environmental community.

The rationale for limiting participation to the Five-plus-Five could be the Arctic Five's belief or position – which may well be shared by the Other Five – that, at least so far, only the Five-plus-Five have a "real interest" within the meaning of Articles 8(3) and (5), and 9(2) of the Fish Stocks Agreement (see subsection 9.4.3). However, these provisions are not fully tailored to the scenario at hand. First of all, neither now nor at the outset of the Five-plus-Five process were there "particular" straddling or highly migratory fish stocks in the high seas portion of the central Arctic Ocean as envisaged in Article 8(5).

Second, neither the Arctic Five nor the Other Five took the view that the Five-plus-Five process was aimed at establishing a new RFMO/A. This would therefore render Article 9(2) non-applicable. Article 8(5) is different, however, as it also contains the phrase "enter into other appropriate arrangements". Furthermore, as argued in subsection 9.5.5, even though the Five-plus-Five did not intend to establish an RFMA and may also not regard the CAOF Agreement as such at present, there are nevertheless good arguments for categorising the CAOF Agreement as an RFMA. The ambiguity on the applicability of the requirement of real interest based on an analysis of the provisions of the Fish Stocks Agreement is nevertheless set aside by Article 10(2) of the CAOF Agreement, which reflects the agreement among the Five-plus-Five to include the requirement of real interest as the only substantive condition for accession. This must necessarily mean that the Five-plus-Five take the view that they meet this requirement as well.

As explained in section 9.2, participation of the EU and Iceland ensures representation of all Arctic states, as the EU also represents mainland Denmark, Finland and Sweden. The proximity of China, Japan and Republic of Korea to the Pacific side of the high seas portion of the central Arctic Ocean – where a commercially viable fishery is likely to be possible first – as well as the significant distant-water fleets and interests of China, the EU, Japan and Republic of Korea and their participation in most of the other RFMO/As listed in subsection 9.4.2[118] are likely to have played a role in their invitation as well. Conversely, there are no indications that

118 See Molenaar, *supra* note 75, at subsection 9.5.1.

their (*de facto*) Observer status with the Arctic Council had any relevance whatsoever. Moreover, inviting the Other Five ensures participation of all members of the overlapping NEAFC, as well as participation or representation of all parties to the "nearby" CBS Convention.[119]

This is not the case, however, for the "nearby" NAFO (Cuba and the Ukraine) and the "nearby" NPFC (Taiwan). As regards Cuba, it may not have been interested in participating anyway, among other things because there are at present no actual fisheries, and Cuba will probably not have the types of fishing vessels needed to participate in such high-latitude fisheries. Due to the events relating to the Crimea and eastern Ukraine in 2014, it can be assumed that it was highly unlikely that Russia would have supported inviting Ukraine, and this has by no means changed since then. A reason for not inviting Taiwan, despite its significant distant-water fleet, interests and capability to engage in high-latitude fishing, could be to avoid having to address the complexities associated with its disputed status under international law in the presence of China. Finally, inviting only the Other Five, and not more states and entities, may also have been motivated by the desire to ensure that the Arctic Five are not outnumbered by non-central Arctic Ocean coastal states and entities, or to keep the negotiations to a manageable size.

9.5.6.2 Participation in the CAOF Agreement

The CAOF Agreement distinguishes between two categories of participants: the nine states and the EU that participated in the negotiations on the CAOF Agreement on the one hand, and other states that could become parties to the CAOF Agreement through accession on the other hand. The first category of participants – often referred to as the "founding fathers" or "(original) signatory States" – has an unconditional right to become party to a treaty. The draft CAOF Agreement discussed during the first meeting already contained this participatory category. Paragraph (1) of Article 9 of the final text lists the ten participants, and paragraph (2) entitles those that have signed the Agreement within 12 months after the ceremony of signature to become parties through "ratification, acceptance or approval at any time". In addition, Article 10(1) provides that all ten participants have an unconditional right to accede to the CAOF Agreement even if they have not signed it.

Accession by other states and entities was not really discussed before the fourth meeting. The successive drafts of the CAOF Agreement had until then included a provision that allowed any state with an interest to accede, without according existing parties any role in that regard. No special arrangements for the

119 The EU and Iceland represent the "missing" Members of NEAFC, and China, Japan and Republic of Korea the "missing" parties to the CBS Convention (*supra* note 27). Poland is also a party to the CBS Convention but, as it is also an EU member state, it would be represented by the EU. The EU will seek to become a party to the CBS Convention "in due time" (cf. Report of the 20th (2015) COP to the CBS Convention, para. 8.1).

participation of Taiwan were included, and none were proposed since then. While several delegations were in favour of keeping the original provision on accession unchanged, the majority eventually preferred to limit accession to those states with a real interest which the parties may decide to invite to accede. The majority's view was subsequently included in the draft text used for the fifth meeting. In view of the unresolved issues on decision-making discussed in subsection 9.5.4, the draft text still contained different types of decision-making rules – consensus, simple majority and two-thirds majority – in bracketed text. Article 10(2) of the final text stipulates: "After the entry into force of this Agreement, the Parties may invite other States with a real interest to accede to this Agreement."

If any states and, if so, how many, will be invited to accede is highly speculative, except for the fact that no further central Arctic Ocean coastal states can be invited as all are already involved. This necessarily means that all accessions will increase the number of high seas fishing states and entities. Even though consensus decision-making gives the Arctic Five a *de facto* veto, it may well be that they will not feel comfortable to be (significantly) outnumbered. None of the current participants are also likely to be keen to invite high seas fishing states capable of becoming significant competitors for the resources. However, some of the Arctic Five could be favourable to inviting non-user states, and some of the Other Five could be favourable to inviting like-minded, but "relatively insignificant" high seas fishing states.[120] An example of the latter category could be the United Kingdom, if and once it has left the EU. Finally, the fact that not only the ten founding fathers are entitled to object to the extension of the duration of the CAOF Agreement pursuant to Article 13(2) – and thereby terminate the Agreement – but new parties have this entitlement as well will mean that the founding fathers will proceed with extreme caution when considering potential new parties.

9.5.6.3 Comparative analysis with participation in selected RFMO/As

The question that understandably arises after the two previous subsections is how participation in the Five-plus-Five process and the (future) CAOF Agreement compares to participation in the 15 other RFMO/As listed in subsection 9.4.2, and their negotiation processes. This comparative analysis builds on my more in-depth research on the formal rules on eligibility requirements and criteria, and procedures laid down in the selected RFMO/As' constitutive instruments or decisions, as well as the subsequent practice in relation to those rules and procedures.[121] Such practice evidently does not yet exist vis-à-vis the CAOF Agreement, as it still needs to enter info force.

Participation in the Five-plus-Five process has been more limited than the negotiation-processes of some of the selected RFMO/As (e.g. SEAFO and

120 See also Rosemary Rayfuse (2018) "Regulating Fisheries in the Central Arctic Ocean: Much Ado About Nothing?" in Niels Vestergaard, Brooks A. Kaiser, Linda Fernandez and Joan Nymand Larsen (eds), *Arctic Marine Resource Governance and Development*. Springer, Cham: 47–48.

121 See Molenaar, *supra* note 75.

SPRFMO), but more inclusive than others (e.g. NEAFC and NPFC). The number of participants (ten) is towards the upper end for non-tuna RFMO/As, and the equal number of coastal states and high seas fishing states and entities is unique. From the perspective of creeping coastal state jurisdiction discussed in section 9.3, there are certainly more troublesome RFMO/As. The negotiation processes for JNRFC, NEAFC and NPFC consisted (almost) exclusively of coastal states. Moreover, at present the membership of JNRFC and NEAFC still consists exclusively of coastal states, and NPFC so far invited only one non-coastal state to accede (Vanuatu) and dismissed the EU's request for an invitation at its 2018 Annual Meeting.

In terms of the substance of the Five-plus-Five process, the fact that the Arctic Five have not used the content of the Oslo Declaration to pursue a "take it or leave it approach" vis-à-vis the Other Five, but have given them a largely equal role – even though with the Declaration as the point of departure – reflects favourably on the openness of the Five-plus-Five process.

As regards the formal rules on eligibility requirements and criteria, the CAOF Agreement is not that unusual either. Most of the non-tuna RFMOs do not have arrangements for the participation of Taiwan, and only four of the 15 constitutive instruments of RFMO/As do not contain a founding-father criterion (GFCM, ICCAT, IOTC and JNRFC). The last really stands apart from all others, because it does not provide for accession at all. As regards GFCM and IOTC, the absence of a founding-father criterion is explained by the fact that they have been established under FAO, and are therefore at any rate open to members and associate members of FAO. It is also interesting to emphasise that founding-father criteria are by no means always fully utilised; not even for RFMOs that are relatively "closed". This concerns, for example, Cuba in relation to NEAFC, and the United Kingdom in relation to WCPFC. The costs of membership must apparently outweigh the benefits. In the case of the CAOF Agreement, however, non-utilisation of the founding-father criterion would have the far-reaching consequence of the Agreement's non-entry into force. A founding father's decision to pursue such a course will therefore be based on a very different cost–benefit analysis. Reference can here be made to the observations in subsection 9.5.5 on the uncertainty surrounding the full extent of Russia's support for the CAOF Agreement.

In addition to a requirement relating to statehood, the CAOF Agreement only contains one substantive requirement: that of real interest. It thereby uses the same terminology as the Fish Stocks Agreement and is the first constitutive instrument of an RFMO/A to do so. This is not necessarily commendable or troublesome, however. Everything will depend on the parties' practice in applying this requirement, and the perspective from which this practice is assessed. The parties have given themselves the widest possible margin of appreciation in, on the one hand, inviting non-user states and flag states engaged in fishing or wishing to do so to accede and, on the other hand, rejecting requests by the same categories of states that wish to be invited to accede. The same result could therefore also have been achieved by not including any substantive criterion at all; similar to the constitutive instruments of ICCAT and NEAFC. In terms of procedure, however, these two RFMOs are in a fundamentally different position. While ICCAT has no approval role in relation to accession (and thereby membership), accession to the NEAFC Convention[122] is only possible if an application to accede is approved by a three-quarters majority of the NEAFC members. In addition to the CAOF Agreement and NEAFC, the following RFMO/As also have an approval role in relation to accession: the CBS Convention, CCAMLR, NPFC and WCPFC.

The litmus test is nevertheless how this approval role is applied in practice, and this practice is actually quite divergent. For instance, CCAMLR members so far rejected only one of 11 applications (by the Cook Islands) but WCPFC members only invited one applicant to accede (the EU) while ignoring repeated requests to be invited by others (e.g. Ecuador, El Salvador and Vietnam). The fact that NPFC – which was only established in 2015 – admitted Vanuatu in 2017 as its first "non-founding-father member" despite the NPFC's "invitation by consensus" procedure, could be interpreted as a sign of its openness. The dismissal of the EU's request for an invitation to accede at the NPFC's subsequent Annual Meeting in 2018 casts doubts on this openness, however.

9.5.7 The role of the Arctic Five

In pursuing their rights and interests (see section 9.3), most of the Arctic Five claimed a special role for the Arctic Five in decision-making and the Agreement's entry into force (see subsection 9.5.4). In addition, the Arctic Five advocated for a reference to the Arctic Five in the Preamble to the Agreement. The first proposal for such a reference was made during the second meeting, when one of the Arctic Five proposed a reference to the Oslo Declaration. This was eventually reflected in the draft of 1 June 2016 used at the start of the third meeting, where a new preambular paragraph "notes" the Oslo Declaration.

At the third meeting, one of the Arctic Five proposed a new preambular paragraph that would underline the special role of the Arctic Five while also referring to the 2008 Ilulissat Declaration. This proposal was not included in the text used at the start of the fourth meeting, but the same Arctic state repeated it during the fourth meeting and this time received support from three others of the Arctic Five. At the same time, however, three of the Other Five opposed the proposal, noting that a reference to the Oslo Declaration was sufficient. As a compromise, the draft of 5 December 2016 included bracketed text with a reference to the "role" of the Arctic Five before a reference to the Oslo Declaration. Based on a proposal of one of the Other Five during the intersessional period, however, the draft used at the start of the fifth meeting read "initiative" instead of "role". As the Preamble was not discussed during the fifth meeting, this terminology was also included in the Chairman's Compromise Proposal of 23 March 2017.

122 *Supra* note 84 at Art. 20(4).

Very early during the sixth meeting and even though there seemed to be agreement that discussions would focus first of all on bracketed text – in particular on the three key unresolved issues, namely the CAOF Agreement Area, decision-making and the Agreement's entry into force – the Arctic state that initiated this debate at the third meeting proposed inclusion of a new preambular paragraph that would emphasise the special role of the Arctic Five with wording modelled on the Preamble to the 1973 Polar Bear Agreement.[123] After eliciting support from two others of the Arctic Five and opposition from two of the Other Five, all delegations agreed to focus first on bracketed text. Once agreement was in essence reached on the package deal on decision-making, entry into force and the Agreement's duration (see subsection 9.5.4) – literally in the last minutes of the negotiation-process – one of the Arctic Five demanded an additional reference to the Arctic Five as part of the package deal. This was supported by all of the other Arctic Five, and the Arctic state that initiated this debate at the third meeting then proposed the following text modelled on the Preamble to the 1973 Polar Bear Agreement:

> Recognizing the special responsibilities and special interests of the central Arctic Ocean coastal States in relation to the conservation and sustainable management of fish stocks in the high seas of the central Arctic Ocean;

One of the Other Five then suggested to remove the words "high seas of the". This raised no objections and thereby concluded the substantive negotiations. The amended text is included in the Preamble to the CAOF Agreement right before the reference to the Oslo Declaration, which reads as follows:

> Noting in this regard the initiative of the central Arctic Ocean coastal States as reflected in the Declaration Concerning the Prevention of Unregulated High Seas Fishing in the Central Arctic Ocean signed on 16 July 2015;

9.6 Conclusions

The CAOF Agreement is in many ways a landmark agreement. Its abstention from high seas fishing – even though qualified and temporary – ensures that such fishing will only commence after the necessary scientific research and monitoring to ensure precautionary and ecosystem-based fisheries management have been undertaken, and the associated institutional framework and substantive conservation and management measures are in place. While the CAOF Agreement could be regarded as an implementation of the rationale of the obligations relating to the application of the precautionary approach to new and exploratory fisheries included in Article 6(6) of the Fish Stocks Agreement – which were based on the

123 See the Agreement on the Conservation of Polar Bears, signed 15 November 1973 and entered into force 26 May 1976, *International Legal Materials* 13–1: 13.

pioneering work of CCAMLR in the waters adjacent to Antarctica at the end of the 1980s – the scale and manner in which the CAOF Agreement does so are unparalleled and could not possibly have been contemplated during the negotiations of the Fish Stocks Agreement.

The CAOF Agreement's significance for the legal regime of the high seas is equally noteworthy. Making the commencement of commercial and exploratory fishing on the high seas portion of the central Arctic Ocean conditional on obtaining prior approval by the MOP – the CAOF Agreement's decision-making body – can be regarded as an important step in the post-World War II process of the gradual transformation of the freedom of the high seas as originally postulated by Grotius, into an increasingly conditional freedom. The currently ongoing BBNJ negotiations are expected to continue that process.

A comparative analysis of participation in the Five-plus-Five process and the CAOF Agreement with participation in the 15 other RFMO/As listed in subsection 9.4.2 and their negotiations gives rise to three main conclusions. First, the invitation-based participation in the Five-plus-Five process was more limited than some of the negotiating processes of the 15 other RFMO/As, but more inclusive than others. Second, the number of participants (ten) is towards the upper end for non-tuna RFMO/As, and the equal number of coastal states and high seas fishing states and entities is unique. From the perspective of creeping coastal state jurisdiction discussed in section 9.3, there are certainly more troublesome RFMO/As. Third, the CAOF Agreement's eligibility requirements and criteria are not that unusual either, except that none of the 15 other RFMO/As explicitly include the substantive requirement of real interest in their constitutive instruments. This is not necessarily commendable or troublesome, however. Everything will depend on the parties' practice in applying this requirement, and the perspective from which this practice is assessed.

The negotiations on the CAOF Agreement were not only driven by the fundamentally different central Arctic Ocean fisheries interests of the Arctic Five on the one hand, and those of the Other Five on the other hand, but also by their broader interests in the domains of international fisheries law, the international law of the sea and the international law relating to the Arctic. A pertinent example of the interaction between these domains, and the multiple levels – global and regional – at which they operated, are the interactions between the BBNJ process and the Five-plus-Five process. Some of the states that participated – or were represented – in both processes were concerned about coastal state assertions in the BBNJ process relating to their special roles, interests or rights in ABNJ adjacent to their maritime zones, and the potential of these assertions to lead to multilateral creeping coastal state jurisdiction. In light of the Arctic Five's assertions of their special role and interests in the central Arctic Ocean – both during the Five-plus-Five process and before – these concerned states were determined to avoid a scenario where successful assertions in the Five-plus-Five process would be used as a precedent in the BBNJ process. Successful assertions in the Five-plus-Five process could also have meant that the "burden" of any abstention from high seas fishing would be borne only by distant water fishing states, and thereby also amount to a manifestation of creeping coastal state jurisdiction.

The willingness of China, the EU, Japan and Republic of Korea to accept the CAOF Agreement's exceptionally precautionary abstention from high seas fishing in the central Arctic Ocean, without any constraints on fishing in adjacent coastal state maritime zones at present, should also be understood in light of their interests in the domain of the international law relating to the Arctic. Given their inferior participatory status in the Arctic Council, the Arctic Council System and the new, more peripheral Arctic bodies, they had a clear interest in bringing the Five-plus-Five process to a successful conclusion, as that will offer the prospect of obtaining an equal participatory status as Arctic states in a legally binding Arctic governance instrument and its decision-making body. However, in light of Russia's lack of enthusiasm for a legally binding outcome during most of the Five-plus-Five process as well as its repeated assertions of a special role and interests of the Arctic Five and related demands for preferential rights, only time will tell if this is really acceptable to Russia. The significance of this is underscored by the fact that the CAOF Agreement can only enter into force once all of the Five-plus-Five have formally adhered to it.

Despite the efforts of most of the Arctic Five to obtain a preferential role and rights for the Arctic Five, the CAOF Agreement only contains a preambular paragraph that recognises their special responsibilities and interests. While the Arctic Five are therefore formally equal to the Other Five under the CAOF Agreement, their fundamentally different fisheries interests in the central Arctic Ocean are likely to strongly influence their participation in consensus decision-making. Optimal use of the CAOF Agreement's full potential in precautionary and ecosystem-based fisheries management will require all of the Five-plus-Five to recognise these different interests and cooperate in good faith to reach the necessary compromises. Only this can avoid the scenario of non-extension of the duration of the CAOF Agreement without one or more RFMOs/As to replace it.

10 The role of transnational knowledge networks and epistemic communities in Arctic shipping governance

Rasmus Gjedssø Bertelsen

10.1 Introduction: Arctic shipping governance adapting to global change

This chapter and research seeks to address the following questions: What is global Arctic shipping governance adapting to? What is global Arctic shipping governance? What are transnational knowledge networks and epistemic communities? What is the function of transnational knowledge networks and epistemic communities in global Arctic shipping governance?[1] A key point for this chapter is the word "adaptive". Global Arctic Shipping governance must adapt to the global environmental and social changes that are shaping the Arctic as the rest of the world: under the impact of climate change, globalisation and power transition. The Arctic is today subject to new interest which reflects changes in the international system, as the Arctic has been deeply affected by developments in the international system for centuries.[2]

This chapter will analyse and discuss the role of transnational knowledge networks and epistemic communities within countries and between countries in this process of adapting global Arctic shipping governance to global change. The research behind this chapter shows that there has been and continues to be a number of partly overlapping transnational knowledge networks within and between countries that shape thinking about Arctic shipping. These transnational knowledge networks may reach the stage of epistemic communities.

The topic of global Arctic shipping often concerns the possibility of new transit shipping routes along the Northern Sea Route (NSR), the Northwest

1 Transnational knowledge networks are here defined as cross-border networks of experts across sectors. The members do not need to share causal and principled beliefs, knowledge basis and interests as do epistemic communities. The definition of transnational knowledge networks is therefore broader and less restrictive than that of epistemic communities. Peter M. Haas (1992) "Introduction: Epistemic Communities and International Policy Coordination" *International Organization* 46–1: 1–35. I include both the more inclusive concept of transnational knowledge networks and the more restrictive concept of epistemic communities because of the variety of transnational knowledge networks mentioned in this chapter.

2 Lassi Heininen and Chris Southcott (eds) (2010) *Globalization and the Circumpolar North*. University of Alaska Press, Fairbanks.

Passage or the Transpolar Route, or it concerns destinational shipping to locations along the Northern Sea Route or more rarely the Northwest Passage. This chapter focuses on destinational shipping for Arctic natural resources. This research looks at the place of the Arctic and particularly global Arctic shipping in broader global change. It looks at how Arctic governance in general and global Arctic shipping governance in particular responds to these broader changes, and especially the role of transnational knowledge networks and epistemic communities in this adaptive Arctic governance. As such this research also seeks to provide lessons from Arctic governance from global governance and vice-versa.

There is a rich literature on the law of the sea on shipping along these sea routes.[3] The international regulatory framework together with international organisations such as the International Maritime Organization (IMO) or international fora such as the Arctic Council provides the fundamental framework for different state and non-state actors in Arctic shipping. UNCLOS sets out the rights and responsibilities of coastal states of the Arctic and the access of other states to Arctic waters. The Polar Code also regulates private actors to protect the environment, lives and vessels. This framework is the basic structure for public and private actors' expectations of other actors' actions. Within this framework remains uncertainties about both environmental (climate change and sea ice) and strategic factors of state and non-state actors' political, regulatory, economic and commercial choices inside and outside the Arctic. The Arctic is affected by rapid climate change as well as globalisation and power transition, where international law by nature evolves slower.

The global changes of climate change, globalisation and power transition puts stress on Arctic governance, also of shipping. All the Arctic Council states are members of the IMO, and many are major shipping nations. Many of the major non-Arctic shipping nations have Observer status in the Arctic Council and are IMO members. A significant problem in global Arctic shipping governance is that the Arctic Council and the IMO have no direct relationship and no mutual observer access, which is diplomatically and politically impossible. According to former IMO Secretary General Sekimizu Koji, it would be valuable for the interested Arctic and non-Arctic nations to have an alternative forum for discussing Arctic shipping.[4]

The need for such alternative fora to diplomatic fora directs the attention to transnational knowledge networks and epistemic communities cutting across borders, disciplines and sectors concerning Arctic shipping. The study of the role of knowledge, knowledge networks and the power over the formulation of

3 Robert C. Beckman, Tore Henriksen, Kristine Dalaker Kraabel, Erik J. Molenaar and J. Ashley Roach (eds) (2017) *Governance of Arctic Shipping: Balancing Rights and Interests of Arctic States and User States.* Brill, Leiden.

4 Koji Sekimizu (2017) "The Polar Code and the Contribution of Non-Arctic States in its Formation and Implementation" Keynote Speech delivered on 7 December 2017 at the Third PCRC International Symposium on the Role of Non-Arctic States/Actors in the Arctic Legal Order-making, Kobe, Japan, 7–9 December 2017.

knowledge is also a research tradition in international relations,[5] and in other fields as political science, sociology, and so on.[6]

The most prominent formal transnational knowledge network on Arctic shipping is the Protection of the Arctic Marine Environment working group (PAME) of the Arctic Council, which in 2009 published the influential Arctic Marine Shipping Assessment.[7] The various Arctic Council member states and Asian Observer states are all important shipping nations with serious national maritime strategy processes. The major non-Arctic shipping nations are Observer states to the Arctic Council, whether the large European shipping nations Germany, France, United Kingdom, Netherlands, Italy, and Spain, or the rapidly growing Asian economies of China, Japan, India, Republic of Korea and Singapore, which are the focus of this chapter. The economic growth of these Asian countries in recent decades is what is driving power transition and globalisation, which global Arctic shipping governance must adapt to. Arctic shipping has been the topic of some of this national maritime strategy work. A very important early example was the Japanese INSROP project on the Northern Sea Route between 1993 and 1999 in cooperation with a Norwegian and Russian institute. The long-term effects in terms of clear and less clear effects of the INSROP study is an interesting case for the effect of such national and to some extent transnational knowledge networks.[8] The Singapore International Maritime Center 2030 Strategic Review is an example of a new national maritime strategy process, where it is interesting to look for Arctic elements.[9]

Shipping is an international, private, legal and economic activity that involves a number of important international private actors in shipping, insurance, finance, and so on. Shipping is an activity with a significant level of risk, which has historically led to a number of risk-management practices, where knowledge plays an

5 Haas (1992), *supra* note 1, at 1–35; Emanuel Adler and Peter M. Haas (1992) "Conclusion: Epistemic Communities, World Order, and the Creation of a Reflective Research Program" *International Organization* 46–1: 367–390; Peter M. Haas (2011) "Epistemic Communities" in *International Encyclopedia of Political Science* edited by Bertrand Badie, Dirk Berg-Schlosser and Leonardo Morlino. Sage, Thousand Oaks, CA: 788–792.

6 Peter Bachrach and Morton S. Baratz (1962) "Two Faces of Power" *American Political Science Review* 56–4: 947–952; Peter Bachrach and Morton S. Baratz (1963) "Decisions and Nondecisions: An Analytical Framework" *American Political Science Review* 57–3: 632–642; Steven Lukes (1974) *Power: A Radical View*. Macmillan, London; Steven Lukes (2007) "Power and the Battle for Hearts and Minds: On the Bluntness of Soft Power" in *Power in World Politics* edited by Felix Berenskoetter and M. J. Williams. Routledge, London: 83–97.

7 Arctic Council (2009) *Arctic Marine Shipping Assessment 2009 Report*. https://oaarchive.arctic-council.org/handle/11374/54 (accessed 6 June 2018)

8 Ship and Ocean Foundation (2001) *The Northern Sea Route: The Shortest Sea Route Linking East Asia and Europe*. The Ship and Ocean Foundation, Tokyo; R. Douglas Brubaker and Claes Lykke Ragner (2010) "A Review of the International Northern Sea Route Program (INSROP) – 10 Years On" *Polar Geography* 33–1/2: 15–38.

9 Maritime and Port Authority Singapore and Maritime Singapore (2017) *The Singapore International Maritime Center 2030: Strategic Review*. Singapore: Maritime and Port Authority Singapore.

important role. Lloyd's of London has played a key role in managing risk through insurance for more than 300 years. Classification societies such as DNV GL also play a key role managing risk through knowledge. It is therefore not surprising that there are also knowledge networks around private economic actors on Arctic shipping with the purpose of managing risk. These knowledge networks are around Lloyd's, the World Economic Forum, the Arctic Economic Council and smaller think-tank initiatives such as The Arctic Institute. This chapter will outline these different knowledge networks on Arctic shipping governance. On this basis, the chapter will finish by discussing the relations between these networks and how these relations can be structured to achieve the aim of an adaptive global Arctic shipping governance.

10.2 Global changes shaping the Arctic and Arctic shipping

Arctic shipping governance is adapting to a framework of complex interacting effects of global environmental and social change. Transnational knowledge networks play a role navigating environmental and social complexities. Climate change is disproportionately impacting the Arctic and decreasing sea ice opening up areas for navigation both time and space wise.[10] Global social changes are also deeply affecting the Arctic. These are globalisation, which here is defined as the compression of time and space between societies,[11] and the twin power transition which is the shift in relative power from Western states to Eastern states and from state to non-state actors.[12] This power transition is largely driven by the strong economic growth especially in East Asia, which started with Japan's strong post-war growth and in recent decades the rise of China.[13]

This chapter emphasises destinational shipping of sailing to an Arctic destination of the Northern Sea Route or the Northwest Passage to collect Arctic oil, liquefied natural gas (LNG) or minerals.[14] The Yamal LNG projects with its enormous investments of 27 billion USD illustrates why destinational shipping is more interesting than the unrealised dreams of transit shipping between Northeast Asia and Western Europe via the Northern Sea Route, which have received disproportionate attention. The Northern Sea Route is of little relevance for

10 Arctic Climate Impact Assessment (ACIA) (2005) *Arctic Climate Impact Assessment: Impacts of a Warming Arctic*. Cambridge University Press, Cambridge; Arctic Council, *Arctic Marine Shipping Assessment 2009 Report*, *supra* note 7.

11 David Harvey (1989) *The Condition of Postmodernity: An Enquiry into the Origins of Cultural Change*. Blackwell, Oxford.

12 Joseph S. Nye Jr. (2011) *The Future of Power*. Public Affairs, New York: 300.

13 Asian Development Bank (2011) *Asia 2050: Realizing the Asian Century*. Asian Development Bank, Singapore.

14 Bloomberg (2017) "Russia Wins in Arctic After U.S. Fails to Kill Giant Gas Project" last modified 14 December 2017. www.bloomberg.com/news/articles/2017-12-14/russia-dreams-big-as-u-s-fails-to-kill-27-billion-gas-project (accessed 20 May 2018).

container transit shipping because of shallow waters and unpredictability.[15] The traditional shipping trunk line via Malacca Strait, Indian Ocean, Middle East and Mediterranean passes Asian economic and population growth centres.[16] The shorter Arctic sea routes passes practically empty lands.

China has paid a high environmental price for its phenomenal economic growth for four decades. Now, China must improve air quality in its urban centres. This sustainable development requires cutting coal-powered energy significantly towards natural gas. Shifting from coal to natural gas is also important for mitigating climate change. Arctic LNG are important sources for this switch in energy source, which connects with key questions of Arctic destinational shipping.

China, Japan and Republic of Korea have large energy security problems. They have very limited domestic energy resources and are very large importers of energy, which especially arrives by sea from the Middle East, where risk of conflict and disruption are high. The sea lanes of the world are at present dominated by the United States Navy, except the NSR. Japan and Republic of Korea are close allies of the United States (US). China is a strategic peer competitor of the US, and in a conflict with the US, it is to be expected that the US would disrupt energy supplies to China. All three very large Northeast Asian economies therefore have incentives to diversify their energy supplies. Arctic LNG providers such as Russia, Norway and possibly in the future Alaska have higher costs than the Middle East, but their political stability is so much higher.[17]

10.3 Governance: politics and knowledge in addition to law

UNCLOS and the Polar Code provide the fundamental framework of state and non-state actors' actions and expectations of others' actions in Arctic shipping, but there are complexities and uncertainties not mitigated by international law. This is where the governance role of transnational knowledge networks and epistemic communities enter. Transnational knowledge networks and epistemic communities between academia, business and government have played and

15 Kentaro Nishimoto (2017) "The Rights and Interests of Japan in regard to Arctic Shipping" in *Governance of Arctic Shipping*, *supra* note 3, at 357–378.

16 Asian Development Bank, *supra* note 13.

17 Xing Li and Rasmus Gjedssø Bertelsen (2013) "The Drivers of Chinese Arctic Interests: Political Stability and Energy and Transportation Security" *Arctic Yearbook 2013*: 1–16; Graham Allison (2017) *Destined for War: Can America and China Escape Thucydides's Trap?* Houghton Mifflin Harcourt, New York: 364; Wensheng Cao and Christoph Bluth (2013) "Challenges and Countermeasures of China's Energy Security" *Energy Policy* 53-C: 381–388; Guy C. K. Leung (2011) "China's Energy Security: Perception and Reality" *Energy Policy* 39–3: 1330–1337; Luo Yixin (2011) "Research on the Current Situations and Countermeasures for the Energy Security in China" *Energy Procedia* 5: 261–265; Zhong Xiang Zhang (2011) "China's Energy Security, the Malacca Dilemma and Responses" *Energy Policy* 39–12: 7612–7615; Xu Yi-chong (2006) "China's Energy Security" *Australian Journal of International Affairs* 60–2: 265–286.

will continue to play a central role in building and co-creating knowledge and understanding of Arctic shipping in a context of global environmental and social change. Universities may play a privileged role as neutral conveners of political or economic interests from governments and business. This section will discuss how these global changes set a framework for the Arctic and Arctic shipping. Before doing so, the section will briefly touch upon governance structures where different governance structures are interlinked in different ways, one way in knowledge and knowledge-holders connecting them as well as co-creation of knowledge in overlapping groups of knowledge-holders.

There is political and diplomatic governance. This governance is in the spheres of multilateralism, where the most important example is the IMO. There is intergovernmental governance as in the Arctic Council. And there are bilateral relations as between Japan and Russia. The political and diplomatic spheres of governance both shape and are shaped by the law of the sea. Private actors act in this framework of governance and contribute to shape it. Olav Schram Stokke points out four generic tasks of governance in general, which also apply to Arctic shipping governance.[18] These four tasks point out where transnational knowledge networks and epistemic communities play an important role supplementing the law of the sea for Arctic shipping governance under conditions of global environmental and social change. According to Stokke, the four generic tasks of governance are with my emphasis on key concepts. These four generic tasks of government speak to Haas and Adler's arguments about the role and contribution of epistemic communities in governance.[19]

First, governance provides "*knowledge* about the severity of the problem addressed by the regime and the effects of various options for dealing with it". This task of governance points directly to Haas and Adler's argument about the role of epistemic communities for mitigating complexity and uncertainty, which is discussed below. Arctic shipping on the NSR is marked by environmental and especially social complexity and uncertainty, where building common knowledge is of value.

Second, governance provides "elaboration of behavioural *norms*, whether soft-law instruments or binding rules". This generic task of governance of elaborating norms point directly to the central problem of international policy coordination under complexity and uncertainty, where actors' mutual uncertainty about other's actions are a major impediment. Discussions about NSR shipping are often characterised by lack of information and uncertainty about especially Russian policy and regulation. Creating common norms between Russia and user states and private users is therefore important for expanding use of the NSR.

18 Olav Schram Stokke (2013) "Regime Interplay in Arctic Shipping Governance: Explaining Regional Niche Selection" *International Environmental Agreements: Politics, Law and Economics* 13–1, 65–85.

19 Haas (1992), *supra* note 1, at 1–35; Adler and Haas (1992), *supra* note 5, at 367–390; Haas (2011), *supra* note 5, at 788–792.

Third, governance supports implementation through funding and capacity-building: "multilateral institutions frequently provide means for facilitating the *implementation* of such norms if some participants would otherwise be unable to heed them, for instance through funding or specific capacity-building programs". Russia and major user states and large, private shipping companies have significant resources for participating in and understanding NSR shipping. Governance through transnational knowledge networks and epistemic communities concerning Arctic shipping creates returns to scales and efficiency for engaging the question of Arctic shipping. Transnational and transdisciplinary knowledge networks and epistemic communities lower the barriers of entry for more marginal state and non-state participants. The examples discussed below will illustrate these efficiencies.

Fourth and finally, governance contributes to "*rule enforcement*, [which] is often a weak point in international governance, since structures for behavioural monitoring, compliance review, and response to rule violation may be weak or non-existent". Here, Haas and Adler's arguments about the effects of epistemic communities are particularly interesting. Epistemic communities are characterised by shared set of normative and principled beliefs (the value basis), shared causal beliefs (derived from analysis), shared notion of validity and a common policy enterprise. In the absence of other mechanisms of rule enforcement, the shared beliefs of Arctic shipping epistemic communities may make a contribution.

10.4 Global Arctic shipping governance by epistemic communities: complexity, uncertainty, interpretation, institutionalisation

Haas and Adler outline basic challenges to international policy coordination and how epistemic communities address these challenges.[20] Their general discussion is relevant to the question of Arctic shipping and the NSR in particular. The basic topic for Haas and Adler is how different state and non-state actors coordinate international policy, which is also the question concerning Arctic shipping and the NSR in particular. For international policy coordination, a central general question is: Where do expectations come from? For developing Arctic shipping and the NSR, the question becomes: Where do expectations about the behaviour and choices of different state and non-state actors come from? What shapes their mutual expectations? This is where transnational knowledge networks and epistemic communities enter.

International policy coordination in general can be challenged by *complexity*, which is the problem of *grasping interactive effects of different actors and factors*. These actors and factors can be both environmental and social. Here it is clear that there is both considerable environmental and social complexity concerning

20 Haas (1992), *supra* note 1, at 1–35; Adler and Haas (1992), *supra* note 5, at 367–390; Haas (2011), *supra* note 5, at 788–792.

Arctic shipping and using the NSR. Much attention has been devoted to the effects of climate change for opening up the NSR (as well as the Northwest Passage and eventually the Transpolar route). The global climate system is naturally a very large, complex system, which means a high degree of complexity and interactive effects in ice conditions for Arctic shipping. This complexity and uncertainty is a major challenge especially to container shipping, which is particularly dependent on reliability and regularity.

The social complexity around Arctic shipping and the NSR is no less than the environmental. The political, economic, security, legal and other factors and actors and their interactions form a global, complex system. The use of NSR depends on Russia's political, economic and security relations with both Western and Asian states, which may be determined by questions completely unrelated to the Arctic, as the Ukraine/Crimea crisis illustrates clearly. The profitability of Arctic oil and gas resources may depend on technological and policy decisions again completely unrelated to the Arctic as the shale oil and gas revolution in the US demonstrated clearly years ago. Russian policies and regulations of the NSR depend on domestic Russian political and economic developments, which are opaque to outsiders. Destinational shipping for Russian Arctic energy resources and raw materials depend on outside decisions of energy policy and energy security as well as global commodity prices, which in themselves are complex, global systems. The dream of Arctic transit shipping between East Asia and Western Europe is in itself part of a global maritime transport system comprising of myriad political, economic, technological and regulatory factors. Both the environmental and social complexity surrounding Arctic shipping point to the serious problem of *uncertainty* for international policy coordination pointed out by Haas and Adler.

The environmental and social complexities surrounding Arctic shipping create conditions of *uncertainty*, which is *strong dependence on other's choices for obtaining goals and great difficulty assessing different outcomes.* Climate change is a product of human political, economic and technological choices at global scale. The user states and non-state actors for Arctic shipping and the NSR are among the greatest sources of greenhouse gasses and those who decide the future climate development. However, the historical, current and future greenhouse gas emissions of significance are separate from the Arctic and decisions on these emissions are also separate from the Arctic in general and Arctic shipping (except the possibilities of replacing coal with Arctic natural gas). For the purposes here, climate change is assumed to be outside the complex system of Arctic shipping. Thus, climate change policy decisions by others are exogenous, which returns us to the complex social system around Arctic shipping and using the NSR.

Haas and Adler point to uncertainty based on the dependence on other's choices and the difficulty of assessing different outcomes. The law of the sea provides a certain framework for predicting other state and non-state actors' choices and predicting outcomes, which depends on assumptions of observing the law of the sea. However, there is still a wide range of choices for state and non-state actors and outcomes within the framework of the law of the sea, which creates profound uncertainty around Arctic shipping and the NSR in particular. There is persistent uncertainty about Russian policy and regulation, and there is great uncertainty about the choices of a vast range of private shipping companies and public and private investors in port infrastructure, navigational aids, chart making, and so on. The challenges of complexity and uncertainty for international policy coordination point to the question of interpretation, which brings us closer to the role of epistemic communities.

A fundamental challenge of governance is international policy coordination which can be hampered by complexity and uncertainty, which is very much the case for Arctic shipping and using the NSR. Facing complexity and uncertainty requires *interpretation* in the sense of interpreting social and physical phenomena, which here are the global environmental (climate change) and social systems surrounding Arctic shipping and using the NSR. Different state and non-state actors involved in Arctic shipping must make interpretations of how the environmental conditions (climate change and ice conditions) will develop as well as how the many other state and non-state actors affecting Arctic shipping and using the NSR will act, while everybody is trying to interpret everybody else. This interpretation points to the structure–agency question of actors interpreting their surrounding structure and (re-)creating this structure through their agency.[21] The various state and non-state actors in Arctic shipping must interpret the political, economic, legal, security and technological structure they are acting within and the policies and strategies of other actors.

Acting with those complex and uncertain structures puts a premium on *knowledge*, which is at the fundamental level of knowledge on cause and effect (both environmental and social) and understanding the level of environmental and social complexity.[22] It is also the understanding on how other state and non-state actors define their interests, formulate policies and make decisions concerning Arctic shipping and the NSR. Transnational knowledge networks and epistemic communities for sharing and co-creating this knowledge are valuable for the next step outlined by Haas and Adler.

Epistemic communities can contribute to *institutionalisation and socialisation*, which address the challenges identified above to international policy coordination. This contribution is also important concerning Arctic shipping and using the NSR as will be pointed out below by presenting state and non-state actor transnational knowledge networks and epistemic communities concerning Arctic shipping. Epistemic communities are social institutions that guide international behaviour and as such address the challenges outlined of complexity and uncertainty around others' decisions and enforcement of rules. The following sections

21 Alexander E. Wendt (1987) "The Agent–Structure Problem in International Relations Theory" *International Organization* 41: 335–370.

22 Dmitry Yumashev et al. (2017) "Towards a Balanced View of Arctic Shipping: Estimating Economic Impacts of Emissions from Increased Traffic on the Northern Sea Route" *Climatic Change* 143–1/2: 143–155.

will discuss whether the various state and non-state actor transnational knowledge networks and epistemic communities contribute to reducing complexity and uncertainty of other actors' decisions concerning Arctic shipping and the NSR, and even contribute to the enforcement of rules, which is a more difficult requirement. A common epistemic framework of knowledge and beliefs around the Arctic shipping and the use of NSR can, according to Haas and Adler, contribute to guide "rational" actions and expectations of different actors around a topic.

Such "rational" actions and expectations based on a common epistemic framework can, according to Haas and Adler, have policy implications through *policy innovation*, where the participants generate policy innovation together. This new policy is *diffused* through the epistemic community, or a wider transnational knowledge network. Policy-makers and decision-makers representing different relevant state and non-state actors may *select policies* for their organisations based on this common epistemic framework. And the shared beliefs and knowledge of the epistemic community leads to *persistence and stability* of these policies, which addresses the original challenges of international policy coordination hampered by complexity and uncertainty. The very limited transit use of the NSR despite great optimism dating back to the Japanese–Norwegian–Russian INSROP project of the 1990s may indicate that the problem of international policy coordination for transit traffic has not been solved. On the other hand, the very large (27 billion USD) investments in the Yamal LNG project and likely follow-up investments in other Russian Arctic LNG projects suggests that complexity and uncertainty have been overcome in these cases.

10.5 Arctic shipping transnational knowledge networks and epistemic communities

The map of the shorter Yokohama–Rotterdam route via the NSR rather than the trunk line of world trade via the Malacca Strait and the Suez Canal have been shown in countless popular and research presentations and publications, however with very limited effect on actual transit shipping. In contrast, especially Chinese investment in Russian Arctic LNG is developing rapidly. These observations suggest from an international policy coordination perspective that problems of complexity and uncertainty have not been solved for Arctic shipping through adequate transnational knowledge networks and epistemic communities. The research behind this chapter has looked at the landscape of Arctic shipping transnational knowledge networks and epistemic communities and shows that there is a plethora of such networks and communities at national and transnational level and connecting state or non-state actors. Below I briefly discuss the most important and most representative transnational knowledge networks, first the state-based and then non-state-actor-based networks. This brief discussion will give a quick overview of how these networks or communities seek to manage risk and mitigate complexity and uncertainty, and some limitations in doing so.

10.5.1 Arctic Council: Protection of Arctic Marine Environment working group (PAME)

Perhaps the most central epistemic community in the field of Arctic shipping based on state, and, to a certain extent, also on non state actors (indigenous communities), is the Protection of Arctic Marine Environment working group (PAME) of the Arctic Council. The Arctic Council working groups are strong examples of epistemic communities in Arctic affairs.[23] The PAME working group produced the well-known 2009 Arctic Marine Shipping Assessment,[24] which illustrates well the process of addressing complexity and uncertainty through a common epistemic framework. The outcome of such a process is logically an Arctic Marine Strategic Plan 2015–2025,[25] which indicates the progress outlined above by Haas and Adler. The PAME working group produces a number of activities and documents that illustrate its role as an epistemic community on Arctic shipping.

10.5.2 Japan: INSROP: an epistemic community on the NSR ahead of its time?

The joint programme of International Northern Sea Route Programme (INSROP) between the Japanese Ship and Ocean Foundation, Norway's Fridtjof Nansen's Institute and the Russian Central Marine Research and Design Institute (CNIIMF) between 1993 and 1999 is a very interesting example of trying to build an epistemic community to make sense of a new and complex environmental (climate change) and social (post-Cold War) system with high levels of uncertainty, but also opportunity. Nishimoto explains how Japan very early on from 1993 through the Nippon Foundation and Ship and Ocean Foundation (SOF) with FNI and CNIIMF pursued "a multi-disciplinary research programme aimed at building knowledge necessary for shipping along the NSR".[26] Nishimoto is exactly describing a transnational knowledge network and epistemic community here. Japan was as such ahead of Chinese and Korean initiatives to build knowledge on the Northern Sea Route.

The INSROP project did not produce the transit shipping it predicted and as such the project was probably ahead of its time. But a very important effect of the project was to train a generation of Japanese, Norwegian and Russian – and others – analysts and researchers to work and work together on the question of using the NSR. These analysts and researchers produced a significant number of publications and outreach.[27]

23 Timo Koivurova, Paula Kankaanpää and Adam Stepien (2015) "Innovative Environmental Protection: Lessons from the Arctic" *Journal of Environmental Law* 27–2: 285–311.

24 Arctic Council (2009) *Arctic Marine Shipping Assessment 2009 Report*, *supra* note 7.

25 Arctic Council (2015) *Arctic Marine Strategic Plan 2015–2025*. Arctic Council, Akureyri.

26 Nishimoto, *supra* note 15, at 358.

27 Ship and Ocean Foundation, *supra* note 8; Brubaker and Ragner, *supra* note 8.

The Ship and Ocean Foundation, turned Ocean Policy Research Foundation, and turned Ocean Policy Research Institute (OPIR) as part of the Sasakawa Peace Foundation, is an interesting example of a body in Japanese policy-making which makes it possible to create a Japanese national knowledge network between academia, business and government. The OPRI has in 2010 sponsored a short-lived Arctic study group. In 2014–2015, there was another short-lived study group, which gave input to the Japanese Arctic policy. From 2016, OPRI has sponsored an ongoing Japanese study group on Arctic shipping.[28] So it is clear that OPRI continues the work of building and maintaining the Japanese epistemic community on Arctic shipping and using the NSR. However, these activities are limited to Japanese state and non-state actors, so they do not contribute to building transnational epistemic communities with state and non-state actors from other Arctic and Asian countries. As such, these OPRI activities do not contribute to addressing complexity and uncertainty challenges.

10.5.3 Singapore: International Maritime Centre 2030 Strategic Review – any role for the Arctic?

Singapore is a very small state without natural resources, but holds an exceptionally important maritime position. Singapore since independence has pursued a strategy of building a highly knowledge-based and globally connected economy, especially in the maritime domain. Singapore is host to some of Asia's highest ranked universities, the National University of Singapore, the Nanyang Technical University and others. These universities work very closely with Singaporean business in this pursuit of the highly knowledge-based and globally connected Singaporean economy.

A key example of Singaporean academia–business cooperation for growing Singaporean high-knowledge-based and high-value business in the Arctic is the cooperation between the National University of Singapore and Keppel Offshore & Marine in developing Arctic offshore installations.[29] A broader Singaporean maritime cooperation is the International Maritime Centre 2030 Strategic Review which brings together government, business and academia, including the Singapore Shipping Association.[30] The strategic review is a fascinating insight

28 On 15 January 2018, the report coming out of the Arctic study group entitled "Important Arctic Challenges and Policies for Japan" has been delivered to the Minister of State for Ocean Policies. www.spf.org/opri-j/news/article_24478.html (accessed 15 May 2018, in Japanese).

29 Zhuo Chen et al. (2017) "Singapore and the Arctic: A Partnership between Academia and Business through Research & Innovation" *KOMtech Technology Review 2017*: 23–31. www.keppelom.com/en/content.aspx?sid=3625 (accessed 15 May 2018).

30 Maritime and Port Authority Singapore and Maritime Singapore (2013) *The Singapore International Maritime Center 2030: Strategic Review*, at 33. www.gov.sg/~/sgpcmedia/media_releases/mpa/press_release/P-20170922-2/attachment/IMC 2030 Strategic Report.PDF (accessed 15 May 2018).

into how one of the most sophisticated maritime centres in the world thinks strategically across government, business and research to strengthen and develop its "London+" position as a very valuable and influential centre for maritime activities. The Arctic is not mentioned in the strategic review, but it would be worthwhile further research to search for the possible role for the Arctic in the various elements of the strategic review.

10.5.4 China: the Polar Silk Road – who are the Chinese epistemic communities?

In light of China's rise and its power transitioning effects at the global stage, there is intense outside speculation about Chinese analysis, policy-making and decision-making circles and procedures, also concerning the Arctic. Outside understanding is limited both by the closed nature of Chinese politics and society and linguistic barriers for non-Chinese readers. It is clear to the outside world that the key Chinese grand strategy project currently and for the foreseeable future is the Belt and Road Initiative linking China through Central Asia and Eurasia and along the traditional maritime trunk line via the Malacca Strait and the Indian Ocean to the Middle East, East Africa and Europe.[31]

Concerning the Arctic, observers were waiting impatiently for a Chinese Arctic policy, which led to much speculation of China's interest and interests in the Arctic. This policy was published in early 2018 with few surprises. At the Arctic Circle Assembly conference in Reykjavik in October 2017, China proposed to make the NSR a Polar Silk Route component of its enormous Belt and Road Initiative grand strategy, which caught much attention. Such announcements from Chinese side raise much outside speculation of Chinese intentions, where closedness of analysis and policy- and decision-making increase complexity and uncertainty for outside actors. There are bilateral and multilateral initiatives that build such Arctic networks and communities. China and Russia have held annual bilateral Arctic dialogues since 2012, followed by occasional Sino-US and Sino-Canadian Arctic dialogues. China and Iceland signed an Arctic research agreement in 2012, which in 2013 led to the China–Nordic Arctic Research Center, a virtual research centre at the Polar Research Institute of China in Shanghai with eight Chinese and ten Nordic member institutions. China, Japan and Republic of Korea have held trilateral Arctic dialogues since 2016.[32] In light of the enormous Chinese investment in and lending to the Yamal LNG project it is clear that there must be deep government and private sector networks between China, Russia, France and Japan.[33] These networks are not visible for the public or research, which raises questions of public accountability.

31 Maximilian Mayer (ed.) (2018) *Rethinking the Silk Road: China's Belt and Road Initiative and Emerging Eurasian Relations*. Palgrave Macmillan, Basingstoke: 287.

32 Ping Su and Maximilian Mayer (2018) "Science Diplomacy and Trust Building: 'Science China' in the Arctic" *Global Policy Special Issue 2018*: 1–5.

33 Bloomberg, *supra* note 14.

10.5.5 Republic of Korea: national knowledge networks around LNG tanker building

Republic of Korea is commercially deeply involved in developing the Russian Arctic LNG resources through the construction of the 15 icebreaking LNG tankers (the Christophe de Margerie class) by Daewoo Shipbuilding & Marine Engineering (DSME) at a total worth of 4.8 billion USD.[34] From participant observation in the 3rd Korea Arctic Academy in 2017 organised by the Korea Maritime Institute and with visits to the Korea Polar Research Institute and Korea Research Institute of Ships and Ocean Engineering, it appears to me that there is a Korean national epistemic community around Arctic shipping and developing the NSR, which is reminiscent of the Japanese OPRI (legacy) activities.

10.5.6 Complexity and uncertainty around Russia's NSR policy and regulation

The key country for Arctic shipping in general and the NSR in particular is naturally Russia. However, it is also from media, literature and observation a great source of complexity and uncertainty for other state and non-state interested parties. Russia's policies and regulations concerning access for outside users and conditions for use of the NSR is the subject of intense speculation, since this greatly affects the interests of other users. Again, the more closed nature of Russian politics and society as well as language barriers create opaqueness for outside observers. Here stronger transnational knowledge networks and epistemic communities between Russian public and private actors and outside actors would be very valuable. In light of the very significant investments in the Yamal LNG project of 27 billion USD, it is also clear that Russian, Chinese, French and Japanese partners have the out-of-sight networks to execute this technologically, financially and politically complex project. It would be very valuable both for researchers and society to know these networks better.

10.5.7 Norwegian national and transnational networks, Maritim21 and CHNL

One small, highly developed Arctic state of particular importance to Arctic shipping and developing the NSR is Norway, which combines being a highly developed, small Nordic Arctic state, a neighbour of Russia to the west of the NSR, with a very large and highly developed global maritime sector. The maritime sector, including offshore oil and gas production, shipping, fisheries and derived industries is extremely important for Norwegian society. As part of national policy-making, the Norwegian government ordered the Maritim21 strategy,

34 Verdict Media Limited (2018) "Christophe De Margerie Class Icebreaking LNG Carriers" *Ship Technology*. www.ship-technology.com/projects/christophe-de-margerie-class-icebreaking-lng-carriers (accessed 15 May 2018).

which was written by an expert group and delivered in November 2016.[35] The strategy touches upon the Arctic in numerous dimensions, but what stands out is the Norwegian composition of the strategy group from academia, business and interest organisations. As such, this strategy work reminds of the Japanese OPRI work, which contributes much to national epistemic community building, but not transnational.

Another Norwegian initiative to be mentioned for its more transnational nature is the Centre for High North Logistics (CHNL), first in Kirkenes, and now at Nord University in Bodø. CHNL was founded in 2008 as an international non-profit foundation initiated by Tschudi Shipping Company in collaboration with the Norwegian Ministry of Foreign Affairs and Det Norske Veritas (DNV). The centre was originally launched as part of the Norwegian national research initiative "The Global Maritime Knowledge Hub" which was initiated by the Norwegian Ship Owners' Association and the Oslo Maritime Network. This Norwegian-based centre is particularly interesting for its range of international partners in Russia, Finland, Republic of Korea, Japan and Alaska, which makes it more of a transnational knowledge network.[36]

10.5.8 Chatham House–Lloyd's Risk Insight Report 2012

The joint Chatham House–Lloyd's Risk Insight Report "Arctic Opening: Opportunity and Risk in the High North" from 2012 is a remarkable case of how private actors at the highest level try to use knowledge to manage risk in the Arctic. Chatham House is one of the world's leading international affairs think tanks and meeting places for confidential discussions of international affairs questions. Its mission is to be

> a world-leading source of independent analysis, informed debate and influential ideas on how to build a prosperous and secure world for all [...] by drawing on its membership to promote open as well as confidential debates about significant developments in international affairs and about the context and content of policy responses.

Lloyd's is the historical centre of maritime insurance and risk management and according to itself "the world's leading specialist insurance market [...] often the first to insure new, unusual or complex risks". The report exactly pointed out knowledge gaps concerning the Arctic and the need for public and private research to fill these gaps.[37]

35 Norges forskningsråd (2016) *Maritim21*. Oslo: Norges forskningsråd.

36 Centre for High North Logistics (CHNL) website. www.chnl.no/?page=1&title=The+International+Gateway+to+Relevant+Knowledge+about+Logistics+in+the+High+North (accessed 15 May 2018).

37 Charles Emmerson and Glada Lahn (2012) *Arctic Opening: Opportunity and Risk in the High North*. Lloyd's, London.

10.5.9 Arctic Economic Council – Marine Transportation

The Arctic Economic Council, which is separate from the Arctic Council, is a good example of global governance in the Arctic as it brings private sector actors and indigenous peoples together to shape governance of economic activities in the region. AEC has four working groups, including one on Maritime Transportation, which is relevant here. It is chaired by a Finnish shipping executive, Mikko Niini, who is well connected in Finnish, Nordic and European shipping affairs, including the board of above-mentioned CHNL. The working group brings together Arctic shipping actors (not listed) and has a work plan with four items, which clearly serve to reduce complexity and uncertainty through common knowledge gathering: 1) information gathering on all the national and international Arctic navigation rules and regulations; their analysis and preparation for possible transport scheme harmonisation; 2) analysis of the status of hydrographic mapping in the Arctic waters and of the operators' priorities; 3) new and additional ongoing processes on environmental regulations related to navigation in the Arctic waters; 4) freedom of trade; 5) administration of the traffic management in the Arctic waters.[38]

10.5.10 The Arctic Institute: the future of Arctic research and policy talent – and shipping

The Arctic Institute plays a useful role for a talented group of young professionals and graduate students to practise policy analysis and advice and reporting their findings. In 2012, Malte Humpert and Andreas Raspotnik of the Arctic Institute published their study "The Future of Arctic Shipping", which still stands for its conclusions.[39] The members of the Arctic Institute are an important part of the academic talent basis of future Arctic epistemic communities on shipping and other policy areas. It is important to remember the temporal and generational aspect to epistemic communities. We saw how the INSROP project served an important role in training a generation of Japanese and international researchers and practitioners to think about the NSR and whether it is relevant for shipping or not. The INSROP generation has moved on career-wise and will eventually retire. Therefore, it is important to continuously see new initiatives that can train successive generations of academic and professional talent to think about Arctic shipping and create epistemic communities. A different question then becomes to connect the generations of Arctic shipping epistemic communities, so that there is both continuity and transmission of experiences as well as innovation.

38 Arctic Economic Council website: "Marine Transportation". https://arcticeconomiccouncil.com/our-work/#collapse-1 (accessed 15 May 2018).

39 The Arctic Institute Center for Circumpolar Security Studies (2012) *The Future of Arctic Shipping* (last modified 11 October 2012). www.thearcticinstitute.org/future-arctic-shipping (accessed 15 May 2018).

10.6 Conclusion

Arctic shipping is potentially very important to global shipping, which is the artery of the world economy. Arctic shipping develops in highly complex and uncertain circumstances of global environmental and social change, which make international policy cooperation especially in developing the NSR particularly challenging. UNCLOS and the Polar Code provide the basic framework for different state and non-state actors to manage such complexity and uncertainty.

Outside the law of the sea framework, there remain many areas where different actors are faced with great complexity and uncertainty about climate change and sea-ice conditions in the Arctic, as well as actions of other public and private actors. The literature on transnational knowledge networks, epistemic communities and governance suggest that such networks and communities can play important roles providing governance and facilitating international policy coordination under significant complexity and uncertainty by producing knowledge, norms, capacity-building and enforcement.

In this chapter, we saw that there has been since the 1990s (INSROP) a number of national and transnational, private and public knowledge networks and epistemic communities on Arctic shipping. Managing risks through knowledge is usually the common and explicit purpose of these networks. It is noteworthy and of concern that some of these networks or communities are either national rather than transnational or outside the purview of academics and the public. Bridging Chinese and Russian knowledge networks and epistemic communities with the outside is particularly important. Some of the networks or communities are either nationally, politically or privately economically interested and may have credibility issues or issues connecting with each other for political and commercial reasons.

In this context, it is my view that universities may play a role as conveners of transnational knowledge networks or epistemic communities because of their political and economic neutrality. Such a mission for universities requires that powerful public or private, political and economic interests understand the value of this role and support it financially and morally.

11 Russia's legislative development pertaining to the Northern Sea Route and its interactions with Sino-Russian Arctic cooperation

Leilei Zou

11.1 Introduction

The effects of climate change are making the Arctic more accessible. In 2017 the International Code for Ships Operating in Polar Waters (Polar Code) adopted by the International Maritime Organization (IMO) came into force. It is a mandatory instrument that regulates polar navigation and provides uniform standards to accommodate the increasing volume of international shipping in the Arctic. The Russian Federation (Russia), with an eagerness fuelled by the economic and strategic incentives to open up the Russian Arctic, demonstrates its willingness to promote international shipping through the Northern Sea Route (NSR).[1] Significant amounts of data have illustrated the advantages of NSR use when compared to the traditional routes, for example via the Suez Channel, as the NSR offers combined benefits of shorter-distance, cost-effective transit and trouble-free maritime security.[2] Thus, the commercial use of the NSR for international shipping is becoming increasingly feasible in environmental, legislative, and economic terms.[3]

1 Claes Lykke Ragner (2009) "The Northern Sea Route" in *Norden Association's Yearbook for 2008* edited by Torsten Hallberg. Arena Norden, Stockholm: 114–127; Barret Weber (2012) "Increased Shipping in the International Arctic? An Overview" *Journal of Maritime Law & Commerce* 43–3: 301–318; Sebastien Pelletier and Frederic Lasserre (2012) "Arctic Shipping: Future Polar Express Seaways? Shipowners' Opinion" *Journal of Maritime Law & Commerce* 43–3: 553–563.

2 Aldo Chircop (2012) "Regulatory Challenges for International Arctic Navigation and Shipping in an Evolving Governance Environment" presented at the annual meeting of the Comite Maritime International, Beijing, 14–19 October 2012; Scott G. Borgerson (2008) "Arctic Meltdown: The Economic and Security Implications of Global Warming" *Foreign Affairs* 87–2: 63–77; Lawson W. Brigham (2017) "The Changing Maritime Arctic and New Marine Operations" in *Governance of Arctic Shipping: Balancing Rights and Interests of Arctic States and User States* edited by Robert C. Beckman, Tore Henriksen, Kristine Dalaker Kraabel, Erik J. Molenaar and J. Ashley Roach. Brill, Leiden: 22.

3 Kentaro Nishimoto (2017) "The Rights and Interests of Japan in regard to Arctic Shipping" in *Governance of Arctic Shipping, supra* note 2, at 359; Zhang Xia, Zou Leilei, Tu Jingfang et al. (2015) "From Mandatory Icebreaker Guiding to a Permission Regime: Changes to

A review into the Russian legislative development pertaining to the NSR reveals that Russian authority to coordinate NSR shipping is less extensive than it was when military ventures were prioritised, multi-year sea ice made longer seasonal navigation unfeasible, and economic prospects from such a route were bleak. However, Arctic routes for international shipping will in all likelihood open up the prosperous prospect of using the Arctic/sub-Arctic all year around. Thus, the opening up of the Arctic routes is well received by those states with proximity to the Arctic, such as Russia, who can benefit from NSR navigation, as well as by user states, such as China, that are heavily reliant on shipping for international trade. Given the existing land- and ocean-based facilities and navigation conditions, the NSR is currently a much favoured Arctic route for immediate use.[4] This chapter will evaluate the development of Russia's Arctic navigation legislation alongside China's Arctic policy and its growing interest in incorporating the Arctic into its global strategy which is driven by the "One Belt One Road Initiative" (referred to as "Initiative"), a recent ambitious global strategy to sustain China's long-term growth potential.[5] In so doing, this chapter will also explore how Sino-Russian NSR cooperation is facilitated and how such cooperation impacts the Arctic and global strategies of both states.

11.2 Russia's NSR legislation

The 1982 UN Convention on the Law of the Sea (UNCLOS) sets forth basic parameters for global navigation regimes,[6] while a variety of IMO instruments provide supplemental specifications.[7] These parameters deal with a wide range of issues including rights and obligations, maritime safety, environmental protection, and port state and flag state control. Since this chapter aims to highlight Russian efforts to promote NSR accessibility and navigation by removing some stringent constraints on its international use, analysis will focus on the legal

the New Russian Legislation of the Northern Sea Route" *Advances in Polar Science* 25–3: 138–146.

4 Zou Leilei, Huang Shuolin and Fu Yu (2014) "A Comparative Study of the Administration for the Northwest Passage and Northern Sea Route" *Chinese Journal of Polar Research* 26–4: 515–521 (in Chinese); Zhang Xia, Yang Huigen and Wang Luo (2017) "Strategic Thinking on China's Involvement in the Development of Arctic Sea Routes" *Polar Research* 28–2: 267–276 (in Chinese).

5 The "One Belt One Road Initiative", firstly articulated by Chinese President Xi Jinping in 2013, has two components, namely, the "Silk Road Economic Belt" (the land-based Silk Road) and the twenty-first-century "Maritime Silk Road" (the ocean-based silk road). https://en.wikipedia.org/wiki/One_Belt_One_Road_Initiative (accessed 25 May 2018).

6 See generally articles in the UNCLOS concerning the innocent passage, transit passage, right of navigation, and protection and preservation of the marine environment.

7 See generally instruments established by the IMO like the International Code for Ships Operating in Polar Waters (Polar Code), the International Convention for the Safety of Life at Sea (SOLAS), the International Convention for the Prevention of Pollution from Ships (MARPOL), and the International Convention on Standards of Training Certification and Watchkeeping for Seafarers (STCW).

framework that Russia used to rely on to exercise its rigid unilateral control over the NSR, its recent legislative development and the motivating factors for this development.

Thus, to answer three questions concerning what, how and why for Russia's legislative development pertaining to the NSR, this section will conduct reviews of both the international and domestic navigation legislative framework, under which Russia set forth its unilateralism in defining the NSR scope and conducting stringent constraints on the NSR navigation. The section will then conduct an examination of Russia's NSR legislative development launched by the federal laws enforced in 2013 on the amendments on the original NSR legislation. The NSR legislative development could be viewed as the signal for Russia's departure from being ambiguous and arbitrary and developing into being accommodating and flexible. Comparative studies are conducted between the original and the most recent legislations under the 2013 amendments in order to determine the most significant Russian legislative development and how this development is still ongoing. Official English versions of Russian legislation are not widely available from Russian official sources, thus versions translated by reliable organisations either dealing with navigation issues or offering NSR information[8] are used for examination into the change of Russian policy on NSR services like the icebreaker assistance. However, the examination of the change of the NSR definition involves a large amount of textual interpretation of the terms in the legislation, thus this chapter will "borrow" the findings from my former research conducted with the assistance from Russian-speaking research partners and published elsewhere. This section ends with an analysis of the drivers of this development, which would serve as the introduction to the next section on China's approach to NSR development and Sino-Russian Arctic cooperation facilitated by NSR development.

11.2.1 International legal framework

The UNCLOS defines baselines and maritime zones, such as the exclusive economic zone (EEZ) and the territorial sea. It also establishes the mandates on national sovereignty and jurisdiction. Although user states enjoy the freedom of navigation through coastal states' EEZs, transit passage through international straits, and innocent passage through territorial seas and some internal

8 This chapter uses English versions of the Russian navigation-relevant legislations from the website of the NSR Administration (NSRA), the Russian government institution that organises navigation in the water area of the NSR. In the case that they are not available on NSRA website, those from the Centre for High North Logistics (CHNL) Information Office are used for examination. The CHNL Information Office was established as a joint initiative in June 2011 between CHNL and Rosatomflot. The objective of this office is to provide businesses and international organisations with relevant and practical information in English for planning and arranging transit voyages on the NSR. Most of its information is collected from various Russian sources, including the NSRA in Moscow.

waters,[9] those rights are subject to specific domestic instruments designed to regulate international navigation for the purpose of environmental protection and maritime safety in the maritime zones of the coastal states.

Article 234 "Ice-covered Areas" of the UNCLOS, also called the "Arctic Exception", accommodates coastal states' broad and extra legislative and enforcement jurisdiction in ice-covered areas.[10] Intended to establish a jurisdiction concerning pollution for the fragile ecosystems of ice-covered areas, Article 234 empowers the coastal states to impose more stringent standards than those generally adopted through the IMO.[11]

The Polar Code, which came into force in 2017, is the binding and mandatory polar-specific navigation standard. Since 1993, the Polar Code has undergone a long evolutionary process coordinated by the IMO. It addresses challenges of maritime safety and environmental protection for ships operating in remote and harsh environments where marine infrastructure is limited or non-existent.

11.2.2 Russian unilateralism under the legal framework

Russia's claim of historic title to Arctic waters dates back to 1960 when the *Structure of the Protection of the State Boundary of the Union of Soviet Socialist Republics* (USSR) was established. In 1965, the USSR Ministry of the Maritime Fleet issued a specific enactment to require mandatory icebreaker assistance and pilotage for the Vilkitskii and Shokalskii Straits, which was extended to other Arctic straits in 1972.[12] However, the *1971 Statute on the Administration of the Northern Sea Route Attached to the Ministry of the Maritime Fleet* was widely recognised as the first document by which the USSR exercised special rights to regulate NSR navigation.[13]

The 1990s were a defining time for Russia's NSR legislation. The *Regulations for Navigation on the Seaways of the Northern Sea Route* were approved by the

9 See Article 8.1 of UNCLOS provides as follows: "where the establishment of a straight baseline in accordance with the method set forth in Article 7 has the effect of enclosing as internal waters areas which had not previously been considered as such, a right of innocent passage as provided in this Convention shall exist in those waters".

10 Erik J. Molenaar (1998) *Coastal State Jurisdiction over Vessel-Source Pollution*. Kluwer Law International, The Hague: 419–421; Aldo Chircop (2017) "The IMO, Its Role under UNCLOS and Its Polar Shipping Regulation" in *Governance of Arctic Shipping*, *supra* note 2, at 132; Erik J. Molenaar (2009) "Arctic Marine Shipping: Overview of the International Legal Framework Gaps and Option" *Journal of Transnational Law & Policy* (2008–2009): 289–326; R. Douglas Brubaker (1996) "Jurisdiction Governing the Straits in Russian Arctic Waters" *INSROP Working Paper* No. 52: IV.3.1.

11 Aldo Chircop (2007) "Climate Change and the Prospects of Increased Navigation in the Canadian Arctic" *World Maritime University Journal of Maritime Affairs* 6–2: 193–205; Myron H. Nordquist et al. (eds) (1991) *United Nations Convention on the Law of the Sea 1982: A Commentary Vol. IV*. Brill, Leiden: 392–398; Molenaar (2009), *supra* note 10, at 305.

12 Jan J. Solski "Russia" in *Governance of Arctic Shipping*, *supra* note 2, at 207–208.

13 Ibid., at 186.

USSR Minister of Merchant Marine in 1990[14] (1990 Regulations) and laid out the legal framework for access to and navigation on the NSR for vessels of all states. A notable aspect of the 1990 Regulations is its definition of the NSR as the "national transport route of the USSR, which is situated within the inland waters, territorial sea (territorial waters), or exclusive economic zone adjoining the USSR northern coast, and includes seaways suitable for guiding ships in ice".[15] This gave rise to opposition from the international community claiming that some Arctic high seas, defined as the NSR portion, fell under the USSR jurisdiction. Furthermore, the *1996 Guide to Navigating through the Northern Sea Route* served as a supplement for the 1990 Regulations. Also the *1996 Regulations for Icebreaker and Pilot Guiding of Vessels through the Northern Sea Route* set forth detailed regulations on the requirement for prior applications for NSR navigation, mandatory icebreaker assistance and pilotage. And finally, the *1996 Requirements for the Design, Equipment, and Supplies of Vessels Navigating the Northern Sea Route* specified requirements for maritime safety and pollution prevention.

The above illustrates that a series of domestic follow-up regulations were established after the enactment of 1990 Regulations. Further, it also points towards Russia's move to safeguard its rights responding to the challenges, from the US in particular, over the legal status of the NSR to be an international strait, eligible for transit passage. As indicated in section 11.2.1, to solidify the NSR jurisdiction, Russia also relied on the UNCLOS which clearly defined regimes for the different maritime zones.

Besides the validity of the Russian definition of the legal status of the NSR, opposition from the international community is also concerned with the applicability of stringent regulations on NSR navigation, and the extent and scope of coastal state powers under Article 234 of the UNCLOS.[16] Most of these controversial issues are regulated through the above domestic legislation. As interpreted by the international community, the then USSR and present Russian Federation imposed regulations unilaterally,[17] going beyond the coastal state jurisdiction

14 The Regulations for Navigation on the Seaways of the Northern Sea Route, as approved by the USSR Minister of Merchant Marine (1990 Regulations), 14 September 1990. www.arctic-lio.com/docs/nsr/legislation/Rules_of_navigation_on_the_seaways_of_the_Northern_Sea_Route.pdf (accessed 16 June 2018).

15 See Clause 1.2 of the 1990 Regulations, ibid.

16 Mi Chenxi (2015) "China's Role in the Governance of the Northeast Passage under New Circumstances" *Pacific Journal* 23–8: 71–79 (in Chinese); Willy Østreng (2010) "The Northern Sea Route and Jurisdictional Controversy" *Ocean Futures* 10. www.arctis-search.com/Northern+Sea+Route+and+Jurisdictional+Controversy&structure=Arctic+Policies+and+Governance (accessed 20 June 2018).

17 Zou, Huang and Fu, *supra* note 4, at 517; Zhang, Yang, and Wang, *supra* note 4, at 271; Aldo Chircop, Ivan Bunik, Moira L.McConnell et al. (2014) "Comparative Perspectives on the Governance of Navigation and Shipping in Canadian and Russian Arctic Waters" *Ocean Yearbook* 28: 291–327.

defined in the UNCLOS, and thus imposed strict restrictions on access to and navigation on the NSR.

11.2.3 Russia's NSR legislative development

The last decade has witnessed an accelerating retreat of Arctic sea ice, accelerating trade interactions between northern America/Europe and eastern Asia, and an accelerating Russian desire for Arctic economic development; meanwhile, the last decade has also witnessed Russia's legislative development pertaining to the NSR.

In 2011, at the International Arctic Forum President Vladimir Putin articulated Russia's interest in turning the NSR into a key commercial route of global importance.[18] To facilitate its desire to develop the NSR into a competitive international shipping route, Russia initiated its NSR legislative development. On 28 January 2013, the *New Federal Law on Amendments to Specific Legislative Acts of the Russian Federation Related to Governmental Regulation of Merchant Shipping in the Water Area of the Northern Sea Route*[19] (2013 Amendments) came into effect. In light of the 2013 Amendments, significant amendments and additions were made to existing domestic navigation-related legislation. For example, new *Rules of Navigation on the Water Area of the Northern Sea Route*[20] (2013 Rules) were enacted to provide detailed regulations on NSR navigation including the application for navigation and services like icebreaker assistance and pilotage,[21] superseding the 1990 Regulations.

Under the 2013 Amendments, the Merchant Marine Code which was formerly enacted in 1999 was amended and provided a new definition of the NSR. A comparative study on the definition of the NSR between the 1990 Regulations and the updated Merchant Marine Code was conducted elsewhere.[22] Two findings from this study are supportive of the argument that Russia's NSR legislation is undergoing

18 Russian President Vladimir Putin's speech at the Second International Arctic Forum in RIA Novosti on 23 September 2011. https://narfu.ru/en/media/news/21110/ (accessed 20 June 2018).

19 Federal Law on Amendments to Specific Legislative Acts of the Russian Federation Related to Governmental Regulation of Merchant Shipping in the Water Area of the Northern Sea Route, as put into force by Federation Council of Russia, 28 January 2013. www.arctic-lio.com/docs/nsr/legislation/federal_law_nsr.pdf (accessed 20 June 2018).

20 Rules of Navigation in the Water Area of the Northern Sea Route, as approved by the order of the Ministry of Transport of Russia (2013 Rules), 17 January 2013. www.nsra.ru/files/fileslist/120-en-rules_perevod_cniimf-13_05_2015.pdf (accessed 20 June 2018).

21 See Clause 2 Procedure of the navigation of ships in the water area of the Northern Sea Route and Clause 3 Rules of the icebreaker assistance of ships in the water area of the Northern Sea Route in 2013 Rules, ibid.

22 See Zhang, Zou, Tu et al., *supra* note 3.

an development and Russia has taken up an accommodating attitude towards international use of the NSR. The first finding is that the eastern boundary of the NSR defined in the updated Merchant Marine Code was confined within the Line of Maritime Demarcation with the US and Cape Dezhnev parallel in Bering Strait, and this new definition of the east boundary avoided disputes with the US in the east.[23] The second finding is concerned with the definition of the northern boundary of the NSR. The 1990 Regulations allowed Russia to exercise its jurisdiction beyond the EEZ in the name of organising NSR navigation, while the updated Merchant Marine Code eliminated this ambiguity by acknowledging the newly defined northern boundary of the NSR to coincide with that of Russia's Arctic EEZ.[24] Other research echoed this finding in that the updated Merchant Marine Code has eliminated the ambiguity concerning the extension of NSR to the high seas, which was put forward by the 1990 Regulations.[25] The above points towards Russia's defining the scope of the NSR within the EEZ boundary and confining its jurisdiction to the EEZ under the new legislation.

A comparative study between the 1990 Regulations and the 2013 Rules reveals that another significant change in the updated legislation is concerned with the regulations on icebreaker assistance. Clause 7.4 in the 1990 Regulation stipulated that "(m)andatory icebreaker guiding of vessels with ice pilot on board each vessel is established" in the straits of Proliv Vil'kitskogo, Proliv Shokal'skogo, Proliv Dmitriya Lapteva, and Proliv Sannikova, where navigational situation and ice conditions were unfavourable. For other regions, Clause 7.4 stipulated that icebreaker guiding may be prescribed "in consideration of ensuring safe navigation and for the purpose of providing the most favourable navigating conditions".[26] As regulated in the 1990 Regulations, icebreaker assistance was mandatory for foreign vessels navigating through certain straits of the NSR. In practice, however, these services were imposed on those vessels navigating through all of the NSR due to the absence of concrete and applicable standards for independent navigation.[27] Different from the 1990 Regulations which requested arbitrary and mandatory icebreaker guiding, the 2013 Rules had no such wording as "mandatory" in the Clause 3 of "Rules of the icebreaker assistance of ships in the water area of the Northern Sea Route".[28] Besides Clause 3 dedicated to specifications on icebreaker assistance, the 2013 Rules provided an Annex concerning "criteria of the admission of ships to the NSR", where independent navigation and

23 Ibid., at 140.
24 Ibid., at 141.
25 Zhang Xia, Yang Huigen and Wang, *supra* note 4, at 271.
26 See Clause 7.4 of 1990 Regulations, *supra* note 14.
27 Zhang, Zou, Tu et al. *supra* note 3, at 143.
28 See Clause 3 of 2013 Rules, *supra* note 20.

navigation with icebreaker assistance were indicated as two modes of ice navigation.[29] An examination into the Annex provisions reveals that the 2013 Rules stipulated clear and feasible standards for the independent navigation in terms of the category of ice strengthening of the vessel, ice conditions, navigation waters and navigation seasons.[30] Thus, the 2013 Rules gave the clear indication of the possibility of independent navigation through the NSR, ruling out the arbitrariness that the 1990 Regulations imposed compulsory icebreaker assistance and its high fee rate on foreign vessels.[31] With the 2013 Rules, the vessels are now charged for the actual assistance they have received[32] rather than being compelled to pay for the service they have not received simply because the vessel is using the NSR for navigation.[33]

The Russian legislative development demonstrates that Russia appears to facilitate accessibility to and navigation on the NSR in the attempt to make the NSR a potentially competitive commercial route of global significance.

11.2.4 Drivers for Russia's NSR legislative development

Russia's desire to facilitate the international commercial use of the NSR is interpreted as the primary driver for its navigation-related legislative development. The question at hand is what drives Russia's desire to facilitate the international commercial use of the NSR. Economic development may rank as the top

29 See Annex 2 Criteria of the admission of ships to the Northern Sea Route in compliance with category of their ice strengthening in 2013 Rules, ibid.

30 See specifications on navigation under 4 categories in Annex 2 Criteria of the admission of ships to the Northern Sea Route in compliance with category of their ice strengthening in 2013 Rules, ibid. Specifications under 4 categories in Annex 2 are: 1) for ships without ice strengthening and with category of ice strengthening Ice1–Ice 3 during the navigation from July to November 15; 2) for ships with category of ice strengthening Arc 4–Arc 9 during the period of navigation from July to November; 3) for ships with category of ice strengthening Arc4–Arc9 during the period of navigation from January to June and in December; 4) for icebreakers with category of ice strengthening Icebreaker 6–Icebreaker 8 during the period of navigation from January to June and in December. www.nsra.ru/en/ofitsialnaya_informatsiya/pravila_plavaniya/fl20.html (accessed 20 June 2018).

31 Zhang, Zou, Tu et al. *supra* note 3, at 143; Zhang, Yang and Wang, *supra* note 4, at 271.

32 See Clause 5.1(4) in Navigation in the water area of the Northern Sea Route: "In compliance with item 5 of article 51 of CCN the fee rate of the icebreaker assistance of ship in the water area of the Northern Sea Route is determined according to the legislation of the Russian Federation about natural monopolies taking into account the capacity of ship, ice class of ship, distance of the escorting and period of navigation", as approved by the order of the Ministry of Transport of Russia, 17 January 2013. www.nsra.ru/en/ofitsialnaya_informatsiya/pravila_plavaniya/fl20.html (accessed 20 June 2018).

33 Xue Guifang and Long Yu (2017) "Equal Treatment and Non-discrimination for User States in Governance of Arctic Shipping: Balancing Rights and Interests of Arctic States and User States" in *Governance of Arctic Shipping*, *supra* note 2, 318–356.

motivating factor. On 27 March 2009, the Russian Security Council released the *Fundamentals of the Russian Federation's Policy in the Arctic for the Period up to 2020 and beyond*. The document is recognised as the first Russian Arctic policy, in which "use [of] the Russian Arctic Zone as a strategic resource base for ... socio-economic development" was prioritised as the top national interest in the Arctic. Approximately 150 resource extraction projects are reported to be forthcoming along the NSR.[34] Considering the abundance of strategically important industrial and mineral resources in the vast Russian Arctic, the ambition of transforming the Russian Arctic into a resource base of national strategic significance will likely substantiate Russia's identity as a leading Arctic power, another long-held Russian ambition.[35] The opening-up of the Arctic begins with the opening-up of the Arctic Ocean, and the NSR will be the newly emerging route of national strategic importance to transport the resources out of the Arctic to international markets.

Russia's awareness that being cooperative and accommodating is the sensible Arctic approach may also serve as a driver for the Russian transformation of its Arctic navigation legislation. From a geopolitical perspective, Russia is isolated from an Arctic community consisting of North Atlantic Treaty Organization (NATO) members with the US leading the pack. Confrontation and vigilance are the routine Russian responses to most Arctic initiatives among Arctic states.[36] For the sake of Arctic security and Arctic strategy fulfilment, international cooperation, rather than confrontation, now comes first. Many recent Russian moves are indicative of its cooperative attitude – it played an active role in the IMO's development of Polar Code;[37] it contributed to the negotiation and adoption of the Central Arctic Ocean Fisheries Agreement;[38] and it proposed the integration of the One Belt One Road Initiative under the Eurasian Economic Union framework,[39] a prelude to the introduction of the Silk Road defined in the

34 Xu Qingchao and Yi Meng (2018) "Silk Road on the Ice: An Economic Passage into the Future Blue Economy" *Social Science Weekly* 1611 (in Chinese). www.shekebao.com.cn (accessed 14 June 2018).

35 Willy Østreng (2010) "The Russian Federation's Arctic Policy" *Ocean Futures* 10. www.arctis-search.com/The+Russian+Federation%E2%80%99s+Arctic+Policy&structure=Arctic+Policies+and+Governance (accessed 18 June 2018).

36 Zou Leilei (2016) "Comparison of Arctic Navigation Administration between Russia and Canada" in *Challenges of the Changing Arctic: Continental Shelf, Navigation, and Fisheries* edited by Myron H. Nordquist, John Norton Moore and Ronan Long. Brill, Leiden: 290.

37 Chircop, *supra* note 10, at 139; Zou Leilei and Fu Yu (2017) "Enlightenment of Arctic Shipping Management to Arctic Fisheries Management" *Chinese Journal of Polar Research* 29–2: 270–278 (in Chinese).

38 See Chapter 9 by Erik Molenaar in this book.

39 See Joint statement between the People's Republic of China and Russian Federation on Synerizing the Silk Road Economic Belt Initiative and the Eurasian Economic Union,

Initiative to the Arctic. Russian scholars also study the transformation of Russia's Arctic strategy and have found this transformation indicative of Russia's departure from the widespread stereotype as a revisionist power in the high north.[40]

11.3 China's interactions with the NSR

With greater accessibility to the Arctic and better knowledge of Arctic values in socio-economic-political perspectives, enhancing the Arctic presence has been one of the concerns for states both within and beyond the Arctic. Ongoing Arctic issues are no longer of a regional nature; instead, they should be interpreted in a much broader global context. There is no necessary correlation between Russia's transformation of Arctic navigation legislation and China's growing interest in the NSR. This being said, a careful examination of China's first official Arctic document, the White Paper of China's Arctic Policy (White Paper) released in early 2018, and the Initiative reveals that the timing of both states' moves matches. After all, the NSR will serve to implement the "rational use of the Arctic",[41] the exact wording from the White Paper; furthermore, the NSR is a potentially important northward component of the "Silk Road on Ice" featured in the Initiative. Since the timing of Russia's NSR legislative development and China's growing interest in the NSR matches, it fosters a mutual understanding that they could be an asset for the fulfilment of each other's strategy at regional and global levels.

A review of China's approach to the NSR reveals that it has undergone some changes to accommodate China's Arctic strategy in the global context. With the mutual understanding of a win–win prospect, both states are exploring how to initiate and carry out Sino-Russian cooperation in the NSR.

11.3.1 China's approach to the NSR

The NSR is recognised as an emerging maritime short-cut in the far north between northern America/Europe and eastern Asia. However, there are still

Moscow, Russia, 8 May 2015. www.xinhuanet.com/english/2015-05/09/c_134222936.htm (accessed 10 June 2018).

40 Alexander Sergunin, Valery Konyshev (2014) "Russia in Search of Its Arctic Strategy: Between Hard and Soft Power?" *The Polar Journal* 4: 69–87; Solski, *supra* note 12, at 188–192.

41 See Clause IV(5) Utilizing Arctic resources in a lawful and rational manner of the White Paper of China's Arctic Policy, The State Council of the People's Republic of China (2018) "China's Arctic Policy", 26 January 2018. http://english.gov.cn/archive/white_paper/2018/01/26/content_281476026660336.htm (accessed 30 January 2018).

many uncertainties and risks concerning schedule reliability, short navigation seasons, and a greater likelihood for navigational hazards.[42] Even though Russia's efforts to transform the NSR into a competitive international maritime passage have been received favourably by potential user states, technical and economic constraints remain. These have adversely impacted on increased use of the NSR.

China, as one of the most important trade states that relies heavily on shipping, has had very few attempts to navigate the NSR so far. In 2012 *Snowdragon*, then the only Chinese icebreaker for polar scientific expeditions, made its first attempt through the NSR. This was followed by *Yongsheng*, a commercial vessel from China Ocean Shipping (Group) Company (COSCO Shipping), which successfully navigated a one-way and a two-way NSR commercial transit in 2013 and 2015, respectively. China's undoubtedly explorative attempts for future NSR use are also strategic in nature: each Arctic attempt from different states can be interpreted as a component of their Arctic strategy or policy; to distinguish from other states, China defines itself as the near-Arctic state,[43] and thus its past NSR attempts can more likely be a follow-up reminder of its role as an important Arctic stakeholder and Arctic user.

However, the situation has changed since "The Belt and Road Forum for International Cooperation" in May 2017, where Russian President Putin proposed the incorporation of the NSR into the "Maritime Silk Road",[44] one key ocean-based component of the "One Belt One Road". The Russian proposal was well received by Chinese President Xi Jinping's confirmation in July 2017, creating the term of "Silk Road on Ice" with the NSR being defined as a significant component.[45] Following this clear message from the Chinese central government, there has been a top-down rush in China to develop the NSR. Such development efforts have included five commercial vessels from COSCO Shipping that resumed their NSR attempts in 2017 – which they last attempted in 2015,[46] and shipbuilding enterprises seeking technical breakthroughs in icebreaker building.[47] These are also indications that China's approach to the NSR is changing – that is, the nature of the weight attached to the NSR attempts has shifted from being symbolic to being substantive.

42 Brigham, *supra* note 2, at 3–23.

43 Lu Junyuan and Zhang Xia (2016) *China's Arctic Interests and Policy*. Current Affairs Publishing House, Beijing: 379–380 (in Chinese).

44 See the speech delivered by Russian President Vladimir Putin at the One Belt One Road International Forum, 14–15 May 2017, Beijing, China. http://en.kremlin.ru/events/president/news/54491 (accessed 30 June 2018).

45 See China, Russia Agree to Jointly Build "Ice Silk Road", as released by Xinhuanet, 1 July 2018. www.xinhuanet.com/english/2017-07/04/c_136417241.htm (accessed 28 June 2018).

46 See Five COSCO Shipping Specialized Vessels Had Passed Arctic Northern Route, as released by COSCO on its website, 21 September 2017. www.coscol.com.cn/en/news/detail.aspx?id=11499 (accessed 28 May 2018).

47 Yan Fenghua (2017) "Opportunities for Chinese Shipbuilding Industry with Wakeup of the Arctic Routes" *China Ship News*, 21 May 2014, at section 1 (in Chinese).

11.3.2 Drivers for China's changing approach

Although China keeps a relatively low profile with regard to Arctic issues,[48] it prioritises the enhancement of its Arctic presence, exhibiting the same mentality as most non-Arctic states. Although there is no immediate prospect that the NSR will be used as an important international transport alternative, China made its first commercial NSR attempt in 2013, the year when Russia dropped its stringent NSR navigation legislations. Considering the limited number of China's attempts, its efforts will be more strategic in nature – made to enhance its Arctic presence – rather than of practical importance for the future commercial use of the NSR.

The Initiative proposed by Chinese President Xi in 2013 is a grand global strategy by which China may highlight its significant role in global economic development in the short term and, hopefully, political development in the long term.[49] The follow-up Silk Road on Ice initiative introduces the Arctic into this grand global strategy in 2017,[50] as reconfirmed in the White Paper of China's Arctic Policy in early 2018. The White Paper highlights the role of the Silk Road on Ice in extending the "Maritime Silk Road" into the Arctic and expresses China's readiness to "participate in the development of Arctic shipping route".[51] However, in the White Paper "Silk Road on Ice" is formally named as "Polar Silk Road". Chinese governmental policies convey a clear message that the role of the NSR in facilitating the Polar Silk Road is acknowledged and that substantive work by the Chinese government will be conducted to enhance NSR development.

Thus, China's approach to the NSR has undergone a significant change, as its attempts to navigate the NSR have evolved from being merely a reminder of its Arctic presence to a signal of Arctic's future substantive and substantial use.

11.3.3 Sino-Russian NSR cooperation

There is not necessarily a causal link between Russia's legislative transformation and China's acknowledgement of the role of the NSR in its Arctic and global strategies; however, the aligning of the timing for the two events supports the

48 Peng Jingchao and Njord Wegge (2014) "China and the Law of the Sea: Implications for Arctic Governance" *The Polar Journal* 4–2: 287–305.

49 Krishnan Raymon and Sriganesh Bhargav (2018) "One Belt One Road" *MHD Supply Chain Sulutions* 48–2: 50–53; Michael M. Du (2016) "China's One Belt One Road Initiative: Context, Focus, Institutions, and Implications" *The Chinese Journal of Global Governance* 2–1: 30–43.

50 See Joint statement between the People's Republic of China and Russian Federation on Synerizing the Silk Road Economic Belt Initiative and the Eurasian Economic Union, *supra* note 39.

51 China's Arctic Policy, *supra* note 41.

understanding that a good partnership in NSR development could be mutually beneficial.

11.3.3.1 Drivers for Sino-Russian NSR cooperation

Sino-Russian NSR cooperation conforms to each state's Arctic and global strategies as described below.

Economic development is highlighted as a priority for the Russian Arctic strategy, as clearly set forth in its governmental documents on Arctic policy and Arctic socioeconomic development.[52] Considering the vast volumes of untapped resources that the Arctic holds,[53] Russia, which possesses a vast Arctic continental shelf, coastline and land, sees the retreating ice as opening up new spatial areas for economic prospecting and exploitation. The liquefied natural gas (LNG) plant on the Yamal Peninsula, the mining project that the Russian government capitalises on by exporting available gas to foreign markets via the NSR, will trigger more economic projects in the Russian Arctic. The NSR is expected to provide reliable transport for the resources derived from these economic projects. With the incentive of more economic projects, accessing the Russian Arctic via the NSR is expected to revive the Russian economy.[54]

Extracting resources from the Arctic complies with the policy of most oil and gas importing states in their efforts to reduce the vulnerability of being subject to energy blackmails from governments in politically unstable areas.[55] China is one of such states; in fact, its thirst for Arctic oil and gas is articulated in its White Paper of Arctic Policy as "utilizing Arctic resources in a lawful and rational manner".[56] The transport of resources out of the Arctic and into the Chinese market via the NSR is the initial step in Sino-Russian Arctic cooperation. Subsequently, the NSR is capable of facilitating Sino-Russian cooperation of different forms and contents into more extensive areas in the Arctic.

52 Basics of the State Policy of the Russian Federation in the Arctic for the Period till 2020 and for a Future Perspective, as adopted by the Russian government, 18 September 2008. https://rg.ru/2009/03/30/arktika-osnovy-dok.html (accessed 8 June 2018); Russian Strategy of the Development of the Arctic Zone and the Provision of National, as adopted by the Russian government, 2 February 2013. http://minec.gov-murman.ru/files/Strategy-azrf.pdf (accessed 8 June 2018); State Programme of Socioeconomic Development of the Arctic Zone of the Russian Federation through to 2020, as adopted by the Russian government, 21 April 2014. http://government.ru/media/files/AtEY-gOHutVc.pdf (accessed 8 June 2018).

53 Circum-Arctic Resource Appraisal (North of the Arctic Circle) Assessment Units GIS Data, as released by U.S. Geological Survey, 2009. http://energy.usgs.gov/arctic/ (accessed 18 May 2018).

54 Heather A. Conley and Caroline Rohloff (2015) *The New Ice Curtain: Russia's Strategic Reach to the Arctic*. Center for Strategic and International Studies, Washington, DC: 24.

55 See Willy Østreng (2010) "On the Geopolitical Significance of the Arctic States", as released by Centre for High North Logistics. www.arctis-search.com/On+the+Geopolitical+Significance+of+the+Arctic+States (accessed 18 June 2018).

56 China's Arctic Policy, *supra* note 41.

The Chinese government is now devoted to promoting the Initiative as a promising means for ensuring economic prosperity over a vast region. The potential for economic prosperity, the selling point of the Initiative, is in line with Russia's Arctic priority. More importantly, the NSR, as a key component of the Silk Road on Ice in the Initiative, is capable of stimulating trade between China and North America/Europe further. Under the Initiative, there are now more economic and strategic incentives for China to collaborate with Russia in developing the NSR to enhance not only China's Arctic strategy but its global strategy as well.[57]

Political considerations are also important drivers for Sino-Russian Arctic cooperation. In April 2014, at the meeting attended by the Russian Security Council members shortly after the adoption of the *State Programme of Socioeconomic Development of the Arctic Zone of the Russian Federation through to 2020*,[58] President Putin announced the Russian ambition of being ahead of other counterparts and establishing a stronger position in the Arctic.[59] Similarly, China maintains ambitious Arctic and global strategies. China has endeavoured to establish its Arctic presence[60] while the Initiative is a much grander strategy to enhance China's global position. Economic development serves as the incentive to boost its reputation and political clout, framing China as the geographic, financial and, hopefully, political centre, with ties radiating toward Europe, Asia and Africa. Sino-Russian joint efforts will, for Russia, enhance its leading Arctic position and relieve pressure from being politically isolated from the NATO in the Arctic, and for China, enhance its Arctic presence and facilitate its economic as well as political strategies via the Initiative.

11.3.3.2 Initiatives for Sino-Russian NSR cooperation

Shipping and navigation have been critical to China both economically and strategically. The Silk Road on Ice in the Initiative and the Arctic economic development that China is involved in rely heavily upon the use of the NSR, which emphasises the significant role that the NSR plays in facilitating China's economic and strategic interests within and beyond the Arctic.

Given the geopolitical circumstances of the Arctic, Russia takes the lead in establishing and guiding the Sino-Russian Arctic cooperation. However, given

57 Silvana Malle (2017) "Russia and China in the 21st Century: Moving towards Cooperative Behavior" *Journal of Eurasian Studies* 8–2: 136–150.

58 State Programme of Socioeconomic Development of the Arctic Zone of the Russian Federation through to 2020, *supra* note 52.

59 See Meeting of the Security Council on State Policy in the Arctic, the speech by Russian President Vladimir Putin at an expanded meeting of the Security Council on the Implementation of Russia's State Policy in the Arctic in the Interests of National Security, 22 April 2014, the Kremlin, Moscow. http://en.kremlin.ru/events/president/news/20845 (accessed 30 June 2018).

60 Yang Jian (2018) "An Interpretation of China's Arctic Policy" *Pacific Journal* 26–3: 1–11 (in Chinese).

China's political influence arising from its large population, significant geographic size, resourceful financial back-ups, potential trading capabilities and vast domestic markets, China also has some say in the Sino-Russian Arctic cooperation. Accordingly, this section will explore the two states' cooperative initiatives in the Arctic.

The Arctic currently holds little infrastructure to support vessels in transit. Thus, to make the NSR a viable shipping route, significant efforts must go to the improvement of navigation aids, port and repair facilities, search and rescue, pollution response, and more. If the Arctic becomes navigable during more months of the year, shorter shipping routes and access to untapped energy resources will incentivise the Chinese government to allocate more investments to Arctic infrastructure improvement. The Yamal LNG project is the initial Sino-Russian cooperation project, where Chinese investment has 29.9 per cent of shares, with 9.9 per cent from China's Silk Road Fund and 20 per cent from the China National Petroleum Corporation, a significant financial back-up and impetus for the project to move forward.

The operational network of meteorological and oceanographic observations in the Arctic, essential for accurate weather and wave forecasting for safe navigation, is extremely sparse. Most NSR portions do not have adequate hydrographic data and therefore lack sufficient charts to support safe navigation. The demand for maritime safety and environmental standards in the fragile Arctic Ocean is high, especially with the introduction of the Polar Code. Resource extraction from the Arctic calls for breakthroughs in prospecting and mining technologies. Techniques concerning ice-class shipbuilding, crew training and icebreaker assistance need updating. The above issues can be addressed to some degree by scientific research, and joint research is always a safe incentive to commence international Arctic cooperation. Given China's substantial existing Arctic research and strong financial and technological back-ups, research cooperation will lead to win–win results.

With the central government acting as the dominant body in both states, Sino-Russian Arctic cooperation could be facilitated in a top-down manner, with initial efforts to respond to Arctic issues emerging within the central government, followed by efforts from local government, the industry sector and the private sector to carry out Arctic endeavours.

11.4 Conclusion

Based on certain climatic, geographical, and human conditions, the NSR offers the promising prospect of developing into a competitive international transport alternative. Both Russia and China find the NSR cooperation capable of facilitating their economic and political strategies within and beyond the Arctic. However, there are also uncertainties and risks surrounding the prospect of using the NSR as an international trade route. Factors relating to those uncertainties and risks include climate change variability, legal and governance situations, changes within domestic strategies, international cooperation within and beyond the Arctic, the application of new shipping and navigation rules and regulations, radical changes in global trade, and more. From the environmental perspective, being aware of issues concerning environmental protection for the uniquely fragile Arctic ecosystem is key. From the political perspective, being cooperative and accommodating is the best method for remedying some of the above uncertainties and risks.

As discussed above, both Russia and China possess motivating factors and initiatives for establishing their NSR cooperation. Similarly, there will be motivating factors and initiatives for NSR cooperation between Russia and any other state interested in using the NSR. Each potential stakeholder has an identity with multiple roles within the NSR, which may include NSR users, Arctic resources purchasers and entities who may bring about potential Arctic environmental disturbance. Whatever a state's role may be, the principal duties of that state are to observe the rules and regulations, give due regard to the interests and rights of other stakeholders, and be cooperative – such duties are also true for Russia and China in their Arctic cooperation.

Part IV

The universality of science and the Arctic Council

12 The Arctic Science Cooperation Agreement

A perspective from non-Arctic actors

Akiho Shibata

12.1 Introduction

On 11 May 2017, at the occasion of the tenth Arctic Council Ministerial Meeting held in Fairbanks, Alaska, the foreign ministers of the eight Arctic states – Canada, Denmark, Finland, Iceland, Norway, the Russian Federation, Sweden and the United States (US) – signed a new Agreement on Enhancing International Arctic Scientific Cooperation (hereinafter Arctic Science Cooperation Agreement or Agreement).[1] Geographically, this new Agreement covers the designated Arctic region as an integral area for the promotion of science, without distinguishing the land, the sea and the airspace.[2] Functionally, this Agreement covers all "Scientific Activities" relating to the Arctic as defined in its Article 1 and promotes international cooperation in such activities. Since the first International Polar Year in 1882, scientists have known that "the Arctic region offered opportunities unparalleled anywhere on the planet for scientific studies of the Earth's physical and natural processes and that promotion of cooperation among nations was essential to the successful accomplishment of research in the Arctic".[3] Because of the geopolitical sensitivities in the Arctic, the perceived need for such cooperation required more than 130 years to materialise into a political consensus to develop a legally binding treaty to promote international Arctic scientific cooperation.[4] Compared with the 1959 Antarctic Treaty which holds a provision on scientific cooperation in the Antarctic, the conclusion of the Arctic Science Cooperation

1 Agreement on Enhancing International Arctic Scientific Cooperation, signed 11 May 2017 and entered into force 23 May 2018. https://oaarchive.arctic-council.org/handle/11374/1916 (accessed 1 July 2018), reproduced in the Appendix of this book.

2 Akiho Shibata (2016) "The Arctic as a Distinct Legal Sphere for Promoting International Scientific Cooperation" *Journal of International Cooperation Studies* 24–1: 45–56 (in Japanese).

3 Words of Karl Weyprecht, cited in Akiho Shibata and Maiko Raita (2017) "An Agreement on Enhancing International Arctic Scientific Cooperation: Only for the Eight Arctic States and Their Scientist?" *Yearbook of Polar Law* 8: 154.

4 Paul Arthur Berkman et al. (2017) "The Arctic Science Agreement Propels Science Diplomacy" *Science* 358: 596–598.

Agreement in 2017 was long overdue. With the swift entering into force of the Agreement on 23 May 2018[5] and due to its effective implementation,[6] a new legal environment will be established that is more conducive for international scientific endeavours relating to the Arctic. These include the urgent scientific analysis of the effects of and possible responses to climate change. The conclusion of the Arctic Science Cooperation Agreement is, therefore, an important milestone for the future of Arctic scientific cooperation.

After recapitulating the legal structure of the Agreement, this chapter examines the way in which this Agreement incorporates the legitimate interests of non-Arctic states and their scientists actively engaged in and contributing to Arctic science. It argues that those provisions relevant to non-Arctic states and their scientists are the result of careful negotiations in the Scientific Cooperation Task Force (SCTF) established under the Arctic Council (AC) with the involvement of non-Arctic actors. This chapter demonstrates that the Arctic Council Observers, namely non-Arctic states and relevant international organisations such as International Arctic Science Committee (IASC), have substantively engaged in the SCTF discussions, despite their lack of decision-making powers. In the discussion, they represented the universal voice of scientists in the sense that Arctic science should be further promoted and its international cooperation be enhanced irrespective of their nationalities. Based on the experience of SCTF negotiations, this chapter ends with a future prospect as well as inherent limitations of the Arctic Council and its subsidiary bodies becoming legitimate law-making forums for those Arctic issues the interests in which go beyond the eight Arctic states.

12.2 The legal structure of the Agreement

12.2.1 Purpose

The establishment of the SCTF and the consequent agreement reached were the offspring of the Fourth International Polar Year (IPY-4) 2007–8.[7] The Agreement in its Preamble recognises the substantial benefits gained through the international cooperation during the IPY-4 including new scientific knowledge, infrastructure and technologies for observation and analysis. It is not that such international Arctic scientific cooperation had been lacking, but *enhancing* such cooperation *through legally binding obligations* is the real purpose of this new Agreement. The Agreement emphasises the importance of using the best available knowledge for decision-making by the governments in areas such as maintaining

5 Arctic Council Secretariat News and Events website: "Scientific Cooperation Agreement enters into force", 21 June 2018. www.arctic-council.org/index.php/en/our-work2/8-news-and-events/488-science-agreement-entry-into-force (accessed 30 June 2018).

6 Malgorzata Smieszek (2017) "The Agreement on Enhancing International Arctic Scientific Cooperation: From Paper to Practice" *Arctic Yearbook* 6: 439–445.

7 For a brief history of the negotiation on the Agreement, see Shibata and Raita, *supra* note 3, at 134–136.

peace, stability and constructive cooperation in the Arctic; the sustainable use of resources; economic development; human health and environmental protection; and actions to mitigate and adapt to climate change. In order to make such decisions based on best available knowledge, the contracting governments considered that, through a legally binding agreement, they needed to "enhance international cooperation in Scientific Activities in order to increase effectiveness and efficiency in the development of scientific knowledge about the Arctic" (Article 2). In other words, for their own interests, the contracting governments agreed to exercise their relevant jurisdiction relating to Arctic science so as to achieve such knowledge development through international cooperation.

12.2.2 Core obligations

The Agreement obliges its Parties to exercise their existing regulatory powers regarding scientific activities in a way more advantageous for Arctic science. This legal nature of the core obligations under the Agreement has not changed over the negotiations.[8] Contrary to the Antarctic Treaty, the Arctic Science Cooperation Agreement does not provide for the freedom of scientific research under international law. During the negotiation of the Agreement within the SCTF, Observer delegations of Germany, France and the United Kingdom, in their joint statement, referred to a general principle of freedom of scientific research and requested that this principle be inserted in the Agreement.[9] However, the final text of the Agreement does not refer to this principle.

More specifically, the Agreement tries to enhance international Arctic scientific cooperation by obliging its Parties to "facilitate" the way in which relevant administrative procedures and legal mechanisms are to be applied and implemented. These facilitative measures would be taken by its Parties for the benefit of the "Scientific Activities" and the "Participants" as defined by the Agreement (see sections 12.2.5 and 12.3.3 below). The Agreement defines the term "facilitate" as "pursuing all necessary procedures, including giving timely consideration and making decisions as expeditiously as possible" (Article 1). This definition is strengthened, compared to the previous draft.[10] Under the customary usage, the obligation to facilitate denotes a passive action not to obstruct something.[11] On the contrary, the term "facilitate" in this Agreement provides a positive obligation

8 For an analysis on the Oslo draft of February 2015, see ibid., at 137–143.

9 Joint Statement of Germany, France and the United Kingdom on the draft of the "Agreement on Enhancing International Arctic Scientific Cooperation" (date unspecified but circulated during the SCTF Reykjavik meeting on 1–2 December 2015) (on file with the author). See also Arctic Council, Task Force on Scientific Cooperation (2015) *Summary submitted by the co-chairs on its VII meeting, Reykjavik, 1–2 December 2015*. https://oaarchive.arctic-council.org/handle/11374/1733 (accessed 1 July 2018).

10 Shibata and Raita, *supra* note 3, at 137.

11 Cf. Article 255 of the United Nations Convention on the Law of the Sea (UNCLOS). See Shibata, *supra* note 2, at 48–49.

on the part of the contracting governments to proactively pursue "all necessary procedures", in addition to a usual negative obligation not to place impediments. At the same time, it is important to note a subtle gradation that has been inserted into the obligation: the straightforward obligation to facilitate is provided in relation to access to research areas (Article 6 (1)), permit processing for marine scientific research (Article 6 (2)), and access to data (Article 7). On the other hand, as to entry and exit of persons, equipment, and material (Article 4) and access to research infrastructure and facilities (Article 5), the obligations are to "use best efforts to facilitate". It is understandable that entry of personnel and their equipment into the territories of contracting parties under Article 4 must also take into account security considerations. Similarly, as to the access to research infrastructure and facilities, Article 5 of the Agreement limits its application to "national" (excluding private) and "civilian" (excluding military) research facilities, and allows security and confidentiality considerations in its implementation. These flexibilities were inserted at the final Ottawa negotiation in July 2016 after careful deliberations. This signifies the seriousness of the signing governments to implement the far-reaching obligation to pursue all necessary procedures to facilitate Arctic science.

12.2.3 Geographic scope

It is significant that the Agreement covers the entire Arctic region as an integrated area for promotion of science, without distinguishing its terrestrial, marine and air spaces. Article 6 provides the obligation of the Parties to facilitate access by Participants to the research areas consisting of terrestrial, coastal, atmospheric and marine areas without distinguishing between them. General international law provides different legal regimes for the land and the sea, for different zones in the sea, and for airspace over the land and territorial sea, and that over the high seas, as well as for outer space. Premised on this differentiation under general international law, including its different treatment of scientific activities in the respective areas, the Agreement requires its contracting governments in all areas under its geographic scope to enhance international scientific cooperation. They shall do so by pursuing all necessary procedures commensurate with their relevant jurisdiction relative to the different areas as provided under general international law. The Agreement, in the context of international scientific cooperation, recognises the Arctic region as a distinct legal sphere requiring integrated treatment.[12] This conceptual underpinning of the Arctic Science Cooperation Agreement corresponds with that of the Antarctic Treaty System.[13]

Geographically, the Agreement provides for three layers of its application. First, a generic term of "the Arctic" denotes a general and widest meaning of the

12 Shibata, *supra* note 2, at 50.

13 Akiho Shibata (2015) "Japan and 100 Years of Antarctic Legal Order: Any Lessons for the Arctic?" *Yearbook of Polar Law* 7: 3–54.

region, without a definition. It is used in key provisions such as Article 2 on the Purpose ("development of scientific knowledge about the Arctic") and Article 1 on the definition of Scientific Activities ("efforts to advance understanding of the Arctic"). The Agreement does not intend to restrict the scope of scientific interest relating to the Arctic to a strictly defined geographic area. Second, the term "territory" appears only once in Article 4 on entry and exit of persons, equipment and material. The term "territory" denotes the entry and exit points for transboundary movements of scientists and related material, where cumbersome immigration, security and taxation procedures are usually applied. Each contracting party to the Agreement shall use its best efforts to facilitate such procedures and make decisions as expeditiously as possible when the Participants as well as their research platforms, material, samples, data and equipment are to enter into and exit from its territory.

Third, the term "Identified Geographic Areas" (IGAs) appears only in Article 5 on access to research infrastructure and facilities and Article 6 on access to research areas. Article 5 obliges its Parties to use their best efforts to facilitate access by the Participants to national civilian research infrastructure and facilities and other logistical services such as transportation for the purpose of conducting Scientific Activities in the IGAs. In other words, the Parties are obliged to facilitate access only with regard to those scientific facilities and other services used for activities undertaken within the IGAs. It should be noted, however, that these facilities might not always be physically situated in the IGAs when the obligation of facilitation applies. For example, a research vessel in the harbour of St Petersburg (outside of IGAs) heading for the Arctic Ocean (within the IGAs) for Scientific Activities may under certain conditions come under the purview of the facilitation obligation under Article 5. The obligation under Article 6 to facilitate access by the Participants to research areas when conducting Scientific Activities applies to all terrestrial, coastal, atmospheric and marine areas of the IGAs. This is significant because, in essence, the vast areas of IGAs (see Figure 12.1) in its totality have been designated as research areas where access by Participants would be promoted and facilitated for the purpose of conducting Scientific Activities. Although such activities must be conducted subject to applicable domestic laws and regulations (Article 10), the Agreement does not foresee the need of additional implementing agreements or arrangements (see Article 3) to "open" a research area within the IGAs.

Knowing the exact geographic extent of the IGAs is crucial not only for the Parties to the Agreement but also for scientists seeking access for fieldwork. IGAs are self-claimed areas described by each of the eight Arctic states and are reflected in Annex I of the Agreement. Annex I constitutes an integral part of the Agreement and is legally binding (Article 14 (1)), and any amendment to it must be by agreement of all the Parties (Article 18 (1)). Thus, once listed in Annex I, the geographic extent of the IGAs becomes a part of the facilitation obligation under Articles 5 and 6 of the Agreement. Denmark, Finland and Iceland designated all of their territories and their marine areas, whereas other five Parties designated only a part of their territories using either certain degrees of north latitude

Figure 12.1 Identified Geographic Areas (IGAs) under the Arctic Science Cooperation Agreement

Source: US Department of State (2017): www.state.gov/e/oes/ocns/opa/arc/278907.htm (accessed 30 September 2018)

(Norway and Sweden) or certain domestic administrative or policy districts/areas as the southern limits of their IGAs. Figure 12.1 depicts the area of IGAs as reflected in Annex I. This map is produced by the United States Department of State to reflect the Agreement.

The self-proclaimed IGAs by the Parties, however, are legally framed by the provision of the chapeau in Annex I. The area described by each Party includes an area over which that Party exercises sovereignty, sovereign rights or jurisdiction, including land and internal waters within that area and the adjacent territorial sea, exclusive economic zone (EEZ) and continental shelf, consistent with international law. Significantly, the chapeau of Annex I provides further that "Identified Geographic Areas also include areas beyond national jurisdiction in the high seas north of 62 degrees north latitude". With this latter provision, the famous high seas portions in the Arctic, namely the Banana Hole in the Norwegian Sea, the Loop Hole in the Barents Sea and the Central Arctic Ocean (CAO), are included in the IGAs.[14] The inclusion of the high seas within the IGAs does have merit when one considers the practical implication of Article 5. It could happen that, for example, a research vessel might be planning to conduct marine scientific research only in the CAO, for which the facilitation of access under Article 5 would be provided only if such vessel conduct Scientific Activities in the area designated as IGAs.

Given that the five Arctic coastal states did indeed designate all land areas facing the Arctic Ocean with their adjacent marine areas as their IGAs, and with the legal consequences of the chapeau in the Annex I, the entire Arctic Ocean including its high seas portion is now legally designated as IGAs. Thus, the access to the entire Arctic Ocean by Participants and their research vessels and other logistical services shall be facilitated under international law. This may be another concrete appeal by the eight Arctic states of "the special role and responsibility of the Arctic states for marine stewardship in the Arctic region".[15]

12.2.4 Arctic marine scientific research and the law of the sea

As the Arctic Science Cooperation Agreement has come to apply widely to the Arctic waters including their high seas, the non-Arctic states and their scientists actively engaged in marine research expressed some concerns as to its relationship with the United Nations Convention on the Law of the Sea (UNCLOS),

14 It should be noted that, according to the Map produced by the United States, the so-called Donut Hole in the Bering Sea is also included in the IGAs, although the Donut is south of 62 degree north latitude. This inclusion may have legal effect if the Map can be considered as an "instrument which was made by one or more parties in connection with the conclusion of the treaty and accepted by the other parties as an instrument related to the treaty" (Article 31 (2) (b) of the Vienna Convention on the Law of Treaties).

15 Arctic Council, Task Force on Arctic Marine Cooperation (2017) *Report to the Ministers of the Task Force on Arctic Marine Cooperation, 11 May 2017*, at 7. See also Tore Henriksen (2016) "The Arctic Ocean, Environmental Stewardship, and the Law of the Sea" *UC Irvine Law Review* 6: 61–82.

particularly its provisions relating to marine scientific research. The eight Arctic states negotiating the Agreement, acknowledging such concerns, repeatedly assured them that the Agreement would not prejudice their rights and obligations under UNCLOS.[16] The Agreement fully takes into account "the relevant provisions of the 1982 UNCLOS, in particular the provisions in Part XIII on marine scientific research as they relate to promoting and facilitating the development and conduct of marine scientific research" (6th preambular paragraph) and provides, in Article 6 (2), that the Parties "shall facilitate the processing of applications to conduct marine scientific research under this Agreement *consistent with* the 1982 UNCLOS" (emphasis added). Article 246 (3) of UNCLOS obliges all its Parties to "establish rules and procedures ensuring that such consent (for marine scientific research projects by other States in their EEZ) will not be delayed or denied unreasonably. Based on such rules and procedures, the Agreement requires its Parties to facilitate the processing of permit applications, that is to pursue all necessary procedures including making decisions as expeditiously as possible. Article 17 (3) of the Agreement provides that "(n)othing in this Agreement shall affect rights and obligations of the Parties under agreements with non-Parties". These rights and obligations, of course, include those under UNCLOS with its non-Arctic state parties. Thus, the Agreement promotes international cooperation in Arctic marine scientific research consistent with the carefully balanced rights and obligations of both coastal states and researching states as regards different zones of the seas as provided in UNCLOS. In light of the reality that the permit processing by coastal states is often delayed and denied,[17] it is significant that the eight Arctic states agreed to facilitate the processing of permits for the specific case of Arctic marine scientific research in their EEZ.

There still remains a question as to how such a special agreement among the eight Arctic states promoting and facilitating marine scientific research in the Arctic waters can be appropriately situated within the legal framework of UNCLOS, particularly as to its balance between universalism and regionalism.[18] In principle, as long as the careful balancing of rights and obligations based on universalism between coastal and researching states as regards marine scientific research has been kept intact, UNCLOS allows the relevant states to agree to exercise their coastal states' jurisdiction in a way more conducive for international cooperation regarding marine scientific research in a particular area of the seas, including regional seas.[19] As Alan Boyle attests, it is more the political will of the relevant

16 Evan Bloom (2014) "The New Arctic Frontier in International Law and Diplomacy" *Keynote Address at Arthur Watts Public International Law Seminar Series, British Institute of International and Comparative Law, London, 19 November 2014* (on file with the author).

17 Shibata and Raita, *supra* note 3, at 141–142, footnotes 28, 29 and 30.

18 Alan Boyle (2000) "Globalism and Regionalism in the Protection of the Marine Environment" in *Protecting the Polar Marine Environment: Law and Policy for Pollution Prevention* edited by Davor Vidas. Cambridge University Press, Cambridge: 19.

19 Alexander Proelss (ed.) (2017) *United Nations Convention on the Law of the Sea: A Commentary*. C.H. Beck, Munich: 1639.

states, rather than its natural or physical conditions, that identifies a certain sea as "regional" where a strengthened cooperation needs to be effectuated. According to Timo Koivurova, since 2005 the eight Arctic states within the Arctic Council have demonstrated such political will to treat the Arctic region requiring special governance. The Arctic Science Cooperation Agreement can be seen as yet another extension of such "paradigm change".[20]

Indeed, Article 243 of UNCLOS obliges all its Parties to cooperate for creation of favourable conditions for the conduct of marine scientific research "through the conclusion of bilateral and multilateral agreements". According to Alfred Soons, such favourable conditions include applying simplified procedures for obtaining permits and a general permission to conduct certain categories of research, but usually based on reciprocity.[21] The Arctic Scientific Cooperation Agreement as regards its application to marine scientific research in the Arctic waters can be seen as a unique implementing agreement at a regional level called for by Article 243 of UNCLOS. Moreover, the Agreement provides a legal possibility to extend its favourable conditions to research vessels, including those flagged to non-Arctic states, conducting marine scientific research within the Arctic waters identified as IGAs (see section 12.3.3 below).

12.2.5 Functional scope: "Scientific Activities"

The Agreement applies to "Scientific Activities" defined as "efforts to advance understanding of the Arctic through scientific research, monitoring and assessment" (Article 1). A previous title of the Agreement was on "Enhancing International Scientific Cooperation *in the Arctic*". However, it was changed after the SCTF Copenhagen meeting in August 2015 to "Enhancing International Arctic Scientific Cooperation", precisely because the Agreement "would not just focus on scientific research *in* the Arctic, but rather on scientific research *on* the Arctic, implying that research on Arctic issues could be done outside of the Arctic".[22] Thus, the examples of Scientific Activities provided in the definition can occur both within and outside of the Arctic, in its widest meaning, as long as they are the efforts to advance understanding of the Arctic in order to develop scientific knowledge about the Arctic (Article 2). The examples of Scientific Activities as provided in Article 1 include planning and implementation of scientific research projects and programmes, expeditions, observations, surveys, modelling and assessment; organising and execution of scientific seminars, workshops and meetings; collecting, processing, analysing and sharing scientific data, ideas, results, methods, and traditional and local knowledge; and preparing publications. Thus,

20 Timo Koivurova (2015) "Can We Conclude an Arctic Treaty?" *Yearbook of Polar Law* 7, 417.

21 Alfred H.A. Soons (1982) *Marine Scientific Research and the Law of the Sea*. T.M.C. Asser Institute, The Hague, 242.

22 Arctic Council, Task Force on Scientific Cooperation (2015) *Summary submitted by the co-chairs on its VI meeting, Copenhagen, 19–20 August 2015*, 1 October 2015 (on file with the author; emphasis in the original).

the Agreement applies to all kinds of scientific activities relating to the Arctic irrespective of their physical place of occurrence. This demonstrates again the perception of the eight Arctic states treating Arctic science as requiring special attention and in its entirety, overcoming artificial territorial boundaries.[23]

12.3 Incorporating the interests of non-Arctic states and their scientists

12.3.1 The negotiation process

The last three SCTF meetings at Reykjavík (December 2015), Arlington (March 2016) and Ottawa (July 2016) devoted substantial time and energy to the discussion on the scope of beneficiaries of the Agreement. In the final stage of the negotiations, the eight Arctic states carefully considered and finally determined how to incorporate the legitimate interests of non-Arctic states and their scientists actively engaged in and contributing to Arctic science. We have identified those legitimate interests as, first, the legal interests recognised under international law, including UNCLOS, of the non-Arctic states active in the Arctic science. Second, the equal treatment of scientists working in the Arctic irrespective of their nationalities – a legitimate expectation recognised by the Arctic scientific communities.[24]

The final Agreement is a closed treaty for the eight Arctic states without an accession clause. Thus, it does not represent "a quantum leap"[25] for the Arctic Council's practice to open the agreements negotiated under its auspices to non-Arctic states. Consequently, the facilitation obligations under the Agreement are imposed only on the eight Arctic Parties, and the legal rights to claim that their nationals and institutions receive benefits under the Agreement and to request rectification if problems persist are enjoyed only by the eight Arctic Parties vis-à-vis other Parties. As to the state-to-state relationship, the well-established doctrine of *res inter alios acta*, or a matter between others does not harm or benefit us, squarely applies to the Agreement.

At the same time, after the eight Arctic states decided in May 2015 to work towards a legally binding instrument for Arctic scientific cooperation,[26] the SCTF co-chairs proactively approached the non-Arctic Observer states and organisations and decided to allow their interventions during the meetings, both orally and through written documents. This is precisely because the need for "non-Arctic states … [to] receive benefits under the Agreement … was supported by several Arctic states".[27] At the Copenhagen meeting in August 2015, ten

23 Shibata, *supra* note 2, at 50–51.

24 Shibata and Raita, *supra* note 3, at 147–158.

25 Shibata, *supra* note 2, at 53.

26 *Iqaluit Declaration on the occasion of the Ninth Ministerial Meeting of the Arctic Council*, 24 April 2015, para. 44.

27 *Summary submitted by the co-chairs on its VI meeting*, *supra* note 22.

Observers were in attendance and some of them made presentations during the meeting.[28] At the Reykjavík meeting, a joint statement with specific textual proposals was submitted by Germany, France and the United Kingdom. The meeting recognised that these proposals have "contributed to the discussion on the draft agreement".[29] The Executive Secretary of IASC also made statements.[30] At the Arlington meeting, Japan[31] and Poland[32] submitted their written statements, and many Observer representatives made oral interventions during the meeting. Even though at around noon of the first day of the two-day meeting the co-chairs declared that there would be no more interventions from the Observers, they were still able to convey their views informally (and maybe more effectively) in the corridors and at receptions and dinner tables.[33] At the final Ottawa meeting, the co-chairs again allowed the Observers to express their views on the negotiating texts, particularly on the provision regarding non-Parties (see section 12.3.4 below).[34] There had been some important improvements made in the relevant texts. As the result, the Agreement can now be said to "extend benefits under the Agreement to non-Parties (including Arctic Council Observer states)".[35] Let us examine more closely these "benefits" that can be extended to non-Arctic states and their scientists under the Agreement.

12.3.2 Importance of cooperation with non-Arctic states

The Agreement explicitly recognises the importance of continuing engagement by non-Parties (that is non-Arctic states) and their research organisations and

28 France, Germany, Italy, Japan, Republic of Korea, United Kingdom, IASC, University of the Arctic (UArctic), North Atlantic Marine Mammal Commission (NAMMCO) and Nordic Council for Ministers (NCM). Arctic Council Secretariat News and Events website: "Scientific Cooperation Task Force (SCTF) meets in Copenhagen". www.arctic-council.org/index.php/en/ our-work2/8-news-and-events/360-sctf-copenhagen (accessed 1 July 2018).

29 Arctic Council Secretariat News and Events website: "Scientific Cooperation Task force (SCTF) meets in Reykjavik". www.arctic-council.org/index.php/en/our-work2/8-news-and-events/379-scientific-cooperation-task-force-sctf-meets-in-reykjavik (accessed 1 July 2018). Six Observers attended the meeting: France, Germany, Republic of Korea, United Kingdom, European Union and IASC. *Summary submitted by the Co-Chairs on its VII meeting*, *supra* note 9.

30 Arctic Council (2016) *Observer Report of International Arctic Science Committee (IASC)*, 30 May 2016. http://hdl.handle.net/11374/1875 (accessed 1 July 2018).

31 Arctic Council (2016) *Observer Report of Japan*, 16 December 2016. http://hdl.handle.net/11374/1868 (accessed 1 July 2018).

32 Arctic Council (2016) *Observer Report of Poland*, 31 May 2016. http://hdl.handle.net/11374/1879 (accessed 1 July 2018).

33 At Arlington, 11 Observers attended the meeting: China, France, Germany, Italy, Japan, Republic of Korea, Poland, United Kingdom, European Union (two delegates), IASC and UArctic.

34 At Ottawa, 12 Observers attended the meeting: China, France, Germany, Italy, Japan, Poland, Republic of Korea, United Kingdom, European Union, IASC, UArctic and WWF.

35 Arctic Council (2017) *Senior Arctic Officials' Report to the Ministers, Fairbanks, Alaska, 11 May 2017*, at 79. http://hdl.handle.net/11374/1909 (accessed 1 July 2018).

scientists for enhancing international Arctic scientific cooperation.[36] Because of this recognition, a proposal from Russia to restrict the scope of Scientific Activities to those "joint or cooperative activities *between the Parties*" was not accepted by other negotiating Parties. Many Observers, including Japan, expressed concerns specifically to this restriction. At the Ottawa meeting, a small contact group led by Norway was established to address this issue, and its resolution was finally achieved.

It became known in the contact group discussion that one of the main reasons that Russia requested the insertion of "cooperative activity" was because its domestic laws required international scientific activities conducted within its land territory to have a Russian partner. Thus, the issue was rather a technical one related to drafting and finding an appropriate language in the Agreement that would not prejudice the requirements under Russian law. The final agreed resolution was to delete all reference to "cooperative activities between the Parties" which had the effect of restricting the functional scope of the Agreement, namely the definition of Scientific Activities. Russian domestic law concerns were addressed instead in the definition of Participants by explicitly inserting the term "partners". Thus, the Agreement covers all Scientific Activities, including those undertaken by and with the cooperation of non-Arctic states and their scientists and, consequently, the benefits of facilitation under the Agreement can be extended to those activities.

12.3.3 "Participants": the beneficiaries of the Agreement

The definition of Participants as the scope of beneficiaries of the Agreement has gained importance, especially for the Observers attending the SCTF meetings. Many of their statements, textual proposals and informal contacts related to this issue. The Participants are the beneficiaries of the Agreement; for example, under Article 4 (facilitation of entry and exit of "persons [...] and equipment of the Participants") and under Article 6 (1) (facilitation of access "by the Participants to [...] areas in the IGAs"). The final agreed text of the definition of Participants reads as follows (underlining has been added):

> "*Participants*" means the Parties' scientific and technological departments and agencies, research centers, universities and colleges, <u>and contractors, grantees and other partners acting with or on behalf of any Party or Parties</u>, involved in Scientific Activities under this Agreement.

The underlined part was the package proposal coming from the contact group led by Norway that discussed the two issues on "cooperative activity" and "Participants" together during the final hours of the Ottawa meeting. The first part

36 Cf. the eleventh preambular paragraph of the Agreement, which recognises "the significant scientific expertise and invaluable contribution to scientific activities being made by non-Parties and specifically by the Arctic Council Permanent Participants and Arctic Council Observers".

of the text is clear that the beneficiaries of the Agreement would be scientific organisations and their scientists having the nationality of and/or the place of their establishment in one of the Parties to the Agreement, namely the eight Arctic states. However, as to the second part of the text, it is the understanding of the negotiating states, including Russia, that this underlined part is independent from the first part. Consequently, "other partners" in the latter part of the text are not conditioned by their legal relationship with the Parties, either by their nationality or their place of establishment. Thus, the beneficiaries of the Agreement shall include scientific partners from non-Arctic states as long as they are "acting with or on behalf of any Party or Parties". For example, a Japanese–Finnish joint scientific team seeking fieldwork in Russia as one of Scientific Activities as defined by the Agreement would benefit the facilitation by the Russian authorities as to their entry into the Russian territory (Article 4), access to Russian national civil research infrastructure in its IGA (Article 5) and access to the research area for the fieldwork within its IGA (Article 6 (1)). Those benefits will equally apply to all members of the team and their equipment, irrespective of their nationalities.

It is true that, under the Agreement, the benefits would accrue to non-Arctic states' scientists only when they are the partners of one or more of the Parties acting with them or on their behalf. The phrase "acting with or on behalf of any Party" does not necessarily require that non-Arctic states' scientists must always be physically with the Party or its representatives in order to benefit the facilitation under the Agreement. For example, a research team composed of all Japanese scientists on the invitation of their Russian counterpart based on a joint research programme with the Russian scientists can benefit from the facilitation provided under Article 4 as to their entry visa. From a more practical point of view, the facilitation measures assumed under Articles 4, 5 and 6 (1) where the Participants are designated as beneficiaries can be implemented almost invariably with some kind of agreement with the relevant territorial or jurisdictional state as a Party to the Agreement. For example, an access to Russian icebreakers or Russian research facilities in its IGA (Article 5) can materialise only with a prior approval by the relevant Russian authorities as to the activities requiring such access. This prior approval by the Russian authorities would most likely be required for all Scientific Activities, including those by the nationals of the Parties to the Agreement. If one can interpret the phrase "partners … acting with or on behalf of any Party" to include those non-Party scientists whose proposed scientific activities have obtained approval by the relevant territorial/jurisdictional Parties, in practical terms, there would be almost no difference between the scientists with the nationality of the eight Arctic states and those of non-Arctic states. With this interpretation, the legitimate expectation of the scientists that they be treated equally irrespective of their nationalities would be practically achieved.

12.3.4 Cooperation with non-Parties

As demonstrated above, with the constructive engagement of non-Arctic Observer states in its negotiation representing the interests of their scientists, the Arctic Science Cooperation Agreement has been fairly successful in eliminating discrimination among the scientists based on their nationalities. At the same time, the distinction between the eight Arctic states as Parties to the Agreement and the non-Arctic states as non-Parties still remains at the state-to-state level. The Agreement does not provide for non-Parties the right to bring legal claims against the Parties. This is a legal consequence of the principle of aforementioned *res inter alios acta*. In other words, non-Arctic states as non-Parties cannot legally claim on behalf of their scientists against an Arctic state as a Party to the Agreement that they be provided with the benefits based on the Agreement. Thus, the benefits that may accrue to scientists from non-Arctic states under the Agreement cannot be said to constitute legal interests protected and enforceable under international law.

The Agreement, however, has endeavoured to fill this legal gap through an innovative provision on "Cooperation with Non-Parties" under Article 17. Contrary to meagre provisions with a similar title in the two previous Agreements negotiated under the auspices of the Arctic Council,[37] Article 17 of the Agreement is rich in its legal and practical significance. It was one of the most controversial provisions during the negotiation, the resolution of which was achieved only at the final Ottawa meeting. Its paragraph 1 declares that the Parties may continue to enhance and facilitate cooperation with non-Parties, whereas, as explained above, its paragraph 3 is a without prejudice clause. The gist of Article 17 lies in its paragraph 2: "Article 17 (2): Parties may in their discretion undertake with non-Parties cooperation described in this Agreement and apply measures consistent with those described in this Agreement in cooperation with non-Parties." Although framed as a discretionary provision, this provision enables the Parties to extend their substantive obligations under the Agreement to the scientific cooperation with non-Arctic states. It formally recognises the possibility to transform the benefits that may accrue to non-Arctic states' Participants under the Agreement to legal interests protected and possibly enforceable under international law. First, Article 17 (2) allows its Parties to "undertake" the cooperation described in the Agreement with non-Arctic states. These are: cooperation as regards entry and exit of persons and equipment (Article 4); access to research infrastructure (Article 5); access to research areas (Article 6); access to data (Article 7); education and career development (Article 8); and traditional and local knowledge (Article 9). Then, Article 17 (2) allows its Parties to "apply measures" described in the Agreement in such cooperation with non-Arctic states. These measures are the facilitative measures, defined as pursuing all necessary procedures, including giving timely consideration and making decisions as expeditiously as possible. The extension of such facilitative measures can be applied individually with specific non-Parties and/or generally with all non-Parties participating in the Scientific Activities as defined in the Agreement.

37 See Article 18 on "Non-Parties" under Agreement on Cooperation on Aeronautical and Maritime Search and Rescue in the Arctic (2011), and Article 17 on "Non-Parties" under Agreement on Cooperation on Marine Oil Pollution Preparedness and Response in the Arctic (2013).

Depending on the legal nature of the decision by the Parties to "undertake" cooperation with and "apply measures" to non-Arctic states, such extension of facilitative measures can be legally binding on the concerned Party and one or more non-Arctic states. One such legal means to extend the benefits of the Agreement to non-Arctic states is the utilisation of bilateral science and technology cooperation agreements (STCAs) concluded by many Arctic and non-Arctic states.[38] For example, the Japan–Russia Science and Technology Cooperation Agreement concluded in 2000 (Japan–Russia STC Agreement)[39] can provide a legal avenue for Russia to implement Article 17 (2) of the Arctic Science Cooperation Agreement towards Japan. Japan may also urge Russia to utilise its STC Agreement to examine the possibility of extending the cooperative measures as provided in the Arctic Science Cooperation Agreement. In fact, in 2015, the Japan–Russia Joint Committee on Scientific and Technological Cooperation established under the Agreement identified Arctic research as one area where both parties have an interest in strengthening the cooperation.[40] In implementation of Article 17 (2) of the Arctic Science Cooperation Agreement, Japan–Russia Joint Committee can further specify the facilitative measures to be applied to Japan as to certain Scientific Activities in which Japanese scientists are involved. On a reciprocal basis, the Committee can also identify relevant measures that Japan can take to promote international Arctic scientific cooperation with Russia, including, for example, access to its research infrastructure, such as its Arctic research vessel *MIRAI* (Article 5) and access to its scientific data relating to the Arctic (Article 7). These agreed measures to "enhance efficiency in the cooperative activities" (Article 6 (1) (d) of the Japan–Russia STC Agreement) can be provided in a legally binding implementing agreement between the two governments and/or in a non-binding memorandum of understanding (MoU) between relevant scientific organisations of the two parties. Even in the latter case, the MoU between scientific organisations is formally based on Japan–Russia STC Agreement, and, therefore, Japan has a legal interest in the appropriate implementation of such MoUs. Thus, through the existing legal mechanisms such as STCAs, the benefits accrued to non-Arctic states' scientists under the Arctic Science Cooperation Agreement can be transformed into legal interests protected and possibly enforceable under international law.

In order for the non-Arctic states to legally benefit from the Agreement, they need separate agreements to that effect with the relevant Arctic states. However,

38 The legal relationship between the Arctic Science Cooperation Agreement and bilateral STCAs has been analysed in Shibata and Raita, *supra* note 3, at 139.

39 Agreement between the Government of Japan and the Government of Russian Federation on Cooperation in Science and Technology, done on 4 September 2000, *Gaimusho Kokuji* (Ministry of Foreign Affairs Notice) No. 458 (24 October 2000, in Japanese and Russian only).

40 Gaimusho (Ministry of Foreign Affairs) website: *The result of the 12th meeting of the Japan–Russia Joint Committee on Scientific and Technological Cooperation*. www.mofa.go.jp/mofaj/press/release/press4_002439.html (accessed 1 July 2018, in Japanese).

this distinction may also be more formal than substantive, because, according to Article 3 of the Agreement, "cooperative activities under this Agreement shall take place pursuant to specific implementing agreements or arrangements concluded between the Parties or Participants". In other words, it is expected that, even among the eight Arctic state Parties to the Agreement, the specific facilitative measures provided under the Agreement would be effectuated in accordance with additional implementing agreements and arrangements. Thus, if the cooperation between Arctic state Parties and non-Arctic states is indeed enhanced as recommended by the Agreement (Article 17 (1)), the benefits arising from facilitative measures under the Agreement would accrue almost invariably upon both the Arctic state Parties and non-Arctic states cooperating with them in Arctic science. This optimism is shared by the eight Arctic Council Foreign Ministers as they emphasised that the "Agreement [...] *confirms* that the Parties have the discretion to extend benefits under the Agreement to non-Parties (including Arctic Council Observer states) when they cooperate with Arctic states".[41]

12.3.5 Review of the Agreement and non-Arctic states

Article 12 of the Agreement establishes a review process to consider the "implementation of this Agreement, including successes achieved and obstacles to implementation, as well as to improve the effectiveness and implementation of this Agreement" (Article 12 (2)). This review will take place in a meeting of the Parties to the Agreement (MoP), most likely convened in conjunction with meetings of the Arctic Council. It also provides that the Parties may decide to invite Arctic Council Permanent Participants and Arctic Council Observers. Here, unlike the two previous Agreements, the Arctic Science Cooperation Agreement, although formally outside of the Arctic Council ambit, establishes an institutional link with the Council.

From the perspective of non-Arctic actors, it is significant, first, that Article 12 (1) explicitly provides that the Arctic Council Observers, including many of the non-Arctic states actively engaged in Arctic science and Arctic scientific organisations such as IASC, can attend the MoP "to observe and provide information". Although they would not be involved in the decision-making, the Agreement recognises the importance of non-Arctic actors' participation and provision of information in considering the effectiveness of the Agreement. Second, the third sentence of Article 12 (1) provides as follows: "Scientific cooperation activities with non-Parties related to Arctic science may be taken into account when reviewing the implementation of this Agreement." In effect, this is an explicit mandate for the MoP to review the implementation of Article 17 on cooperation with non-Parties. As explained above, Article 17 leaves it to the discretion

41 *Senior Arctic Officials' Report to the Ministers, supra* note 35, at 79 (emphasis added). This report is adopted by the AC Ministerial Meeting at Fairbank. *Fairbanks Declaration on the Occasion of the Tenth Ministerial Meeting of the Arctic Council*, 11 May 2017, Fairbanks, Alaska, para. 45.

of the Arctic state Parties to extend the benefits of the Agreement to non-Parties. However, through Article 12 (1), the actual implementation of this discretion would be internationally monitored as an issue of common interest of the Parties. Moreover, this international monitoring would occur with the participation of and information provided from those non-Parties as Arctic Council Observers. This third sentence was inserted in the final Ottawa meeting based on the proposal from Denmark. Japan, during the negotiation of the Agreement, had been requesting that non-Arctic states' interest would also be reflected in the implementation phase of the Agreement. The voice of non-Arctic actors was indeed heard and their interests reflected in the texts of the Arctic Science Cooperation Agreement.

12.4 Conclusion

The Arctic Science Cooperation Agreement sets a new model for Arctic international law-making within the Arctic Council. It is a fact that only the eight Arctic states had the decision-making powers during its negotiation, and that its outcome as a closed treaty will not directly provide legal benefits to non-Arctic states as non-Parties. However, within such limited parameters, the Agreement has succeed in reflecting as much as possible the interests of non-Arctic states and their scientists actively engaged in Arctic science, with substantive inputs from Arctic Council Observer states and organisations during its negotiation in the Science Cooperation Task Force (SCTF), a subsidiary body of the Arctic Council. This new model, of course, is premised on the recognition by the eight Arctic Council member states that the Arctic scientific endeavours can succeed only with the broadest cooperation from all interested and capable states and their scientists, irrespective of whether they are Arctic or non-Arctic.

Compared with the two previous agreements on Arctic search and rescue and Arctic marine oil spill response, for which a limited geographical context was still prevailing, the Arctic Science Cooperation Agreement addressed "the development of scientific knowledge about the Arctic" (Article 2) – an issue of universal significance and interest. The Arctic Council, for the first time in its 20-year history, was faced with a treaty-making exercise within which interests of non-Arctic actors had to be accounted for. In order to respond to this new situation, the procedural and diplomatic ingenuities demonstrated by the co-chairs of the SCTF must be highly appreciated, although most of them, I would suspect, were spontaneous and *ad hoc* decisions. Under the Rules of Procedure, in the Arctic Council's subsidiary bodies, including Task Forces, it is "at the discretion of the Chair, the Observers make statements [...], present written statements, submit documents and provide views on the issues under discussion".[42] In order for the

42 Rule 38, *Arctic Council Rules of Procedure,* most recent version adopted by the Kiruna Ministerial Meeting, 2013. www.arctic-council.org.

Observers to effectively contribute to the discussion and for their interests to be meaningfully heard, the exercise of this discretion by the Chairs should at least be consistent and foreseeable, if not written on paper. This is especially the case for Task Forces with their short lifespan and, unlike the permanent Working Groups, its customary practice of operation difficult to be established and discerned from outside. For example, after the decision by the SCTF co-chairs at the Arlington meeting that the Observers could no longer intervene during the meeting, the Observer delegations were not certain whether they would be allowed the opportunity to speak or submit papers at the next meeting at Ottawa. Some delegations, including Japan, did not think so and, consequently, its mandate for the Ottawa meeting was based on such silence. However, on the contrary, the co-chairs at the Ottawa meeting requested the views of Observers on specific texts of the draft Agreement. Even if we admit that the Arctic Council were an appropriate forum for negotiating a treaty on Arctic scientific cooperation, there certainly is a need of critical (and hopefully open) reflection on its practice and improvements for its future exercise, if and when such opportunity arises for the Arctic Council. From this perspective, the Arctic Council should consider making all negotiating documents of the SCTF publicly available.

More fundamentally, the legitimacy of Arctic Council as an Arctic international law-making forum for subject matters that substantively involve interests of non-Arctic actors must be critically examined. We have already seen the diversification of appropriate and legitimate intergovernmental law-making forums for and related to the Arctic: cf. International Maritime Organisation (IMO) for Polar Code; United Nations for climate change, conservation and sustainable use of biological diversity, persistent organic pollutants (POPs), and mercury; and Arctic Five Plus Five (A5+5) for the Central Arctic Ocean fisheries.[43] Although not yet a law-making forum, the Arctic Science Ministerial (ASM) biennial meetings with twenty-five governments interested in the Arctic science have gained its prominence.[44] The Arctic Council members will continue to be discreet as to the selection of subject matters and their potential legal designs that best suit its forum as a law-making venue. At the same time, the Arctic Council strives to maintain its status as the "preeminent intergovernmental forum for the Arctic Region",[45] and many pressing issues of its governance today cannot be addressed without the substantive involvement and cooperation of non-Arctic actors, like the black carbon problems in the Arctic.

43 See Chapter 8 by Joji Morishita and Chapter 9 by Erik Molenaar in this book for the details of the A5+5 process.

44 See the outcome of the first ASM meeting in 2016 hosted by the United States, United States Arctic Research Commission and Arctic Executive Steering Committee (eds) (2016) *Supporting Arctic Science: A Summary of the White House Arctic Science Ministerial Meeting, September 28, 2016, Washington, DC.* US Arctic Research Commission. Those 25 governments include those of the Faroe Islands, Greenland (separately from Denmark) and the European Union.

45 See 2nd preambular paragraph, *Fairbanks Declaration*, *supra* note 41.

With the experience of the Arctic Science Cooperation Agreement and based on its critical reflection, the time may have come for the Arctic Council to seriously consider the possibility of establishing a law-making process that, while still recognising the special role of Arctic states and its indigenous peoples, would be formally open to interested non-Arctic states and other relevant actors, during the negotiation and/or in its final outcome. A similar discussion arose in the Antarctic Treaty System in the 1970s when the consultative parties were considering the establishment of a fisheries regime in the Southern Ocean, the Convention on the Conservation of Antarctic Marine Living Resources (CCAMLR).[46] CCAMLR was negotiated within the Antarctic Treaty Consultative Meetings with the participation limited to the consultative parties. But it was adopted in a separately convened diplomatic conference where other interested nations, such as West Germany and East Germany, were invited to formally participate. Other interested intergovernmental organisations such as the United Nations Food and Agricultural Organization (FAO) and non-governmental organisations such as the World Conservation Union (IUCN) also participated in the adoption conference as observers. The Convention itself is open to “any State interested in research or harvesting activities in relation to the marine living resources to which this Convention applies”.[47] Depending on the subject matter of the law-making and its legal design, the effective governance of the Arctic may indeed be strengthened if the Arctic Council, while maintaining the initiative of the eight Arctic states and Permanent Participants, has the courage to formally open its law-making processes to relevant non-Arctic actors.

46 Akiho Shibata (2000) “Antarctic Treaty Consultative Meetings in 1970s” *Okayama Law Journal* 49–3/4: 445–464 (in Japanese).
47 Article 29, Convention on the Conservation of Antarctic Marine Living Resources, adopted 20 May 1980 and entered into force 7 April 1982, *United Nations Treaty Series* 1329: 47.

13 State Observers and science cooperation in the Arctic Council

Same same but different?

Sebastian Knecht and Jennifer Spence

13.1 Introduction

The Arctic Council's Observer policy towards non-Arctic states has been largely driven by functional desires. As official Council documents indicate, the primary role of Observers in the most important regional organisation for the circumpolar region is to bring additional resources to the table to help boost the Arctic Council in its mission to "provide a means for promoting cooperation, coordination and interaction among the Arctic states, with the involvement of the Arctic indigenous communities and other Arctic inhabitants on common Arctic issues".[1] To that end, Observers may either hold specialised knowledge and scientific expertise that could help promote the work and output of the Council or serve as multipliers to increase the Council's outreach, help distribute scientific results and promote the Council's political agenda among non-Arctic domestic or international audiences.

The first wave of non-Arctic state admission into the Arctic Council took place shortly after its establishment in 1996 and exclusively included European states, in addition to several non- and inter-governmental organisations. Germany, the Netherlands, Poland and the United Kingdom were admitted in 1998, with France following suit in 2000. All five states had long-established polar research programmes, including research stations located in the Arctic, and were thus able to contribute original data, research and knowledge to the newly founded body.[2] Furthermore, all of them (except for France) had already been Observers to the Arctic Council's predecessor, the Arctic Environmental Protection Strategy (AEPS), and had – together with Japan – joined the International Arctic Science Committee (IASC) in 1991. In brief, there were good reasons for a "European enlargement" of the Arctic Council early on to integrate these non-Arctic states into the work of the forum.

1 Article 1(a), *Ottawa Declaration on the Establishment of the Arctic Council*, 19 September 1996. https://oaarchive.arctic-council.org/bitstream/handle/11374/85/EDOCS-1752-v2-ACMMCA00_Ottawa_1996_Founding_Declaration.PDF?sequence=5&isAllowed=y (accessed 31 July 2018).

2 Ken Coates and Carin Holroyd (2017) "Non-Arctic States and Their Stake in Arctic Sustainability" in *Governing Arctic Change: Global Perspectives* edited by Kathrin Keil and Sebastian Knecht. Palgrave Macmillan, London: 207–228.

The second major wave of non-Arctic state admissions took place in 2013 and opened the institution to five Asian states (as well as Italy). This "Asian enlargement" involving China, India, Japan, Singapore and Republic of Korea presumably had other motivations than previous Observer admissions, and also had more direct and profound consequences for the perception, functionality and effectiveness of the Arctic Council. Rather than a step to solicit additional and particular expertise from Asian Observers, the eight Arctic states mainly sought to increase the reach of the "Arctic messenger"[3] and raise awareness for regional developments and governance challenges among those states that, according to the Arctic Council's own assessment work, had a stake in current Arctic environmental changes that were expected to have ripple effects on Asia and the globe. These states have been crucial in the successful negotiation of international agreements that the Arctic Council worked hard to advance, such as the 2013 Minimata Convention on Mercury and the International Code for Ships operating in Polar Waters (Polar Code) under the International Maritime Organization, both of which entered into force in 2017, or the annual UN climate change conferences.[4]

Although the Arctic Council's Observer policy applies the same rules and procedures to all Observers (though the institution classifies them into "non-Arctic states", "global and regional inter-governmental and inter-parliamentary organisations", and "non-governmental organisations"), the non-Arctic states admitted during these two distinct waves have differed considerably with regard to substance and regularity of their respective contributions to the work of the Arctic Council. Overall, the European Observers are more visible and hold stronger ties to Arctic scientific communities contributing to the Arctic Council's working groups than the Asian Observers.[5] This is surprising given Asian states' longstanding claims and relentless efforts to join the Arctic Council, and puzzling given the institutional reforms initiated by the forum to guarantee their successful integration. Although the same rules apply to all Observers, there are, as has been argued elsewhere, "different worlds of commitment".[6]

This chapter analyses the historical, political and legal context of Observers' admission and integration into Arctic Council affairs, and considers the unintended

3 David P. Stone (2015) *The Changing Arctic Environment: The Arctic Messenger*. Cambridge University Press, Cambridge.

4 Henrik Selin (2017) "Global Environmental Governance and Treaty-Making: The Arctic's Fragmented Voice" in Keil and Knecht, *supra* note 2, at 101–120; Olav Schram Stokke (2015) "Can Asian Involvement Strengthen Arctic Governance?" in *Asian Countries and the Arctic Future* edited by Jian Lunde, Jian Yang and Iselin Stensdal. World Scientific Publishing, Singapore: 51–60.

5 Jennifer Spence (2016) "Finding a Place in the Arctic Council for Non-Arctic Actors: A Social Network Analysis of the Arctic Monitoring and Assessment Programme" in *Arctic Yearbook 2016*, 74–90; Jennifer Spence (2017) "Is a Melting Arctic Making the Arctic Council Too Cool? Exploring the Limits to the Effectiveness of a Boundary Organization" *Review of Policy Research* 34–6: 790–811.

6 Sebastian Knecht (2017). "Exploring Different Levels of Stakeholder Activity in International Institutions: Late Bloomers, Regular Visitors, and Overachievers in Arctic Council Working Groups" in Keil and Knecht, *supra* note 2, at 163–185.

consequences of the admission and integration process following from procedural reforms in the Observer policy. Given the lack of previous research systematically examining sequences of Observer enlargement in the Arctic Council, this chapter sheds light on the changing Observer policy under which the European and the Asian Observers had been admitted in the late 1990s and in 2013 respectively. The legal context is hereby considered a necessary component to better understand why Arctic Council Observers have the same status, but have played different roles in the body. More precisely, the change from a flexible, informal and bottom-up approach to a more rule-based, formalised and top-down approach in the Observer policy may not only impact who gets admitted as an Observer in the first place, but also how Observers participate and what roles they perform following admission. This analysis may also prove useful to better comprehend and assess the functionality of the Council's Observer policy against the backdrop of an ever-increasing pool of interested stakeholders.

13.2 Development and change in the Arctic Council's Observer policy

Institutional rules of procedure (RoP) are usually designed to ensure the appropriate and effective functioning of an organisation's processes, bodies and administration. By joining an institution, the members are expected to observe the RoP and comply with them, even if they may not agree with every specific rule. Rules require a certain level of mutual understanding, acceptance and self-commitment among the parties bound by the rules. They may also be used to facilitate and promote a high degree of inclusiveness of all parties in order to "enable forms of collective action which otherwise would not emerge".[7] Members' adherence to an institution's RoP may not only depend on the presence of internal sanctions or external instruments for rule enforcement to manage non-compliant behaviour, such as international courts' judgments. Compliance may also be contingent on the formulation, comprehensibility and specificity of the rules.

For instance, it makes a difference whether a state attending an intergovernmental institution in the capacity of an Observer is given the freedom to participate, or its participation is explicitly constrained. In the first case, an Observer may be given the opportunity to raise points of order, distribute information and documents or give oral statements during meetings. Making use of this opportunity is an institutional practice articulated in the RoP, not a legal obligation that follows automatically from the Rules.[8] Non-usage does not infringe these rules, and will thus usually not entail any direct political or legal consequences

7 Kenneth A. Shepsle and Barry R. Weingast (1984) "When Do Rules of Procedure Matter?" *The Journal of Politics* 46: 217.

8 For more on this, see Robbie Sabel (2017) *Rules of Procedure at the UN and at Inter-Governmental Conferences, Third Edition*. Cambridge University Press, Cambridge.

for the Observer. If, on the other side, some elements of an international meeting like the decision-making process or voting are reserved for a specific "club", for example the full members of the institution or contracting parties to an agreement, then contestation of such a procedural norm will likely result in political consequences for the party concerned up to the point where the state might be suspended or expelled from the institution. In more colloquial speech, if you do not play by the rulebook, you will not play at all.

Under the RoP of the Arctic Council, a total of 39 Observer states, non-governmental and inter-governmental as well as inter-parliamentary organisations have been admitted between 1998 and 2017. The full record of admissions is presented in Figure 13.1. Notably, the Arctic Council has admitted the same number of actors – thirteen – in each category. This points to the Council's efforts to counteract the impression of a largely state-dominated Council that had emerged after the admission only of Italy and the five Asian states at the 2013 Ministerial Meeting in Kiruna, whereas for instance the applications of Greenpeace, the Association of Polar Early Career Scientists (APECS), the International Association of Oil and Gas Producers (IOGP), the International Hydrographic Organization, the European Union (EU) and the World Meteorological Organization (WMO) had not been approved. While admission also of non-state actors at the 2017 Ministerial Meeting in Fairbanks might be seen as a political strategy of legitimising the Council's admission and Observer policy by balancing out the number of actors in all three Observer categories, it may have the opposite effect with regard to those frequently left out of the Council due to this political pragmatism. In discussions of Observers it is often disregarded that many applications, like those mentioned above, continue to be deferred or rejected at Ministerial Meetings.

For those admitted to the Arctic Council as an Observer, the same rules and conditions apply. Whereas other inter-governmental organisations often distinguish between state and private or non-governmental organisations with respect to their status and participatory rights, all Observers in the Arctic Council are subject to the same conditionality criteria, the same readmission procedure, and the same rules and standards for participation. In light of this, the following discussion may also apply to non-state actors. We nevertheless focus particularly on the state Observers to the Council (on the left of the timeline in Figure 13.1) so as not to mix up the different legal and political statuses of state and non-state actors in international politics, and given the public and political discussions surrounding explicitly non-Arctic states' interest in Arctic affairs.[9]

9 See Piotr Graczyk (2011) "Observers in the Arctic Council – Evolution and Prospects" *Yearbook of Polar Law* 3: 576–633.

Non-Arctic states		NGOs	IGOs, IPOs*
Germany, Netherlands, Poland, UK	1998	IASC, IUCH, NF, WWF	SCPAR*, UNECE, UNEP
France	2000	ACOPS, AWRH, CCU, IASSA	IFRC, IUCN, NCM, NAMMCO
	2002	IWGIA, UArctic	UNDP
	2004	AINA	NEFCO
Spain	2006		
	2009		
	2011		
China, India, Italy, Japan, Singapore, South Korea	2013		
	2015		
Switzerland	2017	NGS, Oceana	ICES, OSPAR, WMO, WNC*

Figure 13.1 Observer accession in the Arctic Council over time[10]

10 NGOs: non-governmental organisations; IGOs: inter-governmental organisations; IPOs: inter-parliamentary organisations; UK: United Kingdom; IASC: International Arctic Science Committee; IUCH: International Union for Circumpolar Health; NF: Northern Forum; WWF: World Wide Fund for Nature; ACOPS: Advisory Committee on Protection of the Sea; AWRH: Association of World Reindeer Herders; CCU: Circumpolar Conservation Union; IASSA: International Arctic Social Sciences Association; IWGIA: International Work Group for Indigenous Affairs; UArctic: University of the Arctic; AINA: Arctic Institute of North

13.3 Arctic Council Observer policy under the 1998 Rules of Procedure

The Arctic Council's RoP have been reformed substantially in the course of the organisation's lifetime. These changes are not simply institutional and procedural adaptations to better accommodate a growing number of non-Arctic states and non-state actors interested in the region. They are also an effective tool to restructure the Arctic Council's relations with third parties in a changing political climate where Arctic governance is increasingly considered a global responsibility and subject to growing recognition that regional and global issues are interconnected.[11]

The original RoP of the Arctic Council were adopted by the eight Arctic states at the first Ministerial Meeting in September 1998 in Iqaluit. The Council's founding document, the 1996 Ottawa Declaration, had instructed that the member states, "as its first order of business, should adopt rules of procedure for its meetings and those of its working groups".[12] The Senior Arctic Officials (SAOs) had in a series of nine meetings prior to the first Ministerial Meeting drafted a first version of the RoP which they had already adopted *ad referendum*, still requiring additional approval by Arctic ministers.[13] In what was probably meant to enable a smooth transition from the predecessor organisation, the Arctic Environmental Protection Strategy, the SAOs had linked the question of Observer admission with the adoption of the Rules of Procedure by listing AEPS Observers[14] in Annex II to the proposed RoP.[15] SAOs informed the Arctic ministers in their report before the 1st Ministerial Meeting that "with the adoption of the Arctic Council Rules of Procedure, the […] accredited Observers to the Arctic Environmental Protection Strategy are accorded Observer status under the Arctic Council".[16]

America; NGS: National Geographic Society; SCPAR: Standing Committee of the Parliamentarians of the Arctic Region; UNECE: United Nations Economic Commission for Europe; UNEP: United Nations Environment Programme; IFRC: International Federation of Red Cross & Red Crescent Societies; IUCN: International Union for the Conservation of Nature; NCM: Nordic Council of Ministers; NAMMCO: North Atlantic Marine Mammal Commission UNDP: United Nations Development Programme; NEFCO: Nordic Environment Finance Corporation; ICES: International Council for the Exploration of the Sea; OSPAR: OSPAR Commission; WMO: World Meteorological Organization; WNC: West Nordic Council.

11 Kathrin Keil and Sebastian Knecht (eds) (2017) *Governing Arctic Change: Global Perspectives*. Palgrave Macmillan, London.

12 *Ottawa Declaration*, *supra* note 1, Article 6.

13 Arctic Council (1998) *Senior Arctic Officials Report to Ministers, Iqaluit, Canada, 17 September 1998*, at 2. https://oaarchive.arctic-council.org/bitstream/handle/11374/2050/IQALUIT_1998_SAO_Report_to_Ministers.pdf?sequence=1&isAllowed=y (accessed 31 July 2018).

14 These were Germany, the Netherlands, Poland, the United Kingdom, the NCM, NF, UNECE, UNEP and IASC.

15 Annex II, *Arctic Council Rules of Procedure*, as adopted by the Arctic Council at the First Arctic Council Ministerial Meeting, Iqaluit, Canada, 17–18 September 1998. https://oaarchive.arctic-council.org/bitstream/handle/11374/1783/EDOCS-3688-v2-ACMMUS02_BARROW_2000_6_SAO_Report_to_Ministers_Annex1_Rules_of_Procedure.pdf?sequence=1 (accessed 31 July 2018).

16 *Senior Arctic Officials Report to Ministers (1998)*, *supra* note 13, at 3.

This strategy of bundling has turned out to be fortunate for those actors listed in Annex II (the previous AEPS Observers), which "were grandfathered in under the Rules"[17] at a time when Observer admission was far from uncontroversial. At the first Ministerial Meeting in 1998, several other inter-governmental and non-governmental organisations had applied for Observer status,[18] of which only three – the World Wide Fund for Nature, the Standing Committee of the Parliamentarians of the Arctic Region and the International Union for Circumpolar Health – were ultimately recommended by SAOs (though not added to Annex II in the RoP), and later admitted by Arctic ministers. Particularly divisive was the decision by the Arctic Council not to admit the North Atlantic Marine Mammal Commission (NAMMCO), an inter-governmental organisation whose membership is composed of the Faroe Islands, Greenland, Iceland and Norway, and hence largely coincides with that of the Arctic Council. Some of these members threatened to block the consensual admission process for any other applicants until NAMMCO was admitted,[19] which increased the pressure on the other Arctic Council member states to accept the organisation as an Observer in 2000 at the Ministerial Meeting in Barrow.

If Arctic ministers at their first Ministerial Meeting in 1998 would have wanted not to admit any of the Observers under Annex II, their only options would have been to reject the proposed RoP as a whole, or delegate the RoP back to SAOs for further negotiation and revision. Given that the Arctic states themselves had defined the adoption of RoP as first and highest priority in the Ottawa Declaration, any decision not to adopt the RoP would have resulted in a severe institutional crisis for this new organisation even before the actual work had begun. The first wave of admissions in 1998 was thus by and large unconditional for these initial Observers.

At that time, the RoP were the only directive source for the Council's Observer policy, and one that lacked precision regarding what Observers were supposed to do and how to do it. The founding Ottawa Declaration had specified the composition of Arctic Council membership, and that non-Arctic states, inter-governmental and inter-parliamentary as well as non-governmental organisations "that the Council determines can contribute to its work" were eligible for Observer status.[20] However, it remained unclear what attributes applicants should have to increase the probability of admission, contribute to the Council's work and deepen their relationship with the Arctic community in practice.

Instead, Observers were mainly supposed to play their part in the literal sense of the word – *observe* the processes of the Arctic Council. The 1998 RoP allowed for their invitation to Ministerial and other meetings of the Council and granted

17 Evan T. Bloom (1999) "Establishment of the Arctic Council" *American Journal of International Law* 93–3: 720.

18 These were the WWF, SCPAR, IUCH, NAMMCO, ACOPS, CCU, IWGIA, the Circumpolar Universities Association (CUA) and the High North Alliance (HNA).

19 *Senior Arctic Officials Report to Ministers (1998)*, *supra* note 13, at 4.

20 *Ottawa Declaration*, *supra* note 1, Article 3.

Observers three basic rights: access to Arctic Council documents, dissemination of own written material, and the opportunity to make oral statements at the discretion of the chair of the meeting.[21] The later requirement of actively participating in Arctic Council subsidiary bodies – working groups, task forces and expert groups – was not yet an essential obligation for Observers, but was reserved for a different category of "experts" to be invited by the chair of the body on a case-by-case basis to "contribute expertise".[22] These experts, in turn, did not have unrestricted access to Arctic Council meetings as Observers beyond the particular meeting they were invited to participate in.

The controversial case of NAMMCO further led to the decision not to admit Observers permanently, but only as long as consensus existed at the biennial Ministerial Meetings.[23] The Arctic states wanted to retain the right to suspend Observer status if a state or organisation "engages in activities which are at odds with the Council's Declaration".[24] The Council's founding declaration contained a number of general provisions that can be summarised as five key commitments to:

a) the well-being of Arctic indigenous communities;
b) sustainable development in the Arctic region;
c) environmental protection of the region;
d) a multilateral approach to regional cooperation;
e) regular interaction on Arctic issues on the ministerial level.[25]

On paper, Observer status lasted for the time between two Ministerial Meetings, and would have ended as soon as only one Arctic state refused to give its consent at such a meeting. However, in practice there was no regular procedure to review the Observer status of states and organisations, and no Observer has ever had its status revoked.

Another crucial aspect of the early Observer policy that stands out is that the authority to assess and ultimately admit new applicants did not exclusively rest with Arctic ministers. Not only did SAOs have a strong impact on the Council's admission policy through preselection and recommendation of suitable candidates, but also the integration of Observers was to a great extent organised from the bottom up rather than the top down. The RoP explicitly allowed for the accreditation of *ad hoc* Observers at specific meetings at all levels of the Council, which gave external actors a chance to discuss issues of mutual concern with Arctic Council officials and indigenous communities' representatives, holding the special status as Permanent Participants (PPs) in the Council. It is no coincidence that many organisations and non-Arctic states that were admitted at Ministerial Meetings as

21 *Arctic Council Rules of Procedure*, *supra* note 15, at 7.
22 Ibid., at 8.
23 Bloom (1999), *supra* note 17, at 720.
24 *Arctic Council Rules of Procedure*, *supra* note 15, at 7.
25 *Ottawa Declaration*, *supra* note 1, at 2.

official Observers had been participating in Arctic Council activities and subsidiary body meetings in the capacity of *ad hoc* Observers before. It stands to reason that their early participation had an influence on later admission decisions.

Moreover, under the initial RoP, the six Arctic Council working groups were not prohibited from admitting their own Observers as long as their processes conformed with the Council's RoP. Under the Operating Guidelines of the Arctic Monitoring and Assessment Programme (AMAP) adopted in September 2000, AMAP was able to assign the special category of *AMAP Observers* to "countries and organizations that can directly contribute to the work of AMAP".[26] This status only applied to activities and projects organised under AMAP and was restricted to a period of two years, after which it would be reassessed by the working group.

13.4 Arctic Council Observer policy under the 2013 Rules of Procedure

The growing international interest in the work of the Arctic Council from both state and non-state actors from the mid-2000s onwards led Arctic Council officials to reconsider the forum's Observer policy and internal processes. Particularly the interest of emerging powers, such as China and India, was initially viewed with suspicion, with concerns raised by some commentators that Asian states' sudden interest in Arctic affairs was the result of hidden agendas, or their intentions were considered ambiguous and not transparent enough. In part, Council officials' concerns stemmed from some non-Arctic states openly questioning the Arctic states' legal position and political responsibility as primary stewards of the region and the geopolitical order organised around the eight Arctic states.[27] On the other hand, these fears disregard the argument that any political drawbacks generated by allowing these states to join the Arctic Council as Observers are lower than potential benefits.[28] After all, Observer status gives the Arctic states far more possibilities to influence non-Arctic states than the other way around.

The rising number of new applications for Observer status resulting from the changing political situation in, and public perception of, the Arctic region, its environmental changes and presumed resource abundance brought to the fore the limitations of the Council's old Observer policy with its low and unclear barriers and expectations. The Arctic Council simply had few plausible reasons why not to admit all these interested parties under the existing RoP. Following the

26 Arctic Monitoring Assessment Programme (2000) *Operating Guidelines for the AMAP*, adopted by the AMAP Working Group in Trondheim, Norway, 5–6 September 2000, at 1. https://oaarchive.arctic-council.org/bitstream/handle/11374/444/ACSAO-FI01_5_1_AMAP_Ope_Guide.pdf?sequence=1&isAllowed=y (accessed 31 July 2018).

27 Per Erik Solli, Elana Wilson Rowe and Wrenn Yennie Lindgren (2013) "Coming into the Cold: Asia's Arctic Interests" *Polar Geography* 36–4: 253–70; P. Whitney Lackenbauer, Adam Lajeunesse, James Manicom and Frédéric Lasserre (2018) *China's Arctic Ambitions and What They Mean for Canada*. University of Calgary Press, Calgary.

28 Stokke (2015), *supra* note 4.

admission of Spain at the Ministerial Meeting in Salekhard in 2006, which was the last state to be given Observer status under the 1998 RoP, the Arctic states responded to the rise in international interest in two ways, first with an indeterminate halt in further enlargement, and second with a substantial reform of the Observer policy prior to new admissions. Although non-Arctic actors like China, Italy and Republic of Korea had applied for Observer status already in advance of the 2009 Ministerial Meeting in Tromsø, they were not admitted until the Ministerial Meeting in 2013 in Kiruna, together with India, Japan and Singapore.

It was also at the 2013 Kiruna meeting that the revised RoP, which substantially reformulated the Observer policy, were adopted by Arctic Council ministers. Overall, the changes made to the Council's Observer policy concern primarily the admission process. Under the new RoP, the admission process was reversed from a flexible bottom-up to a strict top-down approach based on a comprehensive set of political conditionality criteria. The 2013 RoP raised the bar for new Observers. Applicants for Observer status were not only expected to contribute to the work of the Arctic Council, but to further comply with a geopolitical narrative formulated by the Arctic states of what the political order of the Arctic region should be. Taken together, the conditionality criteria set such high standards to obey that some commentators assume "[s]ome of the *Arctic states* would have difficulty in satisfying all of these criteria if they were to apply for observership".[29]

Specifically, the new RoP determine that in their evaluation of prospective Observers Arctic states will assess whether the applicant:

a) accepts and supports the objectives of the Arctic Council defined in the Ottawa declaration;
b) recognizes Arctic states' sovereignty, sovereign rights and jurisdiction in the Arctic;
c) recognizes that an extensive legal framework applies to the Arctic Ocean including, notably, the Law of the Sea, and that this framework provides a solid foundation for responsible management of this ocean;
d) respects the values, interests, culture and traditions of Arctic indigenous peoples and other Arctic inhabitants;
e) has demonstrated a political willingness as well as financial ability to contribute to the work of the Permanent Participants and other Arctic indigenous peoples;
f) has demonstrated their Arctic interests and expertise relevant to the work of the Arctic Council; and
g) has demonstrated a concrete interest and ability to support the work of the Arctic Council, including through partnerships with member states and Permanent Participants bringing Arctic concerns to global decision-making bodies.[30]

29 Terry Fenge and Bernard Funston (2015) *The Practice and Promise of the Arctic Council*. Greenpeace, Amsterdam: 13 (emphasis added).

30 Annex II, *Arctic Council Rules of Procedure*, most recent version adopted by the Kiruna Ministerial Meeting, 2013. www.arctic-council.org (accessed 31 July 2018).

In addition to the requirement to respect the Council's founding Ottawa Declaration as formulated in point (a), which is reminiscent of the suspension clause entailed already in the 1998 RoP, the other criteria revolve around three key issues: acceptance of the international legal framework applicable to the Arctic and Arctic states' sovereign rights that follow particularly from the Law of the Sea,[31] recognition and support of Arctic indigenous communities and those represented in the Council as PPs, and the willingness and competency to promote the work of the Arctic Council. This list of criteria is not finite but can be extended to include other, as yet unspecified criteria. Arctic states can thus on a case-by-case basis decide to deny access even under circumstances where all of the above criteria are fulfilled, thereby tarnishing transparency of the admission process and maintaining a certain degree of political arbitrariness.

The continued deferral of the EU's application is a case in point. The EU has been denied Observer status twice under the 1998 RoP – first in 2009 and again in 2011 – over an EU regulation adopted in 2009 which aimed at banning trade in seal products in the common market.[32] This regulation was criticised, especially by Canadian Inuit and the Canadian government, which did not give its consent to the application of the EU.[33] Poorly timed as the regulation was, it can be read as being incompatible with the purposes of the Arctic Council as laid down in the Ottawa Declaration, particularly the Arctic states' "commitment to the well-being of the inhabitants of the Arctic".[34] The Arctic Council's blockade mentality continued even after the dispute with Canada had been resolved by exempting indigenous seal products from the ban in 2014. At the 2013 Ministerial Meeting and with the new RoP in effect, the EU's application was received "affirmatively" but was nevertheless deferred again "until the Council ministers are agreed by consensus that the concerns of Council members [...] are resolved".[35] Apparently, the EU was seen to generally comply with the new criteria for admission in the 2013 RoP, while some Council members still had reservations.[36] Also after these had been solved in 2014 with the exemption of indigenous seal products, the Arctic Council still deferred the EU's application at the 2015 and 2017 Ministerial Meetings. Since early 2014, a new conflict between the EU and an Arctic Council

31 The terminology "Law of the Sea" is used in the Council's Rules of Procedure over the United Nations Convention on the Law of the Sea (UNCLOS) mainly because the United States of America has not ratified UNCLOS.

32 European Union (2009) "Regulation (EC) No 1007/2009 of the European Parliament and of the Council of 16 September 2009 on Trade in Seal Products" Official Journal of the European Union, Brussels.

33 CBC News (2009) "Canada against EU Entry to Arctic Council because of Seal Trade Ban" last modified 29 April 2009. www.cbc.ca/news/canada/north/canada-against-eu-entry-to-arctic-council-because-of-seal-trade-ban-1.806188 (accessed 31 July 2018).

34 *Ottawa Declaration*, *supra* note 1, at 2.

35 *Kiruna Declaration on the occasion of the Eighth Ministerial Meeting of the Arctic Council*, 15 May 2013, Kiruna, Sweden, at 8.

36 As a consequence, the EU is invited to participate almost in full capacity of an Observer since 2013 although is does not have official Observer status.

member state had emerged replacing the dispute with Canada. Now it was Russia that refused to give its approval of the EU's application over EU sanctions against Russia in reaction to the annexation of the Crimean peninsula and the following crisis in Eastern Ukraine.[37]

Compared to other inter-governmental organisations, the Arctic Council's revised Observer admission policy is formulated in unusually strong and imperative terms, and probably unprecedented in international affairs for the low-profile status of Observers. Other organisations restrict acceptance of observers, if at all, to members of a geographical community or other political institution, but ordinarily do not impose any other political or legal conditions for their participation. The demands of the Arctic Council's Observer policy are further remarkable given that the forum has no legal personality under international law. Acceptance of the admission criteria by an Observer has thus no legal consequences under international law (e.g. regarding current or possible future claims to extended continental shelves in the Arctic Ocean by the littoral states) and neither would any violation have except for the political consequence of presumably losing Observer status. Against this backdrop, it is more constructive for Arctic states to use the Council's Observer policy to socialise interested actors and build consensus around a legal and political order for the region that enables Arctic states to further expand and strengthen their position in the regional governance framework.[38]

A consequence of the conditionality policy was that Arctic ministers were given more control over the admission process. Continuation of *ad hoc* or working group-specific Observer status without prior assessment against the imposed conditionality criteria would have undermined the legitimacy of the new Observer regime and ultimately the authority of the Arctic Council leadership. It was thus logical to abolish the former flexible system entirely and only admit Observers "to the Arctic Council proper" whereas "[s]ubsidiary bodies are not authorized to accredit Observers" anymore.[39] Actors interested in Observer status now have to apply to the standing chairmanship of the Arctic Council, which forwards the application to Arctic states and PPs at least 120 days before a Ministerial Meeting at which the Council may then take a decision based on the criteria above.[40] In accordance with the new Observer admission policy, AMAP revised its Operating

37 Barents Observer (2015) "EU Bid to Become Arctic Council Observer Deferred Again" last modified 4 May 2015. http://barentsobserver.com/en/arctic/2015/05/eu-bid-become-arctic-council-observer-deferred-again-04-05 (accessed 31 July 2018).

38 Piotr Graczyk, Małgorzata Śmieszek, Timo Koivurova and Adam Stępień (2017) "Preparing for the Global Rush: The Arctic Council, Institutional Norms, and Socialisation of Observer Behaviour" in Keil and Knecht, *supra* note 2, at 121–139.

39 *Arctic Council Observer Manual for Subsidiary Bodies*, as adopted by the Arctic Council at the Eight Arctic Council Ministerial Meeting, Kiruna, Sweden, 15 May 2013, at 2. https://oaarchive.arctic-council.org/bitstream/handle/11374/939/EDOCS-3020-v1B-Observer-manual-with-addendum-finalized_Oct2016.PDF (accessed 31 July 2018).

40 *Revised Arctic Council Rules of Procedure*, *supra* note 30, at 13–14.

Guidelines in 2014 to abandon *AMAP Observer* status and only allow Observers admitted by the Arctic Council to contribute to the working group.[41]

Observers like the Asian states, Italy and Switzerland admitted since 2013 under the top-down approach of the new Observer policy are much less assessed according to their scientific suitability than with regard to their political obedience. In the 1998 RoP, applicants for Observer status were asked to submit "a written description of the proposed Observer's ability to contribute to the work of the Arctic Council";[42] a paragraph that has in the 2013 RoP been amended with the addition "and conformity with the criteria listed at paragraph 6 of this Annex" (those above).[43] Some of these conditionality criteria can neither be reasonably nor reliably judged at the admission stage, but become manifest in the everyday interaction with Arctic states and PPs after admission.

With regard to the substance of science cooperation between Arctic and non-Arctic actors in Arctic Council working groups, the overall record is mediocre. Out of 111 projects currently worked on under the six working groups, state and non-state Observers participate in 19 projects (about 17 per cent).[44] From the eight European state Observers, half the group (namely France, Germany, the Netherlands and the United Kingdom) contributes to five initiatives, whereas Italy, Poland and Switzerland have experts involved in two projects each. Spain contributes to three projects. The Asian state Observers show a similar record, also with considerable variation between the five countries. Japan contributes to six projects, China to five and Republic of Korea to four projects. At the lower end stand India and Singapore with two project contributions each.

Among the projects state Observers were or continue to be most actively engaged in are three AMAP projects, the *Adaptation Actions for a Changing Arctic* (AACA) project, the *Sustaining Arctic Observing Networks* (SAON) project and an integrated assessment on air pollution with a special focus on short-lived climate forcers (SLCFs). Other projects include the *Actions for Arctic Biodiversity 2013–2021* implementation plan and the Arctic Migratory Birds Initiative (AMBI) under the Conservation of Arctic Flora and Fauna (CAFF) working group.

Not least due to the limited integration of Observers in working group projects, the Arctic states have implemented further procedural reforms in central aspects of the Observer policy. Most importantly, they introduced a monitoring and assessment system according to which Observers have to express their

41 Arctic Council (2014) *Operating Guidelines for the AMAP Working Group*, submitted to the Senior Arctic Officials meeting in Yellowknife, Canada, 22–23 October 2014, at 1. https://oaarchive.arctic-council.org/bitstream/handle/11374/1383/AC_SAO_CA03_Doc7-2_AMAP_Operating_guidelines.pdf?sequence=1&isAllowed=y (accessed 31 July 2018).

42 *Arctic Council Rules of Procedure, supra* note 15, at 11.

43 *Revised Arctic Council Rules of Procedure, supra* note 30, at 13.

44 Arctic Council (2018) "Amarok 'Maxi-Report' ". Arctic Council Secretariat, Tromsø. *Amarok* is the Arctic Council's project tracking tool maintained and regularly updated by the Arctic Council Secretariat.

continued interest in Observer status with the Arctic Council every four years, and are then being evaluated by Arctic states and PPs with a final decision taken by Arctic states. However, the RoP remain vague as to whether the criteria for readmission following internal review are the same as for the initial admission process. During the review process, which is largely based on a self-monitoring report from Observers about their achievements in relation to the work of the Arctic Council, the Arctic Council chairmanship distributes to Arctic states and PPs "a list of all accredited Observers and up-to-date information on their activities relevant to the work of the Arctic Council".[45] It is unspecified which "activities" inside the Arctic Council or also beyond the reports cover what is considered "relevant", and whether all or only some of the admission criteria listed in Annex II to the RoP are taken into consideration for that purpose.

In practice, it seems that once inside the Council, what matters most for readmission is how well Observers contribute to the work of the Arctic Council. Questions regarding their recognition of the international legal framework, Arctic states' sovereign rights and jurisdiction in the region, or indigenous peoples' interests, values and traditions apparently are left out of consideration. The 14 state and non-state actors reviewed during the US chairmanship of the Arctic Council between 2015 and 2017, all those admitted to the Arctic Council in 1998 and 2000 among which were the European state Observers,[46] were only asked to provide a self-monitoring report indicating any a) past contributions to Arctic Council subsidiary bodies, b) anticipated future contributions to working groups, task forces and expert groups, and c) other relevant contributions to the Council.[47] The reports of these 14 Observers accredited during the first wave of admissions were all received affirmatively, and all reviewed Observers were readmitted.[48]

The Arctic states nevertheless try to ensure that Observers recognise the international legal framework as well as Arctic states' sovereign rights and support Arctic indigenous peoples throughout their time as Observers even though these requirements are not part of the review process. To this end, a minor change in wording occurred with practical implications regarding the possibility to suspend or expel Observer status once granted. While the 1998 RoP made Observer status subject to the consensus of all eight Arctic states at a Ministerial Meeting usually taking place every two years,[49] the 2013 RoP now require tacit consent among

45 *Revised Arctic Council Rules of Procedure*, *supra* note 30, at 13.

46 The 2017 Fairbanks Declaration adopted at the Ministerial Meeting further instructed the SAOs with a review of the remaining Observers under the Finnish chairmanship until the next Ministerial Meeting taking place in 2019 in Rovaniemi.

47 See, for example, Arctic Council (2016) *The United Kingdom's (UK) 2016 Observer Review report*. https://oaarchive.arctic-council.org/handle/11374/1877 (accessed 31 July 2018).

48 *Fairbanks Declaration on the occasion of the Tenth Ministerial Meeting of the Arctic Council*, 11 May 2017, Fairbanks, Alaska, at para. 13.

49 *Arctic Council Rules of Procedure*, *supra* note 15, at 7.

Arctic ministers at all times,[50] thereby increasing the pressure upon the Observers to comply with Arctic Council regulations constantly.

A major innovation of the new Observer policy was that the revised RoP were complemented with an Observer Manual adopted at the same Ministerial Meeting in 2013. This Manual addresses the integration of Observers after admission and shall, in contrast to the RoP regulating the admission process, serve as a guideline primarily for "chairs of subsidiary bodies to run meetings effectively and efficiently to ensure the exchange of information on items under discussion".[51] Nevertheless, the Manual is of special importance to Observers in their attempt to contribute to Arctic Council subsidiary bodies, increasing their chances for readmission.

Generally, soft tools like Manuals enable the Council to maintain procedural agility and undertake reforms as necessary should the integration of Observers not work out as effectively as anticipated. At the same time, the Manual is assumed to have a binding force upon the Observers who could be expelled from a specific meeting (though not the Arctic Council) in case an Observer violates the guidelines.[52] Through this Manual, the Council grants Observers extensive participatory rights in subsidiary bodies to which they are supposed to contribute the most in their role as Observers.[53] To this end, they may "make statements after Arctic States and Permanent Participants, present written statements, submit relevant documents and provide views on the issues under discussion".[54]

The Observer Manual for the first time specifies that Observers are expected "to participate with their expertise, competence and resources primarily in working group meetings and projects".[55] Moreover, the Manual asks chairs of subsidiary body meetings to actively promote the participation and inclusion of Observers in their processes through early notification of scheduled meetings, access to meeting documents, and giving them an opportunity to present their views on the discussion and introducing own project ideas in collaboration with an Arctic state or PP.[56]

Since 2013, the Observer Manual has been amended twice by consensual decision of the SAOs. At a meeting in Anchorage in October 2015, SAOs adopted an Addendum to the Observer Manual in an effort to "provide further specification for the participation of observers, facilitating relevant and meaningful contributions to the work of the Arctic Council, where applicable".[57] The Addendum

50 *Revised Arctic Council Rules of Procedure*, *supra* note 30, at 9.

51 *Arctic Council Observer Manual for Subsidiary Bodies*, *supra* note 39, at 1.

52 Ibid., at 5.

53 *Revised Arctic Council Rules of Procedure*, *supra* note 30, at 9.

54 Ibid.

55 *Arctic Council Observer Manual for Subsidiary Bodies*, *supra* note 39, at 1.

56 Ibid., at 4–5.

57 *Arctic Council Observer Manual for Subsidiary Bodies*, *supra* note 39, and *Addendum*, approved by the Senior Arctic Officials at the Meeting of the Senior Arctic Officials, Anchorage, United States, 20–22 October 2015, at 11.

addresses a variety of procedural issues regarding the organisation and conduct of subsidiary body meetings. Observers shall not only be notified in due time 30 days before a meeting takes place, but shall also receive detailed information about ongoing or planned projects and contact details of project leaders.[58] During gatherings, chairs shall "make every effort" to allow Observers to exercise their participatory rights.[59] The third specification addresses Observers directly and lists several concrete possibilities Observers have at their disposal to contribute to Arctic Council projects, including communicating their own proposals for projects, making financial or in-kind contributions to existing ones, and serving as a host for project meetings.[60]

The second change to the Observer Manual was a minor supplement to this latter aspect adopted in October 2016 by SAOs in Portland, Maine. In a footnote to the question of whether Observers shall be allowed to host a project-specific meeting, the evaluation criteria were made explicit which subsidiary bodies and SAOs should take into account when accepting the offer, which in turn signals to Observers precisely what attributes they need to have in order to be granted permission to host a meeting.[61] Although minor in substance, the two amendments to the Observer Manual can have serious repercussions for the status of Observers, and whether Arctic states perceive that single Observers deserve the status. Arctic states ask Observers in their self-monitoring reports to emphasise specific contributions they have made under the Addendum, which might then influence the final outcome of the review process.[62]

Overall, what has changed with this new policy is that Observers are considered to become more expert-like in their role as contributors in Arctic Council subsidiary bodies. This "scientification" of the Observer status has led to conflated roles of "Observers" and "experts", which were two distinct categories under the 1998 RoP. The latter is now increasingly excluded from Arctic Council meetings. Although the status and conditions for participation of "experts" remain unchanged in the 2013 RoP, the Observer Manual calls upon subsidiary body chairs to "decide on the necessity of a given expert on a meeting-by-meeting basis" precisely because they do not hold Observer status in the Council.[63] If Observers are unwilling or unable to step into their place, the new Observer policy

58 *Addendum* (2015), *supra* note 57, at 11.
59 Ibid., at 12.
60 Ibid., at 13.
61 The following three attributes shall be considered by SAOs and subsidiary bodies in such a case: "Observer capacity to provide relevant subject-matter expertise; Observer capacity to provide a unique value-added contribution to the work of the subsidiary body by hosting the event; Observer hosting as a percentage of overall project or initiative funding." See *Arctic Council Observer Manual for Subsidiary Bodies*, *supra* note 39, and *Addendum*, approved by the Senior Arctic Officials at the Meeting of the Senior Arctic Officials, Portland, Maine, 4 October 2016, at 14.
62 See again *United Kingdom's (UK) 2016 Observer Review report*, *supra* note 47.
63 *Addendum* (2016), *supra* note 61, at 6.

will be detrimental to what it intends and actually produce a dearth of additional expertise and complementary knowledge.

13.5 Discussion

This chapter has shown how Arctic Council Observers differ with respect to their role, recognition and participation in the Arctic Council despite their equal legal status and the non-discriminatory Observer policy of the Arctic Council. Observers are, in short, same same but different. The Arctic Council has managed to adapt to a changing political environment rather quickly and decisively. What was once a flexible and largely informal process organised from the bottom up is now a highly formalised process managed and monitored from the top down.

What stands out from the above discussion of the historical development of the Arctic Council's Observer policy is that in legal terms Observers have always been treated equally, irrespective of when they joined the Arctic Council and whether they have been state or non-state actors applying for Observer status. Despite legal equality, political considerations affect the admission and integration process and prohibit equal treatment. Equality principles can be a valuable source of legality and inclusiveness, but may also create unfair and ineffective processes. It is debatable, for instance, whether the European Observer states admitted under few conditions can and should be reviewed according to new standards imposed after their admission. And the other way around, it is astonishing how norms of inclusion, stewardship and international collaboration have changed in Arctic affairs to a point where the later Asian applicants are measured by other, higher standards than actors admitted before 2013, even though the authority and mission of the Arctic Council have remained more or less unchanged since the forum has been established. The case of the EU's deferred application further shows that full compliance with the conditionality criteria is no guarantee for admission, but that, as Michael Byers notes, "ultimately the decision to exclude or admit will be based on political considerations rather than the (deliberately) ambiguous standards".[64]

If Observers all have the same status, but play different roles, what accounts as a contribution to the Arctic Council, which contribution is valued higher or lower than others, and what if Observers are expected to participate in all areas of the Council's work, but can or only want to contribute in some? These become important questions when it is mainly organisational, financial and in-kind contributions that have been considered in past Observer reviews, and given that the procedural reform set in motion with the revised 2013 Observer policy was meant to harmonise Observer performances to a certain degree.[65]

64 Michael Byers (2013) *International Law and the Arctic*. Cambridge University Press, Cambridge: 236–237.

65 Sebastian Knecht (2016) "Procedural Reform at the Arctic Council: The Amended 2015 Observer Manual" *Polar Record* 52–5: 601–603.

Furthermore, the new Observer policy may also have unintended consequences that stand in stark contrast to its actual purpose. If Observer applications are primarily assessed according to a catalogue of political criteria rather than scientific considerations, the attempt at integrating new Observers in scientific projects of Arctic Council subsidiary bodies, as asked for and supported in the Observer Manual, may be undermined because the interests and ambitions of actors to join the Council may not be aligned with the Council's institutional needs. The need to restructure the Observer policy from a bottom-up to a top-down approach to maintain an authoritative and legitimate Observer system may then result in an increase of those actors literally observing the processes and outcomes of the Arctic Council without contributing much to them.

14 China in the Arctic Council

Existing problems and prospective solutions

Yuanyuan Ren

14.1 Introduction

On 11 May 2017, the Arctic Council (AC) admitted seven new Observers at its 10th Ministerial meeting in Fairbanks, Alaska, United States.[1] Along with this enlargement, the participation of Observers in the Arctic Council will continue to be a major issue surrounding the debates on the reform of the Arctic Council and the role of the Arctic Council in Arctic governance in the coming years. During the period 2015 to 2017, the first Arctic Council's review of Observers also took place, in which the 14 longest-standing Observers in the Council were reviewed.[2] In the next two years, the Senior Arctic Officials (SAOs) of the Arctic Council will conduct another review of the remaining accredited Observers, including the People's Republic of China ("China"), and report the final outcome in 2019.[3]

Against this background, this chapter examines how China has performed in the Arctic Council since it has become a "full" Observer in May 2013. It finds that, although there has been overall improvement, China's participation in the work of the subsidiary bodies[4] of the AC has remained limited. To better illustrate this limitation, this chapter examines China's participation in the work of the Task Forces (TFs) of the Arctic Council as a case study. It suggests that in order to make more substantial contributions to and have a more prominent voice in the

1 *Fairbanks Declaration on the occasion of the Tenth Ministerial Meeting of the Arctic Council*, 11 May 2017, para. 44.

2 Arctic Council (2017) *Senior Arctic Officials' Report to Ministers, Fairbanks, Alaska, United States, 11 May 2017*, at 92. https://oaarchive.arctic-council.org/handle/11374/1909 (accessed 30 March 2018) (the Council found that the Observers reviewed should maintain their Observer status in the Council).

3 *Fairbanks Declaration, supra* note 1, para. 43.

4 The subsidiary bodies of the Arctic Council include: 1) Working Groups; 2) Task Forces; 3) Expert Groups; and 4) such other subsidiary bodies as the Arctic Council may create. *Arctic Council Observer Manual for Subsidiary Bodies*, as adopted by the Arctic Council at the Eighth Arctic Council Ministerial Meeting, Kiruna, Sweden, 15 May 2013, and *Addendum* Approved by the Senior Arctic Officials at the Meeting of the Senior Arctic Officials, Anchorage, United States of America, 20–22 October 2015, and Portland, Maine, United States, 4 October 2016, at 6.

Arctic Council, the Chinese government should pay closer attention to the work of the subsidiary bodies of the Council and accordingly send adequate, more suitable delegates, rather than simply attending the Ministerial and SAO meetings.

Without a proper understanding of the AC and the Council's rules on Observer participation, the understanding of China's participation in the Arctic Council appears incomplete. Therefore, the chapter begins with a brief discussion of the evolution of the AC and the associated recent efforts to strengthen the engagement of non-Arctic Observers. The following section shifts the focus onto China's participation in the Arctic Council and investigates the specific problems with China's performance in it. To complement the existing literature, it concentrates on China's limited participation in the Task Forces of the AC, particularly given that some of these Task Forces have the mandate to draft and conclude special regional agreements for the Arctic. The fourth section discusses possible solutions to strengthen China's participation in the Arctic Council. The last section concludes with final remarks.

14.2 Observers in the Arctic Council

14.2.1 The Arctic Council as an evolving international institution

The Arctic Council is the pre-eminent high-level forum for Arctic cooperation. As a successor to the Arctic Environmental Protection Strategy (AEPS),[5] the Arctic Council was established in September 1996 by the Ottawa Declaration to promote cooperation and coordination on the issues of environmental protection and sustainable development among the eight Arctic states (Canada, Denmark, Finland, Iceland, Norway, Russia, Sweden and the United States of America) and Arctic peoples.[6] Established by a declaration rather than a treaty, the Arctic Council has long been regarded as a soft-law "high-level forum" instead of an international organisation.[7] Nevertheless, in practice, the Council is becoming increasingly similar to an international organisation given its recent improvements in its organisational structure and capacity.[8]

5 Arctic Environmental Protection Strategy, 14 June 1991, *International Legal Materials* 30: 1627.

6 *Ottawa Declaration on the Establishment of the Arctic Council*, 19 September 1996. https://oaarchive.arctic-council.org/bitstream/handle/11374/85/EDOCS-1752-v2-ACM-MCA00_Ottawa_1996_Founding_Declaration.PDF?sequence=5&isAllowed=y (accessed 31 July 2018).

7 See, e.g., Evan T. Bloom (1999) "Establishment of the Arctic Council" *American Journal of International Law* 93–3: 712; Erik J. Molenaar (2012) "Current and Prospective Roles of the Arctic Council System within the Context of the Law of the Sea" *The International Journal of Marine and Coastal Law* 27: 569; Oran Young (2016) "The Arctic Council at Twenty: How to Remain Effective in a Rapidly Changing Environment" *UC Irvine Law Review* 6–1: 107–108.

8 These developments include, but not limited to: the establishment of a standing Arctic Council Secretariat in 2013, refining the rules for Observers' involvement, and negotiating legally

With regard to the functions and roles of the Arctic Council, many agree that a core task and the best function of the Council is its work on providing science-based knowledge about the Arctic to influence multi-level Arctic policy-making.[9] In general, this is done primarily through the work of its six Working Groups (WGs).[10] However, the AC has also been increasingly using short-term Task Forces (TFs)[11] for specific initiatives such as negotiating "hard-law" instruments or highly specialised regional arrangements regarding the Arctic. For example, to date, three of the nine TFs of the Arctic Council that have completed their work and are no longer operational were the negotiating venues for three pan-Arctic treaties: Agreement on Cooperation on Aeronautical and Maritime Search and Rescue in the Arctic (2011);[12] Agreement on Cooperation on Marine Oil Pollution Preparedness and Response in the Arctic (2013);[13] and Agreement on Enhancing International Arctic Scientific Cooperation (2017).[14] Although both the Ottawa Declaration and the Arctic Council Rules of Procedure do not expressly provide for negotiations on legally binding agreements, some scholars

---

binding pan-Arctic agreements under the auspices of the Council. See also Piotr Graczyk and Timo Koivurova (2015) "The Arctic Council" in *Handbook of the Politics of the Arctic* edited by Leif Christian Jensen and Geir Hønneland. Edward Elgar, Cheltenham: 311.

9 See, e.g., Timo Koivurova, Paula Kankaanpää and Adam Stępień (2015) "Innovative Environmental Protection: Lessons from the Arctic" *Journal of Environmental Law* 27: 285–311 (noting that large-scale scientific assessments constitute the core area of the Council's work); Young, *supra* note 7, at 100.

10 The six Working Groups are: Arctic Contaminants Action Programme (ACAP), Arctic Monitoring and Assessment Programme (AMAP), Conservation of Arctic Flora and Fauna (CAFF), Emergency Prevention, Preparedness and Response (EPPR), Protection of the Arctic Marine Environment (PAME), and Sustainable Development Working Group (SDWG). See Arctic Council website: "Working Groups". www.arctic-council.org/index.php/en/about-us/working-groups (accessed 30 March 2018).

11 Within the Arctic Council, Task Forces (TFs) are appointed at the Ministerial meetings to work on specific issues for a limited period of time. Currently, there are two active Task Forces: The Task Force on Arctic Marine Cooperation (TFAMC II) and the Task Force on Improved Connectivity in the Arctic (TFICA). See Arctic Council website: "Task Forces of the Arctic Council". www.arctic-council.org/index.php/en/about-us/subsidiary-bodies/task-forces (accessed 30 March 2018).

12 Agreement on Cooperation on Aeronautical and Maritime Search and Rescue in the Arctic, signed 12 May 2011 and entered into force 19 January 2013. https://oaarchive.arctic-council.org/handle/11374/531 (accessed 30 March 2018) (negotiated within the Task Force on Search and Rescue (TFSR, 2009–2011)).

13 Agreement on Cooperation on Marine Oil Pollution Preparedness and Response in the Arctic, signed 15 May 2013 and entered into force 25 March 2016. https://oaarchive.arctic-council.org/handle/11374/529 (accessed 30 March 2018) (negotiated within the Task Force on Arctic Marine Oil Pollution Preparedness and Response (2011–2013)).

14 Agreement on Enhancing International Arctic Scientific Cooperation, signed 11 May 2017 and entered into force 23 May 2018. https://oaarchive.arctic-council.org/handle/11374/1916 (accessed 1 July 2018), reproduced in the Appendix of this book.

have contended that the founding documents could be interpreted as creating space for such arrangements within the current mandate of the Council.[15] This new practice reflects the growing interest of the Arctic states in a more action-oriented Arctic Council.[16] It also significantly raises the Council's profile in Arctic governance.[17]

Overall, there is no common vision for the Arctic Council's roles and future among different participants and scholars. On the one hand, the Council has been urged to maintain its knowledge-provider and policy-shaping role. On the other hand, the Member States seem committed to expanding the Council's roles from policy-shaping to policy-making.[18] In this regard, several Task Forces of the Council have played a unique role in enhancing the decision-making capacity of the Arctic Council.

14.2.2 The participation of Observers in the Arctic Council

Since 2007, the increasing global attention to the Arctic has whetted the interests of more non-Arctic states and other actors in participating in the work of the Arctic Council.[19] The only way to do so is to gain Observer status[20] in the Arctic Council and to follow the official procedures of the Council.[21] Currently, the Arctic Council's criteria for admitting Observers and the rules on the participation of Observers are primarily listed in three documents: the Ottawa Declaration;[22] the revised Arctic Council Rules of Procedure;[23] and the Arctic Council Observer Manual for Subsidiary Bodies.[24]

15 Piotr Graczyk (2012) "The Arctic Council Inclusive of Non-Arctic Perspectives: Seeking a New Balance" in *The Arctic Council: Its Place in the Future of Arctic Governance* edited by Thomas S. Axworthy, Timo Koivurova and Waliul Hasanat, Munk-Gordon Arctic Security Program. University of Lapland, Toronto: 282; Young, *supra* note 7, at 110.

16 Małgorzata Śmieszek, Adam Stępień and Paula Kankaanpää (2016) "The Recent Arctic Council Assessments: Influential Tools in Policy-Making in the Council and Beyond?" *The Yearbook of Polar Law* 8: 213.

17 See Graczyk and Koivurova, *supra* note 8, at 318.

18 Arctic Council (2013) "Vision for the Arctic", Kiruna, Sweden, 15 May 2013. https://oaarchive.arctic-council.org/handle/11374/287 (accessed 30 March 2018).

19 Koivurova, Kankaanpää and Stępień, *supra* note 9, at 291–292.

20 Observer status in the Arctic Council is open to non-Arctic states, inter-governmental and inter-parliamentary organisation, global and regional non-governmental organisations. *Ottawa Declaration, supra* note 6.

21 Piotr Graczyk (2011) "Observers in the Arctic Council – Evolution and Prospects", *Yearbook of Polar Law* 3: 599.

22 *Ottawa Declaration, supra* note 6.

23 *Arctic Council Rules of Procedure*, most recent version adopted by the Kiruna Ministerial Meeting, 2013. www.arctic-council.org.

24 *Observer Manual, supra* note 4.

According to the documents above, (1) Observership in the Arctic Council is neither *ad hoc* nor "permanent".[25] It lasts only as long as there is a consensus among the Member States and Permanent Participants (PPs),[26] and if the entity that holds an Observer status has not engaged in activities that are in conflict with the Ottawa Declaration and the Rules of Procedure;[27] (2) the participation of Observers is confined to observing the work of the Council, primarily contributing at the Working Group level, making statements at meetings at the discretion of the chair, submitting relevant documents and providing views on the issues under discussion;[28] (3) Observers are allowed to propose projects through an Arctic State or a Permanent Participant, and to make financial contributions to existing and developing projects; however, their financial input cannot be larger than that of the Member States;[29] and (4) Observers can also host project-specific, expert-level workshops or gatherings with the approval of the SAOs on a case-by-case basis.[30]

However, controversies over the involvement of non-Arctic Observers in the operation of the Arctic Council have continued. Some prevalent critiques on the limitations of the current Observer rules of the Council are briefly outlined as follows.

First, some critics have particularly questioned the criteria for admitting Observers to the Arctic Council. For instance, Peiqing Guo has argued that the Council's "three recognitions" criterion,[31] in fact, requires the applicants to recognise Arctic sovereignty and jurisdictional issues which are not settled.[32] Second, the participatory rights of Observers in the Arctic Council are limited, as mentioned above, to the right to contribute at the Working Group level.[33] However, "the working groups do not provide an effective venue for policy dialogues regarding

25 Under the revised Arctic Council Rules of Procedure, every four years, from the date of being granted Observer status, Observers should state affirmatively their continued interest in Observer status in the Arctic Council. Their Observer status will be reviewed at the Ministerial meetings of the Council. The Revised Rules of Procedure, *supra* note 23, Annex 2.

26 In the Arctic Council, the organisations of Arctic indigenous peoples have been granted Permanent Participants status. The Permanent Participants have full consultation rights regarding the Council's negotiations and decisions. Arctic Council website: "Permanent Participants", www.arctic-council.org/index.php/en/about-us/permanent-participants (accessed 30 March 2018).

27 *Revised Rules of Procedure*, *supra* note 23, para. 37.

28 Ibid., para. 38.

29 *Observer Manual*, *supra* note 4, at 13.

30 Ibid., at 14.

31 The "three recognitions" criterion refers to the Observer admission criterion of the Arctic Council that asks an applicant to "recognize Arctic states' sovereignty, sovereignty rights and jurisdictions in the Arctic". *Revised Rules of Procedure*, *supra* note 23, Annex 2: para. 6.

32 Peiqing Guo (2012) "An Analysis of New Criteria for Permanent Observer Status on the Arctic Council and the Road of Non-Arctic States to the Arctic" *KMI International Journal of Maritime Affairs and Fisheries*: 24.

33 *Observer Manual*, *supra* note 4, para. 6.

a range of politically sensitive issues now arising on the Arctic agenda".[34] Moreover, in practice, there is a prohibited area for Observers in the Council, which is actually not provided by the founding document of the Council: the closed meeting of the Heads of Delegation (HoD) of the Arctic States.[35] Lastly, to date, there still exists a lack of detailed guidelines for the efficient incorporation of non-Arctic scientists into the work of the Working Groups,[36] let alone for the engagement of non-Arctic Observers in the work of the Task Forces and other subsidiary bodies of the Council.[37]

Facing growing criticism, since 2015, the Arctic Council has been developing new practices and arrangements to strengthen engagement with the non-Arctic Observers. One important development, in this regard, is to hold Observer Meetings associated with the SAOs meetings. To date, the Council has held four such meetings under the United States Chairmanship II (2015–2017) and the Finnish Chairmanship II (2017–2019).[38] This new channel of communication between the Arctic actors and non-Arctic Observers could allow better engagement of Observers with the Council.

Another notable improvement regarding the engagement with non-Arctic Observers is related to the recent operations of the Task Forces of the Council. As discussed above, the Arctic Council has used the TFs for several specific initiatives such as negotiating legally binding agreements among the eight Arctic states. For a period of time, however, some Arctic states had tended to prevent non-Arctic Observers and Permanent Participants from participating in these TFs[39] by asserting that the special initiatives of TFs may "require unique expertise, in those instances, the composition and mode of operation of the Task

34 Oran R. Young (2012) "Listening to the Voices of Non-Arctic States in Arctic Ocean Governance: A Commentary" in *The Arctic in World Affairs: A North Pacific Dialogue on Arctic Marine Issues* edited by Oran R. Young, Jong-Deog Kim and Yoon-Hyung Kim. Korean Maritime Institute, Seoul. East-West Center, Honolulu: 287.

35 *Observer Manual, supra* note 4, para. 7.1 ("The Head of Delegation of the Arctic States may also at any time meet privately at their direction").

36 In fact, the Council adopted new Common Operating Guidelines for its WGs in December 2016. However, the new Guidelines provide no details on how to involve Observers effectively in the work and procedures of the WGs. See Arctic Council (2016) *Working Group Common Operating Guidelines*, December 2016. www.arctic-council.org/images/PDF_attachments/AC_Org_Docs/December_2016_Common_Operating_Guidelines_FINAL.pdf (accessed 30 March 2018).

37 See also Jong-Deog Kim (2016) "Observer States in the Arctic Council: A Way Forward to Better Cooperation" in *Shared Voices Magazine 2016 Special Issue: Arctic Council at 20.* The UArctic: 53. www.uarctic.org/media/1428309/sharedvoicesmagazine2016specialissuescreen.pdf (accessed 30 March 2018).

38 They are: Special Session on Observer Engagement (Anchorage, 20 October 2015), Special Session on Observer Engagement (Portland, 4 October 2016), Observer Special Session (Oulu, 26 October 2017), and Observer Special Session (Levi, 23 March 2018).

39 Timo Koivurova et al. (2017) "China as an Observer in the Arctic Council" in *Arctic Law and Governance: The Role of China, Finland and the EU* edited by Timo Koivurova, Qin Tianbao, Tapio Nykänen and Sébastien Duyck. Hart Publishing, Oxford: 164.

Force would be determined on a case-by-case basis".[40] For instance, there was an unprecedented controversy over the participation of Observers in the work of the Task Force on Search and Rescue (TFSR, 2009–2011). Some member states were very reluctant to allow non-Arctic states to observe the negotiation process within the TF.[41] Observer states, on the other hand, were frustrated by being denied the right to observe the work of this type of the subsidiary bodies of the Council which is provided by the Council's rules of procedure.[42] Nevertheless, the recent practices of several Task Forces of the Council have shown a greater willingness to involve Observers. For example, the negotiation of the Agreement on Enhancing International Arctic Scientific Cooperation by the work of the Task Force for Enhancing Scientific Cooperation in the Arctic (SCTF, 2013–2017) involved greater engagement with non-Arctic Observers. Many Observers, such as France, Germany, United Kingdom, Japan and Poland, provided constructive opinions on the draft agreement during the negotiations.[43]

Overall, the participation of Observers in the Arctic Council continues to be limited. This is a two-tiered problem: on the one hand, the current Arctic Council rules do not provide detailed guidance on how to make good use of Observer participation. Consequently, there is considerable room to enhance the effectiveness of engaging Observers within the Arctic Council.[44] On the other hand, the Council's recent efforts to improve the communication and engagement with Observers should be applauded. It is now also the turn of Observers, especially non-Arctic Observer states, to prove their capacities and reform their relevant domestic institutions and procedures to contribute more constructively to the work and improvement of the Arctic Council.

14.3 China in the Arctic Council at ten years

Building on the observations and assumptions above, this section turns the focus towards China's participation in the Arctic Council and investigates some specific problems associated with China's performance in the Council. To better illustrate the problems and challenges, the section takes China's participation in the Task Forces of the Arctic Council as a case study.

40 Arctic Council (2011) *Senior Arctic Officials Report to Ministers, Nuuk, Greenland, May 2011*, at 49–50. https://oaarchive.arctic-council.org/handle/11374/1535 (accessed 30 March 2018).

41 See Arctic Council (2009) *Meeting of Senior Arctic Officials, Final Report, Copenhagen, 12–13 November 2009*, para. 5.2.

42 Graczyk, "Observers in the Arctic Council", *supra* note 21, at 612.

43 See generally Bill Vocke Trip Report, Arctic Council Scientific Cooperation Task Force (Eight Meeting), Arlington, Virginia. 3–4 March, 2016. www.arctic-council.org/eppr/wp-content/uploads/2016/04/2016_06_21_TFSC_Meeting_Report_Arlington_March2016.pdf (accessed 30 March 2018). See also Chapter 12 by Akiho Shibata in this book.

44 See also Brandon M. Ray (2016) "Changing the Role of the Observers in the Arctic Council" *Arctic and International Relations Series: The Arctic Council at Twenty* 2: 35–37.

14.3.1 China's admission to the Arctic Council: a brief overview

China's contemporary involvement in the Arctic region started in the 1990s through its conduct of scientific research and expeditions.[45] However, for a long time, China had no direct interaction with the AEPS and its successor, the Arctic Council. In 2006, in light of its increasing interests in the region, China submitted its first application to the Arctic Council to be an Observer.[46] In April 2007, China was granted *ad hoc* Observership.[47] Mainly because of diplomatic efforts of China's Ministry of Foreign Affairs (MFA)[48] the country gained "full" Observership[49] in May 2013.[50]

14.3.2 China's participation in the Arctic Council

14.3.2.1 General improvement and critiques

Since being granted "full" Observer status, China, on the whole, has been engaging more actively in the work of the Arctic Council. For instance, according to the 2016 Observer Report of China to the Council, China had recommended more than 25 experts to the Council, and eight of them had been invited to participate in specific programs operated by the WGs.[51] In the future, China will

45 According to China's Arctic Policy, "China has long been involved in Arctic affairs. In 1925, China joined the Spitsbergen Treaty and started to participate in addressing the Arctic affairs." State Council Information Office of the People's Republic of China (2018) "China's Arctic Policy", 26 January 2018. http://english.gov.cn/archive/white_paper/2018/01/26/content_281476026660336.htm (accessed 30 March 2018).

46 Jia Guide and Shi Wuhong (2014) "On China's Participation in Arctic Governance under New Circumstance" *Global Review* 4: 22 (in Chinese).

47 Arctic Council (2007) "Senior Arctic Officials Meeting, Minutes, Tromsø, Norway, 12–13 April 2007", at 2. https://oaarchive.arctic-council.org/handle/11374/371 (accessed 30 March 2018).

48 See Jerker Hellstrom (2014) *China's Political Priorities in the Nordic Countries.* FOI-R-3879-SE, March 2014. www.foi.se/reportsummary?reportNo=FOI-R—3879—SE (accessed 30 March 2018).

49 On 15 May 2013, China, together with India, Italy, Japan, Singapore and Republic of Korea, was granted Observer status in the Arctic Council. *Kiruna Declaration on the occasion of the Eighth Ministerial Meeting of the Arctic Council*, 15 May 2013, Kiruna, Sweden, at 6. Since there is no longer distinction between *ad hoc* and "permanent" Observers in the Arctic Council, some scholars have used the term "full observer" to describe the current Observer status in the Arctic Council. See, e.g., Timo Koivurova et al., *supra* note 39, at 173.

50 For a detailed discussion on the issue, see Matthew Willis and Duncan Depledge (2015) "How We Learned to Stop Worrying about China's Arctic Ambitions: Understanding China's Admission to the Arctic Council, 2004–2013" in *Handbook of the Politics of the Arctic*, edited by Leif Christian Jensen and Geir Honneland. Edward Elgar, Cheltenham: 388–407.

51 Arctic Council (2016) *China's 2016 Observer Activities Report, 25 November 2016*, at 2–3. https://oaarchive.arctic-council.org/handle/11374/1860 (accessed 30 March 2018).

recommend more experts to deepen its engagement with the WGs of the Council, especially regarding Arctic climate change and environmental protection.[52] Moreover, China has been actively participating in all the Ministerial and SAO meetings since May 2013.[53] In order to further enhance China's contributions to the Council, in November 2016 China appointed its first Special Representative for Arctic Affairs of the MFA, Gao Feng, who also serves as China's Senior Arctic Official (SAO).[54]

At the same time, some scholars have also found certain limitations concerning China's participation and performance in the Arctic Council. For example, Koivurova and others have noted that, while China has regularly attended the meetings at almost all levels of the Council, there is a lack of continuity in its delegations.[55] Furthermore, China's participation in the work of the Working Groups has been very limited. The problems include sending inappropriate delegates and limited scientific communications.[56] Overall, the handful of existing studies on China's participation in the Council have focused more on China's participation in the Ministerial and SAO meetings and its performance in the Working Groups. As a "newcomer", China generally lacks the knowledge and experience on how to substantively engage in the Arctic Council.[57]

14.3.2.2 Exploring the problems: a case study of China's participation in the TFs

This study focuses more on China's engagement with the Task Forces of the Arctic Council, especially because, unlike the WGs, some TFs of the Council have played a unique role in negotiating pan-Arctic agreements under the auspices of the AC. The study finds that China's participation in the work of the TFs of the Council has also been limited, which constitutes a special reason for China's small contributions to the policy-making processes within the Arctic Council. The major problems include: (1) having no delegates at some TF meetings ("nonattendance" problem); (2) lacking continuity and integration of delegations ("discontinuity" problem); and (3) sending inappropriate experts to some TF meetings ("wrong delegates" problem).

52 Arctic Council (2017) "China's Recent Practice on Preventing Marine Pollution in the Arctic" Observer Special Session, Oulu, 26 October 2017. https://oaarchive.arctic-council.org/handle/11374/2102 (accessed 30 March 2018).

53 Xu Hong (2017) "Arctic Governance and China's Participation" *Journal of Boundary and Ocean Studies* 2-2: 7 (in Chinese).

54 *China's Observer Report, supra* note 51, at 3.

55 Koivurova et al., *supra* note 39, at 174–175.

56 Ibid., at 175–178.

57 See also Qin Tianbao and Li Miaomiao (2017) "Strengthening China's Role in the Arctic Council" in *Arctic Law and Governance, supra* note 39 at 26.

Before May 2013, China rarely contributed to the work of the TFs, due to both its *ad hoc* Observer status and the inchoate disapproval of some Arctic states of non-Arctic Observers. In recent years, China has sent more representatives to the meetings of the TFs, albeit not to all. For example, among six meetings of the Task Force on Black Carbon and Methane (TFBCM, 2013–2015), China only sent a natural scientist to the second meeting in December 2013.[58] Among five meetings of the Task Force on Arctic Marine Oil Pollution Prevention (TFOPP, 2013–2015), China only sent two engineers to the first meeting of TFOPP in January 2014.[59] More recently, the Task Force on Arctic Marine Cooperation (TFAMC)[60] was granted a two-year extension on its term to continue to work on negotiating the terms of reference for a potential new subsidiary body of the Arctic Council and identify potential complementary enhancements to the existing Arctic Council mechanism.[61] However, to my knowledge, China has sent no delegates to the meetings of TFAMC-II.[62]

Moreover, even with regard to the participating Chinese representatives, there has been a lack of continuity and integration. For instance, over the course of the work of the Task Force to Facilitate the Circumpolar Business Forum (TFCBF, 2013–2014), the Chinese MFA sent a middle-level diplomat to the third face-to-face meeting of the TFCBF.[63] On other occasions, however, MFA sent only secretary-level staff to the TF meetings.[64] In addition, there has been a high level of

58 Arctic Council TFBCM II (2013) "List of Participants, Stockholm, 12–13 December 2013". https://oaarchive.arctic-council.org/bitstream/handle/11374/818/TFBCM_II_Stockholm_list_of_participants.pdf?sequence=10&isAllowed=y (accessed 30 March 2018).

59 Arctic Council TFOPP (2014) "Task Force on Arctic Marine Oil Pollution Prevention Participants to the Meeting in Oslo, 16–17 January 2014". https://oaarchive.arctic-council.org/handle/11374/817 (accessed 30 March 2018).

60 Arctic Council website: "Task Force on Arctic Marine Cooperation (TFAMC)". https://oaarchive.arctic-council.org/handle/11374/1704 (accessed 30 March 2018).

61 Arctic Council (2017) *Senior Arctic Officials' Report to Ministers, Fairbanks, Alaska, United States, 11 May 2017*, at 80–81. https://oaarchive.arctic-council.org/handle/11374/1909 (accessed 30 March 2018).

62 See Arctic Council (2017) *Summary Report from the First Meeting of TFAMC-II, Helsinki, 14–15 September 2017*. https://oaarchive.arctic-council.org/handle/11374/2081?show=full (accessed 30 March 2018); Arctic Council (2018) *Co-Chairs' Summary: Arctic Council TFAMC-II, 2nd Meeting, Québec City, 15–16 February 2018*. www.sdwg.org/wp-content/uploads/2018/02/2018-02-26_TFAMC-II-2-Quebec-City-2-pager.pdf (accessed 30 March 2018).

63 Arctic Council, Task Force to Facilitate the Creation of a Circumpolar Business Forum (2013) *Report to the Senior Arctic Officials: List of Participants, Helsinki, Finland, 4–5 December 2013*, at 31. https://oaarchive.arctic-council.org/bitstream/handle/11374/1308/TF_TFCBF_Doc01_Report_to_SAOs_December_2013_AC_SAO_CA02.pdf?sequence=1&isAllowed=y (accessed 30 March 2018). (The Chinese delegate was Wen Chen, former Chargé d'affaires ad interim of the Chinese Embassy in Finland).

64 For instance, Wenting Zhao, a secretary of the Department of Treaty and Law of MFA, was sent to attend the 8th meeting of the Task Force for Enhancing Scientific Cooperation in the Arctic (SCTF) in March 2016.

diversity among Chinese representatives attending the meetings of the same TF. For example, among nine meetings of the Task Force for Enhancing Scientific Cooperation in the Arctic (SCTF, 2013–2017), the Chinese government sent a natural scientist from the Ocean University of China to the fourth meeting,[65] a staff-level representative from MFA to the eighth meeting[66] and a deputy director from the Chinese Arctic and Antarctic Administration (CAA) to the ninth SCTF meeting.[67] Although one reason for this diversity problem might be that, unlike WGs, some TFs of the Council have an evolving nature, particularly in terms of their specific agendas and instruments,[68] a problematic aspect in this mode of participation is that the Chinese delegates would not gain enough experience and expertise on the work of the Arctic Council.[69]

Lastly, sometimes China sent experts without appropriate expertise and knowledge to the work of the TFs of the Council. For instance, even though the discussions under several TFs of the Arctic Council are now more related to diplomatic efforts and international legal negotiations, the Chinese government has often sent natural scientists and experts to these critical meetings. A closer look at China's involvement in the work of two recent TFs reveals the problem. One concrete example is China's participation in the work of the TFBCM (2013–2015). According to the Kiruna Declaration, the mandate of the TFBCM is "to develop *arrangements on actions* to achieve enhanced black carbon and methane emission reductions in the Arctic".[70] It was also clearly agreed that Observers

65 The Chinese representative was Dr Xianyao Chen, a physical oceanographer from the Key Laboratory of Physical Oceanography. MOE China, the Ocean University of China.

66 See *supra* note 65.

67 The Chinese delegate was Wei Long, the deputy director of the International Cooperation Division of CAA.

68 For instance, in its first two years, the Task Force for Enhancing Scientific Cooperation in the Arctic (SCTF) focused more on the existing impediments in Arctic scientific cooperation and possible improvement regarding the exchange of data, access to scientific infrastructure and simplification of movement of scientists and their equipment. In 2015, Ministers decided to *extend* the mandate of the SCTF, including to work towards a legally binding agreement on scientific cooperation in the Arctic. Arctic Council (2015) *Senior Arctic Officials' Report to Ministers, Iqaluit, Canada, 24 April 2015*, at 10–11. https://oaarchive.arctic-council.org/handle/11374/494 (accessed 30 March 2018).

Another good example is the work of the Task Force on Arctic Marine Cooperation (TFAMC). According to TFAMC-II's original mandates adopted in May 2017, the TFAMC should continue to work on negotiating the terms of reference for a potential new subsidiary body of the Council *and* identify possible enhancements of existing mechanisms. However, on the second TFAMC-II meeting in February 2018, all delegates supported the change of agendas and agreed to focus on complementary enhancement to the existing Arctic Council mechanism. *TFAMC-II Co-Chairs' Summary 2018, supra* note 62.

69 See also Koivurova et al., *supra* note 39, at 175 (noting that at least for the SAO meetings there seemed to be a high level of diversity among Chinese representatives and questioning how certain persons could gain expertise on the work of the Council).

70 *Kiruna Declaration, supra* note 49, at 3 (emphasis added).

and other stakeholders should have the opportunity to be engaged in the work of the TFBCM.[71] Over the course of the work of the TFBCM, the Co-Chairs particularly invited all delegates, including Observers, to express and discuss their views on a possible *political* agreement as the end product of the Task Force.[72] Eventually, the TFBCM developed an Arctic Council Framework for Action on Enhanced Black Carbon and Methane Emissions Reductions which was submitted to the SAO meeting in April 2015.[73] In this policy-making process, however, China sent only a *natural* scientist who attended the second TFBCM meeting.[74] Unfortunately, similar shortcomings occurred again with China's participation in the negotiation of Agreement on Enhancing International Arctic Scientific Cooperation. The Agreement was negotiated through the work of the SCTF (2013–2017).[75] Besides a lack of continuity in terms of attendance, China continued to send inappropriate delegate(s) to the SCTF meetings. For example, the Chinese delegate to the fourth meeting of the SCTF, who is a physical oceanographer, found that the conversations were actually beyond his area of research interest and expertise.[76]

In sum, although the policy-making processes under some TFs are arguably more flexible and evolving, China has largely failed to comprehend the changing mandates and agendas of some TFs, and has thereby sent inadequate and unsuitable delegates to the respective meetings.

14.4 Possible solutions for China to enhance its performance in the Council

The reasons for China's performance and influence in the Arctic Council being limited are complex. On the whole, notwithstanding that China has recently issued its Arctic Policy,[77] the Chinese government has maintained a cautious attitude concerning its involvement in Arctic affairs, which also involves its participation in the Arctic Council. Another contributing factor is that the participatory rights of Observers in the AC are indeed limited. Furthermore, an important reason is that Chinese polar bureaucracy seems not fully familiar with the detailed

71 Arctic Council Task Force on Black Carbon and Methane (2013) *Summary Report, Introductory Meeting and Scoping Session, Whitehorse, Yukon, 17–19 September 2013.* https://oaarchive.arctic-council.org/bitstream/handle/11374/818/TFBCM_I_Whitehorse_2pager.pdf?sequence=5&isAllowed=y (accessed 30 March 2018).

72 Arctic Council website: "TFBCM Document Portfolio". https://oaarchive.arctic-council.org/handle/11374/818 (accessed 30 March 2018).

73 *Senior Arctic Officials Report Iqaluit (2015)*, Iqaluit (2015) *supra* note 68, at 8–9.

74 *Supra* note 59. (The Chinese delegate was Dr Junying Sun, from Chinese Academy of Meteorological Sciences.)

75 *Supra* note 14.

76 Koivurova, et al., *supra* note 39, at 179 (based on a conversation conducted by Piotr Graczyk with the Chinese expert).

77 *China's Arctic Policy, supra* note 45.

operations of the Council. Moreover, the significance of the work of the AC's subsidiary bodies appears to be not truly understood.

Like other non-Arctic states, China wants its voice to be better heard in the Arctic, particularly regarding trans-regional Arctic issues. In this regard, being an Observer in the Arctic Council provides China with great opportunities to communicate its Arctic concerns and to conduct diplomacy.[78] Nevertheless, it is also fair to say that there is clearly room for China to improve its performance in the AC in the near future. To strengthen China's participation and role in the Arctic Council, a dual approach is proposed for Chinese polar bureaucracy: on the one hand, China should more actively engage in the discussions on the Arctic Council, particularly with regard to the engagement of Observers and the reform of the Arctic Council; on the other hand, China should reform its domestic institutions and relevant procedures in order to better make substantial contributions to the work of the Arctic Council.

14.4.1 Substantially engaging in the discourses of the Arctic Council Reform

To date, China's official statements on the reform of the Arctic Council and the role of China in the Arctic Council have been relatively vague and lacking in detail.[79] Looking forward, China should substantially participate in international dialogues and cooperation on the reform of the Arctic Council and the engagement of Observers. The potential cooperation areas may be as follows: (1) Although it is clear enough that the decision-making of the Arctic Council, at all levels, is the exclusive right of the Member States with the involvement of the Permanent Participants, China can join other Observers' calls to collaborate and promote openness, transparency, and democratic management of the Arctic Council;[80] (2) Efforts can also be made to help the Arctic Council develop a more detailed and balanced mechanism for Observer participation in the operative work of the Council. The inadequate engagement with the scientists and experts from outside the Arctic in the Arctic Council is a two-tiered problem, which is partly due to a lack of detailed requirements and procedures for incorporating non-Arctic scientists into the work. Dialogue helps. For instance, at the Special Session

78 Lu Junyuan and Zhang Xia (2016) *China's Arctic Interests and Policy.* Current Affairs Press, Beijing: 225, 359 (in Chinese).

79 See, e.g., Statement by H.E. Ambassador Lan Lijun at the Meeting between the Swedish Chairmanship of the Arctic Council and Observers, 6 November 2012. www.arctic-council.org/images/PDF_attachments/Observer_DMM_2012/ACOBSDMMSE01_Stockholm_2012_Observer_Meeting_Statement_Ambassador_Lan_Lijun_China.pdf (accessed 30 March 2018); "China's Recent Practice on Preventing Marine Pollution in the Arctic", *supra* note 52.

80 See, e.g., Taisaku Ikeshima (2016) "Japan's Role as an Asian Observer State within and outside the Arctic Council's framework" *Polar Science* 10: 458–462 (suggesting that Japan can play "an AC watcher" role to check Arctic five and the Council's legitimacy and democracy); Kim, *supra* note 37.

on Observer Engagement of the Arctic Council in October 2016, the participating WGs and Observers had suggested that it would be useful to have "profiles" explaining what kind of experts the WGs actually need for their specific work.[81]

14.4.2 Reforming domestic institutions and procedures

Probably more importantly, the Chinese government should reform and integrate its Arctic affairs administrative system to improve China's performance and role in the Arctic Council, particularly with regard to the "discontinuity" problem and "wrong delegates" problem, outlined above.

Currently, multiple government agencies and institutions have a stake in China's Arctic policy-making and in participating in Chinese delegations to international polar meetings.[82] Among them, the Ministry of Foreign Affairs and the State Oceanic Administration (SOA)[83] are two primary agencies in China's Arctic administrative system.[84] More specifically, within the MFA, although the Department of Boundary and Ocean Affairs has Arctic-related mandates, the Department of Treaty and Law usually leads China's delegations to the Arctic fora such as the Arctic Council. At the same time, the SOA coordinates all aspects of China's polar affairs from scientific research to strategic agendas. It now supervises two subsidiary bodies on polar issues: the Chinese Arctic and Antarctic Administration (CAA) and the Polar Research Institute of China (PRIC), and also leads the newly established Polar Science and Technology Committee (PSTC).[85] However, to date, China has lacked a specialised agency to decide and administer its polar engagement.[86]

81 Arctic Council (2016) *Report of the Senior Arctic Officials Plenary Meeting, Portland, Maine, 5–6 October 2016*, para. 12.3. https://oaarchive.arctic-council.org/bitstream/handle/11374/1834/EDOCS-3870-v5-Plenary_report_Portland_SAO_Oct2016.pdf?sequence=1&isAllowed=y (accessed 30 March 2018).

82 Anne-Marie Brady (2017) *China as a Polar Great Power*. Cambridge University Press, Cambridge, MA: 114.

83 It is noteworthy that the SOA has recently been merged into the newly established Ministry of Natural Resources, but its name is reserved for external purposes. Xinhua News (2018) "Explanation of the State Council's Institutional Reform Program", 13 March 2018. The English version is available at: https://new.reorg-research.com/data/documents/20180314/5aa92e5e425fd.pdf (accessed 30 March 2018).

84 This is basically because, in the Chinese bureaucratic system, polar issues are generally categorised as maritime affairs. At the same time, China's participation in the Arctic region is essentially a foreign policy issue.

85 Notwithstanding the existence of Chinese Advisory Committee for Polar Expeditions (1994–), the SOA initiated and administered a new Chinese Polar Science and Technology Committee (PSTC) on 28 December 2017. The main mandates of PSTC include: providing advisory opinions on polar strategies, polar S&T policies and development plans; investigating and proving important polar S&T issues; evaluating key polar programmes, engineering projects and S&T achievements; and initiating and organising international polar fora. SOA website: "Chinese Polar S&T Committee was established in Beijing". www.soa.gov.cn/xw/hyyw_90/201712/t20171228_59760.html (accessed 30 March 2018) (in Chinese).

86 See generally Wu Jun (2005) "A Research on Optimization of the Polar Research Organizational Management Mechanism of Our Country", MA diss., Wuhan University: 37 (in Chinese).

Given this context, China's participation in the Arctic Council has not been well coordinated domestically. At present, China's engagement with the Arctic Council is jointly managed by MFA and SOA: MFA is officially the leading agency that represents China at the political meetings of the Arctic Council;[87] the recruitment of scientists and experts to participate in the work and meetings of the subsidiary bodies of the Council is separately under the charge of the CAA under the SOA.[88] However, there is no regular communication mechanism between MFA and SOA on China's participation in the Council.[89] No substantial coordination and integration efforts have been made by the two bureaucracies on how to accurately understand the functions and agendas of the different subsidiary bodies of the Council and therefrom how to select suitable delegates to different functional meetings of the Council. In this regard, it is worth noting that, since 2011, China has established a loose Arctic-affairs coordination mechanism among several government departments and institutes which are concerned with Arctic issues.[90] Nevertheless, the mechanism has played little role, if any, in coordinating Chinese delegates' participation and performance in the Council. Moreover, with regard to the participation of Chinese scientists and experts in the work of the subsidiary bodies of the Council, there is no additional support from the MFA, and the enthusiasm of Chinese scientists for participation in the work of the Arctic Council is also low.[91] As a consequence, the suitability of a delegate has been of little concern.[92] Lastly, neither the PSTC nor Chinese Advisory Committee for Polar Expeditions[93] has played a role in the selection of Chinese experts participating in the scientific and technical work of the Arctic Council.

Looking forward, a regular communication mechanism should be established at least between MFA and SOA to systematically handle China's participation and role in the Arctic Council. In this regard, the new SAO of China to the Arctic Council should play a stronger role in coordinating and integrating China's participation and activities in the Council. Moreover, in the new context of institutional reform, one way to integrate different departments' work is to establish a stable and consistent Chinese Arctic Task Team to address Arctic affairs,

87 The staff from the SOA also constitutes Chinese delegation members at the political meetings of the Arctic Council.

88 See Chinese Arctic and Antarctic Administration (CAA) website. www.chinare.gov.cn/caa/ (accessed 30 March 2018) (the administrative work includes posting the invitations from the WGs or TFs of the Arctic Council, and setting the deadlines to contact if Chinese scientists are interested in attending the meetings).

89 Personal communication with a Chinese official of CAA (4 December 2017).

90 Xu, *supra* note 53, at 7–8.

91 Personal communication with a Chinese official of CAA (4 December 2017).

92 Ibid.

93 Chinese Advisory Committee for Polar Expeditions, which might also be translated as "the Chinese Advisory Committee for Polar Research", was approved by the Ministry of Science and Technology (MST) and established on 14 October 1994. The Committee has broad mandates, including advising Chinese polar activities, organising polar conferences and evaluating Chinese polar research programmes. Its Secretariat is located at the CAA in Beijing. Currently, it has 15 component members. For detailed information on the membership in English, see Brady, *supra* note 82, at 121–122.

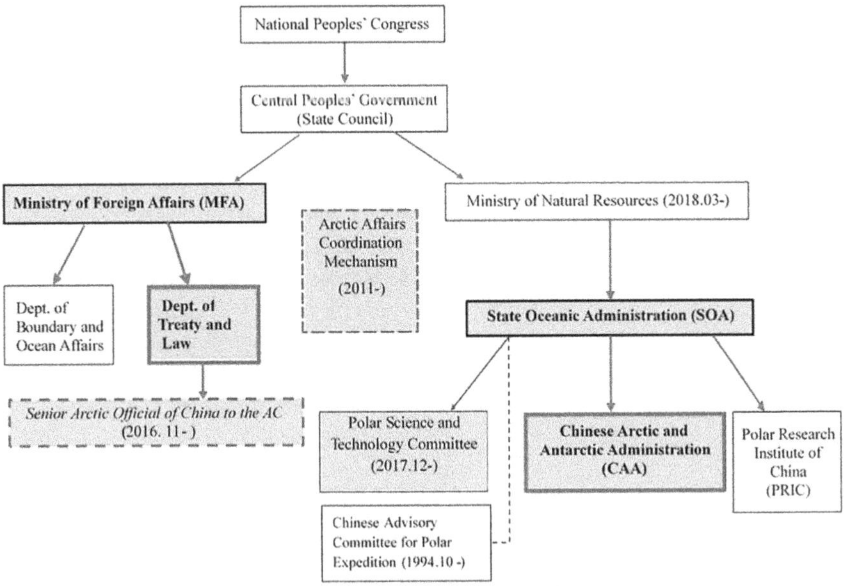

Figure 14.1 China's Arctic administrative system (2018 update)

including China's engagement with the Arctic Council. A formal Arctic (or Arctic Council) Task Team could enable Chinese delegates to better comprehend the work of the Arctic Council and to build up their expertise. Overall, China's polar bureaucracy should pay closer attention to and more actively participate in the work of the subsidiary bodies of the Arctic Council rather than sitting symbolically or speaking rhetorically at the Ministerial and SAO meetings.

14.5 Concluding remarks

Although the Arctic Council is not the only venue where China can carry out its Arctic policy, the Chinese government highly values the primacy of the Council in Arctic governance.[94] However, to date, China's performance and role in the Arctic Council have remained limited. In particular, its participation in the work of the subsidiary bodies of the Arctic Council has been sporadic and insufficiently coordinated domestically.[95] In the ongoing process of domestic institutional reform, the Chinese administration concerning China's participation in

94 *China's Arctic Policy, supra* note 45.

95 It is worth noting that these kinds of problems might not be peculiar to China. See, e.g., Akiho Shibata and Maiko Raita (2016) "An Agreement on Enhancing International Arctic Scientific Cooperation: Only for the Eight Arctic States and Their Scientists?" *The Yearbook of Polar Law* 8: 134, fn. 13 (noting that "Japan's participation as an Observer State in the SCTF was sporadic and not well coordinated internally").

the Council should be further coordinated and improved. On the other hand, as discussed earlier in this chapter, the limited participation of Observers in the work of the Council is a two-tiered problem. It is also due to a lack of detailed guidance and procedures on how to best incorporate non-Arctic scientists and other experts into the work of the Council. For example, some Task Forces clearly have an evolving nature particularly in terms of their specific functions and agendas. Consequently, it could be difficult to discern the nature of discussions at the beginning of the work, especially for Observer representatives. However, to date there are no specific guidelines to efficiently engage Observer experts in the work of the Task Forces. These factors might also be reasons why some Observers delegates in the TFs are not best suited to contribute to the issues under discussion. A related question, then, is whether Observers must send only one delegate per TF meeting or whether they could send a small delegation team with different skills and expertise that might be needed, such as a scientist *and* a diplomat or a legal advisor.

Finally, there are many specific issues on which China can better participate in the Arctic Council as an accredited Observer that are not elaborated upon in this chapter. For example, one of the Council's Observer admission criteria highlights an applicant's efforts to "[bring] Arctic concerns to global decision-making bodies".[96] Given that China has actively engaged with many international institutions concerning Arctic issues, China could and should make its unique contributions with regard to promoting global efforts to address Arctic concerns. Moreover, China should explore specific ways to better engage with Arctic indigenous peoples.[97] Finally, there is no doubt that non-Arctic Observers should shoulder responsibilities while gaining opportunities in the Arctic region. In this regard, China should demonstrate a more substantial commitment to Arctic development, particularly with regard to tackling Arctic climate change and environmental protection. Again, all these efforts can be better made by substantially engaging with the work of the subsidiary bodies of the Arctic Council, rather than by sitting or talking at the Ministerial and SAO meetings.

96 *Revised Rules of Procedure, supra* note 23, Annex 2: para. 6, the criterion (g).

97 See generally Adam Stępień (2017) "Incentives, Practices and Opportunities for Arctic External Actors' Engagement with Indigenous Peoples" in *Arctic Law and Governance, supra* note 39 at 205–231.

Appendix

Agreement on Enhancing International Arctic Scientific Cooperation (2017)

The Government of Canada, the Government of the Kingdom of Denmark, the Government of the Republic of Finland, the Government of Iceland, the Government of the Kingdom of Norway, the Government of the Russian Federation, the Government of the Kingdom of Sweden, and the Government of the United States of America (hereinafter referred to as the "Parties"),

Recognizing the importance of maintaining peace, stability, and constructive cooperation in the Arctic;

Recognizing the importance of the sustainable use of resources, economic development, human health, and environmental protection;

Reiterating the urgent need for increased actions to mitigate and adapt to climate change;

Emphasizing the importance of using the best available knowledge for decision-making;

Noting the importance of international scientific cooperation in that regard;

Fully taking into account the relevant provisions of the 1982 United Nations Convention on the Law of the Sea, in particular the provisions in Part XIII on marine scientific research as they relate to promoting and facilitating the development and conduct of marine scientific research for peaceful purposes;

Recalling the Kiruna Declaration on the occasion of the Eighth Ministerial meeting of the Arctic Council held in May 2013 and the Iqaluit Declaration on the occasion of the Ninth Ministerial meeting of the Arctic Council held in April 2015;

Recognizing the ongoing development of the International Polar Partnership Initiative as determined by the Executive Council of the World Meteorological Organization;

Recognizing the significance of the research priorities as determined by the International Conference on Arctic Research Planning;

Recognizing the efforts of the Arctic Council and its subsidiary bodies;

Recognizing the significant scientific expertise and invaluable contributions to scientific activities being made by non-Parties and specifically by the Arctic Council Permanent Participants and Arctic Council Observers;

Recognizing the substantial benefit gained from the financial and other investments by the Arctic States and other nations in the International Polar Year and its outcomes, including in particular new scientific knowledge, infrastructure and technologies for observation and analysis;

Recognizing the excellent existing scientific cooperation already under way in many organizations and initiatives, such as the Sustaining Arctic Observing Networks, the International Arctic Science Committee, the University of the Arctic, the Forum of Arctic Research Operators, the International Network for Terrestrial Research and Monitoring in the Arctic, the World Meteorological Organization, the International Council for the Exploration of the Sea, the Pacific Arctic Group, the Association of Polar Early Career Scientists, indigenous knowledge institutions, the International Arctic Social Sciences Association, and many others; and

Desiring to contribute to and build upon existing cooperation and make efforts to develop and expand international Arctic scientific cooperation,

Have agreed as follows:

Article 1

Terms and definitions

For the purposes of this Agreement:

"*Facilitate*" means pursuing all necessary procedures, including giving timely consideration and making decisions as expeditiously as possible;

"*Participant*" means the Parties' scientific and technological departments and agencies, research centers, universities and colleges, and contractors, grantees and other partners acting with or on behalf of any Party or Parties, involved in Scientific Activities under this Agreement;

"*Scientific Activities*" means efforts to advance understanding of the Arctic through scientific research, monitoring and assessment. These activities may include, but are not limited to, planning and implementing scientific research projects and programs, expeditions, observations, monitoring initiatives, surveys, modelling, and assessments; training personnel; planning, organizing and executing scientific seminars, symposia, conferences, workshops, and meetings; collecting, processing, analyzing, and sharing scientific data, ideas, results, methods, experiences, and traditional and local knowledge; developing sampling methodologies and protocols; preparing publications; and developing, implementing, and using research support logistics and research infrastructure;

"*Identified Geographic Areas*" means those areas described in Annex 1.

Article 2

Purpose

The purpose of this Agreement is to enhance cooperation in Scientific Activities in order to increase effectiveness and efficiency in the development of scientific knowledge about the Arctic.

Article 3

Intellectual property and other matters

Where appropriate, cooperative activities under this Agreement shall take place pursuant to specific implementing agreements or arrangements concluded between the Parties or Participants pertaining to their activities, particularly the financing of such activities, the use of scientific and research results, facilities, and equipment, and dispute settlement. Through such specific agreements or arrangements, the Parties shall, where appropriate, ensure, either directly or through the Participants, adequate and effective protection and fair allocation of intellectual property rights, in accordance with the applicable laws, regulations, procedures, and policies as well as the international legal obligations of the Parties concerned, and address other matters that may result from activities under this Agreement.

Article 4

Entry and exit of persons, equipment, and material

Each Party shall use its best efforts to facilitate entry to, and exit from, its territory of persons, research platforms, material, samples, data, and equipment of the Participants as needed to advance the objectives of this Agreement.

Article 5

Access to research infrastructure and facilities

The Parties shall use their best efforts to facilitate access by the Participants to national civilian research infrastructure and facilities and logistical services such as transportation and storage of equipment and material for the purpose of conducting Scientific Activities in Identified Geographic Areas under this Agreement.

Article 6

Access to research areas

1. The Parties shall facilitate access by the Participants to terrestrial, coastal, atmospheric, and marine areas in the Identified Geographic Areas, consistent with international law, for the purpose of conducting Scientific Activities.
2. The Parties shall facilitate the processing of applications to conduct marine scientific research under this Agreement consistent with the 1982 United Nations Convention on the Law of the Sea.
3. The Parties also shall facilitate joint Scientific Activities that require airborne scientific data collection in the Identified Geographic Areas, and that are subject to specific implementing agreements or arrangements concluded between the Parties or Participants pertaining to those activities.

Article 7

Access to data

1. The Parties shall facilitate access to scientific information in connection with Scientific Activities under this Agreement.
2. The Parties shall support full and open access to scientific metadata and shall encourage open access to scientific data and data products and published results with minimum time delay, preferably online and free of charge or at no more than the cost of reproduction and delivery.
3. The Parties shall facilitate the distribution and sharing of scientific data and metadata by, as appropriate and to the extent practicable, adhering to commonly accepted standards, formats, protocols, and reporting.

Article 8

Education, career development and training opportunities

The Parties shall promote opportunities to include students at all levels of education, and early career scientists, in the Scientific Activities conducted under this Agreement to foster future generations of researchers and to build capacity and expertise to advance knowledge about the Arctic.

Article 9

Traditional and local knowledge

1. The Parties shall encourage Participants to utilize, as appropriate, traditional and local knowledge in the planning and conduct of Scientific Activities under this Agreement.
2. The Parties shall encourage communication, as appropriate, between holders of traditional and local knowledge and Participants conducting Scientific Activities under this Agreement.
3. The Parties shall encourage holders of traditional and local knowledge, as appropriate, to participate in Scientific Activities under this Agreement.

Article 10

Laws, regulations, procedures, and policies

Activities and obligations under this Agreement shall be conducted subject to applicable international law and the applicable laws, regulations, procedures, and policies of the Parties concerned. For those Parties that have subnational governments, the applicable laws, regulations, procedures, and policies include those of their subnational governments.

Article 11

Resources

1. Unless otherwise agreed, each Party shall bear its own costs deriving from its implementation of this Agreement.
2. Implementation of this Agreement shall be subject to the availability of relevant resources.

Article 12

Review of this Agreement

1. The Parties shall meet no later than one year after the entry into force of this Agreement, as convened by the depositary, and from then on as decided by the Parties. The Parties may elect to convene such meetings in conjunction with meetings of the Arctic Council including inviting Arctic Council Permanent Participants and Arctic Council Observers to observe and provide information. Scientific cooperation activities with non-Parties related to Arctic science may be taken into account when reviewing the implementation of this Agreement.
2. At such meetings the Parties shall consider the implementation of this Agreement, including successes achieved and obstacles to implementation, as well as ways to improve the effectiveness and implementation of this Agreement.

Article 13

Authorities and contact points

Each Party shall designate a competent national authority or authorities as the responsible point of contact for this Agreement. The names of and contact information for the designated points of contact are specified in Annex 2 to this Agreement. Each Party shall promptly inform the other Parties in writing through its competent national authority or authorities and through diplomatic channels of any changes to those designations.

Article 14

Annexes

1. Annex 1 referred to in Article 1 constitutes an integral part of this Agreement and is legally binding.
2. Annex 2 referred to in Article 13 does not constitute an integral part of this Agreement and is not legally binding.
3. At meetings of the Parties referred to in Article 12, the Parties may adopt additional legally non-binding Annexes. Annex 2 referred to in Article 13 may be modified as provided in that Article.

Article 15

Settlement of disputes

The Parties shall resolve any disputes concerning the application or interpretation of this Agreement through direct negotiations.

Article 16

Relationship with other international agreements

Nothing in this Agreement shall be construed as altering the rights or obligations of any Party under other relevant international agreements or international law.

Article 17

Cooperation with non-Parties

1. The Parties may continue to enhance and facilitate cooperation with non-Parties with regard to Arctic science.
2. Parties may in their discretion undertake with non-Parties cooperation described in this Agreement and apply measures consistent with those described in this Agreement in cooperation with non-Parties.
3. Nothing in this Agreement shall affect the rights and obligations of the Parties under agreements with non-Parties, nor preclude cooperation between the Parties and non-Parties.

Article 18

Amendments to this Agreement

1. This Agreement may be amended by written agreement of all the Parties.
2. An amendment shall enter into force 30 days after the date on which the depositary has received the last written notification through diplomatic channels that the Parties have completed the internal procedures required for its entry into force.

Article 19

Provisional application, entry into force, and withdrawal

1. This Agreement may be applied provisionally by any signatory that provides a written statement to the depositary of its intention to do so. Any such signatory shall apply this Agreement provisionally in its relations with any other signatory having made the same notification from the date of its statement or from such other date as indicated in its statement.

2. This Agreement shall enter into force for a period of five years 30 days after the date of receipt by the depositary of the last written notification through diplomatic channels that the Parties have completed the internal procedures required for its entry into force.
3. This Agreement shall be automatically renewed for further periods of five years unless a Party notifies the other Parties in writing at least six months prior to the expiration of the first period of five years or any succeeding period of five years of its intent to withdraw from this Agreement, in which event this Agreement shall continue between the remaining Parties.
4. Any Party may at any time withdraw from this Agreement by sending written notification thereof to the depositary through diplomatic channels at least six months in advance, specifying the effective date of its withdrawal. Withdrawal from this Agreement shall not affect its application among the remaining Parties.
5. Withdrawal from this Agreement by a Party shall not affect the obligations of that Party with regard to activities undertaken under this Agreement where those obligations have arisen prior to the effective date of withdrawal.

Article 20

Depositary

The Government of the Kingdom of Denmark shall be the depositary for this Agreement.

DONE at Fairbanks, Alaska, United States of America this 11th day of May, 2017. This Agreement is established in a single copy in the English, French, and Russian languages, all texts being equally authentic. The working language of this Agreement shall be English, the language in which this Agreement was negotiated. The Depositary shall transmit certified copies of this Agreement to the Parties.

ANNEX 1 – Identified Geographic Areas

Identified Geographic Areas for purposes of this Agreement are described by each Party below and include areas over which a State whose government is a Party to this Agreement exercises sovereignty, sovereign rights or jurisdiction, including land and internal waters within those areas and the adjacent territorial sea, exclusive economic zone, and continental shelf, consistent with international law. Identified Geographic Areas also include areas beyond national jurisdiction in the high seas north of 62 degrees north latitude.

The Parties agree that the Identified Geographic Areas are described solely for the purposes of this Agreement. Nothing in this Agreement shall affect the existence or delineation of any maritime entitlement or the delimitation of any boundary between States in accordance with international law.

CANADA – The territories of Yukon, Northwest Territories, and Nunavut and the adjacent marine areas of Canada.

KINGDOM OF DENMARK – The territory of the Kingdom of Denmark including Greenland and the Faroes and its marine areas above the southern limit of the Greenland exclusive economic zone and the Faroese fisheries zone.

FINLAND – The territory of Finland and its marine areas.

ICELAND – The territory of Iceland and its marine areas.

NORWAY – Marine areas north of 62 degrees north latitude, and land areas north of the Arctic Circle (66.6 degrees north latitude).

RUSSIAN FEDERATION

1. Territory of the Murmansk Region;
2. Territory of the Nenets Autonomous Area;
3. Territory of the Chukchi Autonomous Area;
4. Territory of the Yamalo-Nenets Autonomous Area;
5. Territory of the municipal entity "Vorkuta" (Komi Republic);
6. Territories of Allaikhov Ulus (District), Anabar National (Dolgano-Evenk) Ulus (District), Bulun Ulus (District), Nizhnekolymsk District, Ust-Yan Ulus (District) (Sakha Republic (Yakutia));
7. Territories of the Urban District of Norilsk, Taimyr Dolgan-Nenets Municipal District, Turukhan District (Krasnoyarsk Territory);
8. Territories of the municipal entities "The City of Arkhangelsk", "Mezen Municipal District", "Novaya Zemlya", "The City of Novodvinsk", "Onega Municipal District", "Primorsky Municipal District", "Severodvinsk" (Arkhangelsk region);
9. Lands and islands of the Arctic Ocean, identified in the Resolution of the Presidium of the Central Executive Committee of the USSR dated April 15, 1926 "On the announcement of lands and islands situated in the Arctic Ocean as a territory of the Union of SSR" and other legislative acts of the USSR; as well as adjacent marine areas.

Note: Territories of the municipal entities, listed in the abovementioned items 5–8, identified within the borders as of April 1, 2014.

SWEDEN – The territory of Sweden and its marine areas north of 60.5 degrees north latitude.

UNITED STATES OF AMERICA – All United States territory north of the Arctic Circle and north and west of the boundary formed by the Porcupine, Yukon, and Kuskokwim Rivers; the Aleutian chain; and adjacent marine areas in the Arctic Ocean and the Beaufort, Bering, and Chukchi Seas.

ANNEX 2 – Authorities and contact points

(*not reproduced*)

Agreement To Prevent Unregulated High Seas Fisheries In The Central Arctic Ocean (2018)

The Parties to this Agreement,

Recognizing that until recently ice has generally covered the high seas portion of the central Arctic Ocean on a year-round basis, which has made fishing in those waters impossible, but that ice coverage in that area has diminished in recent years;

Acknowledging that, while the central Arctic Ocean ecosystems have been relatively unexposed to human activities, those ecosystems are changing due to climate change and other phenomena, and that the effects of these changes are not well understood;

Recognizing the crucial role of healthy and sustainable marine ecosystems and fisheries for food and nutrition;

Recognizing the special responsibilities and special interests of the central Arctic Ocean coastal States in relation to the conservation and sustainable management of fish stocks in the central Arctic Ocean;

Noting in this regard the initiative of the central Arctic Ocean coastal States as reflected in the Declaration Concerning the Prevention of Unregulated High Seas Fishing in the Central Arctic Ocean signed on 16 July 2015;

Recalling the principles and provisions of treaties and other international instruments relating to marine fisheries that already apply to the high seas portion of the central Arctic Ocean, including those contained in:

> the United Nations Convention on the Law of the Sea of 10 December 1982 ("the Convention");
>
> the Agreement for the Implementation of the Provisions of the United Nations Convention on the Law of the Sea of 10 December 1982 relating to the Conservation and Management of Straddling Fish Stocks and Highly Migratory Fish Stocks of 4 August 1995 ("the 1995 Agreement"); and
>
> the 1995 Code of Conduct for Responsible Fisheries and other relevant instruments adopted by the Food and Agriculture Organization of the United Nations;

Underlining the importance of ensuring cooperation and coordination between the Parties and the North-East Atlantic Fisheries Commission, which has competence to adopt conservation and management measures in part of the high seas portion of the central Arctic Ocean, and other relevant mechanisms for fisheries management that are established and operated in accordance with international law, as well as with relevant international bodies and programs;

Believing that commercial fishing is unlikely to become viable in the high seas portion of the central Arctic Ocean in the near future and that it is therefore premature under current circumstances to establish any additional regional or subregional fisheries management organizations or arrangements for the high seas portion of the central Arctic Ocean;

Desiring, consistent with the precautionary approach, to prevent the start of unregulated fishing in the high seas portion of the central Arctic Ocean while keeping under regular review the need for additional conservation and management measures;

Recalling the 2007 United Nations Declaramtion on the Rights of Indigenous Peoples;

Recognizing the interests of Arctic residents, including Arctic indigenous peoples, in the long-term conservation and sustainable use of living marine resources and in healthy marine ecosystems in the Arctic Ocean and underlining the importance of involving them and their communities; and

Desiring to promote the use of both scientific knowledge and indigenous and local knowledge of the living marine resources of the Arctic Ocean and the ecosystems in which they occur as a basis for fisheries conservation and management in the high seas portion of the central Arctic Ocean,

Have agreed as follows:

Article 1

Use of Terms

For the purposes of this Agreement:

(a) "Agreement Area" means the single high seas portion of the central Arctic Ocean that is surrounded by waters within which Canada, the Kingdom of Denmark in respect of Greenland, the Kingdom of Norway, the Russian Federation and the United States of America exercise fisheries jurisdiction;
(b) "fish" means species of fish, molluscs and crustaceans except those belonging to sedentary species as defined in Article 77 of the Convention;
(c) "fishing" means searching for, attracting, locating, catching, taking or harvesting fish or any activity that can reasonably be expected to result in the attracting, locating, catching, taking or harvesting of fish;
(d) "commercial fishing" means fishing for commercial purposes;
(e) "exploratory fishing" means fishing for the purpose of assessing the sustainability and feasibility of future commercial fisheries by contributing to scientific data relating to such fisheries;
(f) "vessel" means any vessel used for, equipped to be used for, or intended to be used for fishing.

Article 2

Objective of this Agreement

The objective of this Agreement is to prevent unregulated fishing in the high seas portion of the central Arctic Ocean through the application of precautionary conservation and management measures as part of a long-term strategy to safeguard healthy marine ecosystems and to ensure the conservation and sustainable use of fish stocks.

Article 3

Interim Conservation and Management Measures Concerning Fishing

1. Each Party shall authorize vessels entitled to fly its flag to conduct commercial fishing in the Agreement Area only pursuant to:
   (a) conservation and management measures for the sustainable management of fish stocks adopted by one or more regional or subregional fisheries management organizations or arrangements, that have been or may be established and are operated in accordance with international law to manage such fishing in accordance with recognized international standards, or
   (b) interim conservation and management measures that may be established by the Parties pursuant to Article 5, paragraph 1(c)(ii).
2. The Parties are encouraged to conduct scientific research under the framework of the Joint Program of Scientific Research and Monitoring established pursuant to Article 4 and under their respective national scientific programs.
3. A Party may authorize vessels entitled to fly its flag to carry out exploratory fishing in the Agreement Area only pursuant to conservation and management measures established by the Parties on the basis of Article 5, paragraph 1(d).
4. The Parties shall ensure that their scientific research activities involving the catching of fish in the Agreement Area do not undermine the prevention of unregulated commercial and exploratory fishing and the protection of healthy marine ecosystems. The Parties are encouraged to inform each other about their plans for authorizing such scientific research activities.
5. The Parties shall ensure compliance with the interim measures established by this Article, and with any additional or different interim measures they may establish pursuant to Article 5, paragraph 1(c).
6. Consistent with Article 7 of the 1995 Agreement, coastal States Parties and other Parties shall cooperate to ensure the compatibility of conservation and management measures for fish stocks that occur in areas both within and

beyond national jurisdiction in the central Arctic Ocean in order to ensure conservation and management of those stocks in their entirety.

7. Other than as provided in paragraph 4 above, nothing in this Agreement shall be interpreted to restrict the entitlements of Parties in relation to marine scientific research as reflected in the Convention.

Article 4

Joint Program of Scientific Research and Monitoring

1. The Parties shall facilitate cooperation in scientific activities with the goal of increasing knowledge of the living marine resources of the central Arctic Ocean and the ecosystems in which they occur.
2. The Parties agree to establish, within two years of the entry into force of this Agreement, a Joint Program of Scientific Research and Monitoring with the aim of improving their understanding of the ecosystems of the Agreement Area and, in particular, of determining whether fish stocks might exist in the Agreement Area now or in the future that could be harvested on a sustainable basis and the possible impacts of such fisheries on the ecosystems of the Agreement Area.
3. The Parties shall guide the development, coordination and implementation of the Joint Program of Scientific Research and Monitoring.
4. The Parties shall ensure that the Joint Program of Scientific Research and Monitoring takes into account the work of relevant scientific and technical organizations, bodies and programs, as well as indigenous and local knowledge.
5. As part of the Joint Program of Scientific Research and Monitoring, the Parties shall adopt, within two years of the entry into force of this Agreement, a data sharing protocol and shall share relevant data, directly or through relevant scientific and technical organizations, bodies and programs, in accordance with that protocol.
6. The Parties shall hold joint scientific meetings, in person or otherwise, at least every two years and at least two months in advance of the meetings of the Parties that take place pursuant to Article 5 to present the results of their research, to review the best available scientific information, and to provide timely scientific advice to meetings of the Parties. The Parties shall adopt, within two years of the entry into force of this Agreement, terms of reference and other procedures for the functioning of the joint scientific meetings.

Article 5

Review and Further Implementation

1. The Parties shall meet every two years or more frequently if they so decide. During their meetings, the Parties shall, inter alia:

    (a) review implementation of this Agreement and, when appropriate, consider any issues relating to the duration of this Agreement in accordance with Article 13, paragraph 2;

(b) review all available scientific information developed through the Joint Program of Scientific Research and Monitoring, from the national scientific programs, and from any other relevant sources, including indigenous and local knowledge;

(c) on the basis of the scientific information derived from the Joint Program of Scientific Research and Monitoring, from the national scientific programs, and from other relevant sources, and taking into account relevant fisheries management and ecosystem considerations, including the precautionary approach and potential adverse impacts of fishing on the ecosystems, consider, inter alia, whether the distribution, migration and abundance of fish in the Agreement Area would support a sustainable commercial fishery and, on that basis, determine:

    (i) whether to commence negotiations to establish one or more additional regional or subregional fisheries management organizations or arrangements for managing fishing in the Agreement Area; and
    (ii) whether, once negotiations have commenced pursuant to subparagraph (i) above and once the Parties have agreed on mechanisms to ensure the sustainability of fish stocks, to establish additional or different interim conservation and management measures in respect of those stocks in the Agreement Area.

(d) establish, within three years of the entry into force of this Agreement, conservation and management measures for exploratory fishing in the Agreement Area. The Parties may amend such measures from time to time. These measures shall provide, inter alia, that:

    (i) exploratory fishing shall not undermine the objective of this Agreement;
    (ii) exploratory fishing shall be limited in duration, scope and scale to minimize impacts on fish stocks and ecosystems and shall be subject to standard requirements set forth in the data sharing protocol adopted in accordance with Article 4, paragraph 5;
    (iii) a Party may authorize exploratory fishing only on the basis of sound scientific research and when it is consistent with the Joint Program of Scientific Research and Monitoring and its own national scientific program(s);
    (iv) a Party may authorize exploratory fishing only after it has notified the other Parties of its plans for such fishing and it has provided other Parties an opportunity to comment on those plans; and
    (v) a Party must adequately monitor any exploratory fishing that it has authorized and report the results of such fishing to the other Parties.

2. To promote implementation of this Agreement, including with respect to the Joint Program of Scientific Research and Monitoring and other activities undertaken pursuant to Article 4, the Parties may form committees or similar bodies in which representatives of Arctic communities, including Arctic indigenous peoples, may participate.

Article 6

Decision-Making

1. Decisions of the Parties on questions of procedure shall be taken by a majority of the Parties casting affirmative or negative votes.
2. Decisions of the Parties on questions of substance shall be taken by consensus. For the purpose of this Agreement, "consensus" means the absence of any formal objection made at the time the decision was taken.
3. A question shall be deemed to be of substance if any Party considers it to be of substance.

Article 7

Dispute Settlement

The provisions relating to the settlement of disputes set forth in Part VIII of the 1995 Agreement apply, *mutatis mutandis*, to any dispute between Parties relating to the interpretation or application of this Agreement, whether or not they are also Parties to the 1995 Agreement.

Article 8

Non-Parties

1. The Parties shall encourage non-parties to this Agreement to take measures that are consistent with the provisions of this Agreement.
2. The Parties shall take measures consistent with international law to deter the activities of vessels entitled to fly the flags of non-parties that undermine the effective implementation of this Agreement.

Article 9

Signature

1. This Agreement shall be open for signature at Ilulissat from 3 October 2018 by Canada, the People's Republic of China, the Kingdom of Denmark in respect of the Faroe Islands and Greenland, Iceland, Japan, the Republic of Korea, the Kingdom of Norway, the Russian Federation, the United States of America and the European Union and shall remain open for signature for 12 months following that date.
2. For signatories to this Agreement, this Agreement shall remain open for ratification, acceptance or approval at any time.

Article 10

Accession

1. For the States listed in Article 9, paragraph 1 that have not signed this Agreement, and for the European Union if it has not signed this Agreement, this Agreement shall remain open for accession at any time.
2. After the entry into force of this Agreement, the Parties may invite other States with a real interest to accede to this Agreement.

Article 11

Entry into Force

1. This Agreement shall enter into force 30 days after the date of receipt by the depositary of all instruments of ratification, acceptance, or approval of, or accession to, this Agreement by those States and the European Union listed in Article 9, paragraph 1.
2. After entry into force of this Agreement, it shall enter into force for each State invited to accede pursuant to Article 10, paragraph 2 that has deposited an instrument of accession 30 days after the date of deposit of that instrument.

Article 12

Withdrawal

A Party may withdraw from this Agreement at any time by sending written notification of its withdrawal to the depositary through diplomatic channels, specifying the effective date of its withdrawal, which shall be at least six months after the date of notification. Withdrawal from this Agreement shall not affect its application among the remaining Parties or the duty of the withdrawing Party to fulfill any obligation in this Agreement to which it otherwise would be subject under international law independently of this Agreement.

Article 13

Duration of this Agreement

1. This Agreement shall remain in force for an initial period of 16 years following its entry into force.
2. Following the expiration of the initial period specified in paragraph 1 above, this Agreement shall remain in force for successive five-year extension period(s) unless any Party:

(a) presents a formal objection to an extension of this Agreement at the last meeting of the Parties that takes place prior to expiration of the initial period or any subsequent extension period; or
(b) sends a formal objection to an extension to the depositary in writing no later than six months prior to the expiration of the respective period.

3. The Parties shall provide for an effective transition between this Agreement and any potential new agreement establishing an additional regional or subregional fisheries management organization or arrangement for managing fishing in the Agreement Area so as to safeguard healthy marine ecosystems and ensure the conservation and sustainable use of fish stocks in the Agreement Area.

Article 14

Relation to Other Agreements

1. The Parties recognize that they are and will continue to be bound by their obligations under relevant provisions of international law, including those reflected in the Convention and the 1995 Agreement, and recognize the importance of continuing to cooperate in fulfilling those obligations even in the event that this Agreement expires or is terminated in the absence of any agreement establishing an additional regional or subregional fisheries management organization or arrangement for managing fishing in the Agreement Area.
2. Nothing in this Agreement shall prejudice the positions of any Party with respect to its rights and obligations under international agreements and its positions with respect to any question relating to the law of the sea, including with respect to any position relating to the exercise of rights and jurisdiction in the Arctic Ocean.
3. Nothing in this Agreement shall prejudice the rights, jurisdiction and duties of any Party under relevant provisions of international law as reflected in the Convention or the 1995 Agreement, including the right to propose the commencement of negotiations on the establishment of one or more additional regional or subregional fisheries management organizations or arrangements for the Agreement Area.
4. This Agreement shall not alter the rights and obligations of any Party that arise from other agreements compatible with this Agreement and that do not affect the enjoyment by other Parties of their rights or the performance of their obligations under this Agreement. This Agreement shall neither undermine nor conflict with the role and mandate of any existing international mechanism relating to fisheries management.

Article 15

Depositary

1. The Government of Canada shall be the depositary for this Agreement.
2. Instruments of ratification, acceptance, approval or accession shall be deposited with the depositary.
3. The depositary shall inform all signatories and all Parties of the deposit of all instruments of ratification, acceptance, approval or accession and perform such other functions as are provided for in the 1969 Vienna Convention on the Law of Treaties.

Done at Ilulissat on this 3rd day of October, 2018, in a single original, in the Chinese, English, French and Russian languages, each text being equally authentic.

Index

For Product Safety Concerns and Information please contact our EU representative GPSR@taylorandfrancis.com
Taylor & Francis Verlag GmbH, Kaufingerstraße 24, 80331 München, Germany

www.ingramcontent.com/pod-product-compliance
Ingram Content Group UK Ltd.
Pitfield, Milton Keynes, MK11 3LW, UK
UKHW022013180926
475701UK00003B/348
9781032241272